Library response to urban change

Library response to urban change

A study of the Chicago Public Library

Lowell A. Martin

School of Library Service, Columbia University

assisted by

Terence Crowley

and **Thomas Shaughnessy**

 American Library Association / Chicago 1969

Standard Book Number 8389-0077-1 (1969)

Library of Congress Catalog Card Number 76-104040

Copyright © 1969 by the American Library Association

Printed in the United States of America

A library implies an act of faith
which generations
still in darkness hid
sign in their night
in witness of the dawn

VICTOR HUGO
(Inscription in the central building of the Chicago Public Library)

Survey Staff

Survey Director
LOWELL A. MARTIN

Research Directors
TERENCE CROWLEY
and THOMAS SHAUGHNESSY

Research Associates
WILLIAM KNEEDLER, JOEL LEONARD,
ROSE-ELLEN LEONARD

Research Assistants
YVONNE GREEN, RICHARD JOHNSON,
DALE ANN KNIGHT, PHYLLIS LEVUN,
GERALD WEILAND

Office Manager
MARION STROHM

Secretary
FLORA STROHM

Consultants

Urban Planning
John Duba, Municipal Services Administrator,
  New York City, and former Head, Department of
  Development and Planning, Chicago

Community Relations
Arna Bontemps, former Professor, University
  of Illinois, Circle Campus, Chicago

Adult Education
Cyril O. Houle, Professor, University of Chicago

Children's Service
Effie Lee Morris, Coordinator of Children's
  Services, San Francisco Public Library

Audio-Visual Service
Harold Goldstein, Dean, School of Library Science,
  Florida State University

Technical Library Operations
Maurice F. Tauber, Melvil Dewey Professor of
  Library Service, Columbia University

Computer Applications
Theodore Stein, Data Processing Consultant,
  New York City

Financial Organization
Milton Shulman, Management Consultant, Kaplan,
  Goldman and Co., Chicago

Library Goals
Ervin J. Gaines, Director, Minneapolis Public
  Library
Virginia Mathews, Associate Director,
  National Book Committee

School Relations
Mary Ann Swanson, Head Librarian, Evanston,
  Illinois, Township High School
Elinor Yungmeyer, Consultant, Library Services,
  Oak Park, Illinois, Elementary School

Metropolitan Relations
Lester L. Stoffel, Executive Director, Suburban
  Library System, Western Springs, Illinois

Library Collections
Robert Haverkamp, Dean of Instruction,
  Central YMCA College, Chicago
Hans Lenneberg, former Head, Music
  Department, Brooklyn Public Library
Robb McKenzie, former Head, Popular Library,
  Queens Borough Public Library, New York
Ruth Schoneman, Librarian, The Art Institute of
  Chicago
Richard Seidel, Acquisitions Librarian, University
  of Illinois, Circle Campus, Chicago
Benjamin Weintraub, Assistant Professor, Rutgers
  University
John R. Wood, former Head, Science
  and Technology Department, Queens Borough
  Public Library, New York

Contents

Figures

Tables

Preface

This is the third in a series of studies of the Chicago Public Library, spread over fifty years. The first (*A Library Plan for the Whole City,* adopted in 1916) proposed *expansion,* particularly in branch units. The second (*A Metropolitan Library in Action,* completed in 1939) proposed *quality,* the achieving of recognized standards. The underlying theme of the present report is *adaptability,* the restructuring of the Library in a period of change.

The first report, practical and pragmatic, achieved results. The second, for all its internal excellence, had limited effect. It is hoped that the present effort partakes both of the relevance of the one and of the integrity of the other.

The urban setting today contains a new element not recognized thirty or fifty years ago. The very existence and vitality of the city are challenged; it has within it both the promise of greatness and the seeds of destruction. A library does not stop riots or remove physical deterioration or eradicate prejudice. But an effective library, in its modest way, helps to get at the root causes of the urban problem: people unprepared to take their place in the economic order and people divided by lack of understanding. And an effective library serves to sustain the quality of life for all, not in utilitarian and civic matters alone, but also in the fulfillment of mind and spirit.

The basic premise in this study of the Chicago Public Library, to put it directly at the outset, is that the urban condition calls for something more than "business as usual." Chicago, with other cities, will not be allowed many mistakes; either it will maintain its institutions of communication and understanding, or it will lose power and validity. In the past Chicago could tolerate a mediocre library. Now every urban agency must carry its share and perform at its full potential.

A program of service is presented that calls for the Chicago Public Library to adjust to the people of the city in all their diversity, rather than expecting the people to conform to a standardized institution. But this does not mean a plan that is startling or revolutionary for its own sake; preoccupation with the new and different may be no more relevant than acceptance of the old and familiar. The problem is not to remake our libraries into something other than libraries—a new form of school, a community meeting place, an amusement center—but rather to take the inherent strength of a "library," as a resources center with materials for self-realization, and relate it to the multifarious interests of a society that is reexamining itself. Some of the proposals in this report are no more than a plea for quality in traditional library services, a reaching into capacities inherent in the institution's history. Others are less orthodox, and these are proposed on an experimental basis, with built-in evaluation and planned feedback from the people themselves, because no one can be sure that the untried will be successful. Thus the theme that will appear and reappear —the call to excellence *and* to innovation.

All possible sources of data and means of analysis were used in an attempt to see the

Chicago Public Library whole and clear. Some new methods of library evaluation were applied in an effort to ascertain actual performance and user response. The sources and methods are summarized in the Appendix. But in an enterprise of this nature and scope one comes down, at last, to human judgment. This was group judgment for the most part, arrived at in hours of deliberation, but in the end the final interpretation and the final responsibility properly fall on the survey director alone.

The many consultants and specialists drawn into the deliberations are listed separately on page viii. Some dealt only with their specific areas of expertise, while others—in particular, John Duba, now Municipal Services Administrator of New York City and formerly Commissioner of Development and Planning in Chicago, and Cyril O. Houle, Professor of Education in the University of Chicago—in substance became regular working members of the survey team. The whole project would have been impossible without the services—in the field, at the desk, and over the conference table—of Terence Crowley and Thomas Shaughnessy, young men of the caliber that ensures the future of a profession. As in all tasks of some complexity that are carried through to completion, there was an efficient internal manager, Marion Strohm.

The Board of Directors of the Chicago Public Library commissioned the study, and both the Board and the Acting Librarian supported it at every turn; clearly, they are seeking improvement and not expending their energy in defending the past. The staff of the Library not only cooperated but often contributed extra time and fresh ideas. A citizen's committee of 140 laymen was formed, composed of both civic leaders and active local workers, which met with the survey staff first to review the overall purpose and method, then to study data as these accumulated, and finally to consider the survey recommendations. The Mayor of Chicago attended the final session of the group and pledged support for library development.

All within and without the survey staff were united in a common faith that the library is a means for the individual, whatever his background and aims, to use the record of information, knowledge, and expression available there to help achieve self-development. If the Chicago Public Library can be made to accomplish this for any significant portion of the people in the city, it will in its quiet, personal way make Chicago a better place to live.

LOWELL A. MARTIN

Columbia University
July 1, 1969

Library response to urban change

1 The People of Chicago

A public library is by definition a people's library. The bedrock of planning for urban service is therefore the people of the city, how many there are, who they are, and where they are. The population data presented here for Chicago delineate the "public" for which the Chicago Public Library exists, and the public to be served for the next twenty to thirty years.

Number to Be Served

The population of Chicago when the census is taken in 1970 will be approximately 3,600,000.[1] This is just about what it was twenty years ago, in 1950 (the official figure then was 3,620,962). The city has maintained its total since World War II, unlike other older industrial cities such as Boston, Cleveland, and Saint Louis, which have lost 10 percent or more of their population.

Projections for 1980 and beyond inevitably involve assumptions as to residential movement in and out of the city, the balance of births and deaths among those who remain, and the amount of land and the intensity of land use for residential purposes. One of the sources cited for the 1970 prediction estimates an *increase* of 4.8 percent from 1970 to 1980, up to 3,774,000 inhabitants (Population Research and Training Center), while the other estimates a *decline* in this same decade of 3.4 percent, down to 3,487,000 (Real Estate Research Corporation). The actual figure may well fall somewhere between the two. For purposes of library planning in Chicago, a fairly stable total population can be assumed within the city for the next decade.

Beyond 1980 the picture is unclear. If urban *deterioration* spreads and accelerates, more people will be disposed to move out and fewer to move in. On the other hand, if urban *renewal* spreads and accelerates—as may well occur in the period ahead as the city girds to meet its internal crisis—present residents will stay and others will come in or return. In either case, the population of the city has been maintained recently more by natural increase than by in-migration, and the natural increase will continue in the next decades. The Population Research and Training Center of the University of Chicago estimates a small decline of 1.4 percent from 1980 to 1990, from their prediction of 3,774,000 people in the former year to 3,718,000 in the latter. Official planning for the City rests upon an assumed population in the year 2000 of " . . . up to four million."[2] This report on the Chicago Public Library assumes a fairly stable or

[1]One recognized source gives this prediction of 3,600,000 for 1970 (*Population Projections for the City of Chicago and the Chicago Standard Metropolitan Statistical Area, 1970 and 1980*. Chicago: Population Research and Training Center and Chicago Community Inventory, 1964). Another estimates 3,610,000 (Real Estate Research Corp., *Projections of Population and School Enrollments by Community Area for the City of Chicago, 1970 and 1975*. Chicago: Board of Education of the City of Chicago, 1968).

[2]City of Chicago, Dept. of Development and Planning, *The Comprehensive Plan of Chicago* (Chicago: The Department, 1966), p.21.

slightly increased total population in Chicago in the next twenty to thirty years.

The Chicago metropolitan area as a whole has been increasing rapidly in population, and will continue doing so. The growth rate in the Standard Metropolitan Statistical Area was 20 percent from 1950 to 1960, and is estimated at 17.4 percent from 1960 to 1970, and 18 percent from 1970 to 1980. In the period from 1950 to 1980, when the population of the city itself will remain fairly steady, the total for the metropolitan area will move from 5,177,000 to at least 8,600,000—in other words, in these thirty years as many people will have been added to the suburban districts as live today in the whole central city. In 1950 the city itself accounted for almost 70 percent of the people in the metropolitan area. Today it accounts for just about one-half, and by 1980 it will be in a distinct minority in the total region. This trend serves to underline the importance of region-wide planning, not just for the suburbs so that they can share the strength of the central city but also for library service within Chicago so that it can grow with the burgeoning metropolitan region.

Racial Composition

The color of a person's skin does not determine whether library service is needed or not. There are good and poor readers who are black and good and poor readers who are white. There are predominantly Negro districts within Chicago in which library use is low, and there are predominantly white districts in which library use is equally low. The common denominator is not race but educational level, both in years of schooling achieved and in the quality of education provided.

The 1960 census showed 23.6 percent of the Chicago population to be black. Population studies indicate that the percentage will be approximately 32.0 percent by 1970 and 41.0 percent by 1980. In the *Report of the National Advisory Commission on Civil Disorders* (p.391) it is calculated that Chicago will become over 50 percent Negro by 1984, if present trends continue. In this regard, the official goal has been stated as follows: "The city will seek to change these trends and to achieve harmonious stabilized neighborhoods attractive to families of all races and creeds."[3] Whether this goal is achieved or not, Chicago will still need an effective public library for its people, black and white.

Ethnic Groups

Chicago continues to have neighborhoods with an ethnic identification. Someone has remarked that this is the melting pot that has not melted. A more accurate statement is that the melting process has been slow in some sections and for some people, but it continues, and ethnic neighborhoods will be distinctly less evident in Chicago twenty years from now than they are today.

In 1960 there were 438,392 Chicago residents of foreign birth, one-eighth of the total. This was down from one-quarter of the total in 1930. If we add the native-born children of foreign-born parents, the "foreign stock" in Chicago in 1965 was 1,277,341 persons, 36 percent of the total.[4] Many of the foreign born will continue to live with neighbors of like background, but this will be much less true of their children. Geographic dispersion will tend to accelerate for most groups, and also dilution

[3]Ibid., p.22.

[4]City of Chicago, Dept. of Development and Planning, *The Comprehensive Plan of Chicago, Conditions and Trends: Population, Economy, Land* (Chicago: The Department, 1967), p.15.

of the ethnic stock itself by marriage across national lines.

The one exception is the Spanish-speaking group. The number of Spanish Americans almost tripled in Chicago from 1950 to 1960, from 28,000 to 77,000, and, according to the Human Relations Council, doubled again to 143,000 by 1966. The present approximately 150,000 Chicagoans who are Spanish-speaking, comprising over 4 percent of the total population, constitute a potential library clientele of importance.

Age Distribution

Age is a factor in library planning; the same library resources are not provided for the seven-year old and the seventy-year old. The Chicago Public Library, to cite one example, has been successful with preschool story hours. Children's service, up to age 14, comprises over one-half of the activity of the branches and bookmobiles, as measured by home circulation of books. At a very different age level, senior citizens are an important factor in the on-site use of some library facilities in the city, especially during morning hours.

In one respect, Chicago has a young population. Forty-five percent of the residents are under 25 years of age, and the percentage will go a little higher in the next decade. There are today in the city almost twice as many young people 5–19 years old as there were in 1940 (977,000 as compared with 540,000). In another respect, Chicago has an old population, in that persons 65 or over make up 10 percent of the population, and this will also increase slightly in the next decade. Adults between the ages of 25 and 65 comprise less than half of the population, and will go on doing so through this century.

Library planners in Chicago must therefore set their sights on the following distinct age groups, which will hold fairly well within the indicated ranges over the next twenty years:

375,000–400,000 preschool children
675,000–700,000 children ages 5–14
300,000–325,000 young people ages 15–19
1,700,000–1,800,000 adults ages 20–64
375,000–425,000 senior citizens 65 and over

Sheer numbers of people at different age levels cannot be automatically projected as the base for library use in the future. New forms of communication are appearing, some available through commercial channels (the paperback book is a case in point), and others perhaps through quasi-public sources (such as future electronic access in the home to information banks). The probable effect of new technology on the library program is examined in chapter 8. Another variable is the interrelation among kinds of libraries (such as school and special libraries to the general public library). This changing balance will also be examined as the analysis proceeds.

School and College Enrollment

School enrollment (through 12th grade) will peak in Chicago sometime in the 1970s, and will then fall moderately as the city population in time takes on a less youthful aspect. There are approximately 800,000 children in Chicago schools today—public, parochial, and independent combined. The total will increase toward 850,000 within the next few years and then will fall back below 800,000 by 1980. The division between public and parochial schools is shown in table 1 (but excludes the independent schools, for which reliable enrollment predictions were not located). All these figures would be increased by some 8 percent if the schools were to add a year below the present kindergarten, which is a distinct possibility within the next decade.

Table 1
SCHOOL ENROLLMENT—CITY OF CHICAGO
(in thousands)

	Public K–12	*Parochial K–12*	*Total K–12*
1966	572.6	220.6	793.2
1970	627.2	201.0	828.2
1975	614.9	181.0	795.9
1980	557.4	171.0	728.4

SOURCE: Real Estate Research Corp. *Projections of Population and School Enrollments by Community Area for the City of Chicago, 1970 and 1975,* 1968.

Student use of the public library has increased in recent years, and in Chicago now constitutes 49 percent of total use by persons above 14 years of age, and well over one-half if children are included. The increase has occurred because of larger school enrollments and because of greater instructional demands for students to use resources. Continuation of the latter trend, as school standards increase and as individualized instruction spreads in one form or another, will maintain student library demand at the high school level, even though the number of students below the college level will decrease to some extent by 1980.

College and university enrollment will not slow down but on the contrary will increase through the 1970s. There are 49 college and university campuses within Chicago, and 45 more in the area outside the city. Enrollment in these institutions of higher education was 166,634 in 1965 and 200,618 in 1968.[5] The increase will be rapid in the commuting colleges, which means that more and more college

[5]G. J. Froehlich, *Enrollment in Institutions of Higher Education in Illinois: 1968* (Urbana: Univ. of Illinois Bureau of Institutional Research, 1968), p.9 and 105.

students will attend classes in one location but live in another. They will often seek library resources in the communities where they live and where they have grown up. Present and projected enrollment in two of the larger commuting complexes, the city junior colleges and Circle Campus of the University of Illinois, document this trend. The eight junior colleges had an enrollment of 34,080 in 1968, and are expected to pass the 50,000 mark in 1970. Circle Campus of the University of Illinois had 14,250 students in 1968, and anticipates 25,000 by 1975.

In some form student use of the public library, large as it is at present, can be expected to increase further in the period ahead. The nature of this demand will broaden and deepen, particularly as the number of commuting college students increases. Adequate provision of library resources for the strategic student group, and efficient joint use of public funds in meeting this important social need, both call for collaboration in planning and program among the schools, the colleges, and the public library.

Economic and Job Levels

Chicago for the most part is segregated from an economic point of view. There are the disorganized subsistence-level districts, concentrated in an inverted "L" extending west and south from the central Loop. Further south, and to the southwest and northwest, are stable communities of lower-middle level, occupied by blue-collar and white-collar workers. In the far north and northwest, and far southwest, are homogeneous areas of above-average income. Figure 1 shows this distribution and graduation by economic level from the center to the outskirts. Then in a strip along the lakefront, to a considerable extent to the north

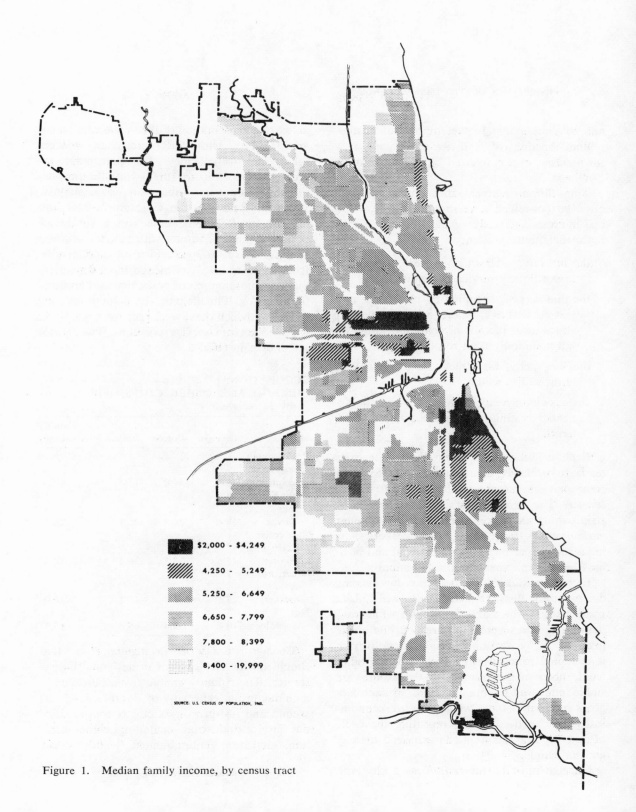

■	$2,000 - $4,249
▨	4,250 - 5,249
▦	5,250 - 6,649
▒	6,650 - 7,799
░	7,800 - 8,399
░	8,400 - 19,999

SOURCE: U.S. CENSUS OF POPULATION, 1960.

Figure 1. Median family income, by census tract

and to some extent to the south, are "cosmopolitan" sections of high-rise apartments, new townhouses, and converted older single-family dwellings.

Thus library service throughout the city must be conceived as responding to the special interests and needs of the residents of different neighborhoods in:

the *inner city,* for which a fresh concept of urban library service is required

the *middle city,* occupied by blue-collar and service workers, where books and other educational records of communication are not commonly used resources

the *outer city,* for which the usual branch libraries are suited

cosmopolitan areas, with varied and sophisticated reading and media tastes and interests.

Each neighborhood within these categories tends to be fairly homogeneous, presenting a somewhat similar group of people for library service. The exception is the "cosmopolitan" strip, along the lake front, where a greater variety occurs, from young office workers sharing a small apartment to professional and business leaders in expensive condominiums.

It is a mistake to equate the low-income disorganized districts exclusively with black residents, and the stable areas with white residents. The one severe slum area outside of the inverted "L," a section in the Uptown district, is occupied primarily by whites. On the other hand, black neighborhoods to the south are stable and well-maintained, and in fact Negroes move into them when they are economically able to do so, thus repeating the cycle of mobility that has long characterized the city and its people.

Chicago must be understood as a city with

an extra representation of blue-collar craftsmen and laborers, with 45.8 percent of workers falling in this category. The percentage increased from 1950 to 1960, while the proportion of white-collar jobs went down slightly. A recent report of the Chicago Commission on Human Relations, based on a survey of 870 firms under contract with the city, showed an increase of 10.7 percent in blue-collar jobs from 1966 to 1967.[6] Chicago has a distinctly higher representation of craftsmen and laborers than Boston, Philadelphia, or Saint Louis, for example, which have a larger percentage in white-collar and service positions. The figures are shown in table 2.

Table 2
OCCUPATIONAL LEVELS—
CHICAGO AND OTHER CITIES, 1960
(by percentages)

	Chicago	Boston	Philadelphia	Saint Louis
Professionals, managers, technicians	16.7	17.0	15.4	10.5
White-collar, sales, clerical	19.4	26.8	25.3	28.2
Blue-collar, craftsmen, laborers	45.8	33.5	39.4	34.6
Other, mostly service workers	7.5	13.3	13.1	16.0
Not available	10.6	9.4	6.8	10.7

Chicago is a city of workingmen, a fact that should not be lost sight of in designing library service. The primary source of employment is manufacturing, especially of durable goods. A second and fast-growing sector is composed of the service industries, including communication, education, entertainment, health, repair

[6]*Human Relations News,* Aug., 1968.

and maintenance, and personal services. Chicago will continue to have a large contingent of skilled workers in the manufacturing and service occupations. However, automation will increase in both manufacturing and service, displacing some present workers who will face increasing need for retraining. Library resources relate to this prospect, with materials in traditional print form, training films, and programmed materials for self-instruction.

Educational Achievement

Amount of education of individuals is closely related to book reading and library use. There is a watershed in book reading somewhere at the level of high school graduation,[7] those not achieving this level not commonly turning to books, while a majority of those at or above high school completion are likely to read one or more books a year.

It sometimes comes as a surprise to learn that, in a city such as Chicago, 25 percent of the adults have education no further than the elementary school (1960 U.S. Census). On the other side, only 14.3 percent have had some college. No more than about 33 percent of adults in Chicago today have achieved or passed the watershed point of high school graduation.

The distribution of adults by educational level is indicated in table 3, and the distribution by education over the city in figure 2. There is a fairly symmetrical distribution by level—by taking nine to eleven years of education as a middle range, slightly over half of adults rank at this level, and the other half divides about evenly above and below this intermediate group. Geographically, the distribu-

[7]Jan Hajda, "An American Paradox: People and Books in the Metropolis" (Ph.D. dissertation, Univ. of Chicago, 1964).

tion also shows a clear pattern—the large central area at the lowest educational level, the intermediate group in a ring around the center, and the upper education group for the most part in the outer ring. Some deviations from the pattern should be noted—the higher education communities in the Near North Side and the Hyde Park-Kenwood-University of Chicago areas, and the lower education districts near the steel mills in the far south. Also to be noted is that while the distribution by schooling bears a relation to distribution by income (see figure 1 on page 5), the low education sections extend well beyond the inner-city blighted area; poverty and limited education should not be thought of as completely coterminous.

Table 3
ADULT POPULATION OF CHICAGO
BY EDUCATIONAL LEVEL, 1965

	Educational level	*Number*	*Percent*
Upper	11 years of schooling and above	842,882	24.3
Middle	9.0-10.9 years of schooling	1,784,180	51.5
Lower	8.9 years and below	838,720	24.2

The educational level of Chicago is below the national average, as shown in table 4. Among larger, older cities it falls midway, with Boston and Philadelphia at a higher level and Baltimore, Cleveland, and Saint Louis at a lower level.

Highly important is the steady increase in educational level of adults in cities, as indicated in table 4. The average in Chicago has increased from 8.5 years of schooling in 1940 to 9.5 in 1950 and to 10.0 by 1960. While it is true that Chicago, by present-day standards, has only a moderate educational level, it actually has an average among adults today about the same as that enjoyed by the suburbs twenty-five to thirty years ago. This upward trend has oc-

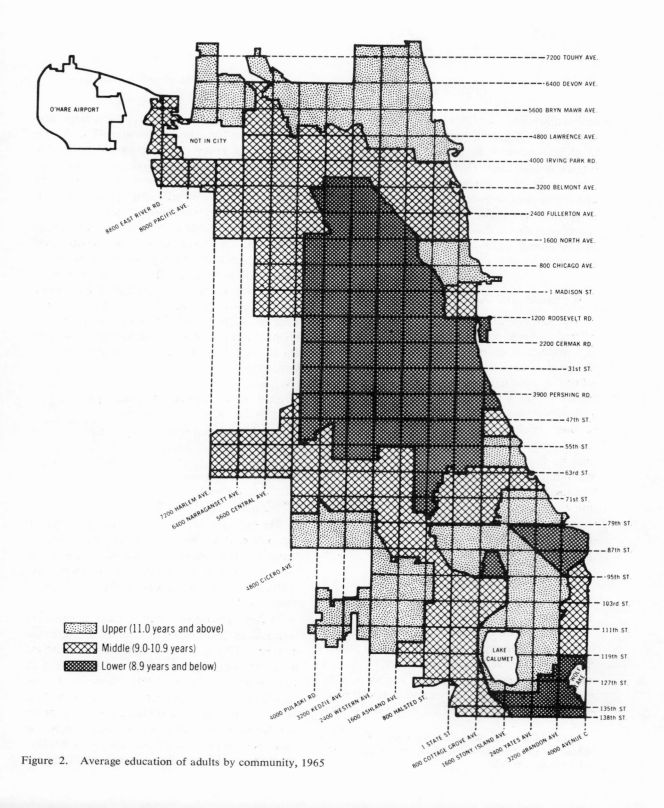

Figure 2. Average education of adults by community, 1965

Table 4
EDUCATIONAL ACHIEVEMENT OF ADULTS
(by average years of schooling completed)

| | *Median Level* | | |
	1940	1950	1960
United States	8.4	9.3	10.7
Boston	8.9	11.0	11.2
Philadelphia	8.2	9.0	10.4
Chicago	8.5	9.5	10.0
St. Louis	8.2	8.7	9.7
Baltimore	7.9	8.6	9.6
Cleveland	8.6	9.4	9.6

curred precisely during those years when the cities have often been characterized as deteriorating. Some city librarians have attributed declining use to the urban crisis, which may have an element of truth, but not because the educational level of the city has been going down.

It is a mistake to think of Chicago as sinking or even of just staying even in educational level of its residents. American society has made significant gains in schooling, the cities included, and this will continue in the future. Many young people, completing high school, are entering the adult community with 12 years of education (as compared with the present average of perhaps 10.5), and some significant numbers are going on to college. A deterrent here is the number of high school dropouts, which was estimated at 36 percent a few years ago,[8] but this negative influence may also be reduced to the extent that urban renewal and social reorganization occur.

Chicago has a million adults who have not completed high school, and they and their families constitute a special and immediate library challenge. On the other side, educational levels

[8]Robert J. Havighurst, *The Public Schools of Chicago* (Chicago: Board of Education of the City of Chicago, 1964), p.204.

continue upward, and by 1980 the Chicago Public Library will be providing service to a population in which a majority of adults will be at least high school graduates.

The Ghetto and Urban Renewal

The crisis of the cities is centered in the ghettos, the areas of extreme physical deterioration and social disorganization. Yet it is not easy to define the ghetto nor to establish its boundaries.

The number of people with subsistence incomes is one indicator. Chicago in 1960 had 483,000 people living in household units with less than $3,000 annual income. But not all of these lived in what are thought of as slum areas, and not all families in recognized slum areas were in this lowest income group.

Perhaps the best basis is to say that in Chicago the following sections show signs of severe physical deterioration and social disorganization: Near West Side, North Lawndale, East Garfield, Douglas, Woodlawn, Oaklawn, Near South Side, and Grand Boulevard. The population in these areas is approximately 600,000 persons, 17 percent of the city total. These are the ghetto residents in the direct sense. Even this is a changing group, for people move out of the slums as they can, and within these areas rehabilitation is being pushed.

Then in addition there are the adjacent areas of rapid transition, as shown in figure 3. One indicator of such areas is an educational level below what would be anticipated from other local social indices—that is, an educational level not commensurate with income level. They are marked by increasing turnover of residents and often by apprehension on the part of those who remain. Depending on definition, these areas contain up to

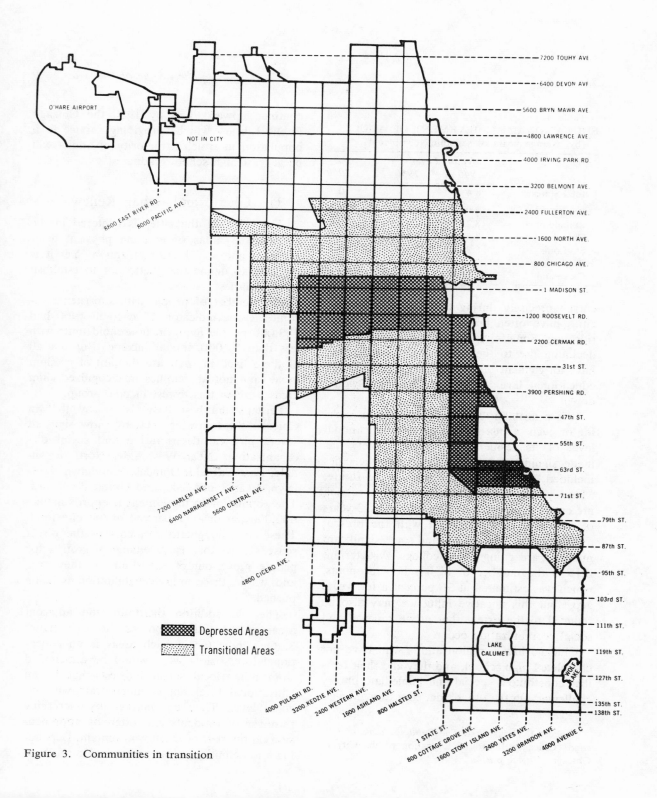

Figure 3.   Communities in transition

1,200,000 people, in addition to the 600,000 in the core slums. Some districts are deteriorating and therefore are potential ghettos, but others are undergoing rapid rehabilitation and will become better rather than poorer residential neighborhoods.

In general terms, several hundred thousand Chicagoans live in slum or near-slum conditions, and a larger number in addition could in time also live in such conditions if countermeasures are not taken. Almost half the people of Chicago are presently or potentially affected by blight in their neighborhoods. This is a measure of the scope of the "slum problem" faced by the Chicago Public Library. The city is "in a race with time," and the Library is one of the runners.

The Department of Development and Planning reports that "housing quality in Chicago has in fact been improving—from 1950 to 1960 the number of dilapidated units was cut by more than 50 percent."[9] A many-faceted renewal program is under way, with the major sites and study areas shown in figure 4.

Not only is the recognized ghetto to the west and south being attacked but also transition areas to the near northwest and near southwest, in an effort to act before slum conditions prevail. Progress is most evident in the Hyde Park-Kenwood district, Prairie Shores-Lake Meadows-South Commons, Lincoln Park, and most recently in the Near West Conservation Area. A close look at these "show-places" reveals that poor people are not the residents; rather the successfully rehabilitated sections are usually enclaves of middle-class occupancy.

[9]City of Chicago, Dept. of Development and Planning, *The Comprehensive Plan of Chicago, Analysis of City Systems* (Chicago: The Department, 1967), v.1, p.16.

On a less concentrated and unofficial basis, neighborhoods within the transition zone are being maintained by local residents, and in some cases new dwelling units are being built on vacant lots. In the long run this could be the more widespread movement. The localized approach may not result in the wholesale removal of older structures and building of new housing projects, but it can, nonetheless, contribute to physical improvement and social stability.

The future of the city is unclear. Urban blight may spread and become a systemic cancer. As the corporate body weakens, the focus of activity and power could conceivably shift to new centers. The assumption in this report is that Chicago has capacity for self-renewal, and, in one form or another, will remain the vital core of its region for at least the remainder of the century. Counter measures against deterioration are being applied, both officially by government and more significantly by local residents themselves. This effort may be stepped up in the period ahead, particularly if a substantial investment of federal funds is made in the constructive forces of the city.

The Chicago Public Library faces a special challenge in the ghetto today. It will also have a special opportunity in whatever rehabilitated areas emerge tomorrow, where, in relatively stable social conditions people of modest means and with ambitions to find their place in contemporary society and participate in its benefits, will live.

Summary

These then are the people which the Chicago Public Library should prepare to serve over the next twenty to thirty years:

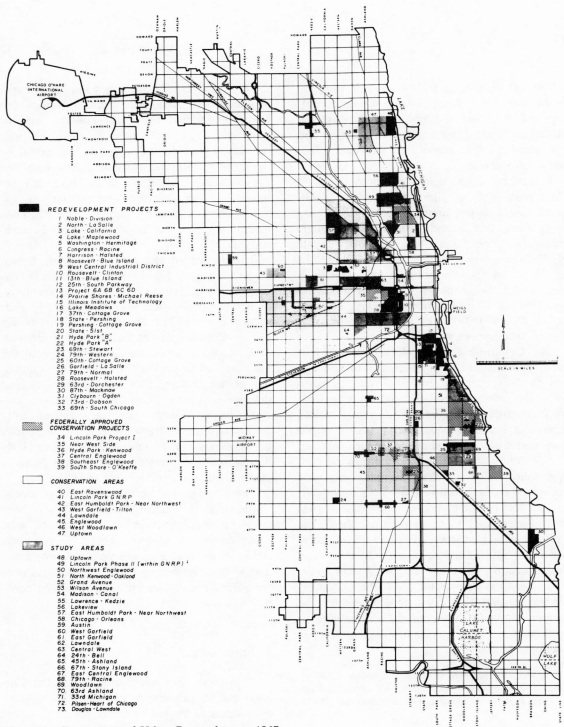

REDEVELOPMENT PROJECTS

1 Noble · Division
2 North · La Salle
3 Lake · California
4 Lake · Maplewood
5 Washington · Hermitage
6 Congress · Racine
7 Harrison · Halsted
8 Roosevelt · Blue Island
9 West Central Industrial District
10 Roosevelt · Clinton
11 13th · Blue Island
12 25th · South Parkway
13 Project 6A 6B 6C 6D
14 Prairie Shores · Michael Reese
15 Illinois Institute of Technology
16 Lake Meadows
17 37th · Cottage Grove
18 State · Pershing
19 Pershing · Cottage Grove
20 State · 51st
21 Hyde Park "B"
22 Hyde Park "A"
23 69th · Stewart
24 79th · Western
25 60th · Cottage Grove
26 Garfield · La Salle
27 79th · Normal
28 Roosevelt · Halsted
29 63rd · Dorchester
30 87th · Macknaw
31 Clybourn · Ogden
32 73rd · Dobson
33 69th · South Chicago

FEDERALLY APPROVED
CONSERVATION PROJECTS

34 Lincoln Park Project I
35 Near West Side
36 Hyde Park · Kenwood
37 Central Englewood
38 Southeast Englewood
39 South Shore · O'Keeffe

CONSERVATION AREAS

40 East Ravenswood
41 Lincoln Park G N R P
42 East Humboldt Park · Near Northwest
43 West Garfield · Tilton
44 Lawndale
45 Englewood
46 West Woodlawn
47 Uptown

STUDY AREAS

48 Uptown
49 Lincoln Park Phase II (within GNRP)
50 Northwest Englewood
51 North Kenwood · Oakland
52 Grand Avenue
53 Wilson Avenue
54 Madison · Canal
55 Lawrence · Kedzie
56 Lakeview
57 East Humboldt Park · Near Northwest
58 Chicago · Orleans
59 Austin
60 West Garfield
61 East Garfield
62 Lawndale
63 Central West
64 24th · Bell
65 45th · Ashland
66 67th · Stony Island
67 East Central Englewood
68 79th · Racine
69 Woodlawn
70 63rd Ashland
71 33rd Michigan
72 Pilsen · Heart of Chicago
73 Douglas · Lawndale

Figure 4.   Department of Urban Renewal areas, 1967

Some 3,600,000–3,700,000 Chicagoans in the next two decades, about at the present level, and possibly moving toward 4 million by the year 2000

Beyond the city proper a metropolitan population that will increase over the next twenty to thirty years toward 7 million, all of whom are of concern to the extent that a large city library has a responsibility beyond its corporate boundaries

Within the city a population that is relatively young at present, but which will balance out and include an older group of substantial size

A population of wide social and cultural range and diversity, with a steadily increasing level of educational achievement

A large population of blue-collar workers, in the semiskilled, skilled, and service trades, in a city and region with its economic life based on industry and manufacturing

A population that includes many of the business and cultural leaders of the Midwest, in a period when both economic and cultural life will be brought under pressure for change

A growing contingent of college students and a sizable group of school children using a wide range of library resources

A mounting group of specialists needed to perform the complex tasks of a technological and interdependent society

A city seeking to meet the urban problems of physical deterioration and social disorganization by means of a rigorous program of urban renewal, both official and indigenous

Now and here today, a half million people caught in severe deterioration and disorganization and demanding extraordinary effort on the part of the public library to help meet the human problems immediately at hand.

These are the people to be served in the remaining years of the century. It can be predicted with assurance that they will be seeking to live better lives by present standards and, in the process, will be using the accumulated record of knowledge, from the library and from other sources.

2 A Public Library for Chicago—Goals and Principles

Two concepts underlie this report on the Chicago Public Library: excellence and innovation. In this age of particular dependence on information and knowledge, the Library must have the capacity to help Chicago capitalize on its opportunities and solve its problems. Then the agency must find new ways to make its resources widely available and used.

A strong public library is not just a matter of prestige for Chicago. A library is a working agency—a service center for people, a source of intelligence for the business, educational, social, governmental, practical, and purely enjoyable life of the city. It should reach not only the affluent and educated, but also the poor and underprivileged who need it most.

General Goals for the Chicago Public Library

The nature of its present and potential contribution must be understood—what the public library is for must be clarified—before the Chicago Public Library can be evaluated as it stands today, and before a program for the future can be developed. Set forth in this chapter are the six social goals which should inspire and guide the agency in the next ten to twenty years. The goals are purposely stated in broad and general terms; they are not precise objectives imposed from above, but inclusive aims reflecting Chicago and its people

and providing ample room for change and emphasis. Within them exact programs are to be designed and then redesigned as time goes on, and priorities established and later adjusted, on the basis of user response.

1. *The Chicago Public Library is to open opportunity for self-development for people at whatever their stage of education and culture.*

   Two key terms animate this underlying public library purpose.

   One is self-development, the growth of the individual from wherever he is to some greater realization of his potential. The public library is the educational agency for the individual, serving *his* communication skills, progressing at *his* rate and speed.

   The individual may seek to satisfy immediate, short-term interests or lifelong ambitions. He may want a better job in one of Chicago's industries, or background on raising his children, or to understand a social problem, or pure pleasure from the works of man's mind and imagination. He may be groping toward pride in the kind of person he is. The individual seeks and the public library provides a means of self-development.

   The other key phrase is "people at whatever their stage of education and culture." This means just what it says, and includes the youngster at the comic-book stage and the adult unfamiliar with books as well as the educated and well-read individual. The library must use the full range of printed and audio-visual resources to serve people at their many stages of development.

If this first goal is to be achieved, the Chicago Public Library will have to become much more varied and flexible than it has been in the past, less prone to stock only an approved middle range of materials, and less rigid in organizing its materials according to standard methods and practices.

2. *The Chicago Public Library is to bring people and resources together, closing the gap between the individual and the record of knowledge.*

The aim is not to promote use of the library just because it is there. The task is to bring knowledge resources and potential users together, a social function which would be needed even if no libraries existed. The test of the Chicago Public Library today is not only the extent to which it provides materials and information, but also the extent to which it disseminates its recorded knowledge among the people of the city.

Informing the people, all people, about the library is a first step. Making libraries inviting and exciting is a next step. Personal, individual guidance is necessary, whether for the youngster who has wandered in and picked up his first book or the oldster looking for fresh interests in retirement. Once again the underprivileged in the city call for extraordinary and innovative effort.

The bringing together of resources and people must go beyond a simple response to the formulated and expressed interest of the individual. The library, in response to public need, is to advocate selected themes and topics. These may be as specific as consumer materials in one community and

art appreciation in another, or as broad as racial tolerance for the city as a whole.

Every outlet of the Chicago system is to select issues of significance to its constituency and "feature" materials on the designated topics; examples are sex education, community control of schools, censorship, the Vietnam war, the drug problem, moral permissiveness. This does not mean that the Library will officially sponsor one or another view or course of action on such matters. But it does mean that the resident in any community will know that if an issue is of concern to him and his fellowmen, he can confidently turn to his public library where he will find not just an occasional publication on the subject somewhere back on the shelves but a wide-ranging, heavily duplicated multimedia presentation brought together and spotlighted for his use. Indeed, he may decide to consult the record precisely because the Library itself has taken first steps to call attention to the question and to proclaim the resources featured in the agency. The selected topics need not all be social issues as such, but should include new vistas of communication—experimental films, underground literature, and the like. Once interest is aroused, strategies for self-development must be indicated, not in the few narrow tracks of the schools, but in hundreds of sequences, to reflect the many ways in which people strive upward. This will be the public library in its unique educational role, not only responding to change but influencing the direction of change.

The Chicago Public Library is not solely to accumulate and organize; it is to select, describe, analyze, display, manipulate, feature, interpret, project, modify, dramatize its resources, connecting them with people. This is the new dimension which the institution must create in the next period, the relating of seeker to source, the stimulation of search, the opening of avenues of individual growth.

3. *The Chicago Public Library is to bring information on the topics of contemporary living into the lives of people.*

The task of the public library is to provide accurate and balanced facts rapidly and in depth for a society increasingly dependent on specific knowledge. The Chicago Public Library is to become the information center for the city, the first place that most people turn either to get reliable facts from the library information bank or to be referred to official, specialized, and professional sources.

Information for whom? For the unemployed dropout and the successful businessman, for the Appalachian family newly arrived at Wilson and Broadway and the cosmopolitan family living in a high-rise apartment on the lake a half-mile east, for the local block officer and the metropolitan civic leader, for the young person going to his first symphony concert and the sophisticated adult comparing experimental dance groups.

For people not accustomed to using authenticated information, the Library must go a step further. It must show the inquirer *how* the information can be used, and help him, at least in the first steps, to use it. For ghetto residents in particular, it is not enough simply to offer reliable information —about jobs, or health, or consumer products, or family affairs—for if information is to be utilized, specific guidance on where and how must be offered, and at times contacts established, whether with a job source, social agency, health clinic or whatever.

Information "centers" are springing up in many specialized locations, such as government agencies and professional associations. The public library will not replace these, but its function is to be the point of first call, the fact resource for the city in its many forms and its rich variety, and the referral center to special-interest sources. The goal as conceived here calls for a more powerful information service than has appeared as yet in the United States.

4. *The Chicago Public Library is to enter into the community and cultural life of the City, serving as a local center through its branch libraries and as a metropolitan center in its central activities.*

A city library, while essentially serving individuals, should not stand apart from the group interests and associations that people develop when they are stimulated. Some of these associations—business and civic groups, for example—flourish independently of the library but they need the resources of the agency; in a sense the Chicago Public Library is the "special library" for these organizations within the City. In some associations such as those devoted to educational objectives the Library should be an active partner, participating in planning and accepting responsibility for its appropriate share of programs. For certain activities, those devoted to literary and cultural life, the Chicago Public Library is a natural center.

Community identification starts in the locality. The public library began as a community agency, close to the people in their local variety. Over the years, as communities shifted and as greater demand for resources appeared on the part of educated individuals, the library grew away from its local roots. Branch libraries in Chicago must get back in working relationship with their neighborhoods. In the many stable areas of the city, this means reestablishing lines of communication. In the disorganized and transition areas, community affiliations are often limited and shifting, but there is no choice in such areas except to build on what constructive forces, no matter how weak, are there.

Many localities are seeking a center for the common lives of their people—to discuss their problems, seek out solutions, share in the culture of their time, and in the process to reestablish group identity. The branch library is a natural center for this purpose, not in any one standard pattern, but in programs adapted to each locality.

Service as a community and cultural center also has a city-wide application. Even as a local neighborhood seeks its identity, so the city as a whole has a common intellectual and cultural life. This dimension of urban living has no common center or focal point in Chicago. A first step should be the establishment by the Chicago Public Library of a cultural information center, to which every Chicagoan can turn for facts about events, people, and resources of the city, the theater, the arts, the music world, and literary affairs.

In time associations will emerge, either centered in the Library or with the Library as an active participant. This will be the library in which people live a part of their intellectual and cultural lives, not simply the reservoir where they go on occasion to get knowledge to use elsewhere.

5. *The Chicago Public Library is to aid and supplement the formal education programs of schools and colleges, by supplying materials for students that cannot be adequately and conveniently provided by the institutions of formal instruction.*

The public library shares responsibility with the schools and colleges for providing

printed, audio, and visual resources for students. However, this is a supplementary function for the public library, to be carried out within an agreed plan and division of responsibility with the formal educational institutions.

The task of the public library is to provide for students those wider and more advanced subject materials which secondary schools and colleges cannot or will not maintain. The public library thus becomes the comprehensive subject resource which students use first while still in school and then on through adult life when they are no longer formal students.

Students through the master's level should be able to turn to the Chicago Public Library for these wider sources, and the Library should consciously provide collections and buildings for the purpose. This will call for collections at a higher level than are now maintained either in the main building or the regional branches, and within reach of students. It will also call for extensive study locations within libraries, particularly in low-income areas where facilities for study at home are limited or lacking. For a part of his library and media needs, the more extensive subject sources short of research materials, the advanced high school student and the commuting college student in particular would depend on the Chicago Public Library.

6. *The Chicago Public Library is to provide specialized resources to sustain the complex life of a great city.*

Chicago and its metropolitan area are the center for a concentration of specialized activities, in business, manufacturing, the professions, government, education, and the arts.

These activities increasingly depend on recorded knowledge, for basic understanding and for immediate facts. Without access to library resources, the affairs of the city, public and private, would have to be conducted without knowledge of what others have learned and without the data on which sound decisions must rest. Various agencies—universities, business firms, government itself—maintain libraries for this purpose. Chicago is blessed with two research libraries, the John Crerar Library for science and the Newberry Library for aspects of the humanities. But various gaps remain at the level of advanced and specialized resources. The Chicago Public Library has responsibility, across the board, for service to the economic, educational, and cultural life of the city, to supplement existing collections where needed, to fill gaps where necessary.

Specialized interests come down to individuals. People in Chicago develop concern about or enthusiasm for topics associated with their occupations or their intellectual interests or their leisure-time activities. These range from an unconventional hobby to delight in experimental literary expression, from special study of some far corner of the world to the history of their own city. As private citizens they do not have corporate libraries to turn to, nor are they members of a university community. The Chicago Public Library is their library, even if they have interests shared by only a limited number of Chicagoans.

The public library cannot realistically aspire to complete research collections in all possible fields. But it has a responsibility to go well beyond the level of the casual adult reader and the student at the high school and early college levels. Even as the Chicago Public Library must become an agency that reaches into the ghetto, to serve the people there, so it must also develop resources and services for the individual of specialized tastes,

whatever his locality. This must be the library for Chicago at its economic and cultural growing edge.

These stated goals imply certain other aims or possible roles which the Chicago Public Library would *not* seek to achieve, except in certain specifically defined areas where it has a unique and continuing contribution to make.

In this formulation the Library would not be an agency of formal group instruction, whether in educational-academic or in cultural-recreational areas. These are the proper responsibility of the schools, colleges, and local educational centers, with which the Chicago Public Library should maintain close association and working relations. The Library may organize group activities explicitly to stimulate and guide the use of its books, films, records, and other resources, but group instruction as such is not central to its mission.

Similarly, the Chicago Public Library is not to serve as a school library, in the sense of providing a curricular collection and multiple copies for school assignments. The public library will be the planned resource for students when they seek to use a comprehensive subject library.

The objectives as set forth do not stress the provision of advanced research collections. These are the proper responsibility of university libraries and such special institutions as the Newberry and Crerar libraries. However, to achieve its goals the Chicago Public Library will have to increase the level and scope of its central resources substantially to serve the many special interests of Chicagoans and the growing number of commuting students up through the master's level. The Library should build distinctive research resources for the Midwest in selected fields such as urban affairs and Negro literature.

Finally, the Library will not serve as a social

welfare agency, advising people on the solutions to their problems. These are the proper functions of guidance and medical centers and of personnel maintained and trained for this purpose. However, local branches should have the best published material dealing with personal and family questions, and the central collection should serve as a resource for the social workers themselves. The public library would seek to bridge the gap between people and specialized services available to them by providing explicit information about how they can be used.

There is more than ample room for imagination, innovation, and fresh approaches to library service in the six basic objectives, from which the people's library agency should not be diverted by ventures into formal instruction, advanced research, or provision of welfare services. Chicago needs a *better library,* not an ineffectual library that tries its hand at what other agencies do better. The mission of the library is to bring impact, effectiveness, and quality into its job of providing the recorded resources of knowledge and getting them used.

Principles Implied in the Goals

This compact statement of social goals for the Chicago Public Library suggests several principles which must be applied rigorously and continuously if the Library is to meet the needs of the city. These are accessibility, usability, flexibility, multimedia provision, individualized service, and user-community orientation in determining resources and services. They apply across the board, in the large central facility and in the smallest branch. Unless these principles are applied, the goals will not be achieved.

ACCESSIBILITY

Libraries are used if the effort required to reach them is within the motivation of potential users. Beyond that point, no building however monumental nor any service however modern will be used to the extent justified by the investment necessary to build and operate them.

There is no standard distance which users will travel to use a public library, precisely because there is no standard user. Because motivation to read differs, effort expended to get to a library differs. Every public library decides, consciously or unconsciously, how many of its constituents it will serve by how close the outlets it provides are to people.

The spacing of outlets must be reconsidered and the standard service radius of a mile questioned, particularly in disorganized neighborhoods. Convenience of access is particularly important when motivation is weak. At its lowest level, it is necessary to bring resources out where people gather or wait, rather than to expect them to come into a branch at a distance. The Chicago Public Library has been reaching out, putting books in welfare centers, medical clinics, jury rooms, juvenile court waiting rooms, most recently in low-income housing projects and at street corners in the summer "Story Caravan."

Accessibility is determined by visibility as well as by distance. If people are to use the public library they must know where it is and what it has to offer. This awareness starts with location at the crossroads, in the middle of shopping and related activities. It extends to publicity about the library; every Chicagoan should be reached and informed about where his library is and what it has for him. It includes the image of the institution, not as a remote storehouse, but as a communication agency committed to the interests of the people.

Accessibility is not solely geographical. Materials brought functionally close to people, in their place of employment, where they gather for special interests, in locations where they are confined (hospitals, for example), also are used. This was the concept behind the "deposit collections" of the Chicago Public Library, but the program now needs revitalization. The principle is books where people are.

USABILITY

Libraries are difficult for people to use. If any librarian doubts this, he would do well to read the direct, immediate reports of the experiences of a public panel of users who went into the Chicago Public Library as part of this survey and simply tried to locate resources and obtain information. Difficulty in use applies to the educated and experienced person, but even more to the individual of limited background.

From the moment that the user enters the library, whether the central building on Michigan Avenue or the smallest branch, the plan of service should be clear and self-evident. Identification and directional signs should abound. Informed and concerned staff should be immediately available. Organization of materials on the shelves should be from the standpoint of use. Kinds of varieties of resources should be identified and conditions of use proclaimed.

Usability also depends on old-fashioned courtesy and helpfulness of staff. Public library service is by definition service to and for people. Staff should be selected on this basis, informed in no uncertain terms that courtesy and helpfulness are required on the job, disciplined if they fail to display these simple virtues, and dismissed for cause if they persist. No tenure or other considerations can prevail over the requirement that government workers serve cooperatively with the people that government is maintained to serve.

Usability extends to the creation of a stimulating library environment. Display of resources in a public library is as important as their selection. Exhibits are in themselves a form of communication and can be related to library holdings. Visual and audio materials can be presented in their own right and also related to printed resources. The subject content of even a small branch library is so rich and varied that no special measure of imagination should be needed to make it come alive. Even as a museum is a place of art, so a library should be a place of the ideas and expression of man, set forth to attract, stimulate, and guide the user.

FLEXIBILITY

The city library, to carry out its mission, must be sensitive to all kinds and levels of people, and must work with them at whatever stage they are in the process of self-development. Chicago, for example, has several hundred thousand well-educated, highly-cultured "cosmopolitans," in Hyde Park-Kenwood, the Near North Side, the Lincoln Park areas, for whom the standard branch and the usual local collection are not suited. The agency must "tune in" at this level and encompass more sophisticated, intellectual, avant-garde holdings. Chicago also has several hundred thousand people just starting to use the printed page for communication, for which the standard branch once again is not suited. The library equally must "reach out" to them, even if this means the stocking of materials which it ceased to buy a generation ago when the earlier immigrants began moving up to more "approved" publications.

The theme is people in their great variety.

The library must respond with flexibility and sensitivity, and not harden into bureaucracy. It will not reach its city unless it has staff that knows this variety, makes a commitment, focuses effort on distinct groups and levels, and designs different programs for each. Standard patterns should be avoided in branch libraries. Today much the same kind of collection sits on the shelves of all branches in Chicago, no matter what the variations in community background and educational levels. In some localities the standard collection is appropriate and is heavily used; in some localities the subject collection stands virtually unused. In these latter instances rotating collections rather than permanent acquisitions, tested to determine local response, would at once serve the locality more flexibly and stretch the tax dollar further. Standard provision of branches in Chicago has progressed over the years to the point where whole branch buildings now virtually stand outside the community and its interests, reflecting an earlier day but unsuited to present needs, and experiencing only a fraction of their former use.

Final and rigid programs are not laid down in this report. Professional librarians are far from knowing all the answers concerning urban library service, and outside surveyors would be presumptuous if they thought they could prescribe in full detail what Chicago needs for the next decades. What is stressed throughout the report are experimental and pilot projects, to determine feasibility and response, and from which new structures of service can be built on the basis of verified experience.

MULTIMEDIA PROVISION

Library theory and standards accept audio-visual materials, but in practice only as an adjunct to the book-centered library. This can be illustrated by the holdings of the average community branch in Chicago: 35,000 hardbound books, 500 paperbacks (a recent addition), 75 magazine subscriptions, 4 drawers of pamphlets and documents (little used), 150 recordings (another recent addition), and occasional film showings. Each form of material stands separate from and unrelated to the others.

The social goals presented here require a multimedia approach on the part of the Chicago Public Library. Each of the media and forms is to be considered, evaluated, and provided on an equal basis with the others; the user should be as able to get from the library a performance of a play on film or recording as the original text in book form; he should as readily find a magazine as a book· about ceramics; he should be as able to see a quality print of a painter as to read about him in a book. In fact, if the film or the record or the print or the pamphlet is more suited to a particular audience, it should be acquired first in that form. Some library agencies in neighborhoods where reading is very limited might be much less collections of books and much more other media. The "other" could stay within print but vary in physical form—for example, more extensive use of magazines and pamphlets in low-education neighborhoods; or the library unit where suited to the local people could be more visual than graphic, more sound than print.

The several media and forms are to be interrelated, the book with the photograph or model, the poem with the recording, the background publication with the newest government survey on the same topic, the recorded story with the children's book. It must be as possible to *hear* or to *view* in the library as it is to open a ·book and read, even if this means turntables and earphones in each branch and individual viewing screens scattered through the main building. Materials must be shown as fits their forms and functions, for example, continuous showings of a sequence of vocational guidance films or of filmed children's classics, educational exhibits and models (the book in three dimensions) adjacent to related reading materials, the filmstrip on life in Biafra or on the process of photosynthesis in plants with an individual, illuminated viewer.

The Chicago Public Library in this next period, if it is to bring the record of knowledge to all its people, must be multimedia at its core and not just at its fringes. Anything less will leave the Library on the sidelines as new and sensitive means of communication open.

INDIVIDUALIZED SERVICE

The goals set forth will not be achieved unless a librarian mediates between individual and resources, helping each person find his way through the world of print and film and recorded sound. Such guidance is particularly needed by the individual unaccustomed to books and libraries. The right suggestion at the right time can spark the interest of the young child. The teen-ager can be caught up in the world of learning, if the topic to be learned is genuinely within his interest and if the book recommended for the purpose is suited to his abilities. The adult of limited education similarly stands uncertain before the shelves of a library and needs human mediation.

While individuals become more at home in the world of books through experience, even the well-educated and well-read need individualized service as they venture into new territory. This may be the high school honors student ready to go beyond the school cur-

riculum. It may be the citizen who wants more first-hand accounts of the issues of the day than he finds in his newspaper and convenient magazines, or the businessman studying a new market, or the graduate student branching out into a related field.

A library to be effective must be logically organized and have all possible aids to use. But in the end it must have staff able to help the individual. The cost for such service is substantial, but once provided it prepares the person to go forward under his own initiative. There is no choice except to release this initiative which, once released, will thrive on the rich resources of the library.

USER-COMMUNITY ORIENTATION

Libraries readily become institution-oriented rather than people-oriented. Old methods and materials are used to meet new needs. The integrity of existing collections and the continuation of established staffing patterns are often the underlying determinant of service decisions.

Reaching into the ghettos is again a case in point, but one could equally use young sophisticated cosmopolitans as an example. The hard fact is that little in verified professional theory or in the librarian's usual experience provides the answers to serving the blighted areas in the heart of the city. There is no alternative except to open contact with and get feedback directly from the people. Librarians should be circulating among local residents, learning about their concerns and interests, talking to local leaders, participating in organizations, trying out sample materials to determine response or lack of it. This does not mean suppression of all library initiative or abdication of all selection standards. The librarian is the one to probe and suggest and experiment. Once promising lines of service and resources are uncovered he will be the locality's expert on what to acquire and how to organize it, which is the role of the librarian in any setting.

Similarly the efforts of the public library should be coordinated with the programs of other agencies. No institution or service alone is going to eliminate urban blight. The concept behind the Model Cities approach is joint and coordinated attack by all services. One source for determining what the library should provide is to learn what school, health and welfare, and other agencies are trying to do. In this respect the library's role will be that of provider of intelligence resources for goals established by larger institutions, which is what school and college and business libraries do.

Rather than depending solely on standard professional practices, built up from experience that may no longer be valid, the librarian must make fresh contact and build user-oriented and community-oriented programs. This concept is a key consideration in the revitalization of the Chicago Public Library, because the institution has grown away from its clientele, both present and potential.

Conclusion

A library, like other organizations of workers, must have goals to achieve and principles for guidance. Without this animating force, an agency becomes bureaucratic, following established patterns without enthusiasm and without concern for the people served. Initiative becomes dulled, standards of performance become lax. Younger staff members are particularly affected, because they seek purpose in their work, not having become complacent through long years of experience.

The Chicago Public Library pointedly needs a sense of mission at this stage of its development. It has been publicly criticized and would like to prove its worth. It has been repressed and would like to show its power. It has capacities of staff and resources which should be mobilized.

This statement of goals and principles is offered as a rallying point. The formulation here is not intended as a final doctrine to be adopted without reflection or review. On the contrary, it is more a starting point and a set of general directions. The statement should be systematically discussed and sharpened and modified, by staff members young and old, both to improve the goals themselves and to pull the staff together in common cause. Then the goals and principles should be applied throughout the library program, in a statement of book selection policy, in developing community activities, in relating media to print. The objectives and guiding tenets also open new staffing patterns in requiring professionally-trained people other than librarians, for example, and in utilizing local people as librarian's aides to provide individual service.

The Chicago Public Library can be significant in its city. Chicago desperately needs a library that will bring the record of facts and knowledge and wisdom and expression into the lives of people. The wellspring of such an agency is not buildings or even money, but clear purpose and complete commitment.

3 User Groups and Service Policies

The population characteristics set forth in chapter 1 establish the shape and limits of library service in Chicago, the landscape that must be comprehended in broad outline and major contours. Reader groups, present and potential, constitute fixed points within the landscape, centers to which library service should lead. Because librarians may not appreciate the vista in its broad sweep, or set their sights on identifiable targets within it, public library service often seems unfocused and not directly related to the interests and issues before distinct segments within the population.

To understand present clientele and to sense potential user groups is that much more difficult when the setting is urban. In the city are the vital forces that mold a society, and here also are the tension points where problems form. Both trends and problems lead to change. Particularly in the urban setting is the library program called upon for flexibility; failing that the institution may turn in upon itself and away from the mass of people.

This chapter is devoted to two questions: who uses the Chicago Public Library, and what should be the broad outlines of the Library's service policies toward existing and possible user groups? The Chicago library landscape will be sketched in by means of general statistics showing user response to present service programs. A variety of groups found in the urban setting will then be indicated, some now reached by the Library and others whose response has been limited. This will lead to proposals for broad policies which should

guide the Chicago Public Library in the period ahead.

The policy proposals derive from the statement of library purposes and principles formulated in chapter 2. Succeeding chapters then set forth a program to carry out the policies. The starting point here is the people of Chicago and the library response to them.

Use of the Chicago Public Library

The total picture for the Chicago Public Library is occupied, in the foreground by the people of the city, 3,600,000 in number, and in the background by more than that number again in the metropolitan area. At the fringes, but still part of the picture, are additional people in northern Illinois, southern Wisconsin, and northwestern Indiana. The total region will be dealt with in chapter 11, "Metropolitan Library Relations."

Oddly enough, public libraries do not customarily maintain statistics that show how many different people use them and who these people are. Existing records do not provide an answer to the fundamental question of how many Chicagoans are reached by the Chicago Public Library. It was necessary to build up such essential figures from various records and from direct studies of library users. An explanation must therefore be given of how the data in table 5 were obtained.

The base was the Library's file of registrants, listing individuals who have obtained a card to borrow materials for home use. The

Library maintains a continuous count of this file, which stood at 697,802 in 1968. Registered borrowers are classified into two groups: children 5–14 years of age (259,939), and persons 15 and above (437,923). Names are removed at the end of a three-year registration period, so these almost 700,000 people are individuals who have used the institution at least once in this period, users in the broadest sense. But the registration base must be adjusted for several reasons. The file includes non-Chicagoans who are eligible to obtain cards from the Chicago Public Library without charge. The Library itself identified 69,745 such individuals in a count of registrants for five weeks in the spring of 1966. Use studies for this survey in December 1968 confirmed this figure, which identified 22 percent of Central Library and just under 5 percent of branch users as living outside of Chicago.

Nonresident use differs markedly between children and adults (only 6,000 of the out-of-city registrants are at the juvenile level), so that the decrease for nonresidents is not uniform by age levels. For determination of use by Chicagoans alone, nonresidents were removed from the base. A further adjustment had to be made because it is not necessary to be a registrant to visit the Library and use the resources on the premises. Use studies made in a sample period in 1968 revealed that 12.9 percent of children and 19.8 percent of adults who come into the Library do not have library cards; this was determined by direct questioning of children and by a question on a questionnaire to adults. In this case the noncardholders (estimated at 106,000 individuals) were added to the registration base. Finally, the Library has no age breakdown beyond children and adults, but the user study provided information about the age spread of adults as well as about other social characteristics. The results of this information concerning the age of actual users was applied to the registration base to "force" an estimated age distribution.

The result of these several manipulations are the data in table 5 on the number of city residents reached by the Chicago Public Library. For a total population base, estimates for 1970 are used on the supposition that these figures are closer to present reality than the 1960 census returns.

The Library directly serves a little over one-fifth (22.3 percent) of the city population 5 years of age and over (20.4 percent if the number of users is projected against the total city population, including infants). When the registration base from which these figures start is considered, it might be best to say that the

Table 5
CHICAGO RESIDENTS USING THE CHICAGO PUBLIC LIBRARY, BY AGE LEVELS

	Library users, 1968	Estimated Chicago population, 1970*	Percent of group using the Library
Children 5–14	286,697	687,000	41.7
Young Adults 15–19	168,405	290,000	57.8
Adults 20–39	172,886	915,000	18.9
Adults 40–59	77,036	812,000	9.5
Adults 60 and over	29,560	533,000	5.6
Total	734,584	3,237,000	22.3

*City of Chicago, Dept. of Development and Planning, *Comprehensive Plan of Chicago, Conditions and Trends: Population, Economy, Land* (Chicago: The Department, 1967), p.41. These statistics are close to the 1964 projections of the Population Research and Training Center of The University of Chicago, as reported in *Population Projections for the City of Chicago and the Chicago Standard Metropolitan Statistical Area, 1970 and 1980* (Chicago: The Center, 1964), p.24.

Library "barely reaches" or "touches" one in five Chicagoans of an age to use library resources. Comparisons with the percentage of people reached in other cities is not feasible because of the lack of data, but a forthcoming report in the Deiches series based on the Enoch Pratt Free Library in Baltimore will show a 28.4 percent response in that city, comparable to the 20.4 percent figure for Chicago.

Various characteristics of the 734,000 Chicago library users serve to indicate the response by various segments in the population. Almost two-fifths (38.7 percent) are children 14 years of age or under. Another 22.9 percent are in the 15–19 school-age group, so that 62 percent of the users of the Chicago Public Library are under 20 years of age. The additional adult users fall largely in the 20–39 group, with only 10.5 percent between 40 and 59, and 4.1 percent 60 or over. The users of the Library are essentially a youthful group.

Over one-half are students using the Library for schoolwork. This is true of many of the almost 300,000 juvenile users. It also applies to 49.3 percent of library visitors 15 years of age and older. Consequently, the Chicago Public Library is to a significant extent an agency for formal students. If the children of elementary school age and students in the older group were removed, the Library would have approximately one-quarter million users rather than the present three-quarters million. Stated differently, a realistic assessment of adult library use in Chicago shows that some 254,000 persons no longer in school of approximately 2,100,000 Chicagoans in this category use the agency. Thus, the Library reaches only one in eight out-of-school adults, 12.5 percent of the total in the city. This statistic alone should make library planners and policy makers hospitable to fresh approaches and new concepts of service.

Library users in Chicago have formal education well above the average, as has been found in past studies of public library use.[1] College graduates constitute 27.5 percent of the adult clientele of the Chicago Public Library, but are only 6 percent of the adult population of the city. On the other hand, adults who have not gone beyond elementary school constitute under 2 percent of library users, but almost 20 percent of Chicago residents. Similarly, the largest occupational groups among library users, other than students, are members of the professions. Educational achievement is the underlying determinant. If education is held constant, even the decline in library use with age reflected in table 5 (page 25) is markedly reduced; a college graduate over 60 years of age is almost as likely as a college graduate under 40 to use the public library.

In chapter 1 the steady increase in the educational level of adults in Chicago was noted. In a sense the city is catching up with its library and will make greater demands upon it as time goes by. Part of the concern of this study is how the Library, rather than wait until this occurs, can go back to where the people are, to meet them at their various stages of development and go forward together with them. This should be an underlying principle of library policy in the next decade.

Contact between the Library and persons of limited education has already been made, despite the statistics that indicate substantial education on the part of users. It should be remembered that all such figures are averages or measures of central tendency. The Chicago Public Library does reach adults who are not high school graduates, at least 20,000 of them. While chapter 5 will show that three-quarters or more of branch library home circulation

[1]Bernard Berelson, *The Library's Public* (New York: Columbia Univ. Pr., 1950), p.24.

of books occurs in comfortable communities of middle or upper educational levels, 463,865 books were taken out for home use during 1968 in the areas defined as severe slums in chapter 1. By the same token, while its clientele is generally youthful, the institution serves almost 30,000 Chicagoans over 60 years of age. Library use in the end is an individual act, represented by the single child or single adult in communication with a book, picture, film, or recording. The social impact of the Library is not measured by a head count alone.

For what kinds of materials do people come to the Library? The answer is as diverse as the users themselves. Direct questioning of individuals in the Library shows an emphasis on subject material, books about something. Only 10.8 percent of persons 15 years of age and over coming to the Chicago Public Library were seeking contemporary fiction. By and large the users want material in the broad middle range that the collections offer—not very elementary publications on the one hand nor very specialized monographs on the other, not very commercial films on the one side nor very experimental films on the other, neither small-group magazines nor highly scholarly journals, neither the throwaway directions for installing home appliances nor research reports in offprint form. The Library occupies a middle ground, and those who seek a standard range of subject publications, starting with students, naturally respond. This does not prove that other materials, more elementary and ephemeral or more specialized and elite, would not be used if provided. Some people respond to what the Library offers—those who believe that the institution does not have what they want or have found by experience that the material they seek is lacking simply do not come.

Among those who do come, how many actually find what they want? On being asked when leaving, 60.5 percent said they were well satisfied, 26.7 percent indicated that they were partially satisfied, and 12.8 gave a distinctly negative response. The degree of satisfaction is a little less in the Central Library than in the branches, not because the collection is weaker but because the users' needs and expectations are greater. Four out of ten patrons, in branches as well as the Central Library, requested help in some form from a staff member. Of those who did, 79 percent found the staff "helpful," 14.5 percent "somewhat helpful," and 6.5 percent "not helpful."

On balance, the record is somewhat favorable. A city educational and cultural agency that has 450,000 satisfied customers and another 190,000 whose needs have been partially met has clearly established a place for itself. So far as it goes, and for those who use it, the Chicago Public Library is an institution of some genuine significance.

In an effort to determine actual performance by librarians when users seek help, a panel of "anonymous shoppers" was used.[2] A considerable range of questions was presented both in the Central Library and the branches; these were designed to test the accuracy of information provided, skill of staff in reference searching, awareness of current trends and publications, background of book knowledge, and disposition of staff to follow up or follow through on inquiries. Panel members also supplied narrative accounts of steps involved and treatment accorded them in such transactions as the issuance of a library card and guidance to the location of materials. Staff performance varied widely. Some staff members displayed background, judgment, and empathy with the inquirer; others were casual, disinterested, and inaccurate. A few questions on which performance was clearly deficient will serve to

[2]This technique is described in the Appendix.

indicate why some library users are dissatisfied with the service provided:

Who is the current Secretary of the United States Department of Health, Education and Welfare? (Asked four months after John W. Gardner had resigned.)

In ten agencies of the Library, the correct answer was given by one branch and the Central Library; incorrect answers were given by seven branches, and one believed that a change had occurred but could not find the name of new appointee.

What is the most recent population estimate you have for the United States?

In ten agencies, the answer varied from 179,323,175 to 208,874,000; staff members seldom reported the source they consulted.

Could you tell me how many countries belong to the United Nations?

Ten agencies, including the Central Library, gave a total of five different answers, none correct.

I saw a Sherlock Holmes movie called "The Pearl of Death" last night. What was the name of the book or story it was made from?

Nine agencies, including the Central Library and all three regional branches, were unable to answer. A subbranch did supply the correct answer. One branch responded with a sharp "How would I know?"

What are the first two names of O. J. Simpson, a football player?

Three of ten agencies located the answer; three others suggested that the inquirer call the *Chicago Tribune.*

Other questions involved advice on books or recommendations on material to consult. Responses by staff members varied from enthusiastic and intelligent to perfunctory and uninformed to such inquiries as "I just moved to Chicago. Can you recommend any background material about the city?" and "My nephew, he's fifteen years old, has read and liked Salinger's *Catcher in the Rye.* What other title along this line can you suggest that I get as a gift for him?" No branch tested was able to help in the last question. To keep the record in balance, it must be noted that some staff performance was at a high level; for example, to the somewhat complicated question, "I understand large areas in Michigan are being burned over to save the Kirtland's warbler from extinction. What area is involved, where is it, and how large is it?," thorough and current material was provided in the Central Library.

On the basis of several hundred responses to a variety of questions asked by a panel of "shoppers" of quite different backgrounds, the following list of shortcomings of staff performance was compiled: minimal interest in exactly what the inquirer is seeking, failure to recognize fairly well-known titles, undue dependence on somewhat outdated books rather than on current reports in answering requests for recent information, a concept of resources limited to the book or at most the book and the magazine rather than to the full range of communication media, and lack of initiative on the part of staff in seeking material from another source if the local library does not have it.

Another general criticism to be made of direct staff service to users is failure to follow up to determine if the inquirer has actually obtained what he wanted—a little as though the doctor prescribed without determining whether the fever went down or the teacher instructed without testing whether students understood. And unfortunately, both the user reports and the "shopper" reports contained a recurring theme of impersonal and sometimes curt treatment by staff members.

The present study in essence is an attempt to show how more can be done for the 450,000 satisfied users of the Chicago Public Library, to identify means of improving service to some 300,000 patrons who are not fully satisfied, and to determine how the Library can be of value to at least some of the 2,500,000 Chicagoans it does not reach at present.

Service to Children

The Chicago Public Library serves approximately 285,000 children of elementary-school age in the city, but does not reach another 400,000. Youngsters make up 38.7 percent of present users of the Library. They are relatively heavy users; the average juvenile registrant borrowed 14 books during 1968, as compared with 9 for the average adult registrant—on a per capita (as distinct from a per registrant) basis, each child in Chicago took out over 7 books and each adult under 2 books. In all but 8 of the 62 branches and subbranches, circulation to children of age 14 and under was greater than circulation to all users above this age, and in 19 of the branches children's circulation constitutes two-thirds or more of the total. Youngsters are also by far the largest participants in group activities conducted by the Library, accounting for almost 200,000 attendances during 1968 at story hours, film showings, class visits, and similar activities. The Chicago Public Library is to a significant extent a children's agency.

Here is a distinct user group which the Library has clearly recognized, built into its service programs, and provided for in its buildings—in other words, a group for which service has been intensified. Designated staff members serve as specialists for children, and throughout the branches they are the only reader-group specialists. Unlike the adult collections, the children's resources showed generally high holdings on the checklists used for evaluation purposes. An extra measure of individual stimulation and guidance is given to youngsters as they enter and explore the world of print. A rich tradition and high standards have marked this aspect of the Library's program. As a result of this intensification over the years, materials and services provided for children constitute one of the more impressive dimensions of the Library's program.

Yet a distinct decline has recently appeared in children's use of the Chicago Public Library. From 1960 to 1968 the home circulation of library books to children decreased by 21 percent. This in itself indicates a downward drift, but a startling figure comes to light when the recent increase in children in the city is taken into account. In 1960 Chicago had 584,012 children and the Library circulated 6,062,000 books to juveniles—*13˙ per child*; in 1968 the city had approximately 650,000 children and the Library circulated 4,783,000 volumes to juveniles—*7.3 per child*. Over half of the branches continued to show a decline in children's use in 1968 as compared with 1967, although the branches as a whole experienced a 4.3 percent gain in circulation to all users. Bookmobile circulation, which is 79 percent juvenile, has shown a 37 percent decrease in the 1960–1968 period. Here again flat statistical counts are not the full measure of service rendered, but, particularly for children's use, home circulation is a valid indicator of response. A fundamental shift is occurring which must be considered in reviewing library policy.

No definite research evidence exists on reasons for the decline in public library use by children which has occurred elsewhere as well as Chicago. Various likely factors can be cited, and some combination of these no doubt accounts for the situation in Chicago. It is not known whether total children's reading has been increasing, decreasing, or remaining the same, and therefore one cannot judge whether the decrease in public library use does or does not reflect a general decline.

One factor for the decline may be television; the population group from 5 to 14 years of age is one of the first full generations of television viewers, accustomed to devoting time to this medium since their very early years. On the other hand, the research findings on this relationship are well outlined in this quotation from a recent summary: "In 1954 Witty reported that television reduced children's reading. In the 1959 study he was not so sure of this. By 1965 he found children were reading a little more than before television."[3] Another factor may be the growing affluence on the part of many families, combined with the availability of children's books in a wide variety of commercial locations, not only bookstores but also supermarkets, drug stores, and department stores, so that an increasing proportion of children's reading material may be provided directly by family purchase. Both of these influences will continue; the role of television is unlikely to be reduced, and a standard of living which enables many families to buy some of the publications read by children will prevail.

Another and crucial influence is the establishment and growth of libraries in the schools. This development is important in its own right, and will in any event continue as part of the educational improvement of the schools. The policy question therefore arises of proper provision and utilization of two publicly supported agencies for children's book and media re-

sources. This should neither be settled by defense or aggression on the part of either agency, nor on the basis of economy in the narrow sense, but by determining what is best for the children.

Certain facts of logistics in the situation must be kept in mind: the number of branch libraries in Chicago is 62, but the number of elementary schools (public, parochial, and independent combined) is 550. Not every one of these schools has an organized library collection and qualified personnel, but this is true of most of the 450 public schools and of an increasing number of the others. There are thus some seven to eight times as many children's libraries in the schools as in the neighborhoods. Further, most children must attend school, including the 400,000 now not reached by the public library.

Various counter considerations must also be weighed. One is the oft-repeated argument that the school is closed during late afternoon, evening, and Saturday hours and during the summer months. This limitation would be removed if the "lighted schoolhouse" concept of the Chicago Board of Education were to be realized. Even without this, school buildings could be designed so that the library would remain open after school hours. It might even be possible to staff the single facility with school personnel during the school day and with public library personnel at other times. If the question of keeping the school library open for longer hours were the only point at issue, it would be best to proceed promptly to shift children's service to the schools as a matter of policy.

Another consideration is educational rather than practical. Children's librarians in public libraries make a distinction between the voluntary reading that occurs in their agencies and the required reading in the schools. The dis-

[3]Mary Jane Gray, "The Effect of Home Televiewing on School Children," *Elementary English*, 46:306–7 (March 1969).

tinction is challenged by school librarians, who point to educational goals, school media center standards, and the improving school library collections, in all of which aims and practices are broad enough to encompass both the child doing his language arts homework under duress and the child reading a fantasy for the fun of it. The distinction applies where school library resources are limited and meet only immediate curricular needs, but it loses force as the school resources build up to become even broader and richer than those of the public library.

The distinction has particular application in ghetto areas. A person who has not visited in slum schools or talked with slum parents does not realize the depth of suspicion and antagonism directed against the schools by local residents. To some in these areas the schools stand for all that is coercive and depersonalized in present-day education. One example of the gulf between people and institution is the 60 pages of criticism leveled at local schools by residents of the Lawndale area in Chicago's application for a Model Cities grant. Any overt policy to depend primarily or exclusively on school libraries as the source of materials for children in the severely depressed areas of Chicago would at this time both run counter to the capabilities of the schools and to the deeply felt attitudes of those children and their parents.

The policy proposed on children's service for the Chicago Public Library is that the matter be handled in two distinct steps, the short run extending over the next decade to 1980 and the long run extending beyond. In the long run, a greater concentration of media service to children should not only be tolerated but actively encouraged in the schools, for the benefit of education and of the individual alike. With joint planning between the schools and the public library the transition can be con-

trolled and phased to avoid disruption of service. From the standpoint of the public library this will mean reallocation of money, staff, and resources away from children's service, while building service for young adults in transition between school and community and services for the many adult groups now reached only to a marginal extent.

But two realistic conditions argue against decelerating of the public library children's service in the immediate future. The hard fact is that libraries in Chicago schools have been slow to develop and are by no means ready to start to carry the double load. As brought out in chapter 11, "Metropolitan Library Relations," support of school libraries in the city has been far short of national standards. Currently the public school system is facing a financial crisis that has led to threats of severe cuts in teaching staff, and the archdiocesan system is considering the closing of selected schools. This leads to the heart of the matter —that it is the children of Chicago who would be hurt by any cutback at this time, planned or unplanned, in public library children's service. The blow would fall hardest in low-education areas, because it is precisely here that school facilities are most substandard, and here also that there is a psychological gulf between child and school. There is a long-range relationship to be worked out between the two educational agencies, in the interest of sound educational planning, but the task now is to serve the present generation of children.

This report therefore advocates not a diminution or even a leveling off of the public library effort to reach children in the next decade, but actually a further intensification of this service. This view is embodied throughout the recommended program. It is an important factor in the proposal for more storefront branches. It is the rationale for the recommendation to recruit local people and train them to give individualized service. It is implicit in the suggested reestablishment of the position of Coordinator of Children's Service. This is a considered decision, in the face of the reality of Chicago's needs and facilities, to get to children now with a range of communication resources provided by an agency that they will use, and to postpone any decision for early curtailment of public library provision for young readers.

This policy should prevail for the years immediately ahead, probably over the next decade. The whole situation should be formally reviewed no later than 1980 to see if the time has come to concentrate more of children's media service in the institution that they visit every school day. In the interval the development of elementary school libraries should proceed apace. All proposals for intensification of public library provision for children in this report do not involve long-term commitments or buildings that will last well beyond 1980. A joint interagency committee between the public library and the schools proposed elsewhere should take the initiative in keeping this matter under review and should start making plans well before 1980 to avoid a disjointed situation. But the children are there now in the many neighborhoods of the city, the public library has shown that it can reach almost half of them, and the agency must muster every means, traditional and unorthodox, in an effort to reach as many of the others as possible. This is not necessarily a policy that should apply in other cities, but it is what is required by the conditions in Chicago and for the children on its streets.

Within the present service program for children in the Chicago Public Library, the one area that does not display vitality is the "senior" section for young people in the 7th and 8th grades, the 13 and 14-year-olds. Relatively few activities are aimed at this level, and these older children do not respond to story hours and to film showings for youngsters. There is in the branches a selection of books designated as the "senior" collection. While this represents an effort to provide more advanced children's books and some selected subject publications for these young teen-agers, in practice it imposes limitations and restrictions on individuals just starting to reach out to a wider world. Intended as a little longer rope to give the older child wider play, the "senior" collection often holds him back, for the titles in these collections do not reflect the wider subject interests of the television generation nor the broader social curiosity of young teen-agers. The Library permits 7th and 8th graders to use adult books when needed, i.e., it occasionally permits teen-agers to engage in adult activities but treats them essentially as children. As a result, for older children the library ceases to be a place of personal exploration and excitement and becomes more a necessary tool for completing assigned schoolwork. Thus is set the pattern of library utilization as a duty to be carried out so long as the young person engages in formal education, to be dropped along with homework and term papers by many when formal education ends.

An adjustment in the level and range of children's and young people's service in the Chicago Public Library is therefore proposed. Children's service should extend to the 6th grade and age 12, rather than the 8th grade and age 14. Children's cards should be issued up to the age of 12, after which the young person is to receive an adult card. A fresh teen-age program would then commence with the beginning of the teens and extend well into the high school years, as described below. In other words, children will be treated as children, and teen-agers as young adults, without holding back the 13- and 14-year olds.

Service to Young Adults

Young people in the teen years (ages 15–19) constitute a second distinct public library user group. The response by these young people is greater than that for any other age level, including children; 57.8 percent of young adults are public library users, as against 41.7 percent of Chicago's youngsters. Over one-third of the users of the adult sections of the Chicago Public Library are between 15 and 19 years of age—36.9 percent of Central Library patrons and 39 percent of branch patrons. This group bulks large in the statistics and also bulks large in visible users when one observes either the Central Library or branches during after-school, evening, and Saturday hours. Data for another large city indicate that high school students and individuals in the early college years make more intensive use of the public library than others; they stay in the building for a longer period of time, make heavier use of card catalogs and bibliographic aids, and call more on staff members for help and guidance.[4]

Heavy use of the public library by young people results chiefly from a combination of two factors: their need for resources related to school work, and their interest in gathering with other young people. This is a strong educational and social combination, which will probably serve to retain this group as public library users in the period ahead. Secondary school libraries are expanding, as are those in elementary schools, but the resource and media centers at the upper level have had a longer

period of development; yet public library use by students remains high. The educational principles of less dependence on a single textbook and more on a range of resources, and of individualization of instruction in the form of accelerated and special-purpose classes and of individual and group projects, long advocated in theory, have in recent years increasingly become realities. This age range also includes the growing group in junior and community colleges and in the first year or two of four-year colleges, in many of which library resources are somewhat limited. In contrast with the trend and prediction for children, public library use in Chicago by teen-agers is likely to remain substantial and may increase in the next years.

One negative note to be entered in the record is that in the most severely depressed ghetto neighborhoods it is among this young people's group that library use (or at least branch library use) declines most. In these areas children's use is down to some extent, as is also adult use; but the most noticeable difference, as disorganization grows, is that the teen-agers do not appear within the branch, except occasionally as they may be roving through the neighborhood. Up to a certain point young people are the most conspicuous of library patrons in low-income sections; beyond that point they are notably absent. Evidently some of the young people are out on the street, and others hesitate to move through the locality because of gang rivalries. One index of social disorganization in a neighborhood is the extent to which young people of high school age have abandoned their local branch library.

Although teen-agers constitute one of the largest user groups of the Chicago Public Library, the agency makes only limited provision for them as a distinct group. There is a small

[4]Lowell A. Martin, *Students and the Pratt Library: Challenge and Opportunity* (Baltimore: Enoch Pratt Free Library, 1963), p.28.

young adult collection used by both younger and older readers in the Central Library. It is a book collection exclusively and does not provide the range of graphic, visual, and aural media with which young people now grow up. The few staff members assigned to this collection are the only public librarians in Chicago who give primary attention to this predominant group. Each branch has several cases of books labeled for young adults, but these collections are fairly static both in titles included and in limited response by teen-agers. The concept behind the young adult collection is not that of opening the world in all its rich variety to young seekers but more one of protecting them from complexity beyond their grasp; the titles are the easier ones containing information and values which teen-agers, according to their elders, should cherish and not those that young people themselves would term "relevant" or that deal with the issues in which they actually have concern. A check was made in a sample of branches as to titles held on the 1968 American Library Association *Best Books for Young Adults*; the range of holdings of these eminent and current books for this age range was from 17.8 to 60.7 percent, and the average 40 percent. The branches have no personnel to work primarily with young people.

Service to members of the 15 to 19 age group is essentially provided as part of the regular library program for adults. Teen-agers use the subject collections in the Central Library and in branches, they turn to the regular reference librarians for information, and they occasionally (very occasionally) seek guidance on reading from the adult staff. For part of the library needs of young people this "integrated" plan has much to commend it. Young adults seek a widening range of resources which can be matched only by large collec-

tions, and they should learn to use the total institution. This applies particularly to their activity as students. But this plan also means that the library has little special appeal to young people and does not particularly reflect their attitudes and interests and values as teenagers. There are no staff members to whom they can readily relate and no aspects of the institution with which they can identify. The ambiance of an ordered adult world prevails, and it is not an atmosphere with which the young person has empathy. As young people they are welcome, or at least tolerated, in a library world made for adults. The young adult is predominant in public library use but he is the forgotten person in library planning and staffing.

Public library service to teen-agers in Chicago should be intensified. The basic concept should not be separating or protecting young people from the larger world, but rather of opening avenues and strategies of exploration out into that world. The concept should not be that of instilling established values but of helping young people build their own values which conceivably could be superior to those of a society that falls somewhere short of perfection. The emphasis should not be on circumscribed and permanent collections as such. On the contrary it is recommended that the young adult "collections" in both the Central Library and the branches be abolished and replaced with changing, youth-oriented, multimedia environments. Emphasis is to be on staff to work with young people, in tune with their outlook, sympathetic to their problems, dedicated to working with them in the way that children's librarians are dedicated to working with youngsters. Some of these are to be professional librarians, young in attitude if not necessarily in years; others are to be selected young people themselves—high school juniors and seniors to work with younger teen-agers, college students on a part-time basis to work with older high school students.

Staff is emphasized because effective contact with the younger generation is more a human matter of attitude and commitment than a matter of supplying a prescribed collection, particularly one selected by older librarians. Teen-agers are being told by parents, teachers, and the society at large what they ought to be doing. The underlying purpose advocated for the Chicago Public Library is that of providing opportunity for self-development for young and old. Young adult librarians and library workers who are themselves young adults, would provide the necessary bridge between the recorded wisdom of generations past or passing to the generation that will be in control before the century is ended.

How much the public library might be used by teen-agers, other than for prescribed reading and school work, has not been determined in Chicago or elsewhere. One view is that they do all the serious reading for their formal education that they are disposed to do and are not inclined to give free time to the same activity. This assumes that all reading is done by young people under duress. Yet a recent national poll among high schoolers, as one straw in the wind, revealed a substantial demand for "underground" literature, precisely that material which is outside the usual bibliographic records consulted by librarians. This view assumes further that library communication must be in the form of print. It is conceivable that a range of media, books included, could be assembled to serve the interests of curiosity, excitement, and even rebellion. The answer will not be known until the public library develops an anticipatory service program for young people.

The overall direction of development recom-

mended in this report will result in improved service for young people at several levels and in several dimensions. A strengthened subject collection in the Central Library will be used by the advanced teen-ager engaged in special study. The 10 regional library centers proposed over the city will be first and foremost students' libraries. A new kind of young person's staff member is suggested for these centers, the "students' librarian," to stay in close touch with school needs and developments and to serve the high school and college individual when he comes to the center—the students' point of contact and guidance within these relatively large libraries, helping him to move from the collection of perhaps 25,000 volumes in the school or twice that in the junior college to the regional resources of 175,000–200,000 volumes. The multimedia environments proposed, for adults of all ages, in the Central Library and in the regional centers, may well arouse the greatest response from young people who are growing up surrounded by the new forms. At the local level, in the neighborhoods, service for teen-agers is to take its place alongside children's service, with two professional young adult librarians on each task force team for sections of the city, and technicians and indigenous personnel working with teen-agers in local branches and adjacent neighborhoods. Some of the proposed experimental storefront installations—for black cultural centers, for self-learning environments, for study locations in neighborhoods where study space is lacking in the homes—have the young person prominently in mind. Finally, there is to be a system-wide position of Coordinator of Young Adult Service. Thus, in traditional service, in new efforts, and in administrative structure the teen-age library user is to have his place.

The Chicago Public Library has made only

limited special provision, both in collection and staff for young people, despite their considerable prominence among library users. A more positive policy is now urged to bring the strategic group at the high school and junior college levels into focus in the service plans for the Chicago Public Library, in anticipation of their even greater response to a program that presents contemporary communication as a stirring and provocative experience.

As in the case of children's facilities, young adult service in the public library should be reviewed and appraised in 1980, in the light of its vitality at that time, and in the light of the development of libraries in the high schools and in the junior colleges during the interval. Here again unnecessary duplication of resources is to be avoided, and the fullest strengthening of the libraries in educational institutions is advocated. In time the young adult program in the public library could concentrate on the transition of the young person from school to adult life by stressing the library as a means of lifelong interplay with what his fellowmen have to say; but for the present the public library is needed by him both as student and as maturing individual.

Service to Adults

The 1970 census will show approximately 2,100,000 Chicagoans 20 years of age or over who are not full-time students (plus some 200,000 at the adult level who are giving much or all of their time to formal education). Of these 2 million or more out-of-school adults, the Chicago Public Library now reaches some 250,000, or 12 to 13 percent.

At the adult level needs and interests take on all the diversity of humankind. The public library response typically has been relatively general in its desire to provide for much if not all of adult variety. As a result, there are at least a few representatives of most elements and levels of the population among library users. Consequently few if any groups visualize the public library as a primary and essential agency. Still another consequence is that out-of-school adult users constitute a middle range, being neither the undereducated nor the specialized, neither the person just reaching up to the social reservoir of recorded knowledge nor the sophisticate of refined tastes who may be contributing to it.

The underlying policy advocated in this report is that the Chicago Public Library retain its multipurpose, multidimensional philosophy, but add literally scores of "specialties" to carry and intensify service to the identifiable groups and segments within the population. The institution is to remain egalitarian, with doors open and resources available to those with credentials and to those without, to those affiliated with businesses and organizations as well as to the completely unaffiliated person. But it is not merely to stand and wait with a miscellaneous program to which 12 percent of the adult out-of-school population responds, managing by themselves to find or put together services of relevance to them from within the assemblage of resources accumulated by the Library. Rather the Chicago Public Library is to become a congery of special libraries adapted to the distinct groups and interests that characterize the diverse urban population.

The collections and service agencies are the broad base of the Library. Chapter 4 deals with the foundation and center, the Central Library; chapter 5 describes the extension program and the branches throughout the city. These various units are the starting points. What happens within them is to be planned for and related to groups of rich variety and contrast. For every identifiable segment of any size, whether the business community or senior citizens, whether the ghetto poor or the high-rise rich, designated staff members are to have a special concern and a clear responsibility and a planned program. And they are to get outside the four walls of the Library, mixing with each target group, learning their needs and problems at first hand, leading them back to the fixed starting points, bringing materials out to them as necessary, and in the process adjusting the library to the people as much as bringing the people to a preordained library.

Where the Chicago Public Library has singled out distinct groups, set priorities and focused service, precisely at these points it displays at least a degree of strength. The most notable example is the collection, staff, and program for children. Another example is subject service in the Central Library. The analysis in the next chapter will reveal many weaknesses in the subject departments, in collections, staff, and departmental structure. But subject service, as a form of specialization, constitutes one of the positive features of the Library. The individual seeking science publications, history journals, art reproductions, or education materials has a part of the agency which is his. The large, scattered, amorphous institution thus becomes psychologically and functionally accessible for the person who reads and studies along subject lines. It will be proposed that the subject structure be at once simplified to five broad departments and within the departments intensified for more specific interest groups.

Once a distinguishable group (defined by age or subject or interest) has been identified and separated from other users, various "service builders" can be brought into play. Pertinent materials can be assembled—in substance a special library created within the framework of the larger institution. Resources can be changed as the group changes. The arrangement of materials can be adjusted to user habits, rather than following a technical prototype. Selected staff can be assigned, with appropriate formal background (as in the case of a subject department), with distinctive training (as in the case of a children's room), with appropriate attitudes and commitments (as in the case of ghetto service). Helpful lists and bibliographies can be made, aimed at a target audience rather than trying to appeal to all and sundry. Special equipment or physical facilities such as listening stations for music lovers and small discussion rooms for senior citizens may be indicated. Contact can more readily be made with individuals, whether they are those who naturally gravitate to the special service provided or are representatives of the group out in the field, to promote further response. Such contact also provides feedback from users which in turn can be applied to further improvement and sharpening of service. Research can be designed to investigate problems and potentialities. The library oriented toward users takes on a relevance and variety that is lacking in an agency turned in upon its collection as a reservoir.

This does not mean a central library with hundreds of physically separate divisions among which the user must wander and risk getting lost. On the contrary, the arrangement proposed for a new building in chapter 4 would be more open and flowing and interconnected than at present, with subsections large and small within a clear overall plan. For some groups and purposes not a separate physical area so much as a concerned, informed, and available staff worker is indicated—the librarian in the Humanities Department who specializes in the drama (for the theatergoer as much as for the student), the staff member in the Social Sciences Department who is thoroughly familiar with the literature of urban redevelopment (for the city planner as well as for the concerned citizen), the "expert" on the Orient in the History and Travel Department, the employee in the Science Department who knows the resources in steel and chemical technology as foundation stones of Chicago's industry. The point is not so much to separate but more to focus and intensify.

The possibilities for special library service within a multidimensional library are multifarious and extend well beyond subjects as such. Broad population groups come immediately to mind—businessmen, parents, teachers, craftsmen. There are age groups, whether young marrieds expecting children or old marrieds whose children in turn are married. There are persons with disabilities, such as blindness and physical handicaps. And there are interest groups that cut across age ranges, such as those seeking intellectual and avant-garde publications. Functional library services can be the basis for specialization and intensification—for example, a telephone reference center for quick-information inquiries, a bibliographic office for those starting on extensive literature searches, a guidance staff for those browsing among the many contemporary products of man's mind. Once a group is differentiated from the mass, once a settlement is discovered in the landscape, library roads can be cut to it, and over such roads materials suited to their destination can move. This is very different from building a central storehouse to which an occasional seeker comes to see if he can find anything of value.

But identification of groups and intensification of service for them is not the end of service planning. Library use is an individual act, not a group function. Library service to be effective must be individual service. This is true for the youngster wandering before the shelves and for the oldster with free time on his hands wondering what the library may have for him. It is true for the undereducated adult looking for material on buying food and clothes and for the holder of a graduate degree seeking the bibliographic record of a new field he wants to explore.

The Chicago Public Library presents one contact point for adults—the general-purpose service desk in each subject department and in each branch which can handle a range of inquiries from pure location questions (where are the science magazines?); quick-information questions (Who is the president of the German Republic?); more complex reference questions (Can you help me identify a painting I saw of a crucifixion showing a yellow Christ and cherry trees in the background?); aid in using the collection (How do you find a magazine article on sensitivity training?); to guidance through the labyrinth of bibliographic sources (What collections of Chicago-area authors exist in the United States?). The same service point handles whatever advice in reading is provided. Formerly the Chicago Public Library maintained a Readers' Advisor service for the latter purpose, with specialized staff devoted to preparing individualized programs of reading. This responsibility has since been diffused, deintensified, and absorbed into the single "Reference Desk." In the process the provision of reading guidance by the public library has all but disappeared.

By and large these all-purpose reference desks, on the evidence of unobtrusive testing for this study, do better with specific factual inquiries and much less well with bibliographic and reading guidance questions. Except that he may get inaccurate information, the quick-fact inquirer is likely to feel satisfied with the service rendered. On the other hand, the person seeking advice and guidance in use of resources and materials to read is likely to feel that the librarian he deals with has limited background in the subject of interest and less inclination to find out enough about it to be of help.

Unless the Chicago Public Library moves toward sharper focus on distinguishable service groups, and toward more sensitive and thorough ministration to the individual members of groups, it will remain an institution for a distinct minority of adults, and indeed may lose more of its present clientele. Special libraries are available to serve some of the reader groups able to finance and provide their own resources. Many others need specialized service, which they will either get from intensified and individualized public library provision, or from other sources which they will find or create, or go lacking as they have in the past. The underlying policy being advocated is library service *in* the lives of people, as against distant and standardized service to which a small minority of out-of-school adults have the motivation or sophistication to go in an effort to find a portion of the prototype that fits them as individuals.

This all comes down to a cliché. People are diverse; library service must be diverse if it is to be meaningful to people.

Service to the Disadvantaged

One of the important groups for which library policies must be set is the people in the ghetto. The problem of the slum districts goes far beyond physical deterioration—which is more a symbol than a cause of social disorganization—to basic human needs of pride, identity, and economic competence. Effective education is at least as important as adequate housing, and education outside the school and classroom may be at least as promising as

formal instruction, hence the obligation to see what the public library can contribute.

Hardheaded realism is the first requirement for the design of a library program with impact. Many of the adults in the slums have limited education, and the data show that library users tend to be people with substantial education. Many of the ghetto dwellers make little use of printed materials, and the library at present is primarily an agency of print. The slum resident is often indifferent to and even suspicious of established organizations, and the library is one of the traditional institutions.

It is therefore small wonder that the severely disadvantaged in Chicago have not responded on any wide scale to the typical program provided by the Chicago Public Library. Home circulation from the branches in the several sections identified in chapter 1 as most deteriorated is less than one book per capita in a year, as compared with over three in other sections of the city. The number of reference questions asked of the branches is also smaller in the slums, but it is interesting that the ratio of difference is not as great as for circulation, which indicates some tendency on the part of disadvantaged persons to turn to the public library for information.

Small as the sample is, it is instructive to note some of the characteristics of library use by adults who are not high school graduates. The user study made in December 1968 showed that such individuals do not travel as far to a branch library as do high school and college graduates. They were somewhat more interested in getting fiction publications. They use the card catalog distinctly less than more educated individuals, and are only half as likely to ask for help from the staff. When questioned on leaving as to whether they had found what they wanted, an unusually large proportion of this group did not respond, expressing neither satisfaction nor dissatisfaction. The small number who sought assistance from staff members were almost uniform in rating the service as "helpful." The picture that emerges is that of the undereducated adult library user who is uncertain of what to expect, unaccustomed to standard library organization, disinclined to seek help, and grateful for whatever he can find.

Yet even with this data it is a mistake to stereotype the ghetto resident and assume that this represents understanding. Poor people have widely varying interests, different degrees of motivation, and sometimes unusual levels of communication skills. It may well be that the library will first reach the less disadvantaged among slum dwellers, whatever the definition of "disadvantaged" is. It is unlikely that any library program will reach all or most people in the ghetto, but this is no more reason for not making the effort than it is for the city as a whole.

Rather than speculate whether and how much the poor and undereducated will respond, librarians would do well to examine themselves and their own institution. To a great extent the public library has become an institution for the many students and educated individuals in our society. Those who already have the advantage of education seek out the library, and the library responds by providing to some extent what educated people want.

The data in this report indicate that over the years the Chicago Public Library has been putting an undue share of its resources into the outlying sections of the city and not enough into the disadvantaged areas. Most of the new branch buildings have been constructed in the outer city. The sites for future construction, either purchased or under consideration, are six to eight miles or more from the Loop. Staff is disproportionately assigned to the outer

sections. Of 24 bookmobile stops, 16 are out beyond a six mile circle.

The Chicago Public Library has recently taken some fresh approaches to the inner city with the summer "Story Caravan," the creation of several community coordinator positions, a demonstration program in the Lawndale area, a recently-financed children's library center in Woodlawn, and the opening of children's libraries in low-income housing project apartments. Such innovations and experimental programs are steps in the right direction and reflect a concern for the inner city. However, some of these are single and short-term projects, financed by special grant funds, whereas the larger part of the regular program and the major share of ongoing branch expenditures from city appropriations go to the more favored communities.

As a matter of basic policy, the Chicago Public Library should mobilize and intensify service for the disadvantaged sections of the city. There should be no illusion that a modest effort will achieve marked results, nor any expectation that a short-term project will effect immediate change. Some individuals have argued that the problems posed by bringing library service to low-education areas are so great that the effort is doomed to failure; but the position taken in this study is that all people are striving upward in their way, that library resources sensitively selected and imaginatively presented may be useful in this striving, and that, in any case, the attempt must be made and should not be abandoned until it has been tried on a substantial scale for a sustained period.

No one can draw a finished blueprint for library service that will be effective in the ghetto. No single approach but rather a multi-front campaign is indicated. All efforts should be thought of as experimental and subject to change. Evaluation is to be built into these special activities, and a hard look must be taken along the way to determine whether progress is being made.

In succeeding chapters the following elements of a ghetto program are set forth as part of the ongoing service of the Chicago Public Library:

Opening of 20 to 25 small, flexible storefront branch libraries in severely depressed areas, to bring library service within the immediate neighborhood of every resident

Some of the new storefront branches are primarily to be information centers, others cultural centers, and still others student centers to provide the necessary experimental approach

Tripling of the staff assignments in the inner city, the greater proportion of such additional staff to be primarily made up of indigenous personnel hired from local communities and given intensive in-service training

Within storefront libraries, sufficient staff to provide individual assistance to every user— every person entering to be greeted and offered help

Establishment of two high-powered task forces in the ghetto, one for the west side and one for the south side, to be made up of a team of nine or ten professionals, including children's librarians, young people's librarians, an adult specialist, an information specialist, one or more community workers, and an audio-visual specialist

A library bus to circulate on schedule through the streets picking up children, young people, and adults, and transporting them to the local library, later returning them to their street corners

Vans to move through the streets, each devoted to a particular topic, such as job information or consumer information, with resources on the topic (leaflets, magazines, government publications) both for consultation and for free distribution, and to carry a person qualified to give such information directly

A "republication office" in the Chicago Public Library to take resources in topics where simplified presentations are lacking and prepare them in leaflet, folder, or pamphlet form for use in the ghetto areas.

The ghetto program as envisioned amounts to a two-front campaign, one to bring users *in* to conveniently located library outlets, and the other to bring the library *out* to the people, on the street and in the block. It applies to the black ghetto and to other poverty areas occupied by Spanish-speaking people and by Appalachian whites.

Experimentation is the keynote of the program for the ghettos. As one example, a "self-teaching center" depending primarily upon nonbook materials might be devised for young people and adults. Here educational films on selected themes would be shown continuously and in series (on speaking, arithmetic, vocations, historical figures, science topics); single-purpose films and "teaching" records would be available for individual viewing and listening; single-page and small leaflet handouts would be prepared on the themes presented; programmed material would be available for those moved to systematic study. Then a sample of individuals is to be followed up, to see if the "learning center" really amounts to more than an amusement stop.

A principle that must run throughout this program is planning with local residents and organizations. The topics to be stressed, the kinds of staff to be used, the schedules for service must be worked out in consultation with the people to be served. Emphasis within program is to be determined by what other educational and social services are and are not doing. This is not to be librarians telling the ghetto dweller what he should do—on the contrary, it is to be the librarian responding to local conditions and providing the materials that people want in the locations where they will use them.

Conclusion

A fundamental redirection of public library policy is proposed. At present the Chicago Public Library provides a combination of (1) specialized service to children, (2) resources for students (not so much by plan as by default), and (3) general, middle-range publications for adults. The first of these will decline as school libraries develop. The second will also be affected by growth in school and college libraries. The third is increasingly handled by commercial resources in an affluent society.

The proposed redirection calls for the Chicago Public Library to shift from its present undifferentiated, middle-range function to the provision of the specialized library services needed by broad segments of the metropolitan population. The proposed specialized nature of the public library can be understood from an historical perspective. Before and after World War I, the Chicago Public Library, along with other city libraries, provided large quantities of "light" fiction—western, mystery, detective stories, and romances—for persons of limited education. In time such publications became widely available in economical format and convenient distribution outlets, so that the public library was less needed for that purpose. During the decades after World War II,

adults on the average attained greater education and developed more sophisticated and more varied reading tastes. The public library moved up to this middle range of reading, in the form of bestsellers, writings of recognized authors, and popular nonfiction (biography, travel, political commentary, and nontechnical psychology have been perennial favorites). Currently several trends are making this general function obsolete—magazines increasingly cater to this audience, paperbacks now cover this range as well as the earlier "light" fiction, and in an economy of abundance many of the people who have an interest in this broad middle range of publication also have the money to buy what they want.

The roles played in the past by the public library are increasingly provided outside the institution. Thus the direction proposed here for the Chicago Public Library is toward a series of specialized, discrete target programs for the remainder of the century. Specifically these are: (1) advanced resources for the many "specialists" not affiliated with universities or large special libraries, (2) cultural resources for the more intellectual and experimental segment of society, (3) basic, utilitarian and self-development resources for the urban underprivileged, (4) information service in a period dependent on facts and data, (5) subject and educational provision for students and adults, and (6) provision of audio-visual resources in which interest now runs high but for which the distribution system is limited other than the bland fare of television. The appraisal and the programs outlined in the following pages seek to turn the Chicago Public Library in these directions.

4 Central Library

The central unit of the Chicago Public Library plays several roles in the life of the city. It is the flagship of the library enterprise, with resources in depth and the command headquarters. It is also a "local" library for people associated with the business and retail center of Chicago.

As Chicago's major resource center, the Central Library has the dual function of serving readers and media users who come directly to it for advanced and specialized materials and of standing behind and reinforcing the collections in the branches. This applies not only to books and journals but also to government publications, technical reports, films, sheet music, and sound recordings. At this level it has a metropolitan responsibility that extends beyond the boundaries of the city; 22 percent of the users of the central unit are not residents of Chicago, and by state legislation it is the official Research and Reference Center for northern Illinois.

To the extent that Chicago has an information or intelligence center, the Main Library serves that role. Inquirers turn to it in person and by telephone. Ideally it also serves as the channel for access to information available in other agencies, both in Chicago and elsewhere.

For some groups and purposes, the central agency serves as a special or academic library, comparable to those in business, industry, and institutions of higher education. It provides data as well as documents for the downtown business community, by maintaining extensive collections of patent records and a range of business and financial data services. As a resource for the city's large college population, the central collection offers a last chance to obtain material needed for term papers. For individual specialists the Central Library is a place to scan old newspapers on microfilm, search scholarly journals, and locate arcane books.

As a "local" agency for the people working or visiting in or near Chicago's Loop, the Central Library also plays the role of a branch or community library. People come to this large center to select leisure reading, as they do in branches. They turn to it as a source of specific factual information. Students use it as a study and resource center. In one aspect of its function as general-purpose library, the central building houses a 20,000-volume "Popular Library." And from time to time there are exhibitions of recognized artists, live concerts, film showings, and lectures.

Thus the Central Library should be seen not so much as a single building and one large collection, but more as a series of libraries, organized in different ways, with varying purposes, and serving people of many levels. The different and sometimes contrasting functions will be identified in the analysis that follows and consideration given to how these functions

Sources of information for this chapter included interviews with department heads, departmental reports, questionnaires to professional staff members, collection analysis by 6 subject bibliographers, checking of standard lists, user studies in a sample week, unobtrusive measures of staff performance, and related sources described in the Appendix.

relate to each other, which require priority, and which might better be provided in other parts of the library system.

Service Departments

When the Chicago Public Library opened its present central building in 1897, its resources and services were divided into a "Reference" department and a "Shelf" department. Except for frequently used encyclopedias, almanacs, and manuals, most materials were on closed shelves and not directly accessible to the public. The user consulted the card catalog and submitted requests for the items he wanted; these then were obtained by a staff member if on the shelves.

Gradually over the years the material in closed stacks was made more accessible. An open-shelf collection was established in 1916. Subject collections began to be separated into "Rooms," starting with Art and Music and Civics. Other types of service departments appeared in the form of a Teachers' Room and a children's division (Thomas Hughes Room), and in the form of units devoted to patents, newspapers, and visual materials. In these latter instances the unifying concept was either a distinct reader group or form of material rather that subject content. By the time of the 1938 survey, eight service divisions existed in addition to the Reference, Shelf, and Circulation Departments.

The 1938 report recommended further subject departmentation.[1] No action to effect this recommendation was taken for ten years, until the appointment of a new Chief Librarian. Then six subject departments evolved or were created

---

[1]Carleton B. Joeckel and Leon Carnovsky. *A Metropolitan Library in Action* (Chicago: Univ. of Chicago Pr., 1940), p.253.

between 1952 and 1964. Three of these—Social Sciences, Education, and Applied Sciences and Technology—grew out of preexisting service units: the Civics and Documents Division, the Teachers' Room, and the Patents Room. Subject departments also were established for Natural Science and Useful Arts, and for History and Travel. Finally, the remaining miscellaneous group made up of religion, philosophy, psychology, linguistics, literature, and biography was designated as the Humanities Department.

The existing service divisions of the Central Library can be grouped under four categories, based on subject content, function, reader or interest group, and form of material:

Subject Departments

> Applied Science and Technology
> Art
> Education
> History and Travel
> Humanities (including Foreign Languages)
> Music
> Natural Science and Useful Arts
> Social Sciences and Business

Function Departments

> Reference
> Circulation

Reader Departments

> Popular Library (including Young Adult)
> Thomas Hughes (for children)

Form Departments

> Newspapers
> Visual Materials

SUBJECT DEPARTMENTS

The organization and reorganization of the eight subject departments represents one of the most definite service efforts in the recent history of the Chicago Public Library. This development was pushed in the face of tremendous odds—a lack of staff with subject background and a rigid building with load-bearing interior walls that could not be moved or eliminated to house new functions. Indeed subject departmentation was carried beyond the recommendations of the 1938 survey report, presumably to provide a "full circle of knowledge" able to serve readers of all subject interests.

To a degree the subject departments display the service advantages of this kind of organization. Resources are placed on open shelves to provide distinct subject collections directly available to the reader. Different forms of resources in a subject area—reference books, circulating books, magazines, and, to a limited extent, government documents and technical reports—are brought together instead of being widely scattered in the building. Reading space becomes a series of rooms adjacent to the assembled collections rather than being off in a huge reading area. Each division has its own card catalog. By no means least important, staff members with interest in a given subject field and in some cases with appropriate formal education are assigned to the several subject departments. This is an expensive form of service organization, but its advantages outweigh its costs.

Such is the theory of subject departmentation, which amounts to the establishment of distinct "special" libraries within the larger whole, as advocated in chapter 3, which deals with service policies. But in Chicago various compromises growing out of the historical evolution of such units in the Chicago Public Library or imposed by its seventy-year-old building were made.

Rather than assembling all materials on a subject in one location, the Chicago plan permits only about half such material to be brought together in the subject rooms. For the remainder the earlier method of consulting the catalog, preparing a written request, and having a staff member go into the closed stacks for the desired material must be used. Several of the departments are not in single rooms but are actually in a series of rooms. Policy is unclear and inconsistent regarding inclusion of nonbook materials in the subject departments. Only 8 percent of staff members have master's degrees in subject fields, and one-third of these are stationed in branches; none of the subject department heads have advanced degrees in their assigned fields, and three are not college graduates.

The structure or logic of the divisions among subjects has also been affected by history and by available physical quarters. Some departments such as Music and Education are quite discrete and circumscribed, while others such as Humanities and Social Sciences are broad and inclusive. A unit such as Education stands outside of the large Social Sciences Department but Business stands within. The Humanities Department is not only comprehensive, but it has within it a Foreign Language Division that is not limited to humanities. While both the Social Sciences and Humanities Departments are broad in scope, the science and technology area is divided into two separate departments. Such variations in organizational principles are reflected in the comments of the 15.6 percent of the Central Library's patrons who report that they find the central service structure hard to use.

Limitations in physical quarters and relationships add to the problems. The Natural Science and Applied Science Departments are at opposite ends of the building from one another. The Education Department and the children's division both with resources used by teachers are separated by two floors. Circulating books in

Humanities are on one floor but reference books in Humanities are on another. On the other hand, Art and Music appropriately have been placed adjacent to each other. The fourth floor houses the related departments of Social Science, History, and Education, although a large general reading room and large stairwells separate them from each other.

The Humanities Department poses a particular problem because it is incomplete as a subject unit. It lacks a complete catalog of its holdings and its reference books are still in the Reference Department. In addition it has a special space problem in that less than one-fourth of its collection stands on open shelves.

Still another problem in the central service structure is the Reference Department. Formerly the heart of the user program, the center to which many readers turned first, it has progressively declined in function as the subject rooms developed. Its role will be further eroded when the reference books on literature and philosophy are transferred (as they should be) to the Humanities Department. The Reference Department is becoming an anomaly in the service structure. Yet the Central Library desperately needs both a focal point for quick information (requested in person and by telephone) and a center to which the new user and the intersubject user can turn for bibliographical guidance. Such patrons at present seldom know of the general reference unit. The department itself is unclear as to its function, is not well geared either for ready reference or bibliographic guidance, and is not publicized as the source of such services.

POPULAR LIBRARY AND YOUNG ADULT DIVISION

These two related collections are organized for a different purpose and clientele than the subject departments. They are designed for groups of readers with similar interests that cut across subject lines, on the one hand for those who follow contemporary and relatively popular publications, and on the other for the interests of individuals in the middle-teen years. Both collections contain titles selected for their respective patrons, duplicated to meet volume demand. They are staffed for the most part by college graduates with English majors and an interest in popular literature, who provide advice and guidance to their varied users.

The concept of the Popular Library is sound from the user standpoint. This is a service for the Loop worker or shopper, the commuter, and the suburban visitor, who have seen reviews or heard of books they would like to read, or who want to see what contemporary publishing provides to catch their interest. These are the users who are prepared to spend a little time and effort to obtain current titles if conveniently provided. The Popular Library supplies such materials and the Loop visitor responds. The ratio of annual circulation to volumes in the Popular Library is approximately ten to one, several times the ratio for other departments.

The validity of a separate collection for "young adults" is another story. Just what should go into a separate selection for a person 16 years old as compared with an individual 26 or 56 years old is not clear. A case might be made for a distinct section for young teenagers in some branches, if such a section is not designed to restrict and protect the young person from the larger world which he should be entering; but users in the central building are mostly young secretaries and young sales people (the high school students using the Central Library come mainly for subject materials). The idea that such individuals have more restricted interests or read at a distinct level is open to challenge. In practice the

Young Adult section is used by readers of popular material, old and young, as an adjunct to the adjacent Popular Library.

Both collections represent fragments or compromises resulting from limited space and limited concepts. They are located along a wide corridor. Quarters are very restricted, so that both the number of different titles and the number of duplicate copies of titles are severely limited. Of the contemporary printed output which the diverse population of the center of a large city might seek, only a portion is provided. The books are placed on crowded shelves, not displayed in exhibits and on tables to create an appealing book environment. There is no place to sit down to sample a book or compare titles. The scope of media presented is limited essentially to books; the rich variety of pamphlet and document and magazine—and beyond them of picture and sound and film—are entirely lacking.

Clearly the Popular Library serves a purpose; thus ample and imaginative provision should be made for it in a new building. Even in the present quarters, better use could be made of space. The Young Adult collection should be joined with it to form a single Popular Library that would occupy the combined area in which they are now located and spill over into the corridor at either end in an informal series of book displays and circulating collections. The space now taken up by the Public Relations Office could also be used, with that function located either on the fifth floor when the recommendation made elsewhere in this report (page 168 in chapter 7) for a Library Processing Center outside the Loop is carried out or in rented quarters across the street. Chicagoans have shown that they want a central Popular Library collection; better provision should be made for this high-volume use.

VISUAL MATERIALS CENTER

This is essentially a motion-picture film unit, with a substantial collection of 1,200 prints. In 1968, 270 movie prints were added, and 212 in 1967, which represents an outlay of close to $100,000 on this resource in two years. Almost 50,000 circulations of movie prints occurred in 1968, an active turnover of 50 per year. The total reported audience viewing these films in 1968 was an impressive 2,017,082, equivalent to more than half the total population of Chicago. This figure must be interpreted; it derives from group showings (often several hundred persons at one viewing) and includes many repeat viewers (as when the same class group sees a series of films over the year, with the audience for each print included many times in the total).

The films fall primarily in the educational and documentary categories, including children's stories, classroom instruction films, and material of relatively wide appeal for community groups. Recently special attention has been given to titles relating to black culture and to urban problems. Training films either for teaching of skills or for business-industrial use are in a distinct minority, as are shorter "single-purpose" prints. Feature films are not acquired and material is not kept retrospectively, so that the collection in no way covers the history of the motion picture. Artistic and experimental films are acquired only in exceptional cases, so that the collection also does not cover cinema art. Only 16mm materials are stocked; 8mm prints which are increasing in number and which can be shown by the individual on home-movie equipment are not available. The collection has recently been weeded for outdated and worn prints.

Circulation of films is exclusively to schools, organizations, and groups; the material does not circulate to individuals. There are 2,700 organizations registered to borrow films, although the active and regular group is considerably smaller. By far the largest groups of users are schools and teachers; the Chicago Public Library is virtually the film agency for many of the nonpublic schools, and for the public system it supplements the in-system resources.

A small collection of filmstrips is maintained, with 123 items added in 1968. There exists on the market a rich variety of such material, not only for classroom but also for community and discussion group purposes, which has not been acquired by the Library. A small collection of 6,000 slides also is maintained, but no additions were made to this resource in 1968. The use of these visual materials constitutes only a fraction of the service load of the Center, the bulk of which is devoted to motion-picture films. Its "visual" resources do not extend to picture collections or to framed art reproductions.

The Center does have a book collection (1,385 volumes) relating to the film, and it subscribes to 47 periodicals on the topic. From these resources an active information-reference service is given—on types and sources of films, on the history and casts of commercial movies, on critical reviews—to the extent of 163,625 inquiries in 1968. While the print-oriented subject departments have seldom drawn visual material into their resources, the Visual Materials Center from its side utilizes books and magazines, and is the stronger for it.

Assembling of programs and series of films is done for the branch libraries, but not for outside film users. A library-sponsored series in the central building is handled entirely by the Center; this is usually built around such standard themes as travel and nature and has a weekly audience averaging over 200.

The sad story of space for service in the central building must be repeated for the Visual Materials Center—location in a remote part of the building, grossly limited storage space, workroom up a long and narrow staircase, no facilities for the viewing of films by the public. The unit gives the impression of being temporarily installed in the vestibule area of the section of the building originally designed for the activities of the Grand Army of the Republic.

The concept behind film service in the Chicago Public Library is that of a separate adjunct to the central enterprise of providing books and giving "regular" library service. The special form of the visual material and its need for special handling and storage set it apart from the mainstream. Regular departments and the branches are thus relieved of this unorthodox medium, except when a specific program is held. The user does not come upon visual materials as he follows his subject interests or browses among contemporary publications; he must be a "film user" and seek out this special form. Conversely, the Visual Materials Center does not reach out to users through its special medium. Materials in film form are not prepared to describe the Library or facilitate its use. Newer types of equipment, such as rearview projectors for continuous visual display, are not promoted. Films stand apart in a world auxiliary to the printed book.

Interestingly enough, the prevailing concept leads to a basically different orientation to the film patron, as compared with the usual book-oriented divisions; while the subject departments and branches serve individuals first and classes and groups only incidentally (for example, they explicitly reject the group reading item in the form of multiple copies of textbooks), the Visual Materials Center serves classes and organizations, providing what in substance is the group text in film form; thus the individual acting solely for himself seldom has occasion to contact the Department. In its basic print services the Library relates primarily to individuals; in its nonprint services, off in a distinct category, it relates only to schools and organizations.

Film provision by the Chicago Public Library, as far as it goes, is a valuable service. It does not extend to the individual. It does not permeate the library system. It does not reach for the new and experimental. Except for the poor physical quarters allocated to the Visual Materials Center, it represents a sound level of traditional library film provision.

Central Collections

The total collection of the Chicago Public Library passed the 4 million mark in early 1969, counting books (including paperbacks), documents and pamphlets, bound periodicals, recordings, slides and films, music scores, maps, and microfilm reels. Books constitute a little under three-fourths of the total, and almost a half million of these are in paperback

form, so that the collection of hardbound volumes is now approaching 2,500,000. However, the number of different book titles in the entire system is less than 250,000, a reflection of the heavy duplication of items purchased. Coming down to the Central Library, the main building holds approximately 700,000 hardbound books, an equal number of documents and pamphlets, 50,000 records, 40,000 maps, 30,000 sheets of music, and 16,000 microfilm reels, besides lesser numbers of slides, films and filmstrips, for a total of a little under 2 million items, almost one-half of the Library's complete collection.

Several factors make it impossible to furnish more precise figures short of a separate and itemized count in every section of the Library. While a running total is kept of materials acquired, breakdowns—as for example of paperbound books—are only general. There is a distinct disparity between accessioned volumes and shelflisted volumes, because paperbacks are not shelflisted; this introduces a new approach to volume accountability. Over a period of time the basis for enumerating holdings has changed; thus a decision in 1961 added 120,000 government documents to the

Figure 5. Total volumes in library, 1948–68

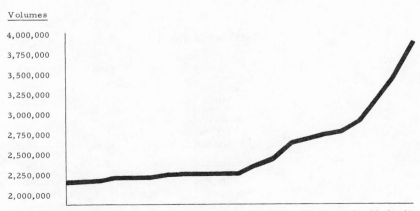

Volumes

4,000,000
3,750,000
3,500,000
3,250,000
3,000,000
2,750,000
2,500,000
2,250,000
2,000,000

1948 49 50 51 52 53 54 55 56 57 58 59 60 61 62 63 64 65 66 67 68

total. Another factor is loss and theft of books. Deductions because of loss are caught after a lapse of time, when inventories are taken, but the increasing rate of theft means that the Library at any given time has a smaller number of volumes than the official figures indicate.

The count of annual acquisitions is definite and shows the growth of the collection. Total size has doubled, from 2 million volumes to 4 million volumes, in twenty years (figure 5). The average annual gross accessions was just over 200,000 for the ten years following 1948, with a lesser annual increase in the total count because of substantial discarding in this period. From 1958 to 1965 the average annual accessions rose to almost 300,000, and from 1965 to 1968 to 536,000 annually, the most recent increase a result of state financial aid. A policy

of expanded purchasing has been followed in a period during which total staff remained stable and the number of professionals declined.

The increase in gross acquisitions is by no means wholly related to greater scope and depth of the central subject collections. Duplication of titles has increased and accounts for a portion of the higher figures. Paperback volumes constitute a larger share of the accessions in recent years, and the adverse of this will shortly be apparent in an increased quantity of discards. Also, a change in policy on fiction has occurred, from high selectivity of fewer than 500 different titles annually during the 1950s to almost 1400 in 1968 (plus heavy duplication in many instances).

The qualitative evaluation of a collection as

Table 6

COMPARISON OF SUBJECT BREAKDOWNS—
SUBJECT DEPARTMENTS AND *BOOKS FOR COLLEGE LIBRARIES*

Main Library subject departments	Percentage of Main Library volumes*	Percentage of titles in Books for College Libraries*	Categories
Humanities	39.8	41.1	Literature, Religion, Philosophy, Psychology
History & Travel	13.7	18.7	History
Social Sciences, Education	19.4	20.8	Social Science
Art, Music	7.7	7.5	Fine Arts
Applied Science and Technology, Natural Science	14.6	9.5	Science
Reference	4.8	2.4	Reference

*It has been assumed that the volume/title ratio in the various subject departments and categories is approximately the same; the Survey was unable to find evidence for or against this assumption.

large and as complex as that contained in the Central Library must use a variety of approaches and measures and even then will inevitably be suggestive rather than definitive. Standard checklists do not suffice for a resource of this scope. A combination of three types of measures was used: the reactions of users, extensive checklists, and evaluations by specialists. The specialists included six "subject bibliographers" and three experts for reference resources, children's materials, and audio-visual materials.

Four out of ten Central Library users (41.1 percent) expressed some degree of dissatisfaction with the institution. Of these, 59.8 percent cited "lack of books" as the reason for dissatisfaction. Combining those who found what they wanted with those who did not succeed in doing so, one of four (24.6 percent) users of the central unit of the Chicago Public Library reported that the collection does not have the books they need. In judging the import of this response, it must be remembered that many people who formerly sought material at the Library, but found it lacking, would not be likely to be in the sample of users studied for this survey in December 1968; in other words, many users have probably already been lost if one-fourth of present users cannot find what they need.

In that students at the upper high school and college levels constitute almost half of Central Library users, it was reasoned that a representative sample from a comprehensive bibliography for college and university undergraduate libraries would provide one appropriate basis for judging the collection. Fortunately, such a list was published in 1967 by the American Library Association. Entitled *Books for College Libraries,* this 53,400-title compilation was a buying guide for a core collection on each of three new campuses of

the University of California. The list was comprehensive enough to include basic books in most academic subjects at an undergraduate level as well as "areas not in a college curriculum."

A further check on the validity of the list was possible by comparing the distribution of subject emphasis in the list with the proportions for subject departments in the Main Library. Table 6 shows that only two subject areas differ as much as 5 percent—History and Travel with 5 percent less and the Science departments with 5 percent more.

Turning to the list itself, there are included in table 7 only those subjects which had, with a 5 percent sample, at least 50 titles. The overall percentage of holdings was approximately 66 percent, or two of every three books listed. Music and education come out at the top; it will be noted later (page 61) that these are the two departments that exhibit the clearest

Table 7
HOLDINGS OF TITLES IN *BOOKS FOR COLLEGE LIBRARIES*—Selected subjects

Subjects	Percentage held
Music	88
Education	82
Geography and Anthropology	80
History of United States	78
General History	76
General Literature	73
Sociology	73
Political Science	72
Bibliography and Library Science	71
Fine Arts	70
American Literature	69
Philosophy and Psychology	65
Economics	61
English Literature	60
Religion	59
French Literature	54
History of Asia	54
All Subjects	65.7

service programs and identification with user groups. The lowest holdings on the academic list were found for a miscellaneous group of subjects which includes Asian history, French literature, and religion.

Examination of the data shows that in some areas the size of the sample is too small to permit generalization about the individual subject covered. For example, no conclusions can be made about the adequacy of the library's collections in Scandinavian history or botany, simply because there were too few titles held to allow a judgment. To sample further the holdings in history areas which seemed surprisingly low, a 25 percent sample was checked with few changes in results; for example, Canadian and Mexican history still scored less than 45 percent.

Another way of looking at the Main Library holdings is to arrange the results on the college checklist by department. Table 8 shows that the three smallest departments score highest. It seems reasonable to expect that music would score well since the number of new music titles in English published each year is much smaller than in other fields. With a smaller number of books to consider, the chances of selecting the "basic" items should be correspondingly larger. In the Education and Art departments,

Table 8
DEPARTMENT HOLDINGS IN *BOOKS FOR COLLEGE LIBRARIES*

Departments	Percentage held
Music	88
Education	82
Art	70
History and Travel	60
Social Science and Business	65
Humanities	64
Natural Science and Useful Arts	63
Applied Science and Technology	56

each book selector must evaluate about 3 percent of the total output of new titles, still a much lower figure than that for the other departments.

The relatively poorer showing made by both the Science and the Technology departments can partially be attributed to the influence of the John Crerar Library and the consequent diminishment of the public library's interest in these areas. Until 1962 the Crerar Library was across the street from the Central Library, and patrons interested in science and technology could be referred there with the knowledge that they would be almost certain to find what they were looking for, if it was printed. Crerar was, and is, a reference library, so that individuals seeking circulating books still had to depend on the public library. When Crerar moved to the campus of the Illinois Institute of Technology, several miles south of the Loop, the many downtown science users who would not or could not travel to the new location were forced to try the Central Library. The figures suggest that in comparison with other patron groups they were not very adequately served.

The checklist used was purposely chosen as basic and related to a large Central Library user group. While every title need not be held, a strong collection would be expected to have most of the items. Overall holdings of less than two-thirds, and in some important topics of less than one-half, suggest that the Central Library lacks a significant portion of the foundation titles that it should have. Analysis of the missing titles shows a disproportionate number of British publications, foreign-language works in subject fields, and university press books.

To update *Books for College Libraries* (which had a cutoff date of 1964) and also to provide a further check on the reliability of the findings, the four annual lists of "Outstanding Academic Books" published by *Choice* were checked completely. Since *Books for College Libraries* specifically cites *Choice* to explain its cutoff date, the two sources do not overlap. As shown in table 9, the difference in Central Library holdings from the basic list to the supplemental lists was less than 2 percent. In addition to substantiating the reliability of the basic checklist figure, this table shows that the substantial increase in book funds brought about by state aid in the 1965–1968 period has not resulted in the purchase of substantially larger numbers of academic "Outstanding Books," despite the fact that at least some of the money has come from funds intended to strengthen the library's reference and research capacity.

Table 9
HOLDINGS OF "OUTSTANDING BOOKS" FROM *CHOICE*

Year	Titles listed	Titles held	Percentage held
1964	297	251	85
1965	443	308	70
1966	687	438	64
1967	888	566	64
Total	2315	1563	67.5

Evaluation by checklists is only one aspect of total collection evaluation. Checking reveals which titles of a selected list the library has, but there are inevitable gaps in list coverage, and the results give no indication of holdings outside the list. Another drawback of such lists is that all titles have equal weight, so that the omission of a vital book may be offset by the holding of a marginal one. Only informed judgment can supply the subjective evaluation needed to supplement checklist figures.

The best judgment about departmental collections comes from "subject specialists," indi-

viduals with broad bibliographical background who are either working in the field or who have reason to be knowledgeable about it. Three of the specialists have had experience in their subject areas in large metropolitan public libraries. Another has experience as a university acquisitions librarian, one is a professor of library science, one the librarian of an art institute, and the single nonlibrarian is a community college dean who evaluated the education collection.

Each evaluator was asked to probe for strength and weakness beyond the items on checklists, and to judge the parameters of the collection in subject scope and depth. Each was given a background statement on levels of collections, using high school, junior college, senior college, master's and doctoral research levels as indicators. Parallels were drawn between such academic stages and the interests of nonstudent users of a large collection; the nonacademic aspects were emphasized as particularly important, since these are hardest to evaluate by checklists. No limits were placed on approaches or methods, as can be seen by the broad variety used—expanded portions of checklists (both published and personal), shelf and shelflist inspection, observation of patterns in reference assignment, catalog inspection by subject category, and personal interviews with department heads. The following sample evaluations, then, are personal and subjective, but they are based on informed background and consistent with other findings.

The collection in the Education Department comprises the most consistent holdings, both in monographs and journals. Of the journals listed in the *Education Index,* 94 percent are held, with substantial back files of most. This collection has little if any research strength, but it has not been built to serve at this level. Students through the college years and individuals in education classes find a considerable range of relevant material. Resources are also adequate for many of the needs of teachers and parents. A factor in this field is that high school students do not customarily study education as such, so that the way has been clear to build the collection at a somewhat higher level. Greater depth at various points is needed if the collection is to be of consistent value to graduate students in formal education and in adult education.

The Music Department also shows considerable scope in English-language materials at the college and "music lover" levels. However, reference copies of standard monographs and expensive anthologies are missing. An inconsistent policy becomes evident in collecting works by and about major musicians and composers—of 40 English-language biographies of Handel, the department holds only ten. Less than half of the journals in the *Music Index* are held. Foreign-language titles are inadequately represented, both in monographic and journal form, a lack of particular import in music because of the predominance of publishing in languages other than English.

The collection in the Art Department is distinctly uneven, even granting the existence of the library of the Art Institute (which is no longer open to nonmembers). In the domestic and applied arts (interior decoration, antiques, handicrafts, and the like) the collection can serve the serious and systematic reader, but in many classical fields—German sculpture, French architecture, Italian furniture, for example—resources could not serve the college student or the adult pursuing an art interest. Catalogs of prints, drawings, individual artists, and national art resources are infrequent. A check of Chamberlain's *Guide to Art Reference Books* showed a 29 percent holding, with reference resources especially weak in "Prints and Engravings," "Documents and Sources," and "Archives and Letters." Only 41 percent of *Art Index* titles are subscribed to, and nonindexed periodicals are discarded although they would have value for persons going beyond the first level of art resources.

The History Department has the Poole collection covering the late 19th and early 20th centuries, which has some research strength, but the collection has not been maintained and some of the serial publications have been allowed to lapse. This special collection should either be maintained or transferred to another library that will take care of it; at present it is less used than its strength justifies, and it is deteriorating physically. There are also long runs of 19th century periodicals and some strength in Chicago and Illinois history. For most aspects of history, outside of the occasional special holdings, the collection is at a beginning college level. For example, of titles on the French Revolution in *Guide to Historical Literature,* the collection holds 50 percent of the English-language titles and 14 percent of those in foreign languages. In Latin-American history, 126 out of 216 titles in English are held (58 percent); if the larger number of items in Spanish were included, the percentage would be much less.

Both Natural Science and Applied Technology for the most part include resources up to the junior college and hobbyist level but not beyond. The one exception is the distinguished collection of patent records in the Applied Science and Technology Department. Advanced undergraduate titles of the type needed by science and engineering students going beyond the first college courses and by adults going beyond an introductory level are lacking. In some cases where standard works at this level are owned, a reference copy is not held, so that the reader is handicapped in advanced study. Applied and hobby interests are somewhat better covered. Journals are limited in numbers (less than 50 percent of *Applied Science and Technology Index* items held), as are British publications on science. Obviously outdated books stand on the open shelves.

The first impression reported of Literature resources is the number of obscure or second-rate titles for which multiple copies stand on the shelves: 18 copies of a scholarly *festschrift,* 8 copies of a study comparing translations of *Faust,* 13 copies of a scholarly reprint—and, at another level, 9 copies of Jacques Deval's *Tonight in Samarkand* (a third-rate play of a dozen years ago), 11 copies of Budd Shulberg's *Across the Everglades* (a minor movie script), 5 copies of *Poets of North Carolina* (an anthology of only provincial value). The fiction shelves have many unused duplicates of best-sellers of five and ten years ago, yet the scope of holdings of contemporary fiction is limited because of a long-standing policy (recently changed) of buying no more than 25 percent of the fiction titles published. Books on high school reading lists abound, but topics not at the high school and beginning college levels—recent poetry, for example, and literary criticism—are weak. British and other English-language titles published outside the United States are seldom acquired. Small but important United States presses (such as City Lights, Red Dust, Eakins, Swallow, Black Sparrow) are thinly represented. There is some evidence of apparent reluctance to collect very controversial authors such as Lawrence Ferlinghetti and Edna O'Brien, a policy understandable for a branch collection but not for the central resource of a large city. Uneven coverage is also evident in philosophy—for example, on existentialism the limited scope and depth of holdings by

and about Heidegger, Jaspers, and Sartre is not consistent with the prominence of these individuals. On the other hand, as one indicator in religion, a check of the bibliography on ecumenism in Robert Brown's *The Ecumenical Revolution* (1967) showed fairly good representation in the Humanities Department.

Thus the pattern builds up from subject to subject of a collection geared to the basic and intermediate student and to the general reader who does not delve very deeply into specific topics. Library users at these levels are numerous and important, but the regional branches should be the agencies to serve them. When these users come to dominate selection policies for the central collection, a lowering of level results and a gap at advanced and specialized levels opens in the library resources of the city. The main collection of the Chicago Public Library, with few exceptions, must be characterized as somewhere at the junior or intermediate college level which is usually built up in cities much smaller than Chicago, but not as a collection with the reference and subject area capacities suitable for a great metropolitan center.

Various factors in policies, in building, and in staff account for the limitations of the central collection. This starts with concept of purpose. Service department heads were unable to present a clear picture of the level of resources they were seeking to maintain or the kinds of users they aimed to serve. In substance they react to those who come. Because the intermediate or regional level of service in Chicago is available to only about 15 percent of the people of the city in the districts where they live, high school and beginning college students naturally turn to the central unit and dominate the visible audience. The Central Library by default is responding to this group.

During 1968, under the leadership of the

Assistant Librarian in charge of the Central Library, initial steps were taken by the department heads to compose a statement of aims and standards for the main collection. Although this is an opportunity to stand back and consider basic purpose in relation to the rest of the library system, to other resources in the Chicago area, and to emerging needs of the city and of the region, thus far the project has dealt more with questions and problems within the present service structure and level. The first need is not so much to do better what has been done in the past but to consider what the distinctive and long-term function of the Central Library should be. The recent designation of the Chicago Public Library as a "research and reference" center for northern Illinois underlines this need. In fact it is not just the metropolitan area that lacks a "research and reference" library center; Chicago itself does not really have such a facility at present.

Various long-standing practices and exclusions in collection building tend to perpetuate the limitations of central library resources in Chicago, despite a doubling of the book budget in the past five years. As one example, little effort is made to acquire English-language publications issued by foreign publishers. Of this group, British, Canadian, and Australian publications are most significant. The gaps in British reference works, indexes, monographs, and serials are widespread and serious. Since the one jobber used by the Library is not contractually responsible for supplying advance copies in this area, the book selectors must rely more on review media and scholarly journals. Of the many British reviewing media, only the *Times Literary Supplement* was mentioned by selectors with any frequency. College-oriented selection aids (*Choice, Books Abroad*), which include British publications, are not used regularly, and the review sections

of scholarly journals, which cover the foreign publications, are not regularly scanned.

Foreign-language material accounts for significant gaps in the collections of the Music Department, the Art Department, the History and Travel Department, and the Reference Department. Collection consultants pointed out generally weak areas as well as specific titles for many of the departments. The attitude that "the patrons won't accept" foreign-language materials reflects a confusion about appropriate patron groups for the Central Library and the proper use of this type of material. The foreign-language selectors do reasonably well in the belletristic fields included in the Humanities Department but do not attempt to cover the broad areas of the social sciences, history, science, and the arts.

University press publications, except for the most popular ones, are not well represented. Fewer than 20 university presses are on standing order, and this list has not been reviewed in several years. Books from these sources, often more specialized and less reviewed than trade books, are highly significant for the patron group which the Central Library should be serving. A combination of increased numbers of review books plus more consistent coverage of scholarly journals and year-end reviews is needed to improve coverage in this important area.

Nontrade imprints published in the United States include a wide range of less-known publishers. While much of the nontrade output is vanity publishing, pseudoscientific treatises, and similar ephemera, there is a significant literature of specialized publishers in many subject fields which deserves to be held. Part of this material is put out by small private presses whose quality varies widely, part of it is the "underground" material which sometimes gains in scholarly value as time goes on, part of it is intended for a particular business or professional group. Some specialized music material is not easily handled through regular channels. As a whole, nontrade United States imprints potentially have a sizable readership and some enduring worth. It is the sort of library material which could support investigation into concrete poetry, the politics of confrontation, or specialized business management techniques, to name only a few topics of current concern.

For the most part, department heads have elected to control their collection level themselves and do not involve the departmental staffs in actual selection. Most departments do not regularly assign a range of popular and scholarly journals to staff members for review reading. The few professional staff memberships and journals received or read by staff, and their very limited participation in the local chapter of the Special Libraries Association, further underline the lack of sensitivity to current developments and publications of a specialized nature.

A final source of titles for consideration is donation. Every major public library receives countless gift books, some of which should be immediately disposed of or sold to dealers. Nonetheless, there are occasional gifts of individual volumes, sets, or whole libraries which are valuable. At the Chicago Public Library there is no central gift processing unit, although the Humanities Department assumes responsibility for handling most gifts. Some use is being made of gifts both by adding to the collection and by sale, but problems remain in the present arrangement. A significant collection donated to the Art Department remains unprocessed after several years. Many gifts are discarded and disposed of from branches and a few central library departments without ever being checked against appropriate bibliographies. Examinations of the discard bins revealed some gift

books of obvious value. Another tendency is to avoid single copy gift titles on the grounds that they are too expensive to add.

Once review titles and printed reviews are collected for the selectors, another set of assumptions comes into play. The most critical of these is that if a title is worth buying at all, it should be purchased in a minimum of three copies. The widespread reluctance to purchase single copies, except for reference sets and very expensive items, has built up over the years because of several claimed factors. A single copy of a new title is expensive to add to the collection when compared with the outlay required to process multiple copies of a single title. Staff shortages, cataloging arrearages, and emphasis on mass-circulation titles all tend to give this point of view added weight. Further, a single copy takes longer to process. Although scheduled in with multiple copy titles, the normal tendency is to process the quantity items first and the single items last. Finally, a single copy is likely to be stolen. This opinion, voiced by several department heads, points up the need for better security.

The bias against single-copy acquisition built up over the years to the point where three copies of a title came to be the working minimum. What was not taken into account was the inevitable narrowing of the range of titles which has been putting artificial boundaries on the effective level of strength for the subject collections. Policy dictated the aim of satisfying the average patron with an average need, and thereby neglected the uncommon patron with an uncommon need.

One further complication in collection building has been a lack of understanding of the changing limits and emphases in acquisition at the Newberry and Crerar libraries. The 1897 agreement to divide subject areas among the three "public" libraries has never been formally reviewed or updated, and the very considerable modifications of subject responsibility adopted over the years by Newberry and Crerar have not been taken into account. History and Travel, for example, has apparently made no attempt to coordinate its selection policy with Newberry's relinquishing of the postcolonial period in Latin-American history. The two science departments have eschewed rapid development in periodical holdings partly because of Crerar coverage, despite the unique importance of serials in this field. The joint plan among the three libraries has been and will continue to be beneficial, but a misunderstanding of its actual application has prompted the public library to hold back, thereby opening gaps in the total of Chicago's resources.

A final important cause of the weakness in Central Library collections has been the lack of consistent effort in using standard bibliographies as a basis for continuing evaluation and for retrospective building of collections. A lack of staff has contributed to the general disinclination to use such specialized sources, but more important has been the widespread rejection of the need to purchase out-of-print titles. While some effort has been made by the Humanities Department to compile want lists, six years elapsed between the last two such lists. Only in the History and Travel Department is there any consistent perusal of the offerings of second-hand dealers. Department heads have apparently been disillusioned by the failure of previous attempts to buy from out-of-print catalogs, and are frustrated by the special requirements for quick checking and ordering of this type of material. Underlying the whole problem is limitation in bibliographic background and sophistication on the part of the subject staff.

A final useful resource of the Central Library that should be mentioned is the newspaper collection, with 125 domestic and 25 foreign papers received. For many titles the issues of recent years are on microfilm, and film readers are at hand. A unique service is provided, the copying of a single item in a newspaper when requested by telephone and mailing it to the requester without charge. But even in this division full potential is not realized. Old bound newspapers have not been microfilmed and are steadily deteriorating, some in a warehouse with a severe moisture problem.

In general the Library has not searched out ways to utilize reduced format for appropriate resources, other than newspapers. Microfilm would help in preserving both older newspapers and older journals. Newer microforms, particularly microfiche at high reduction ratios, offer an opportunity to get long runs of magazines, for example, into compact and convenient compass, and at the same time to save shelf space which is at a premium. The current emergence of holography as a means for even more compact storage should be watched for practical applications in the next few years.

Central Library Service

Departmental structure and collection resources, combined with guides to the collection such as catalogs and indexes, are the components of service for the user who can find his own way. For such individuals the library is a supermarket or cafeteria which the patron uses without much help. The criteria are functional organization, goods within easy reach, clear labelling, and an ample stock.

But for many actual and potential library users this impersonal structure constitutes an obstacle course that requires excessive time and effort. Some try the course, find it taxing or unproductive, and join the large group of nonusers. Others persist because they have no alternative. A broad thread of frustration runs through free responses of samples of library users. Table 10 summarizes the problems most frequently cited.

Table 10
PROBLEMS IN CENTRAL LIBRARY USE

Problems cited most frequently	Percentage of users
Lack of materials needed	24.6
Difficulty in locating materials	21.6
Finding space to read and study	10.3
Finding right subject department	6.4
Getting assistance from staff	4.1

Sources of frustration can be in the user as well as in the agency. People may be unsure what they are seeking; they may have little skill in using libraries; they may turn to the wrong library, expecting service beyond its capacity. But by definition the public library should seek to serve people as they are and to smooth the path. One of the key provisions for the purpose is direct staff-to-user service.

It is precisely such personal, individual service that is most difficult to evaluate. The user himself tends to be grateful for any help he can get. Four out of five patrons of the Central Library, who did turn to staff, rated the assistance received as helpful. Another user group questioned were special librarians in Chicago, who have occasion to turn to the public library as the large collection in their vicinity. Here, where expectations were higher, the response was more critical. One-third of the special librarians surveyed commented on the poor attitudes or capacities of staff members handling telephone inquiries, one going so far as to note "grudging help even after the individual was aware that another library was requesting assistance." The reports of the panel of anonymous users, who did not themselves seek to judge whether personal service was satisfactory or not but rather were instructed to write down exactly what occurred, revealed a variety of shortcomings and limitations in help provided. If librarians at the service point could see themselves as the user sees them, at the least there would likely be an improvement in visible attitude and effort.

One recurring problem is the blind and uninformed referral—that is, the staff member contacted cannot help the inquirer and refers him to another individual or department presumed able to do so. Too often such referrals turn out to be dead ends; while they get the user away from the staff member's desk, they do not result in the service desired. This problem turns up at various points. When persons telephone in to determine if the Library has a specific title, the usual procedure is for the reference librarian receiving the call to check the card catalog to verify whether the item is held and if so in what department; the tendency, however, is to guess departmental location and refer on that basis, which led to wrong guesses in several test instances. Referrals of users within the building also proved to be incorrect, partly due to incomplete knowledge on the part of staff members as to exactly what other departments possess. Inquiries at the building entrances that do not clearly fit a subject area are customarily directed to the Reference Department, and then referred again from there, with an additional chance for misdirection. The general reference staff, of all groups, should be informed about total library resources, because so many inquiries start at that point; but there has been heavy turnover in this staff and new appointees have almost no opportunity to become oriented to other departments, much less to go through a sequence of rotation among these units.

Add to the conditions described above the complication of closely related departments being separated physically (for example, the problem of deciding whether a topic is in Natural Science or Applied Science) and the lack of clear policy on some collection matters (as the problem of the location of government publications, most of which are in the Social Sciences Department but some are also in subject departments), and it is small wonder that the batting average in referrals leaves something to be desired. Of course the situation could be corrected by a basic sense of concern on the part of any staff member contacted, who could call ahead if he is not completely sure of the accuracy of his response and who, in any case, should alert a department that a particular inquirer is being referred; such responsibility and follow-up were most uncommon.

Even as staff exhibited lack of knowledge about other departments, so also ignorance concerning other library resources in the Chicago area was evident. One referral noted was to the Newberry Library for material on a recent period in Mexican history, evidently made in ignorance that Newberry has explicitly stopped collecting Latin-American history after the colonial period. Questions concerning the history of Chicago are often referred to the Municipal Reference Library when the Chicago Historical Society Library is the appropriate source. A request for a map source was referred to an out-of-town service instead of to a comprehensive map store a few blocks away. In general little stimulus is given subject librarians to learn about resources in other agencies, and they are not inclined to do so on their own.

It should be added that such probing of actual performance is unusual in library evaluation and not common in staff supervision in libraries. The Chicago Public Library may be no more derelict than other libraries in this respect, and in fact a research study in another section of the country revealed similar short-comings in the reference service provided.[2] But this is of small comfort to the frustrated user.

Some special services exist but have not been brought to sharp focus and full force. Business information provided by the Social Sciences Department is a case in point. The necessary resources are there: the trade and industrial directories, the various financial information services, 72 percent of the magazines indexed in *Business Periodicals Index,* some company reports, a back-up collection of government documents, and a large run of United States and foreign telephone directories. But the potential has not been realized, and the service does not rank high in the Chicago business community, primarily for lack of staff. Clerical personnel must handle telephone inquiries in this department. Consideration has been given to discontinuation of the telephone directory service—because there are so many inquiries! A more constructive alternative would be to put this specific information service from 600 directories high on the priority list for automated information control.

Lack of contact with agencies, organizations, and leading individuals in subject fields characterizes most of the Central Library departments. Education maintains regular contact with teachers, Applied Science with lawyers about its patent service, and Art and Music with some groups and leaders in their fields. But for the most part neither department heads nor subject librarians are active as individuals in the fields in which they give service. They do not join relevant groups nor participate much in activities in the city. No regular and concerted program exists to bring publicity

[2]Terence Crowley, "The Effectiveness of Information Service in Medium Size Public Libraries" (Unpublished Ph.D. dissertation, New Brunswick, N.J.: Rutgers, The State Univ., 1968).

about subject resources to interested groups. Thus there is little feedback from subject users. The various business, scientific, scholarly, and cultural communities exist in their spheres, and the library in another; contact is made only when an individual comes to the central materials resource to see if it might have something of value for him. Where there are perhaps a half-dozen lines out from the Library to the subject community in all its variety, there should be literally a hundred lines, and indeed many of these groups should be so familiar with the Central Library that each considers one or another subject room as its library.

In special programs for distinct user groups, the smaller subject departments exhibit some degree of activity. The Education Department maintains Great Books discussion groups, with one series now continuing for a quarter century. This department also has a reader's advisory and delivery service for shut-ins. The Music Department arranges for live and recorded concerts, although the latter are not well attended. The Art Department maintains a continuing series of art exhibits. The patent service of the Applied Science and Technology Department is notable, and includes copying facilities. Exhibits for quick pass-through viewing are mounted in the first-floor corridor. Lectures and film showings during the noon period often draw near-capacity attendance. Together these activities give life and lift to a passive program of subject service and a ponderous and unappealing building.

Central Building

Any criticism of the main building of the Chicago Public Library, and any suggestion that it be replaced, immediately arouses a storm of protest on the grounds that the structure is a historical landmark and should be preserved. This could lead to an unfortunate dilemma—modern library service or a historical monument. One group stresses the needs of readers and information seekers, and sees an aging and unadaptable structure without architectural distinction; the other stresses a symbol of the past, and does not consider the users preparing for a changing world. Only Chicago can make the decision between the two, depending on whether it looks forward or back.

Several generations of Chicagoans have now been handicapped because of the city's nonfunctional central library building. It was not functionally designed as a library when it was built between 1892 and 1897, but rather was a modification of the Boston Public Library building, which in turn was copied from an Italian palace. The study of the Chicago Public Library thirty years ago condemned the building. The present report can only repeat the story, and propose alternative ways for Chicago to get a library building equal to its needs in the period ahead.

The catalog of shortcomings of the main library building is long and dreary: the total space is one-half of what is needed, related departments are scattered in the building, subject books are shelved far from the departments in which they are used, there is no way to go from one end of the building to the other on the second and third floors, excess space is wasted in long corridors, reading rooms serve as passageways from one public department to another, and the main public catalog stands in a stairwell. The subject structure of central facilities represents the most forward-looking step in library service in Chicago in recent decades, but the subject plan has had to be compromised to fit the rigid confines of the building with its immovable load-bearing walls. There was no choice, for example, except to divide the functionally unified science and technology section into two separate areas located at opposite ends of the building. Even with such compromises it was still necessary to put subject departments not into a single room or space but into two or more adjoining rooms, as is shown in figure 6. The Music Department and the History and Travel Department are each in three rooms, which makes supervision difficult and necessitates extra staff desks to service the rooms.

The effect is not just the technical violation of a neat service plan that would delight the librarian. It is the public that suffers. One of the most frequent complaints registered by a sample of several thousand users questioned for this survey was difficulty in using the central building: "Can't find where things are," "I get lost," "How do you use this madhouse?"

Space for staff is crowded to the point where productivity is affected. In the business office, nine people work in a space of 600 square feet, along with the financial and business records of the Library; the Business Manager, one of two senior officers under the Librarian, has a semipartitioned office 6 feet square. The other senior officer, the Assistant Librarian in charge of the Central Library, has semipartitioned space of similar size in which she can talk to one person but not to two or more. Several subject department heads cannot have their own desk because there is simply no room available. The staff work space in the History and Travel Department is 5 feet wide, and similar space in other departments is almost as cramped. Staff members must often take their work to reading tables, thus reducing the public space available. Clerical employees in the processing operations on the fifth floor (now handling over 500,000 pieces a year) work several to a table among mounds of books. Add to these crowded and inefficient working conditions the fact that the fifth floor is a sweatbox in the summer and either overheated or drafty in the winter, and it is small wonder that a serious morale problem exists among clerical staff in the processing sections.

Lighting in the principal reading rooms and stack areas is far below recommended levels and cannot be corrected because of dependence on direct current. Average footcandles in reading rooms on the fourth floor ranged from 30 to 40; the recommended level begins at 70.

The air in the Library is not conditioned

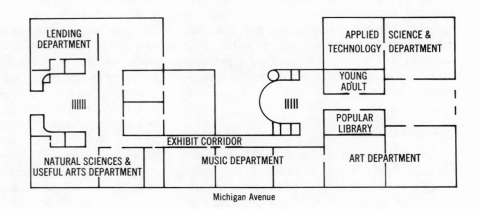

Figure 6. Central Library—first floor

LENDING DEPARTMENT

APPLIED TECHNOLOGY

SCIENCE & DEPARTMENT

YOUNG ADULT

POPULAR LIBRARY

EXHIBIT CORRIDOR

NATURAL SCIENCES & USEFUL ARTS DEPARTMENT

MUSIC DEPARTMENT

ART DEPARTMENT

Michigan Avenue

or cleaned in any way, causing the stack areas to collect dirt rapidly. Excessively dry air in winter is steadily deteriorating the paper in valuable 19th-century books and journals, a process that cannot be reversed.

In sum, the physical environment of the Main Library is often a significantly diminishing factor rather than a positive contribution to the variety of patron uses. Further, the promise of future technology will be thwarted by the building's limitations of space and the immovability of its walls. Not only do Chicagoans now lack the physical setting appropriate for advanced use of library materials, but with the present building it is highly unlikely that they will be afforded the advantage of modern library service utilizing electronic technology. Closed-circuit TV, "wet" carrels plugged into central computers (already found in schools), information storage and retrieval—all of these require more than electric cables, and are unlikely prospects in a building constructed well before the Wright brothers flew their first plane.

A search was made in architectural journals and histories of architecture, and in accounts of outstanding buildings in Chicago; no record could be found attesting to the architectural distinction or significance of the central library building. The one special feature is the mosaic tilework around the staircase at the south entrance and in the ceiling of the third-floor rotunda. Relatively few people see the tile work on the staircase; by count 94 percent of visitors use the elevators to get to the upper floors. The ceiling in the rotunda is seen if users look up at it—in fact it is always pointed out to groups visiting the building—but at eye level this area very much shows its age. If feasible, some portion of the mosaic tilework should be incorporated into the entranceway or one of the readings rooms in a new building.

In 1967 the Library Board commissioned a study to determine if the existing building could be modernized.[3] The firm of Holabird and Root did not recommend such action, but they did show that if the City wanted to retain the present facade for historical reasons, the interior could be rebuilt and some added space gained for an expenditure of over $10,000,000, probably 15 to 20 percent more by 1970. The plan provides for 370,000 square feet of space; the present study shows that 480,000 square feet are needed, even if the book-handling and cataloging operations are transferred (as they should be in any case) to a warehouse and processing building outside the Loop. Further, the Holabird and Root plan, by adding a separate book stack, violated a basic principle of modern library building design—that of bringing books and readers together rather than putting resources off into stack areas. Such an arrangement also adds substantially to the costs of operation, because staff must be employed to go into the stacks to get books for readers. This would be somewhat similar to a department store that puts most of its merchandise back in a stock room and then must send its sales staff to get items as customers request them.

A different plan was presented in a recent issue of *Inland Architect*.[4] It calls for a stack area to the rear of the present building, connecting to a new office building on Wabash Avenue. Placing a book stack area further out to the rear would create an even greater resources-user separation than the Holabird and Root plan, and it would seek to marry a seventy-year-old veteran to a brand-new structure.

[3]Holabird and Root, "Chicago Public Library, Central Library Renovation Analysis" (unpublished architectural presentation, 1967).

[4]John Hartray, and Norman Johnson, "A Plan to Save and Improve Chicago's Central Library," *Inland Architect* 13, no.2:22–25 (Feb. 1969).

The Central Library building has a strategic location. It is an integral part of the business-financial-professional-retail center of Chicago. Both local and commuting transportation lines are adjacent or convenient, and there is a large parking area across the street. The proposed shuttle subway from the near north side to the Loop and out to the campus of the University of Illinois will pass nearby. Any new building should be either on or adjacent to the present site. It is the strategic location that accounts in part for the present heavy use of the building, and full return will be obtained from future investments for construction if this essential advantage is retained.

Conclusions

A gap has opened in library provision in Chicago, between the research collections in the Crerar, Newberry, and university libraries on the one hand and the limited resources now in the central unit of the Chicago Public Library on the other. Chicago lacks a collection of broad scope and depth for advanced students, specialists, and "citizen scholars" unaffiliated with universities.

Two conditions within the Chicago Public Library have contributed to this gap—lack of space in the present central building, and lack of intermediate-level regional branches throughout the city. The second condition forces high school and beginning college students to go to the central building, so that it is used more as an intermediate library rather than as the advanced capstone of a city-wide system. Another but outside factor of importance has been a succession of modifications to the seventy-year-old agreement with the Crerar and Newberry libraries over the years; Crerar has long since stopped collecting in the social sciences, Newberry has withdrawn from some of its former fields, and the Chicago Public Library has been unable to move into the vacuum.

This gap has developed during a period when specialized library resources are increasingly needed. When the library opened late in the 19th century, and proceeded shortly to acquire some distinctive holdings in history, literature, and bibliography, such resources were intended for a small scholarly group. Before and after World War I the institution shifted its priorities to the branches and the nonspecialized needs of a city filling with immigrants and with persons moving up the economic scale. The Library was severely hit by the depression (in 1932 total expenditures for books fell below $15,000) precisely when public demand on it for both practical and recreational materials was at a peak. By the time World War II had been endured, and a measure of recovery achieved, a new student demand descended on the agency as a result of sharp increases in the number of high school and college students and of reforms in education. At each stage the Central Library reacted to user groups that should have been provided for elsewhere in the system, in the process turning first in one direction and then in another. At no time did the Library concentrate upon what should have been its unique role in the central building, that of providing specialized resources and subject service in depth to a city moving steadily into a technological age.

The creation of subject departments in the 1950s and 1960s showed a recognition of the need, but the effort had several strikes against it from the beginning—the building did not have enough space and was not genuinely adaptable to this modern structure of service; staff lacked both subject and bibliographic background; acquisition policies for books and periodicals remained as though the central collection was continuing as a large popular library and intermediate student resource; and contact was not opened with the subject organizations and interests of the city. No overall standards or philosophy emerged to guide the building of a strong subject collection.

At the same time, other components of modern central library service were brought into existence, but shortly their growth also was stunted. To serve the nonspecialized interests of people coming to the center of a large metropolitan region, the Popular Library was created and installed in a hallway. To provide new forms of materials the Visual Materials Department was established and then limited in practice to classroom and similar films.

Provision of information service is another telling case in point. This is one of the essentials of contemporary library service and is proposed in chapter 2 as a major social goal of the Chicago Public Library. The various units of the Central Library handle information inquiries on demand, both in the Reference Department and the subject rooms. However, no unit specializes in quick-information service and no staff group concentrates on it. Information work is interspersed at the general-purpose desks with more complex reference searches, bibliographic checking, and reading advice. There is no center for telephone information inquiries, and test performances in this regard were particularly uneven. Lacking a central unit organized for the purpose, the branch outlets have no clear place to turn to back up their limited reference capacities.

The Chicago Public Library has the elements of strong central service in embryo—subject departments, a current-publications division, information and bibliographical service. But these have been abridged and aborted and compromised in practice, partly as a consequence of shortcomings in other parts of the system and partly because of limitations in concept, staff, and building. Some parts of the foundation are there; the task now is to strengthen the pilings and build the superstructure of a metropolitan library center.

Program for the Central Library

The role and functions which the main building should play in the service program of the Chicago Public Library have been implied in the preceding pages and can be summarized as follows:

1. To provide hard copy and audio-visual access to basic and advanced knowledge of every subject field, for

    College and university students through the master's level

    Adults pursuing knowledge systematically and in depth

    The nonacademic businessman, professional person, advanced technician and other specialists.

2. To provide bibliographic access to the available record in or out of the Chicago Public Library, for

    Individual students and nonstudents

    Staff of the Library for collection building

    Other libraries in the Chicago area.

3. To provide information service drawing on the rich resources of the Library and of the total Chicago area, for

    Residents in all walks of life

    Officers and workers in business, industry, government, the professions

Persons interested in cultural and educational events and resources

Organizations and agencies.

4. To provide access to the rich and exciting
variety of contemporary publication, in
all forms, for

Workers and visitors in Chicago's business and retail center

Persons living adjacent to the Loop

Families throughout the city.

5. To provide personal assistance to the
many kinds and levels of people turning
to this central resource, in

Locating and evaluating specialized
materials

Extracting information as needed

Browsing through the world of contemporary expression.

Recommendations

The following recommendations, extending
from collection to service to building, constitute an overall design for a new library center
for Chicago.

*The central collection of the Chicago Public
Library should be rapidly built up into
a resource at the advanced collegiate and
specialized levels, equal to the demands
of a major city and metropolitan center.*

The starting point is a statement of selection policy which recognizes and proclaims
the responsibility of the Library at this level.
This includes the scientific and technological
fields, and history, despite the existence of
the Crerar and Newberry libraries; the level
advocated stops short of rare and advanced
research resources. To achieve the deeper
and broader collection needed by the city
and the region, the number of different new
titles acquired annually should increase from

the average of 14,000 for the past three
years to approximately 25,000. This number
will include selected British and foreign-
language publications. As the total of different United States titles published increases
in the future, acquisitions should be kept
at about two-thirds of the annual output.

A special effort should be made to gather
underground press publications, with as complete coverage as possible of titles produced
in the Chicago area. As advanced treatises
are acquired, one copy should be placed on
the reference shelves to broaden the ency-
clopedia, dictionary, and handbook scope of
subject reference materials now available.

Standing orders for the complete issue of
selected publishers should be increased ten-
fold, to approximately 200. The rule-of-
thumb of a "three-copy minimum" must be
eliminated. A gift-screening process is needed
which will insure that no gift of potential
value, received either at Central or branches,
is discarded without being examined by a
subject specialist. The periodical list should
be increased from the present total of 2,600
titles to 6,000, adding 20 percent more items
per year over each of the next five years.

As a preliminary for the buildup, guidelines are needed and should be applied for
the systematic discard of outdated and outmoded items and of excessive numbers of
duplicate copies now in the collection. The
essential aim is advancement from the
present intermediate level, which will be
handled in a series of regional library centers
throughout the city, to a distinctive collection of breadth and depth, short of doctoral
and postdoctoral research resources.

*The Chicago Public Library should assume
responsibility for research resources in a
few selected fields not covered elsewhere
in the Chicago area.*

At the very advanced and rare-book level,
Chicago has a variety of special and university libraries, and all efforts should be ex-

erted to make them available to qualified scholars. The public library should not aspire to original doctoral and research laboratory material in the sciences, history, art, and most of the basic social science fields. However, certain of the social sciences are not well covered in the region, and the Chicago Public Library should consider entering these areas on a phased and selective basis. The interdisciplinary area of urban problems and planning above the level found in the Municipal Reference Library comes to mind. Another possibility is Negro literature, on which the Library has a start, and for which no outstanding collection exists in the Midwest. Fields of research collection should be adopted only after thorough checking of resources already in the Chicago area, and not until the base of advanced and specialized material has been extended. In some cases special private funds might be found for specific topics of research collecting.

Subject departments are to be reorganized to connect related areas and to provide for more topical specialties.

The present subject structure is uneven and in time could become restrictive. Five relatively broad departments are proposed: science and technology, social sciences, history and travel, art and music, and humanities. This brings such smaller offshoots as applied science, music, and education within a broad and balanced structure. Within these broad departments, clear subdivisions should exist not only for education, music, and engineering but for other topics as well.

A "subdivision" will mean a physical unit within the larger department, with an identifiable collection and one or more staff members specializing in the topic area. In addition to education, a strong subunit for business service should be built in the Social Sciences Department. In the Science and Technology Department, besides the existing patents unit, there should be staff members and collections in some depth organized around the industries of Chicago. The Art Department calls for an expert in the visual arts on the one hand and the household arts on the other, plus music division specialists. History and Travel should have specialized staff members for broad regions of the world such as Africa and Asia. The Humanities Department in particular, with its many and disparate topics, needs subdivisions and designated staff members for philosophy, psychology, religion, and the major aspects of literature.

The subdivisions need not be permanent but would change or be modified depending on dominant interests. Staff members within the divisions, selected for subject background, would be responsible for building collections and for contacts out in the city in their respective fields. The object of this organization is to present a simple and clear-cut overall plan to the user, and at the same time to provide depth of service within more circumscribed fields.

An Information-Bibliographic Center is to be established to provide excellence in two essential and related library services.

In substance this will be a reorganization of the present Reference Department. Humanities reference service would properly go to the subject department. The Information-Bibliographic Center would provide service at several levels, cutting across subject lines. The first level or point of contact would be "Reception," assistance to and direction of the visitor on entrance. The next level would be "Information," to supply quick, general reference, and would be provided both in response to personal inquiry and by telephone. This is to be an intensive service, modeled on Information SVP of France. Telephone access would be available from 7:00 A.M. to 11:00 P.M., a schedule which in itself would call this unique facility to the attention of Chicagoans. Standing behind the ready-reference desk would be "line backers" in the form of professional reference consultants. Also cutting across subject lines would be bibliography service in depth, for the advanced reader. At this level a broad specialization of staff will be needed, in the social, scientific, and humanities areas. These bibliographers would also aid in building subject collections, particularly in retrospective buying of noncontemporary materials. The unifying function of the Information-Bibliographic Center is that of providing guidance in using the library or extracting information from its resources, rather than subject consultation and study by users.

To provide a new environment for nonsubject users, a Contemporary Media Center and a Family Materials Center are to be created.

Once again, these proposed units are to grow out of existing service divisions. The Contemporary Media Center is the Popular Library enlarged, transformed, and vitalized. A minimum of 20,000 square feet is recommended, half of a floor in the present building, which serves again to underline the need for a new building. The concept behind the Contemporary Media Center should be broader than the idea of current-interest publications that characterizes the present Popular Library. The aim should be to create a new library environment for all who are alert to the trends, expressions, and problems around them. The range of contemporary publication would be spread out before the visitor, in fresh and inviting arrangements, not stuffed in long rows on shelves. Users would browse through the current record of knowledge, sit down and read for a period if so disposed, listen to tapes not solely of music but of speeches, lectures, current-topic comments, watch continuously-scheduled educational and experimental films, even visit with authors, film makers, and others who would be a regular

feature of the library environment. The provision of general-interest magazines would be extensive and inviting. Publications of government and organizations would be carefully selected and attractively displayed. The newest social reports would be available in quantity, for purchase as well as borrowing if the reader prefers. The proposed environment would combine the best features of a bookstore, a museum, a theater, and a library. For the individual responding to the world around him and curious concerning man's creations, the Contemporary Media Center would be one of the most exciting places in Chicago, and, as a bonus, he could take part of this world home.

The concept of the Family Materials Center would be similar, except that the audience would be specifically children, young people, and parents. Again book and magazine and pamphlet and record and film and exhibit and working model would be intermingled. Visiting the Materials Center would be as pleasant for a family as a visit to the zoo, except that it would have more variety and by its nature would encourage frequent visits. The Media Center and the Family Center should be adjacent to each other, so that both parents and young people could readily wander between the two.

In a new building both Centers should be on the first floor, immediately available to the casual visitor and in fact visible to passers-by on the street. A library is not all solemn study; the Media and Family Centers would be places of stimulus, variety, and entertainment—centers of culture in the liveliest sense.

Audio-visual materials, while retaining bases in separate departments, are to become an integral part of all agencies throughout the library system.

Films at present are in the Visual Materials Department and recordings in the Music and Foreign Language Departments. Both should continue and be strengthened as centers of nonbook materials, the film department in particular with 8mm film for home use, the music division with new, light-arm turntables for listening on the premises. But films and recordings that specifically deal with subject areas—art, or history, or science, or literature—should be housed and serviced in the subject departments. Every subject department is to have a staff member especially assigned to audio-visual resources, and other subject staff members are to receive in-service training in new media.

Certain forms will tend to predominate in different departments—charts and maps and diagrams in Social Sciences, films and filmstrips in History and Travel, nonmusical recordings in Humanities, single-purpose films and models in Science. Staff in both the Visual Materials Center and the audio-visual specialist in each subject department will assemble film programs for individuals as well as for groups and organizations. We have entered a period of multimedia communications; filmed and recorded material in subject fields should no more stand separate in a library than the magazines and pamphlets of those fields. By the same token, in presenting current "publications" the Library should no more be limited to those in print form than is a school or a home—thus the proposal to establish a multiform Contemporary Media Center.

Staff members of several distinct levels and specialties are to be recruited and trained for this more specialized and diversified Central Library.

At present service is given by two groups of staff members—clerical workers for circulation and related activities, and professionals for readers service. Some technicians (see chapter 6, "Personnel") are used for the latter purpose, but not in job assignments differentiated from the regular and full range of user inquiry. The program for the Central Library presented here calls for diversification and adjustment to varied reader groups. Staff levels and assignments should reflect this diversity. In addition to clerical personnel for record maintenance, provision should be made for the following:

Receptionists to direct and guide users entering the Library

Information technicians for those seeking specific reference service

Reading guides to move among the users of the media centers

Professional information consultants backing up the information technicians

Bibliographers to help advanced readers entering an area of literature

Subject librarians to provide information and guidance to users in subject fields.

The first class would be Technicians, given a period of intensive in-service training. The information aides and reading guides would be selected college graduates (Technicians II) working under senior librarians. The reference consultants would be professional librarians, and the last two specialized staff groups professional librarians with graduate subject training.

Finally, to achieve central library service equal to the demands of Chicago in the remainder of this century, a new central building is needed.

The present building cannot in itself be adapted to the need. The plan for retaining the outside walls and completely rebuilding the interior is an expensive way to get another structure without enough space. Adding to the present building will also involve substantial outlays and will leave Chicago with a half-new and half-old library.

There is more than one way and place to get a new central building. It would be a mistake to cling to any one plan, and thus penalize the several hundred thousand Chicagoans who use the building every year.

In considering alternatives, Chicago has an opportunity to "think big." The library is one of its major educational-cultural institutions, and the Michigan Avenue frontage from Washington to Randolph one of its choicest sites. The survey team favors the first alternative below, because at one stroke it would meet criteria of library service, economic feasibility, and beautification of the City. Two other alternatives are offered which would also result in a library structure adequate for the next fifty years.

1. *Clearance of all or most of the complete block bounded by Michigan, Washington, Wabash, Randolph; construction of a combined library and office tower building immediately west of the present library; the present library building to be removed when the adjacent new structure is completed and a plaza opened up where the library now stands.*

   A combined library and office structure should not be rejected because it is unorthodox. It would be designed to provide an eight-floor library as a base, with a setback office tower rising above. The building would stand on a plaza a hundred feet deep along Michigan Avenue, providing a distinctive Chicago showplace. The combined tower, constituting one of the choicest office locations in Chicago, makes the whole plan economically feasible. Here is the net result:

   a new, modern central library at a location of maximum usefulness

   appropriate commercial use of a prime site

   financing of the library structure over a period of years by tax return from the office tower

   opening of a gracious plaza, breaking the wall of the west side of Michigan Avenue and providing space in which people can move (short of crossing the multilane artery of Michigan Avenue)

   no interruption of library service, because the present library building would function while the new building is constructed.

2. *The next best solution is simply to build a new eight-story structure where the library now stands, retaining the tile and marble staircase and ceiling within the new building.*

   As compared with the first proposal, this alternative would have the advantage of not involving buildings presently on Wabash Avenue. It would also permit saving of the distinctive tile and marble entrance and stairway at the Washington Street end and the decorative ceiling in the third-floor rotunda, although some part of this work should be incorporated in a new building, whatever alternative is selected. On the other hand, a library building on the present site probably could not be combined with an office tower, because of the limited size of the plot, so that the economic advantage and tax return of the first alternative would be lost. To get sufficient space on each floor (60,000 square feet is needed) it would be necessary to bridge over Garland Court to the west. Finally, this alternative would interrupt library service for two years while the new library is constructed.

3. *Construction of a library building on another nearby site, while preserving the present building for nonlibrary use.*

Two possibilities have been suggested, the north side of Randolph Street across from the present building, and the half block to the east of the Civic Center and fronting on the south side of Randolph Street. The first could probably be acquired from the Harding estate (the old Crerar building) if the Harding collection were to be shifted to the present public library, and it should be possible to obtain adjacent properties without too great cost. The site near the Civic Center can evidently be assembled. If enough land were acquired, a combined library and office building might be feasible in either case. Under this plan the present library building would remain, and some source would have to be found for continued maintenance of a structure now seventy years old.

Whatever the alternative, a new central library building for Chicago will require 480,000 square feet. Assuming a plot such as any one of those proposed above, some 60,000 square feet will be possible on each floor, making for an eight-story structure. Actually a larger plot would be desirable, permitting 100,000 square feet on each level, and resulting in a five-story structure, but this should not be achieved by compromising with location. A library building somewhere west or south of the Loop, where a larger piece of land could be acquired, would be a mistake for the paramount reason that it would not serve as many Chicagoans.

The 480,000 square footage has been built up piece-by-piece for the service areas, book space, and administrative and auxiliary quarters needed in a central library building for the next several decades. This is more than double the present space of 196,000 square feet. The

space elements are shown in table 11. Bookstack space is not listed separately because footage for service departments includes space for their collections. Construction costs for such a building will be almost $17 million for the structure itself (compared with the

Table 11
SPACE NEEDS OF NEW CENTRAL BUILDING*

Functional area	Square footage
Reception and guidance	1,000
Circulation control (including registration)	14,000†
Contemporary Media Center (including film unit)	24,000
Family Materials Center (including children's and young people's resources)	20,000
Information-Bibliographic Center	25,000
Five broad subject departments (3 at 45,000, 2 at 35,000)	205,000
Special collections (such as Negro Literature and Urban Planning)	30,000
Exhibit space (2,000 square feet on first floor, 1,000 square feet on each of six additional service floors)	8,000
Assembly and meeting areas (small auditorium seating 200 and 4 smaller meeting rooms)	20,000
Administration offices	26,000
Computer-Communication Center	9,000
Central work areas (spaced through building)	20,000
Utilities and engineering	12,000
Delivery and shipping	8,000
Staff lounges	6,000
Public washrooms	4,000
Entrance, corridors, elevators, escalators	48,000
Total	480,000

*Technical Services (acquisition, cataloging, binding) in separate building outside of Loop area.

†One-half of circulation space on first floor for public contact, one-half elsewhere in the building for records control.

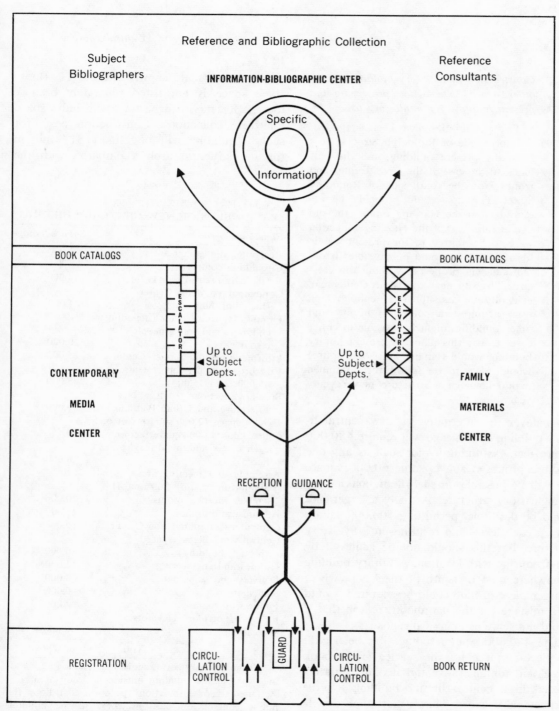

Figure 7.   Relation of proposed Central Library service units—first floor

$11–$12 million cost of rehabilitating the present building which, according to the Holabird and Root plan, would still be short of needed space by 100,000 square feet); new furnishings, shelving, and equipment will add another 20 percent to costs.

Figure 7 shows how the proposed stages of service, as a user enters the building, could be worked out on the lower levels of a new structure. This is a theoretical layout that would have to be fitted into actual space and dimensions. The visitor enters through channels which provide entrance and exit control without imposing turnstiles. Two reception islands are directly ahead for those needing guidance, yet so located that users not seeking immediate assistance can readily move around or between them. During slow periods one station would be manned, at normal times two stations, and if lines should form a "floor walker" could readily assist. Each station would have a large building diagram to show the inquirer where he should go, and he would be handed a map with his destination circled. Registration is to one side of the entrance and book return to the other, both located immediately adjacent to the media centers for browsing and casual reading. New registrants waiting for cards would be invited to visit the centers, and would be notified when their card is ready by means of a lighted number panel. The Contemporary Media Center and the Family Materials Center flow out from the control and reception areas. The Information-Bibliographic Center would ideally also be on the main floor, but if plot dimensions limit space to 50,000–60,000 square feet per floor, this would not be possible—in which case the unit would be directly up a central escalator. Subject departments would then be on the levels above, one or two to a floor. Thus the total layout would lead and guide the new user and the regular user

entering new fields, while providing ready and logical access to the veteran who knows his way in the world of print, film, and other media.

Chicago is overdue for an adequate, functional, modern central library building. Service to this city and region will not be fully achieved until this occurs. However, by no means do all positive steps for central service wait on a new physical setting. Such an intangible but essential quality as true service commitment on the part of every staff member—an attitude sympathetic with the "customer" and concerned to be sure that he gets what he seeks—could and should be started at once. Collection building and rebuilding is a long haul at best, and should also be started immediately. The Reference Department is not in an ideal location for a stepped-up specific information and telephone service, but nonetheless it could double or triple its impact right where it is. The Popular Library is severely restricted in space but it is in a convenient location within the building, and better use of its present area could be made by means of a free-flowing plan for a single collection that would spread out into adjacent hallway areas and the office quarters of the public relations group. Some subject departments are so overcrowded that they could not hope to cope with additional audio-visual materials in their topical fields, but others could make progress in present quarters; for example, the Education Department has room for the purpose, and this would be a suitable pioneer to experiment with multimedia provision that could later be adapted by other departments.

Physical quarters can markedly advance or deter library service, but they are not the heart of the matter. Staff and resources are of the essence, and these must be developed in the central unit of the Chicago Public Library, whether in a bright new building or in the present cramped and cumbersome structure.

5 Library Service throughout Chicago

The Chicago Public Library maintains 62 branch units of various sizes to bring materials and services close to people, in the localities where they live. Further extension of service is provided by 24 regularly scheduled stops of four "traveling branches" or bookmobiles (a fifth mobile unit was added early in 1969), plus approximately 300 small deposit collections in convenient locations, from housing developments to industrial plants. Another related service is provided by the Department of Books for the Blind and Physically Handicapped, which gets its resources out to people by means of the United States mails.

Fifty-six percent of the total staff and 70 percent of book funds are assigned to these several services outside the central building. The extension agencies account for over 80 percent of the home circulation of materials (7,931,960 items in 1968) and for 40 percent of the information and reference questions asked by users (1,800,000 inquiries per year). In 1968, services outside the central building required almost $5,600,000 in direct outlay, 53 percent of total expenditures. The extension program over the city is therefore the "other half" of public library service in Chicago—the

first half being the central building with its service and administrative facilities—and in some respects it is the larger half.

In this chapter the branch program will be analyzed first. Overall use and spacing between units will be described for the several types of branches together. Then attention will be given separately to the three kinds or levels of branch agencies which Chicago maintains. Briefer analysis will follow of bookmobiles, deposit stations, and service to the blind. Conclusions and recommendations will be submitted together for the several types of service, thus in the end treating the various forms of extension as parts of a single pattern.

Number of Branches

Branch libraries in Chicago are classified in three categories or levels: regional branches, regular branches, and subbranches. The first are the superunits (with collections of 75,000–120,000 volumes); the second, the standard units (most within a 25,000–50,000 volume range); and the third, the smaller outposts (averaging less than 20,000 volumes). Their distribution over the city is shown in figure 8.

In the last 30 years,[1] the total number of

Sources of information for this chapter included visits to all regional and regular branches and 12 subbranches, user studies in a sample of branches, consultation with community leaders, questionnaires to all professional staff members, checklists of titles, attendance counts, trips on bookmobiles, and related sources described in the Appendix.

[1] A thirty-year span was used because a major study of the Chicago Public Library was conducted in 1938. For the history of branches before 1938, see that study, Carleton B. Joeckel and Leon Carnovsky, *A Metropolitan Library in Action* (Chicago: Univ. of Chicago Pr., 1940).

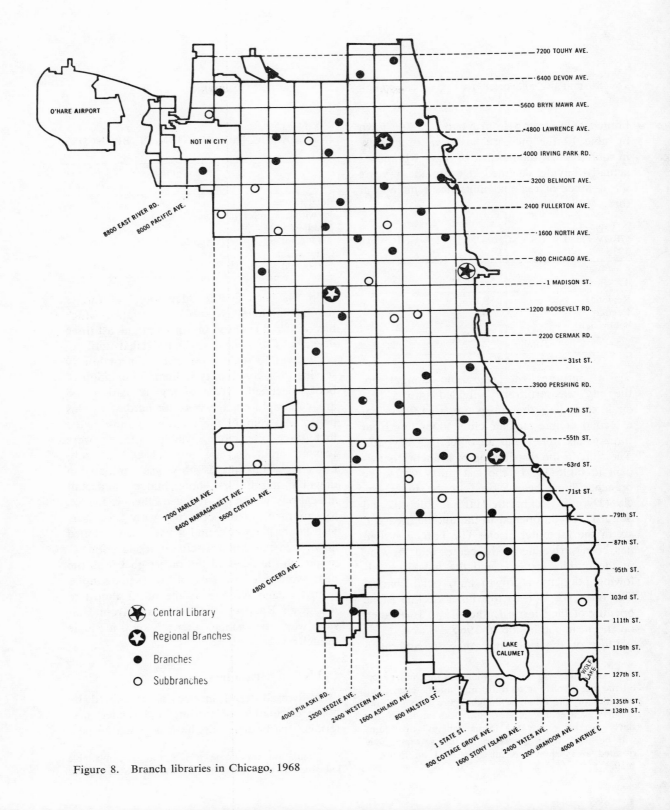

O'HARE AIRPORT

NOT IN CITY

7200 TOUHY AVE.
6400 DEVON AVE.
5600 BRYN MAWR AVE.
4800 LAWRENCE AVE.
4000 IRVING PARK RD.
3200 BELMONT AVE.
2400 FULLERTON AVE.
1600 NORTH AVE.
800 CHICAGO AVE.
1 MADISON ST.
1200 ROOSEVELT RD.
2200 CERMAK RD.
31st ST.
3900 PERSHING RD.
47th ST.
55th ST.
63rd ST.
71st ST.
79th ST.
87th ST.
95th ST.
103rd ST.
111th ST.
119th ST.
127th ST.
135th ST.
138th ST.

8800 EAST RIVER RD.
8000 PACIFIC AVE.

7200 HARLEM AVE.
6400 NARRAGANSETT AVE.
5600 CENTRAL AVE.

4800 CICERO AVE.

4000 PULASKI RD.
3200 KEDZIE AVE.
2400 WESTERN AVE.
1600 ASHLAND AVE.
800 HALSTED ST.

1 STATE ST.
800 COTTAGE GROVE AVE.
1600 STONY ISLAND AVE.
2400 YATES AVE.
3200 BRANDON AVE.
4000 AVENUE O

LAKE CALUMET

WOLF LAKE

⊛ Central Library

★ Regional Branches

● Branches

○ Subbranches

Figure 8.   Branch libraries in Chicago, 1968

branches has grown from 54 to 62. As shown in table 12 the increase has been exclusively in subbranches, the number of regular branches actually having declined. During these years the number of regional units has remained at three.

Table 12
GROWTH IN BRANCH UNITS IN CHICAGO, 1938–68

Type of Branch	Number in 1938	Number in 1968
Regional	3	3
Regular	42	38
Subbranch	9	21
Total	54	62

For purposes of geographic comparison, the city was arbitrarily divided into a first circle extending three miles out from the Loop, a second or intermediate circle extending from three to six miles, and an outer ring beyond.[2] The shift in the distribution of branches is evident in table 13. In the last thirty years five branches have been closed in the inner circle (Dvorak, Eckhardt, Hardin, Pulaski, and Seward), seven opened in the middle area and six in the far outer circle. The branch system has been shriveling in the center and growing in the middle distance and the outskirts, following population growth and social change. The one exception to this inner decline is the opening of the Martin Luther King, Jr. Branch on the near south side in 1967.

Most of the shift in branch to subbranch

[2]These circles do not correspond to the "inner city" on the one hand nor to uniformly middle-class communities on the other, although figure 1, p.5, shows a fairly even economic gradation from center to outskirts. In this report the terms "ghetto" or "slum" will be used when referring to the severely deteriorated areas shown as an inverted L in figure 3, p.10.

Table 13
GEOGRAPHIC DISTRIBUTION OF BRANCHES, 1938–68

Area	Number in 1938	Number in 1968
Inner Circle (within 3 miles)	9	4
Middle Circle (3–6 miles)	11	18
Outer Circle (beyond 6 miles)	34	40

ratio has been due to "demotion" of former regular branches to subbranch status, which has occurred in seven instances in the last three decades. The policy which prevailed until recently was to scale down provision of library service in a community if home circulation of books declined. Areas of low education and areas of rapid change were hit hardest by this policy. All four of the remaining units in the first three-mile circle, which formerly were regular branches, are now classed as subbranches. Thus the Library itself initiated a downhill spiral. First, book budgets and staff allocations would be reduced, then reduction to subbranch status occurred with fewer service hours per week, and if use still continued downward the unit was closed. Today, for example, in the heart of the oldest ghetto on the near west side, an area of two square miles from Chicago Avenue on the north almost to Roosevelt Road on the south, and from Halsted west to Damen, there is not a single branch.

Use of Branches

In overall trend in use, as measured by home circulation of reading and related materials,[3] the branch units have declined 29 per-

[3]Circulation for home use is the best available indicator of total use for the branches. Statistics on

cent since 1938, while central circulation use increased by 34 percent (see figure 9). The fall-off in the branches was steady during and after World War II. A partial recovery occurred during the 1950s. Circulation in the branches held fairly even in the first years of the present decade, but fell again during 1965, 1966, and 1967. In the past year, 1968, branch circulation turned around and increased by 4.6 percent, almost all of the gain in adult use. Overall the trend has been down, despite fluctuations at different periods.

Various factors are related to the decline in branch use. Availability of books through commercial channels has increased sharply in the past thirty years. Television has become

almost universal for diversional purposes. This is also the period when blight spread in some parts of the city, people have moved to the suburbs in increasing numbers, and those who moved tended to be from the better-educated groups.

But references to "deterioration" in the city do not tell the whole story. As noted in the background chapter (chapter 1), "The People of Chicago," the average educational level of adults in the city *increased* from approximately 8.0 years of schooling in 1940 to almost 10.5 at present. The number of elementary and secondary students has risen some 50 percent, and the increase has been even greater at the college level, particularly in commuting students who frequently use public as well as academic libraries. It is too easy an explanation to say simply that the city has declined, and the public library along with it. An alternate hypothesis is that the city has changed but the Library has not kept pace.

A breakdown of the drop in circulation from branches shows the greatest loss over the thirty

---

attendance and the number of information-reference inquiries have not been kept on a comparable basis over this thirty-year period. Librarians who have worked in branches for some time have the impression that total attendance has varied directly with circulation, but the number of information-reference inquiries, in their opinion, has not declined as rapidly as circulation.

Figure 9. Book circulation, 1938–68

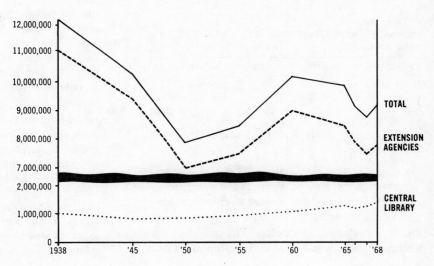

years to be in adult fiction. Nonfiction circulation to students and adults remains almost the same today as at the time of the earlier study in the late 1930s. A close-up of branch circulation since 1960 shows a downward trend in use by children, while both fiction and nonfiction issues to adults remained fairly stable. In this recent period juvenile circulation decreased by 21 percent while adult circulation increased slightly.

Both because of growing deterioration in parts of Chicago and of reduced provision of facilities by the Library in these same areas, use has declined sharply in the older central parts of the city, as is shown in table 14. Middle-city branch use, in the ring three to six miles from the Loop, has also declined in these same three decades, but not as much as in the inner area. Growth in use has been greatest in the outer sections, to the north, northwest, southwest, and south. This is understandable in view of growing population in these sections, the relatively high educational level of their residents, and the opening of new community libraries and construction of new branch buildings.

Table 14
BRANCH CIRCULATION BY CITY AREAS, 1938 AND 1968

	1938	*1968*	*Change*
Inner branches (within 3 miles)	771,419	156,389	−79 percent
Middle branches (3–6 miles)	3,091,867	1,552,869	−49 percent
Outer branches (beyond 6 miles)	4,572,483	5,185,592	+16 percent

Table 15 shows the present average circulation of all branches and volume of information inquiry in the three circles. The middle-area libraries typically have twice the circulation use of inner-area branches, and the outer-area libraries three times the circulation. For information and reference inquiries, the demand is also heavier in the middle and outer areas, but the difference is much less than for circulation, indicating a greater tendency for inner-city dwellers to call on the library for answers to questions than for books to read.

Table 15
AVERAGE USE OF BRANCHES, 1968

Location	*Average annual home circulation*	*Average number of information questions*
Inner Circle	39,099	27,043
Middle Circle	89,580	30,148
Outer Circle	126,478	44,420

The analysis must be carried further, to individual branches. As indicated in chapter 1, Chicago is a city of great diversity. Response by Chicagoans to their branch libraries depends on the individual community, as can be seen in thumbnail sketches of several local outlets.

Chicago Lawn   Area of comfortable homes on the southwest side; attractive branch building constructed 1960; home circulation almost 300,000 in 1968 (second largest of regular branches) plus 80,000 information-reference inquiries; serves unofficially as regional center for large area lacking a regional branch.

Douglas   In the heart of west-side ghetto area; older building, constructed 1930; use has declined sharply with physical deterioration of community and danger in the streets; home circulation 38,024 in 1968, 13 percent of that of Chicago Lawn; used primarily by children, high school students as well as adults make little use; now the site of an experimental program in library-community relations, with some upturn in use.

Blackstone In the Hyde Park-Kenwood re-newal area; oldest of branch buildings, con-structed 1904; use declined over consider-able period, now turning upward—circulation increased 19 percent in 1968; about 60–40 division in use by children and adults; a library that is making a comeback.

Bezazian Rapidly changing Uptown area on north side; building constructed 1957; use down in last ten years, but now holding even and turned back up over 150,000 circulation in 1968; 40–60 division in use by children and adults (the reverse of most branches); substantial use by senior citizens; experi-mental work with Appalachian white neigh-borhood.

New City Storefront branch in Back-of-the-Yards area; older population, young people not staying; use sliding steadily down, to 60,000 circulation in 1968; overcrowded with books and uninviting as place to browse, read, or study.

Oriole Park A subbranch on the far northwest side; located in rented store directly in shop-ping center with ample parking; circulates almost 150,000 books per year, more than 27 of the 38 regular branches; crowded, lively, active.

Hegewisch Another subbranch, serving a resi-dential pocket on extreme south side, hemmed in by steel mills; small but steady use by children and young students, at 45,000 circulation level in 1968; not in touch with young parents in new homes at edge of neighborhood.

What emerges is a general pattern of use, reflecting response to the Chicago Library's branch program as presently conceived. The standard branch is relatively well used in the more substantial communities by the several groups in the population—children, students, and adults. In the moderate-income neighbor-hoods, where blue-collar families live, children

and students are in evidence but adult use is down. In the inner city, children's patronage constitutes two-thirds or more of branch use, students continue to turn to the agency if they can move through the streets without fear of gangs, and adult use becomes very small (table 16).

Table 16
BRANCH USE BY READER GROUPS IN TYPES OF COMMUNITIES

Reader group	Outer city	Middle city	Inner city
Children	+	+	0
Students	+	+	—
Adults	0	—	—

+ Substantial use   0 Moderate use   — Limited use

User studies undertaken in the branches for this survey provided further information about response among adults. The younger group aged 14 to 25 comprise 50 percent of the "adult" users. Students account for 43 percent of response among adults. While the Library as a whole serves a predominantly youthful cli-entele, this applies even more to the branches.

Branch users were questioned about their satisfaction with library resources and services. The direct question—"Did you find what you came for?"—elicited the replies shown in table 17 from a sample of branch users over 14 years of age. The ratio of satisfaction runs about 67 percent for most units, but is down as low as only 56 percent at Northtown Branch,

Table 17
SATISFACTION OF USERS WITH BRANCH LIBRARIES

Response	Percentage
Satisfied	62.6
Partially satisfied	20.7
Not satisfied	16.7

despite a collection above average in size; this is an example of a high-education community for which even a large branch is not sufficient. An indicative variation in response occurs in the subbranches—on the one hand, more of the users report that they found what they came for (presumably those seeking what these smaller units do have); on the other hand, one-quarter report definitely not finding what they came for—the partially satisfied group is down from 21 to 9 percent. Respondents were then asked if they had requested help from the library staff; 53 percent said that they had done so. Seventy-five percent found the staff helpful, but the remainder still did not find the library experience satisfying, even with this assistance.

Spacing of Branches

Table 18 provides some indication of the "density" of branch libraries in Chicago—the average number of people served per unit—by comparison with several other cities. Obviously any interpretation of this comparison should take into account the differences in

Table 18
POPULATION SERVED PER BRANCH LIBRARY*
(Chicago and seven benchmark cities)

City	Average population served per branch
Detroit	64,601
Chicago	*58,409*
Philadelphia	52,866
Los Angeles	48,280
Baltimore	41,031
Saint Louis	34,501
Cleveland	23,494
Boston	21,912

*Includes branches and subbranches. Based on 1968 population estimates of Market Guide of *Editor and Publisher.*

density of population, portion of land area devoted to residential purposes, and variations in transportation facilities in different cities. New York City was not included because of its unique pattern and density of population distribution. The comparison shows that Chicago tends to serve more people per branch than any of the seven other cities, except Detroit. A typical Chicago branch outlet serves 58,409 residents; the average for the seven benchmark cities is 40,955.

More important than comparison with other cities is the practical question of how far branch outlets are from Chicagoans where they live, the actual distance that people must travel to get to a library. The standard usually accepted for urban branches is a maximum of one mile of travel distance, which results in branch spacing every two miles. This criterion has been followed by the Chicago Public Library in planning its branch program and is set down in official plans for the city of Chicago.[4]

Use studies—showing actual distance traveled by a sample group of users—conducted for this survey raise serious doubts as to whether distance alone, and particularly one standard distance figure, should determine the spacing of branch libraries. The one-mile figure meets the needs and habits of people in some sections of the city but not in others, as shown by the following five conclusions based upon a study of actual distance traveled:

1. The one-mile figure fairly well fits adults in single-dwelling and small-apartment communities outside the disorganized slum areas.

2. In the newer outlying areas, where local travel is mostly by automobile and near-suburban mobility prevails, a distance of

[4]City of Chicago, Dept. of Development and Planning, *The Comprehensive Plan of Chicago* (Chicago: the Department, 1966), p.49.

one and one-half miles is within actual reach of most adults and fits their pattern of use of retail, professional, and public services.

3. In densely populated and disorganized neighborhoods in the inner city, travel distance by adults to a branch library is less than one mile except in rare cases.

4. In high-rise, high-income areas, such as the lakefront area from the Near North Side eight miles up to Rogers Park, the usual one-mile standard must also be modified because travel patterns of the apartment dwellers are lateral back and forth to the Loop and not into the adjacent communities to the west.

5. For children the usual one-mile distance standard is too high, to some extent in stable communities where youngsters will go unaccompanied up to three-quarters of a mile, more markedly so in slum districts where youngsters seldom go more than a half-mile to the library.

The one-mile standard can therefore be expanded somewhat in the outer areas but it should be contracted in the inner city. More important in the latter sections, as we shall see as the analysis proceeds, is bringing library resources functionally close to people, where they gather on the block or in the daily pattern of their lives.

Arbitrary drawing of a one-mile circle about each of the 62 existing branches in Chicago shows that approximately 16 percent of the population of the city (a little over 500,-000 people) is still not within the accepted range.[5] Bookmobile stops interspersed between branches reduce this unserved group. On the other hand, when the more limited mobility of

children in all sections and of adults in the inner city are taken into account, at least one Chicagoan in five does not really have access to branch library service. This conclusion applies to any type or size of branch unit. It will shortly become clear that a substantially larger number of residents are not within reasonable reach of a *regional* branch.

Regional Branches

Chicago in the 1920s and 1930s pioneered the concept of regional branches, which has since been picked up in different forms in several large cities. The regional units were conceived as superbranches, distinctly larger than the regular community units, but still only a fraction of the size of the Central Library. They were to serve individuals seeking more extensive collections than in the regular branches, whether reference resources, bibliographical material, subject books, or more specialized and older periodicals. They had an extra complement of reference and advisory staff members. Also the stronger regional collections were intended to serve as the first source of interbranch loans, providing materials for brief periods when users in localities seeking specialized resources found it difficult to use the regional unit directly.

Three regionals were established, one for each main section of the city, located some six miles from the center. It was evidently assumed that people would be willing to travel four to five miles or more from the outlying communities to use these superbranches.

Each of the three shortly established a distinct service role intermediate between the neighborhood branches on the one hand and the central building on the other. In 1940, for example, each regional circulated 450,000–500,000 books (half as many as the Central

---

[5]Calculations of population within arbitrary circles can only be approximate, because such lines cut across census tracts.

Library, and more than double the average of regular branches). Each served as a study center for large numbers of readers and answered 100,000 or more information and reference inquiries. Moreover, each regional loaned some 10,000 volumes to local branches on request from individual readers.

Over the last thirty years severe physical deterioration and social disorganization have overtaken two of the three regionals—Woodlawn on the south side and Legler on the west. Use by nearby patrons fell off. Travel from other neighborhoods into these depressed areas declined sharply. While home circulation of books is not the full measure of regional library effectiveness, it is one indicator of use, and the figures in table 19 show the drastic decline that has occurred in two of the three units. The relatively large buildings still remain, the extra large collections have been preserved and supplemented—but relatively few users respond. Thus does social change affect a logical plan.

Table 19
REGIONAL BRANCH CIRCULATION OF BOOKS

Regional branch	1940	1950	1968
Hild	454,453	293,187	337,421
Legler	474,954	280,992	72,625
Woodlawn	501,568	280,896	62,646

One of the three, Hild, remains as a functioning regional branch. It therefore provides one example to test whether the regional concept is still valid, assuming its location in a relatively stable area. Home circulation of books has held up and increased somewhat since 1950. Reading and study use within the building remains heavy. Reference and information help is regularly requested (88,000 inquiries per year). Only guidance in reading has declined. The building continues to be crowded for study and reference use on the premises.

The Hild collection has doubled from its original size and now contains almost 120,000 volumes. Despite this scope, it showed only moderate holdings in a battery of checklists applied to test resources, as shown in table 20. While complete holding of the titles on any checklist cannot be expected, each checklist contains only popular and nonspecialized titles which might reasonably be included in a general collection. The holdings at Hild (in some cases down to one-quarter of a list) do not reflect a strong collection, particularly for a regional center. By and large the collection now at Hild can be characterized as being somewhat above a good high school collection, but not equal to the demands of the college-educated adults and the college level students who are turning to this resource and who will increase in numbers in the coming years.

Table 20
REGIONAL HOLDINGS ON SELECTED CHECKLISTS OF TITLES

Checklist	Percentage held	
	Hild Regional	Average other two regionals
Basic "Opening Day" collection at college level, compiled by *Choice* (1,766 titles)	60.0	57.0
Subject lists:		
Negro in the U.S. (304)	72.3	70.7
Temper of the Times (124)	61.6	57.0
Contemporary Soviet (33)	54.5	34.8
Recent books:		
ALA Notable Books, 1967 (65)	67.7	60.0
Sci-Tech Books, 1967 (100)	24.0	18.5
Business Books, 1967 (52)	25.0	16.3

A user study, conducted in December 1968, showed that almost one-half (49.4 percent) of the adult patrons of Hild Regional are under 25 years of age, and 43.3 percent are full-time students. In the other two less-used regionals, persons under 25 comprise 65.5 percent of the adult users, and students 57.6 percent. Within the predominant student group, college students who live at home bulked almost as large as high school students. Only 12 percent of the Hild users were seeking current fiction; the rest turned to subject publications and older standard titles. Regional use therefore is characterized by younger adult readers, students, and seekers of nonfiction subject resources.

User satisfaction was also analyzed at Hild. A little less than two-thirds (62.7 percent) of the adult users reported that they obtained what they came for, which means that 37.3 percent were unsatisfied or only partly satisfied. Lack of satisfaction was distributed evenly between young adults under 25 and older users. The dissatisfaction was not with staff but with the resources available. The Hild personnel were given an extra vote of confidence, with 92 percent of users terming the staff "helpful," whereas this rating was given to staff by only 72.7 percent of patrons in the two other regionals.

Most users of this one fully functioning regional branch regularly came up to two miles to use the facility, and somewhat fewer numbers came from another mile out. Beyond three miles the response was thin and scattered. Just under one-half reported fairly regular use of other libraries—in schools, colleges, and business locations—these were assembling "systems" of resources for themselves—while others depended primarily on this regional unit.

In summary, Hild today, as in the past, is serving as a superbranch. While use by adults has fallen off somewhat, this decline has been counterbalanced by increased student use, particularly by commuting college students. Although the collection has grown, it has not kept pace with increasing publication on the one hand and more varied user demand on the other. Despite the original assumptions as to how far people would come to such an extra-strong branch, today Hild serves roughly from Belmont Avenue to Devon and from the lake to Pulaski Road. It does not serve the several-mile-long strip to the south, between Belmont Avenue and the Near North Side, nor does it serve the very populous and extensive area west of Pulaski Road which constitutes the large northwest section of the city.

The example of Hild suggests that the regional concept still is viable today, if several conditions are met. Location of a regional unit must be reasonably convenient and in a stable area. There must be parking available, because a substantial number of regional patrons come by automobile. Collections must be larger than originally conceived, to reflect the wider range of publication and the more intensive demands of readers. Ample seating space must be provided, because a larger unit of this kind is heavily used as a reference facility within the building as well as a source of circulation of materials for home use. The demand for larger collections and more study space will probably continue in the future as the rate of publication increases and the needs of advanced students and adult subject readers become more specialized.

For all practical purposes, regional libraries have an effective service radius of three miles. This area should not be conceived as circular, extending to an equal distance in all directions. On the contrary, both man-made and natural barriers—expressways, industrial areas, railroad tracks, rivers—influence travel patterns and delimit service boundaries. At present, with only one regional unit really functioning and serving an area of less than 30 square miles, only some 15 percent of Chicagoans really have convenient access to regional-level service. If the effective "reach" of these units were five to six miles, three would suffice to serve most of the city, but with an actual effective radius of half that distance, Chicago needs additional regional centers.

Regular Branches

Thirty-eight of the extension units are classed as regular branches. Here is the heart of the branch program, which the regional branches reinforce and the subbranches and traveling branches supplement. It is therefore necessary to look closely at these agencies to see what they do and how they relate to their communities.

BRANCH SERVICE AND URBAN COMMUNITIES

Despite differences in size, the kinds of resources provided and types of service rendered are surprisingly uniform from branch to branch. There is either a separate room or a distinct section for children. A staff member— either a professional, a librarian-in-training, or a college graduate technician—is assigned to work exclusively with children. An active program of preschool classes, story hours, recording sessions, and film showings is maintained for youngsters. Except for three branches, the proportion of circulation accounted for by children is over 50 percent of the total, and in 20 of the 38 branches the juvenile proportion is over 60 percent. The annual turnover (average number of circulations per year) of juvenile books is 5.0 as compared with 3.5 for adult materials. The branches first and foremost are children's libraries.

There is also a "Young Adult" section made up of several cases of books, arranged by interest groupings rather than by the regular Dewey Decimal Classification. The response of teen-agers to this special collection is limited. Some branch librarians find the section useful as a ready source of subject materials not too advanced in reading level.

The bulk of the collection is composed of adult books, divided into fiction and nonfiction. An effort is made, within the limits of the size of the branch, to provide a few titles in each of the many subject fields, plus the materials especially needed by high school students. In 21 of the 38 branches the annual circulation of adult nonfiction is under 20,000, which reflects the relatively small use of this large part of the collection. In most branches the average adult nonfiction book circulates fewer than three times per year, and even this average turnover is higher than really applies to many of the volumes on the nonfiction shelves because the turnover is decidedly greater for a small number of very recent titles and for volumes in special displays. In retailing terminology, the adult nonfiction collection in at least half the branches comprises "merchandise that does not move."

Usually a few racks of paperback books are featured by branches, and these are popular. A section of "recent publications" in hard cover also is maintained in most instances. Display racks usually have selected titles on current-interest topics (such as Christmas, vacations, cooking, sports), but in many branches the chosen topics are routine and unimaginative and the racks are not kept filled with suitable titles. The typical adult branch patron frequently turns to these several special sections rather than seeking out subject materials on specific topics on the nonfiction shelves.

The branches contain magazine collections

ranging from 50 to 125 subscriptions, the titles covered being the picture magazines (*Life, Look*), the news weeklies (*Time, Newsweek, U.S. News and World Report*), the established monthlies (*Atlantic, Harper's*), home and fashion publications, and a smattering of hobby and subject titles. Usually back issues are kept two years for reference purposes. There is likely to be a pamphlet collection in several file drawers, occasionally used for recent information. A standard selection of 150 recordings was introduced in 1967 into most branches and is well used in the middle- and upper-income communities, except where it has been filed away in an inconspicuous location with no identification or promotion. The records are not so popular in low-income neighborhoods, in part because the selection stresses classical "high-brow" music and in part because many homes in these areas do not have record players (only one branch has turntables for listening to records).

Where meeting space is available in branches, children's programs are held regularly and adult programs occasionally. Book discussions are responded to by adults in some neighborhoods and, once started, may continue for several years. Film showings for adults are generally not popular, often being attended by only a handful of older persons. Citizenship classes, for which the branch simply supplies the meeting place, are held in some sections.

All in all the average branch in Chicago is a rather stereotyped agency. This is not due to the physical quarters, which are either in modern buildings, still usable older buildings, or fairly well-maintained rented space. There is simply little to attract or stimulate the user once he comes through the door. In front of him is a formidable circulation desk. There are few directional signs to help orient him. Staff stands ready to handle specific information

questions and the explicit requests of students but not to promote or guide reading and media use. Books line the walls, stand in additional stacks, and, in some instances, are piled on the tables—books which tend to look old because the newer ones are out in circulation; some even look dull when they are relatively new because their colorful dust jackets are not retained.

In terms of community relations, most branches stand aloof and separate within their localities. Only a few branch librarians were found who serve actively in local organizations and seek out contact with groups that do not use the library. Children's librarians do visit schools and arrange for class groups to visit the branch (3,000 class groups in 1968, with a total branch attendance of 72,000 children). The children's librarians also reach out to nursery schools for preschool story hours and film showings, and they have organized several parent discussion groups. But for the most part the branches are libraries within four walls, not community agencies interacting with their constituencies. This lack of interplay has several effects: people have limited opportunity to learn about the library and what it can do for them, the branch staff has limited opportunity to learn about the community and what it really wants, and change occurring in the community is viewed from afar rather than experienced.

Change in the nature, level, and interests of local residents is not a phenomenon limited to the extreme slum areas. Mobility is characteristic well out into the areas in transition, where older residents are moving out and newer ones coming in. Upgrading as well as downgrading of neighborhoods is occurring; some people are moving out to the suburbs and others are moving back in. Branch librarians are aware in a general way of these changes, but when the question is raised as to what corresponding adjustments have been made in the branch, starting with the collection, the response is most limited. When the branch librarians are asked what special efforts have been made simply to inform the new people that they have a library and where it is, the response again is limited and passive.

The foregoing critical comments apply to the regular service programs in most branches. These criticisms must be tempered by the genuine effort put forth by the library administration during 1968 to find a way out of the standard pattern, particularly in underprivileged neighborhoods. These fresh efforts will shortly be described because of their significance and to balance the total picture of library extension in Chicago.

The analysis to this point reveals a need for adjustment and innovation *within* many branches, and at the same time an invigorated relationship *outside* in the communities to be served. Probably neither one nor the other will by itself suffice to revitalize branch service. A balanced and mutual reinforcement must be developed between change within and change without by means of regular interplay between institution and people.

HOURS OF SERVICE

The regular branches are open 68½ hours per week, including all weekday mornings and afternoons and five evenings, Monday through Friday. Although this is a long and demanding schedule in terms of number of staff required to meet service schedules (which means that it is an expensive schedule), it provides generous hours of service to the public. The question is whether such long hours are actually needed. On branch visits for this study during weekday morning hours (other than Saturdays) there sometimes were more staff

members on duty than library users, the exceptions being localities in which senior citizens tend to congregate in the branch during this time of day. On the other side, in some areas evening use has fallen off considerably, and in these same instances staff members point to the danger of going into near-empty streets when the agency closes at 9:00 P.M.

Figure 10 shows the relatively small morning use of branches, and the early evening fall-off in unstable communities. An average attendance of 35 from 9 A.M. until noon in a sample of all branches, and of 27 from 7:00 P.M. to 9:00 P.M. in branches in unstable localities, raises the question of whether the 68½-hour schedule makes the best use of staff and time in relation to service rendered. Serious consideration should be given to using the present 49-hour schedule of subbranches as a base for most branches, and extending this base to more evening and morning hours in agencies where the volume of use cannot be handled within the more restricted schedule.

BOOK COLLECTIONS

The collections in branches vary considerably in size. Seven have collections a little over 50,000 volumes, while three have under 20,000. The average collection in 1968 was 37,985 volumes.

Despite variations in size, common aims and standards are reported by branch librarians as their basis for building collections, and their expressed views are confirmed by the materials on the shelves. They seek first to maintain a balanced subject collection, with one or more titles on each topic that may be asked for. When the branch librarians are asked, "How strong is your collection, and what are its weaknesses?" the response is in terms of subjects covered and not covered. They may have suitable holdings in history but too little in

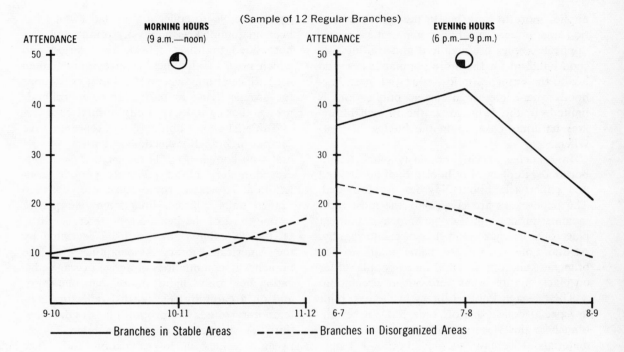

Figure 10. Branch attendance

science—and they will correct the unbalance as soon as budgets permit. Or they are stronger in literature than in religion, but are now correcting this situation. By the same line of reasoning there is a reluctance to withdraw books from the nonfiction shelves, because this may open gaps. If shelf space is completely gone, selected items are moved back into the workroom or other handy storage area, where they can be retrieved quickly. The basic conception is that of the sound foundation or balanced framework, as complete as funds will permit.

To this foundation are added titles to meet several specific user needs. The demands of high school students are noted and followed to some extent. Even the smaller branches have several shelves of collections of one-act plays

and of essays, a long row of Shakespeare's plays, and added copies in the sections on countries. The fiction shelves primarily contain titles on school lists plus remaining copies of popular publications of yesteryear. Responsiveness to student demands is fairly uniform among the many branches, because students with similar assignments come into most of the outlets.

Another user group catered to is made up of the readers of bestsellers. The Library is selective in its purchase of fiction—1,329 of the 1,822 new fiction titles issued in 1968 were bought—so that some of the more ephemeral of the publications on the bestseller lists are not made available. Most of the books reviewed in the newspapers are stocked. This applies more to branches in the middle-education and upper-education communities, where duplicate copies are acquired and waiting lists soon build up for the more popular issues, and less to the branches in low-education neighborhoods where interest in current publications is limited. In the latter areas the branch librarians naturally ease up in the buying of best-sellers.

In branches serving primarily black neighborhoods, duplicates of books, both hardbound and paperback, about Negroes are provided. The paperbacks are given only the most rudimentary processing; they go into a prominent place on wire racks, and they circulate rapidly. At the time visits were being made to the branches, all copies of the more popular titles on black culture often were out in circulation.

The Chicago Public Library in the past built up special collections of some note in certain branches: the Masaryk collection of Slovakian materials at Toman (the neighborhood is now becoming Spanish-speaking), the Swedish collection at Logan Square (the majority of the Swedish group has moved away from this area), the Negro collection at Hall (which has been maintained as a physical entity but was not added to for a considerable period and which now, of all times, receives only limited use). Special language and cultural collections for groups living in particular neighborhoods are another casualty of a city in flux.

Table 21 shows holdings, in a representative sample of branch collections, of titles on several well-known lists. These include both reference materials and relatively popular contemporary titles of some substance. Chicago branch units typically hold from one-quarter to one-third of the items on the reference lists. Of the "Notable Books in 1967" selected by the American Library Association,[6] even the branches in communities of above-average education held only slightly more than one-third, and on a carefully selected list reflecting contemporary trends the proportion is under one-third. A distinction is made in table 21 between holdings in low-education and other communities, not because either group should necessarily have more or less strength in reference or contemporary materials, but simply to see if there is a difference of any significance in resources between the two. In general the agencies in higher-education sections held one-third to one-half of the titles on these particular lists, while the level in low-education sections was under one-third, reflecting the smaller collections in the latter branches. In any case, the data suggest limited strength in standard reference and current interest publications in Chicago branch libraries.

When checklists are used that apply more to certain kinds of branches, the results are more varied. Thus, on the recognized New

Table 21
BRANCH HOLDINGS OF STANDARD LISTS OF TITLES—Percentage held

Checklist	Middle- to high- education communities	Low- education communities
Reference Book List for Branch Libraries (Queens Borough Public Library)	33.6	25.5
ALA Notable Books, 1967	36.9	29.2
ALA Best Books for Teens, 1967	50.0	32.2
Temper of the Times (New York Public Library)	32.0	23.1

[6]1967 was used rather than 1968 to be sure that there was adequate time for the Library to acquire the titles.

York Public Library list of books by and about Negroes, Chicago branches in black communities held a fairly substantial 61.5 percent. But on a list of "Books for Adults Beginning to Read," assembled by the Committee on Reading Improvement of the American Library Association, the same branches held only 33.0 percent. In higher-education communities, holdings of only 20.2 percent of standard titles on American history and of 22.6 percent of controversial books listed by the Intellectual Freedom Committee of the American Library Association were found. These data reflect limitations of resources in both the outer and the inner city branches.

Standard checklists were not used extensively because observation of the great variety and diversity of Chicago communities suggested that there may be relatively few "needs" that apply uniformly. If the criterion for branches is representative and balanced holding of a wide range of publications, then standard checklists are valid measuring instruments, but if the criterion is adaptability and suitability to localities, then such lists are not particularly relevant. Their use here on Chicago branches does indicate only limited success in achieving the goals which the selectors have set for themselves, those of broad subject coverage and representative holdings in contemporary publications.

A title-by-title analysis turned up specific variations in resources not related to local communities, indicated here by a few examples. The most recent automobile repair manual in several branches is for 1966, so that the agencies can offer no information on repairing more recent models. No branch purchased any of the several titles on consumer credit on the 1967 *Library Journal* list of the best business books. Fewer than half of the branches own a copy of Marshall McLuhan's *Understanding Media*. A large branch in a high-education area did not buy copies of poetry by W. H. Auden and John Ciardi appearing on the 1967 Notable Books list, nor does it have a copy of the award-winning 1967 Broadway play, *Rosencrantz and Guildenstern are Dead*. On the other hand, a subbranch recently purchased a book on Indian life in the Rocky Mountains during the 19th century, while a ghetto branch selected *Quarter Horses, a History of Two Centuries*.

Apart from such oddities, there remains a basic paradox in provision and use of the adult nonfiction base of branch collections. Subject scope and depth are limited. It might therefore be assumed that what is there would be used intensively—if one is thirsty he drinks the water he can get—but these are precisely the least used volumes in the collections. The explanation is that it now takes a substantial ready-to-serve capacity before a subject collection can begin really to function at this level, and, even with recent additions to the collections, an average branch does not come up to the requisite level. The well is not used if it cannot supply more than a trickle.

It would be oversimple and unjustified to dismiss the branch collections as weak. When 30,000 or 40,000 or more volumes are assembled with care, they naturally have utility for some readers at some times. It is more that the branch adult collections fall betwixt and between. They aspire to be balanced subject collections but, given restrictions in money and space, they often lack specific topics and titles. They are used by students, but are built on curricular needs only to a limited extent, and the selectors have little contact with schools or with teachers. They are turned to as browsing collections by adults who like to read, yet they are not selective enough or appealing enough or organized in a way to be effective for this purpose. While some effort is made to meet local interests, the narrowing effect of the book selection procedure (see chapter 7), the limited knowledge on the part of branch librarians of their communities, and the preoccupation with more or less complete subject coverage all militate against variation in any depth from branch to branch. The result is an assemblage of titles to which no exception can be taken individually, but not a collection that can be clearly related to social purposes or to local user groups.

One alternative is to continue on the present course, continuously building up the branch subject collections and in time enlarging branch quarters, hoping somehow to achieve adequate subject collections in every outlet. If this choice is made, it must be remembered that subject interests are not static or circumscribed, but become steadily wider and deeper on the part of educated adults, high school students, and commuting college students. The other alternative is to consciously restrict the scope of adult resources in regular branches by converting them into appealing libraries for selected contemporary materials in localities that have an interest in such material and into experimental agencies in communities that are not oriented towards books and reading. Under this alternative there would have to be collections elsewhere in the city, such as regional centers of sufficient number to serve all Chicagoans, to which subject readers could turn.

The story is different for children's collections in branches. Juvenile books account for 46 percent of the branch resources overall (927,000 volumes in total), the proportion going over 50 percent in the smaller agencies. The average branch juvenile collection is just under 15,000 volumes.

The purposes and functions of the children's collections are more clear-cut and less com-plicated than those for adult resources. Books are acquired first to serve the child's pleasure in reading and in exploring the world through print. This is a tradition which was built up by the former Director of Children's Service and which has been carried forward by the regional children's coordinators. Then there are the materials in the form of reference titles and subject books needed for school work. For children of elementary-school age the range and diversity of resources needed is not as great as for more advanced students, so that adequate response to need and demand is not as difficult. The children's collections provide an appealing browsing experience for younger readers and are at the same time a fairly reliable source for elementary reference and beginning research papers. In addition the service provision of both individual guidance and group programs (story hours, film showings, and the like) stimulates the use of resources by this group of users.

In general the juvenile collections were rated at an adequate or above-average level by a consultant knowledgeable in children's books. Checklists confirmed the general judgment. Thus, Hild Branch held 82.9 percent of titles in Eakin's *Good Books for Children,* and the holdings of other branches ranged from 62 percent to 69 percent. Juvenile books constitute a more circumscribed body of literature than is the case with adult books, criteria for selection among the titles published are clear-cut, and the children's coordinators and librarians have applied the criteria consistently. Children's collections in the Chicago branch libraries (as well as in the Thomas Hughes Room in the central building) are one of the strong points of the institution.

BRANCH BUILDINGS

Twenty-two of the 38 branches are in buildings designed for library use, constructed and owned by the city; the three regionals are also in their own structures—a total of 25 branch buildings.

Fifteen of the branch buildings were constructed prior to World War II, three before World War I, four in the 1920s, and eight in the 1930s and early 1940s. The earlier structures have the stately and formidable appearance of the premodern period of architectural design, but despite their age are still usable buildings in fair repair. Somewhat more contemporary design was introduced in the 1930s, particularly in the Hall and Woodlawn branches. The first structure with a distinctly modern flavor—low silhouette, street-level entrance, large glass wall areas—was the South Chicago Branch built in 1941.

A policy of branch building construction has received high priority since World War II and continues to do so at present (figure 11). A new branch building has opened in each of the last three years, 1966, 1967, and 1968. Three more structures are now underway. Sites have been acquired for four additional buildings. It is in construction that action in the development of library service in Chicago has been centered in recent years.

Thinking again in terms of circles three miles out and six miles out, seven of the ten buildings constructed since World War II are in the outer ring and three in the middle ring. Of the three under construction, two are in the outer ring and one is in the middle. All four for which sites have been acquired are in the far circle.

Clearly this building program is aimed primarily at the outer ring of the city, a priority that results from several factors and pressures. The buildings in some instances bring services to newer communities that previously lacked any library facilities. The outer districts are usually upper-education areas, which are the sections that respond to the standard branch program (five of the seven "outer" buildings of the past dozen years have annual circulations of over 200,000). Being in newer and stable communities, the buildings are not subject to early physical decline in the vicinity. And they often get started as the result of organized and persistent solicitation on the part of the local community and of its representatives in the City Council. Each new building represents an investment of approximately a half-million dollars for site, construction, and furnishings.

The policy raises several questions. Is the priority need of the Chicago Public Library new buildings in outlying areas? Is the future form of branch library service clear enough, in view of changing technology, to continue the investment in structures that will last for fifty years? In view of expanding school libraries which will increasingly meet the media needs of both younger children and older students, who together constitute two-thirds of present branch users, should branch buildings be as large as the structures built recently? Are future social developments, traffic, and shopping patterns stable enough to make long-term commitments to local library locations? Such questions concerning prospective change, which no one can answer easily for a time twenty-five or fifty years ahead, should caution public library planners against freezing the extension program over a city into fixed physical plants.

Further, physical structures tend to set service priorities. Where the buildings are, there books and staff go. For the most part new buildings are constructed in the middle- and upper-income areas, because here is where capital investment seems more justified. Then money for service follows. In Chicago, as in other large cities, it is primarily special grant

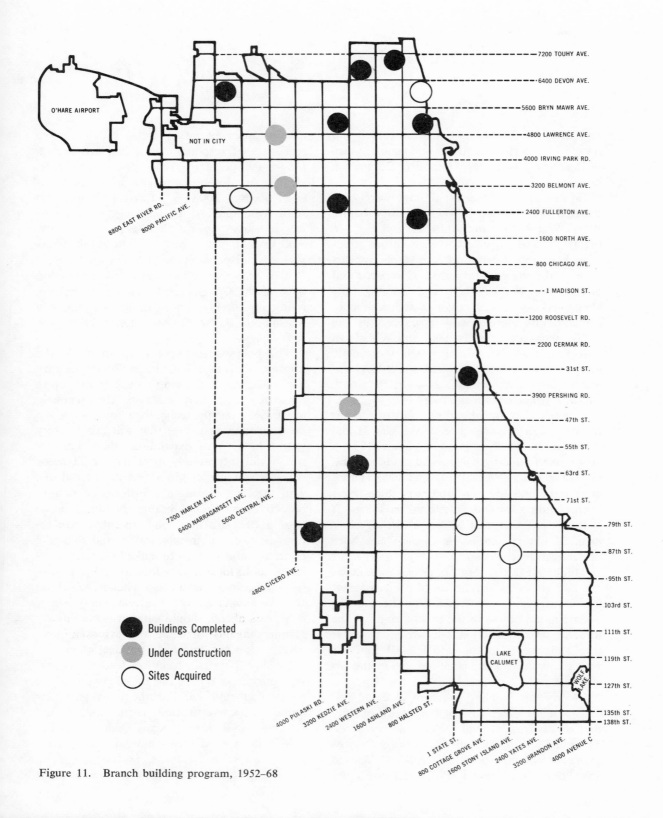

Figure 11. Branch building program, 1952–68

funds that are used for experimental programs in the ghettos, while the bulk of regular on-going money flows into the established library buildings farther out.

A standardized one-floor plan providing 9,000 to 11,000 square feet of space has been used for Chicago branch buildings constructed in recent years. With the entrance on the long side of a rectangle, there is directly inside the entrance a circulation area and back of it an assembly room. Children's and adult reading and book areas stand to each side, and work, staff, and storage space are fitted into the corners and back sections of the rectangle. It is an economical plan from the standpoint of construction, because it involves little excavation and requires no space for corridors and stairwells. The plan is logical, open from the service standpoint, and functional, except for the presence of a formidable circulation desk and the prime location given the meeting room in use only a few hours a week. In the future, where buildings are justified, this assembly-room space should be designed for multipurpose use to house, for example, listening installations, individual film-viewing facilities, and other activities which gain from some separation from public service areas. The space would still be usable for group meetings and film showings at scheduled times. Though furnishing is attractive in the newer branches, it is somewhat standardized and institutional in variety and arrangement. Color is subdued and is yet to be used with warmth and verve.

The criteria for branch building locations are clear enough, but they are not easy to apply consistently in the hard competition for prime land space. Table 22 presents a rating by the survey team on location criteria for structures built since World War II. The somewhat earlier buildings—Logan Square (1952) and Bezazian

(1957)—being on side streets, violated the primary standard of location on a major thoroughfare; they also were built in districts which shortly after showed signs of physical deterioration. Chicago Lawn (1960) and North-town (1962) come close to achieving location criteria, except that they do not rate high on parking, a criterion seldom achieved for Chicago branches. The two most recently opened branches also raise locational questions—King Branch (1967) because it stands between two communities of distinctly different economic level, and Roden (1968) because it is at the edge of rather than within a major shopping district. The sites recently acquired would get about the same score; several come reasonably close to criteria, always excepting parking (Brighton Park and Jefferson Park are examples), but others (such as West Belmont) are just enough off center to be out of the heaviest line of traffic.

Of the regional branches, two of the three present structures are in deteriorated locations. One of these, Woodlawn, is not large enough for regional service, in any case, and need not figure in future regional plans. The other, Legler, does have considerable space, is strategically located with respect to public transportation, and can figure as a regional center when stabilization in the immediate neighborhood is achieved. The third, Hild Regional Branch, has a continuing role to play, if its entire space can be used for regional service and if adjacent off-street parking can be obtained.

It has usually been assumed that the same criteria apply to the location of regional and regular branches, but this needs review and modification. The use of Hild Regional has continued at a high level for almost thirty years, although it is not immediately adjacent to a large shopping area. At the regional level, as we have seen, use is for sustained subject reading and often involves study time within the building. A visit to such a unit tends more to be a trip for its own purpose rather than in conjunction with shopping or when passing by. Future regionals will need large sites, 25,000 feet or more, and they must have ample parking. Putting these several considerations together, regional center locations need not necessarily be in direct competition with prime commercial and retail sites, although convenience of access by both automobile and public transportation is essential and placement at or very near a major intersection is desirable. On the assumption that rail facilities may be revived to help meet the demands of urban transportation (surface mass transit in connection with automobile freeways), attention should also be given to locations adjacent to rapid transit stations.

For regional library centers, location on a main thoroughfare but away from shopping can be considered. Also possible, where sufficient land for off-street parking cannot be acquired, is rooftop parking, which is relatively inexpensive and can be more readily controlled than surface facilities.

Because regional centers will serve relatively large sections of the city, the additional factor of major barriers to movement must be taken into account. Chicago has various industrial corridors (among them one to the southwest and another to the northwest) which separate large sections of the city from each other, and at certain points major parks and wide expressways have the same effect. Figure 12

Table 22
RATINGS OF LOCATIONS OF RECENT BRANCH BUILDINGS
(check indicates criterion is achieved to a reasonable degree)

Location Criteria	Branches Constructed Since World War II									
	Logan Square	Beza-zian	Rogers Park	Chi-cago Lawn	Lincoln Park	North-town	Albany Park	Scotts-dale	Martin Luther King, Jr.	Norwood Park
On main thoroughfare			x	x	x	x	x	x	x	x
At or near major intersection				x		x			x	
In a large shopping district				x		x			x	
Adequate parking	x							x		
Convenient public transportation			x	x	x	x	x	x	x	x
Adjacent to residential area	x	x	x	x		x	x	x	x	x
Stabilized area			x	x		x	x	x		x

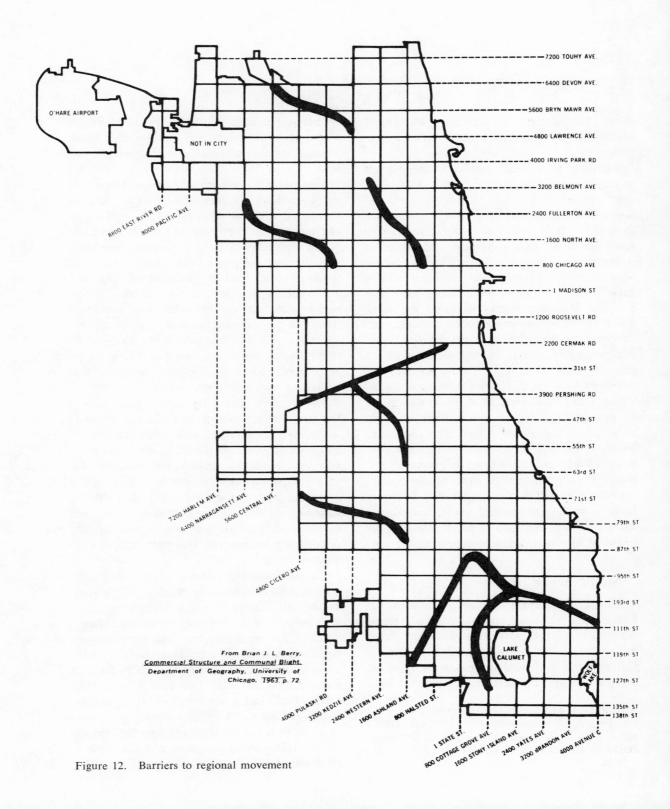

O'HARE AIRPORT

NOT IN CITY

LAKE CALUMET

WOLF LAKE

7200 TOUHY AVE.
6400 DEVON AVE.
5600 BRYN MAWR AVE.
4800 LAWRENCE AVE.
4000 IRVING PARK RD
3200 BELMONT AVE
2400 FULLERTON AVE.
1600 NORTH AVE.
800 CHICAGO AVE.
1 MADISON ST
1200 ROOSEVELT RD
2200 CERMAK RD
31st ST
3900 PERSHING RD
47th ST
55th ST
63rd ST
71st ST
79th ST
87th ST
95th ST
103rd ST
111th ST
119th ST
127th ST
135th ST
138th ST

8800 EAST RIVER RD
8000 PACIFIC AVE

7200 HARLEM AVE
6400 NARRAGANSETT AVE
5600 CENTRAL AVE

4800 CICERO AVE

4000 PULASKI RD
3200 KEDZIE AVE
2400 WESTERN AVE
1600 ASHLAND AVE
800 HALSTED ST.

1 STATE ST.
800 COTTAGE GROVE AVE.
1600 STONY ISLAND AVE
2400 YATES AVE
3200 BRANDON AVE
4000 AVENUE C

From Brian J. L. Berry,
Commercial Structure and Communal Blight.
Department of Geography, University of
Chicago, 1963 p. 72.

Figure 12. Barriers to regional movement

shows the barriers to consumer movement which may be assumed to apply also to regional use.

Situation of regional centers in or adjacent to large educational clusters planned for Chicago[7] will in some cases afford suitable location (the proposed north side cluster adjacent to Waller High School and the complex far south on Stony Island Avenue). However, it is essential that regional library centers be located directly on major thoroughfares and not back in among a group of buildings that may be dark at night. School locations for community branches are conceivable, and one such experimental installation might be tried, but this possibility should be approached with an extra measure of caution. The problem is not primarily location within the building and providing access and heat at night—these could be properly planned in a new structure—but rather that the same criteria that apply to location and use of schools do not apply to branch libraries. Unless care is exercised, the public library will end up with school-housed agencies that will be the delight of the planner because of their theoretical multipurpose utilization, but which in actual practice are simply not used by the community after school hours.

Subbranches

The 21 subbranches are small libraries that either were demoted from "regular" status when use slipped seriously or which never were able to rise above a modest beginning. But apparently there has been a moratorium on promotions and demotions; several sub-

branches are near or above the 100,000 annual circulation mark, and, on the other hand, several regular branches are well below this level.

Compared to regular branches, subbranches are open fewer hours (49 hours per week as compared with 68½), they have smaller collections (15,187 volumes on the average compared with 37,985 for the regular branches), and they are managed by experienced clerical workers rather than by professional librarians. Subbranches are located in rented quarters and by policy do not have their own buildings. They are not autonomous units but are administratively attached to a parent branch of which the librarian provides general supervision, selects books for the collection, and furnishes substitute staff when necessary.

On the other hand, the subbranches exhibit the same program elements as the regular units —children's collection and activities, young adult section, standard but smaller adult fiction and nonfiction collections, selected displays of paperbacks and newer books, and a reference-information desk. In other words, they are not different in kind but in size, and even this differential does not apply with any consistency because of the wide variation in amount of use.

The subbranches serve a purpose within the present extension plan for reaching all sections of the city. Some bring facilities to separate communities with limited population (Hegewisch is an example), some fill gaps between regular agencies (as does Near North), some build up with growing communities in the outskirts (such as West Belmont), some (like Oriole Park) take advantage of strategic locations, and some (Altgeld, for example) serve self-contained housing developments. They do so at a distinctly lower unit cost for services rendered than applies to regular branches

[7] Donald J. Leu and I. Carl Candoli, "Design for the Future; a Recommended Long-Range Educational Plan for Chicago," mimeographed (Chicago: Board of Education of the City of Chicago, 1968), 1:D-26.

whether measured in number of user visits, reference questions asked and answered, or items circulated for home use. Two common criticisms of many subbranches are that their quarters are unduly crowded with books (primarily due to the effort to maintain an adult nonfiction collection), and that the amount of seating is usually limited.

A brief description of one subbranch in a slum section will serve to exemplify the group. The Madison subbranch is the first library outlet directly west of the business center of Chicago, three miles from the Loop. It is located on a main street in a store which is almost the only remaining structure on its block since the fires of early 1968. The subbranch librarian is an experienced clerk from the local area. The collection numbers 21,000 volumes (somewhat larger than the average subbranch), 13,000 volumes being juvenile books. The unit circulated 34,188 items in 1968, up somewhat from the previous year despite the period of severe disturbance in April of that year and the unusual uneasiness thereafter. Eighty-three percent of the home circulation is of juvenile books for children to age 14. Total circulation is almost the same as in the large Douglas Branch in the same area. There is small but steady use on the premises by adults. Informal assistance is given both younger and older readers by a staff that has become familiar with resources through experience. Only limited provision is made of media other than books. From one standpoint this is a very modest library indeed; from another standpoint it is an oasis in a troubled area, particularly for the children in its immediate neighborhood.

With the possibility of a less stereotyped and more flexible branch and community library program in the offing, there is little reason to continue the distinction between branch and subbranch. Some of the subunits should

be substantially increased in size; some regular branches would better have smaller collections selected specifically for their particular localities. The future program should provide local library facilities, of different sizes and characteristics, one in Rogers Park and a different one in South Chicago and still a different one in Garfield Ridge and again in the ghetto, but all called by the name of neighborhood or community library. From the analysis of both branches and subbranches emerges the fundamental importance of greater variation among outlets in different communities; the future success of the branch program depends in significant measure on whether genuine diversity is achieved.

Bookmobiles and Deposit Collections

Beyond the branches, the Chicago Public Library brings books to people by means of "traveling branches" and by means of collections deposited in business firms, hospitals, and other locations. The bookmobiles are an extension of branch service which reaches out to where people live. The deposit collections introduce a new basis of extension, a functional approach to readers where they congregate for special purposes. The two come together and overlap in the schools, which in some instances are used for bookmobile stops and in others are the locations of classroom deposit collections.

TRAVELING BRANCHES

Mobile service started in Chicago in 1939 with a small trailer, called "Books on Wheels," which in the summer was pulled to playgrounds. It has since grown to five traveling branches (the last added in early 1969), a special multimedia van for the Lawndale demonstration program, and a summer "Story Caravan" unit. The bookmobiles are bulky vanlike vehicles with space for 4,000 books and a dozen readers.

Twenty-four full-day stops are made by the bookmobiles, and six more are currently being added with the new unit. The stops are made at weekly intervals at locations between branches and in neighborhoods cut off from ready access to stationary facilities. The actual stops are in shopping centers and school parking lots and at housing projects and settlement houses. Table 23 indicates the distribution of stops as between the inner, middle, and outer sections of the city, (i.e., three miles out, three to six miles, and beyond), and shows an emphasis upon the outlying areas.

Table 23
DISTRIBUTION OF BOOKMOBILE STOPS

Section of city	Number of stops
Inner Circle (within 3 miles)	6
Middle Circle (3–6 miles)	3
Outer Circle (over 6 miles)	16

Essentially the bookmobile service points are gap-fillers in the extension system, particularly for children who cannot readily get to branches. Such stations may be thought of as forerunners of subbranches, but the sequence from mobile to stationary outlet has seldom occurred. In reality bookmobile locations are determined by local community demand and pressure, rather than by a predetermined plan. This accounts in part for the large number of stops in outlying neighborhoods where people are more prone to organize to obtain public services.

Staff members on the traveling units are clerical, except for occasional technicians, and usually number two or three in addition to a driver. The service is essentially circulation of books—only a few reference books are carried, and staff seldom has time to help readers

with information inquiries. The mobile units do not usually carry magazines or records. Readers can request books from the main and regional collections, but this service is used only to a small extent (an average of two books per full-day stop).

Overall, the use of the bookmobiles has been declining from a peak circulation in 1960 of 565,870 volumes to 354,077 in 1968, a drop of 37 percent. The traveling branches are primarily children's agencies. Circulation from these units was 79 percent juvenile in 1968, yet it is in use by children that the recent decline occurred. Beyond this the moderate use by adults is for popular fiction, with some call for how-to and home-fixit publications.

To summarize, bookmobile service is aimed at the common denominator of children's reading and of best-seller and popular fiction for adults. There is limited variation in what is provided from community to community. As books are circulated each day, the stock on the mobile unit is replenished with similar titles from central bookmobile collections. These units are not customarily used to provide collections specifically selected for particular communities, such as neighborhoods of limited reading response.

Experimental use was made of an older bookmobile in the summer of 1968. Named the Story Caravan, it was equipped with facilities for sound and for showing films, and filled with children's books. The vehicle stopped at housing projects in low-income areas. Gay music was played, films shown, and stories told. Response by children was enthusiastic. Visitors to the Story Caravan on location remarked that at times the same tune was played over and over, and the stories had to be postponed while the available staff worked exclusively at circulating books. But promising principles are exemplified in this venture: the selection of materials for a clearly envisioned purpose, the delivery of such materials directly to potential users, and the presentation of those materials with a flair.

The regular bookmobiles operate from and are administered by four separate offices—the three regional libraries and the central children's department. Four separate collections are maintained to stock the mobile units. At present responsibility for them is divided, yet the bookmobile stops which each of the four offices supply are intermingled through the city.

The traveling branches have served a purpose in filling gaps in branch provision and have undoubtedly helped to bring books into the lives of children in some localities. They should continue to serve this purpose where the branches do not reach. However, as existing gaps are filled by the provision of branch units, the value of mobile collections will not come to an end. Bookmobiles have qualities which are an asset in the urban setting—they have the ability to move through the streets, to stop where people congregate, to alter purposes rapidly, to change collections overnight. They have a high potential as special-purpose outposts, to be moved from point to point as circumstances require. The 1967 summer Story Caravan in Chicago was an example of this use of bookmobiles, in that a mobile unit was entirely reconditioned and programmed to serve a special audience.

DEPOSIT COLLECTIONS

A business deposit collection has been maintained by the Chicago Public Library for employees of Marshall Field and Company since 1911. Similar collections are provided on request in other business houses, industrial plants, clubs and organizations, hospitals, settlement houses, and summer camps. Another division of the deposit program provides collections in schools.

Deposit collections are provided by request only. They are not aggressively promoted, nor are they nurtured once installed. Content is fairly standardized, as is the case with the adult sections of bookmobile collections, and stresses popular fiction and self-help titles to some extent. Usually of some 400–500 volumes in size, deposit collections are similar in titles provided to what one finds in a medium-sized paperback installation in railroad and bus stations and smaller than the paperback sections of more substantial bookstores. Constituting a unique resource for the working person some years ago, they are now a small part of the wide provision of popular recreational reading materials available through commercial channels.

The total number of deposit collections numbered 286 in 1968, down from 433 ten years before (table 24). The units in business houses and industries have declined by 50 percent in this period, and the collections in schools have

Table 24
NUMBER OF DEPOSIT COLLECTIONS, 1958 AND 1968

Year	Public stations	Businesses, unions	Organizations, settlements	Hospitals	Summer camps	Public schools	Parochial, private schools	Total
1958	7	42	20	26	57	141	140	433
1968	1	21	55	17	24	30	138	286

declined almost as rapidly. The installations in hospitals and summer camps have also declined in number. The deposit program as it is presently conceived appears to be foundering.

In the public schools there remains only a remnant of the former program; public school deposits will shortly disappear of themselves. This is clearly associated with the establishment of school libraries. In the parochial and independent schools, where the growth of school libraries has not been so rapid, the number of deposit units has remained fairly stable, but here also school libraries can be expected to appear and expand.

A growing aspect of the deposit program is in collections for clubs and organizations. These normally have a program of some kind, and rather than simply accepting general reading materials they seek resources that support their adopted purposes. Another new dimension of deposit work that has been developed in Chicago is in service to the disadvantaged—collections in infant welfare stations and in waiting rooms of courthouses, and most recently the somewhat larger installations (in a sense, very small branches) in apartments within housing developments. These also display the ingredients of a rather specific purpose (recreation and popular information in the waiting-room collections, aid to study for young children in the apartment collections), and of very great accessibility (where people must wait as well as in the same building in which children live).

These several developments provide a key to future opportunities. The deposit concept can continue as it has in the past, with the service running downhill and in time disappearing. Or the function of deposit collections can be replanned and refocused, from convenient provision of diversional reading to special-purpose collections for distinctly defined groups. The revised concept applies to people of many backgrounds, not just to the culturally deprived. It will call for identification of needs, design of programs, and informed selection of materials. The service will have to be promoted rather than remain, as in the past, passively waiting for requests. It will require much more varied collections, with subject materials at different levels selected for audiences of sharply defined interests. Deposit collections in the future may in some cases be short-term, to be used during the life of a project, rather than long-term in all cases. There is a potential for functional extension of library resources to people for special purposes which is not now being realized.

One key to effective functional extension is responsiveness to what the people and the community want. Scouts for the deposit program should be down in the neighborhoods to be served, particularly in the ghetto areas, listening to people, asking about what is needed, trying out some sample books and pamphlets to determine response. Mistakes will be made, modifications must occur once resources are actually provided, but rather than guess at what will be used from the confines of an office, or send out a standardized collection because presumably it was wanted at some locations at some time in the past, the determination of what goes into deposit collections should be based on direct contact with the groups to be served. With this approach the deposit program can not only revitalize its own activity but also can serve as an advance guard and a trial balloon for the whole extension effort.

In bringing books and other resources into the lives of Chicagoans, which is a basic purpose of the Chicago Public Library, the deposit program has a definite contribution to make, particularly for people who are not so much members of geographic communities as they are of various interest communities. Under imaginative administration the deposit program can be an innovative force within the Library.

Service to the Blind

The Department of Books for the Blind and Physically Handicapped is a regional agency of the Library of Congress, with responsibility for service throughout the State of Illinois. It stocks books in Braille, in talking book form, and on magnetic tape. Readers request material by mail or telephone, and the books are delivered by mail (without charge, by act of Congress).

Most of the collection is furnished by the Division of the Blind of the Library of Congress, also without cost. The Department purchases a relatively small number of additional titles and duplicates from the American Printing House for the Blind and the Johanna Bureau. There are 7,000 titles in Braille, 4,500 in recorded Talking Books, and 3,500 on tape —when duplicates among the several forms are eliminated, this amounts to about 10,000 different titles in all. An effort is made to get other titles for brief loans from the Library of Congress as requested. In addition the Department has approximately 100 periodicals in forms appropriate for blind users.

Just under 40 percent of the blind persons in Chicago are registered for library service, and a little under 30 percent from outside the city (see table 25). Roughly half the registrants called on the Department in 1968. All these figures are approximations, because individuals are counted separately if they use more than one form of material for the blind. Once an individual becomes a regular user, he is likely to depend heavily on the service; the average

Table 25
USERS OF SERVICE FOR THE BLIND, 1968

Location	"Blind" persons*	Registered borrowers	Users in 1968
Chicago	7,000	2,783	1,386
Illinois residents outside Chicago	13,000	4,320	2,392
	20,000	7,103	3,778

*Using the usual estimate of 1 "blind" person in 500 of the population: *Standards for Library Services for the Blind and Physically Handicapped.* Commission on Standards and Accreditation of Services for the Blind, 1965, p.2.

user in 1968 borrowed 36 items, books and periodicals combined.

Adults constitute 90 percent of the users. Resources have not been built up for younger persons who are blind, many of whom get their materials through the schools they attend. The predominant emphasis is on recreational reading for adults. This was the concept in the basic Pratt-Smoot Bill of 1931, but since then both federal legislation and policies of the Library of Congress have extended the program to younger readers and broadened it to include educational and subject titles. The service for the blind in the Chicago Public Library has not expanded on any scale into these new dimensions.

Talking books, on records, account for the largest share of the collections and the lion's share of use (table 26). Braille is no longer the backbone of the collection. Magnetic tapes are increasing in number and use and may be expected to occupy a larger place in the future. Fifty-nine percent of the talking-book registrants used the service in 1968 and 65 percent of the tape registrants, but only 27 percent of those in the records for Braille materials. The average talking-book user borrowed 44 items, and the Braille user 13 items. Clearly communication of books by sound bulks much larger for blind persons using the library than communication by tactile sense.

Table 26
REGISTRANTS AND USE, BY TYPES OF MATERIAL, 1968

	Talking books	Braille books	Magnetic tapes
Registrants	4,918	2,275	492
Users	2,928	628	318
Circulation	131,595	8,239	1,124

The national standards of the Commission on Standards and Accreditation of Services to the Blind call for an administrative librarian plus one professional staff member for each 750 registered readers (a total of nine in the case of Chicago if registrants are used as the base, or of five if recent borrowers are used), plus two nonprofessional staff members to each professional (at least ten in the case of Chicago). Actually the Department has one professional administrator, one Head Library Clerk, and ten additional clerical workers.

Clearly professional staff is in short supply, and this is reflected in the service program. The collection has not been built beyond the materials from the Library of Congress. No provision is made for sending materials systematically to regular users; each item must be requested individually. Only limited reference service is provided. Publicity for the service is very limited. Actually, for the staff available, a reasonable standard of regular service is maintained for these patrons.

No provision is made in Chicago for a center to which blind readers could come to confer with librarians and listen to or examine the materials available and thus begin to use libraries as is the case for sighted readers. The present quarters in the basement of the Hild

Regional Branch do not have space for the purpose, the area within the building could not be made accessible to blind persons without very considerable expense, and the building is not in a central location. In any case the full space at Hild will be needed for regular library service. New quarters should be found for the department in order to provide direct access for blind readers who are mobile, either in a new central library building or in conjunction with a centrally-located service agency for the blind.

Service to the physically handicapped was inaugurated in 1967. To date there are only a little over 100 users to whom talking books are sent. In Chicago, as elsewhere, the severely handicapped individual who cannot get to a library is in substance still cut off from library facilities.

Additional trained staff is needed. This should include at least one more professional, and several technicians who are college graduates and who could be given in-service training in the resources now held by the department. Service to the physically handicapped remains to be developed. The Chicago Public Library has the responsibility for extending service to all who seek self-development by means of recorded knowledge, especially to the blind and the physically handicapped who are cut off from ready access to the reservoir of information, ideas, and expression.

Administrative Organization of Branch Service

The Chicago Public Library has developed an unusual administrative structure for its branch libraries. Prior to the establishment of the three regional units in the 1920s and 1930s, all branches were administered by an Assistant Librarian located at headquarters, with local authority delegated to the librarian of each branch. A Supervisor of Children's Service was responsible for the program for younger readers throughout the branches.

Along with the service concept of the regionals, there developed a parallel administrative plan. The three librarians of the regional branches were given management responsibility for the various branches located in their areas. Subsequently the separate position of Regional Librarian was created, dividing the region-wide responsibilities from the direction of the regional library as a service center. Three regional children's coordinators also were appointed. At this stage the branch program was administratively unified and coordinated at headquarters by a single officer, and was managed in the field in a decentralized structure for three large sections of the city.

When the position of Assistant Librarian in charge of Branches became vacant in 1937, no new appointment was made. The regional librarians were each given full responsibility for their areas, reporting directly to the Chief Librarian. Similarly, the central children's coordinator was not replaced on retirement, and the three regional children's librarians handle this level of service in their area, also reporting directly to the Chief Librarian. A fourth coordinator for children's service within the central building was later appointed; this individual handles some system-wide children's service matters but without system-wide authority or responsibility.

Thus, at present the 62 branches are administered by three regional librarians, with children's service coordinated by three regional children's officers, all six of whom report to the Chief Librarian. No senior officer devotes full attention to all branches and service to the city as a whole. By dividing branch responsibility in three, this plan militates against the emergence of any one strong branch leader to carry the whole city system forward. It also places an extra burden directly on the Chief Librarian.

Each regional administrator works with a major geographic section of Chicago—one for the north and part of the northwest side, another for the west side along with some adjacent northwest and southwest areas, and the third for the south side, the southeast, and part of the southwest section. The number of branches in each region is shown in table 27.

Table 27
NUMBER OF BRANCH LIBRARIES BY REGIONS

Regional group	Branches	Subbranches	Total
North	15	5	20
West	11	7	18
South	15	9	24

The distinguishing factor is geographical. The regional areas are not distinct as to kinds of communities included or types of library services needed. Each has areas of low and high educational background, each has communities of varying ethnic traditions, and each has some very large and very small branches. This means that each regional librarian must encompass the full range of service levels and variations, as against having special interest and capacity in service to the inner city or to the middle areas or to the outer ring. In actual practice regional administrators inevitably have preferences and antipathies that are reflected in the kinds of community service that are given high and low priority. This is not an administrative structure that would facilitate, for example, a concerted effort in new service to the ghetto, because the inner city is in substance divided into three parts.

The regional librarians carry full responsibility for the installations and service in their region, from the broadest considerations of long-range development to immediate day-to-day problems. They seek to plan for their areas and to lead the way to greater accomplishment. They must supervise their various units, and should guide them toward appropriate modifications in program and resources. From among the titles selected for purchase by the Central Library subject departments, they designate those that may be considered for acquisition by the branch librarians. They participate in personnel assignments and transfers, whether of a senior branch librarian or of a junior book shelver, and this responsibility has increased since the Assistant Librarian for Personnel retired in 1966 and has not been replaced. The regional librarians handle relations between the branches and the central activities. They are turned to with all immediate problems arising in branch and extension service—the recalcitrant staff member in an individual branch, the breakdown of the bookmobile, the incident in a branch building, a change in working schedule. And along the way each must watch to keep in step with the other two, in the many matters for which formal policies do not exist. Small wonder that in practice it is the immediate and emergency problems that preempt attention and energy, while the larger concerns of the branch program are put aside or rest uneasily at the edge of consciousness.

Overall unified administration of the branch and extension library programs in Chicago is needed. At the same time, in a system of this size and a city of this diversity, decentralized responsibility and variations in program are also essential. A substantial restructuring of extension service administration is suggested below, to provide the leadership and the local autonomy required to meet both present and emerging needs.

Conclusions

The branches of the Chicago Public Library have played an important role in bringing library services close to most of the people of Chicago. Local units, within neighborhoods and regions of the city, will continue to play a strategic role in the future. The existing branch system provides a well-developed starting point for branch and extension provision for the next twenty to thirty years.

However, library needs have changed, communities have changed, publication and communication media have changed, formal education has increased, and new methods of electronic communication for library resources are in prospect. The total branch program of the Chicago Public Library needs replanning as to functions of branches, number and spacing, size, and relationships among units.

Here are nineteen of the factors which dictate a new branch library program in Chicago:

1. The 59 local branches, large and small, are seeking to perform a wide range of library services beyond their capacity, particularly in the provision of adult subject collections, and as a result are not providing any services at full potential.

2. The local branches, large and small, follow a standardized program and are not genuinely and flexibly adjusted to the communities they seek to serve; this applies particularly to the ghetto areas.

3. Community relations and local identity of branches have been withering, in part because of change and disorganization in communities, in part because librarians stay mostly within the four walls of the libraries.

4. Increasingly in the next period the branch service will be affected by and should be

planned in connection with growing school and college libraries and impending cultural-educational complexes or centers.

5. The spacing of branches, on a one-mile service radius, does not conform to the variations in distance and use patterns in areas of different densities and different degrees of social organization.

6. It is clear that a greater number of local outlets are necessary in the inner city, not to provide large, standard subject collections, but to make available resources (films, records, pamphlets, magazines, as well as selected books) needed by local residents, information to meet their inquiries, and individual guidance in use of resources.

7. The regional branches are not large enough or varied enough in resources to meet either the present-day or the emerging needs of adult subject readers and of students at the upper high school and junior college levels.

8. The three existing regional branches make this level of service accessible to only 40 percent of the people in Chicago; and two of the three are not functioning as regionals because of severe deterioration in their immediate neighborhoods, so that in reality only 15 percent of Chicagoans have regional service.

9. This limited availability of regional-level resources in turn drives many high school students to the central building, thereby pulling down the proper level of service provision at the Central Library.

10. Except in children's service, the branches do not provide an inviting and stimulating book and communication environment for present and potential users; this is a matter of program more than of physical quarters.

11. By the same token, the challenge to pro-

fessional staff, particularly younger members, has been limited in branches; and the kinds and levels of staff members provided in local agencies serving different functions need review.

12. The priority given construction of new branch buildings is questionable, because it benefits mostly the outlying areas, and results in structures that may well be outmoded in ten or twenty years; funds for branch construction would better be used to provide regional centers over the whole city.

13. More local agencies adapted to the localities served, enticing and exciting as centers for communities, should be provided; this can be accomplished in rented quarters and in commercial structures built to library specifications and leased for ten years or less.

14. Criteria for branch location also need review in the light of changes in travel patterns, variations in such patterns among communities, and differences in functions among branches.

15. Electronic communication and automatic access to materials at a distance, which will develop in the next ten years, will change the functions of individual branches and also will alter the potential relations and interconnections between all units of the system.

16. The present structure of the regional administration of branch library service, divided in three separate divisions, is not suitable for coping with general and long-range problems and is placing an undue burden on the office of Chief Librarian.

17. The straight geographical definition of regions does not facilitate planning and provision of programs for groups and communities marked by varying economic, educational, and cultural backgrounds.

18. Geographical and functional extension of library services (branches on the one hand, deposit and special-collection programs on the other hand) have been separated in administration with the result that these two related means for bringing resources to people have not been developed jointly to their full potential.

19. Service to the blind and physically handicapped has stayed within the limited scope of the federal program and reaches only a small portion of these special groups cut off from usual library resources.

Proposed Extension Program

The various underlying principles set forth earlier for future development of the Chicago Public Library apply with full force to the branch and extension program: flexibility, experimentation, community identification, multimedia provision, and individuality of service. An additional principle that must be added for branches and other extension agencies is planned relationship to the Central Library and among the various outlets; a branch is not a library separate and distinct to itself, but a unit within a city-wide system.

Certain guidelines for developing branch and extension service will first be set forth, and then applied in a service and administrative program for the city:

Clear distinction between regional centers and branches

It is proposed that the regional and regular branch distinction which has characterized the Chicago extension program for some time be retained and sharpened. Separate functions should apply to each, as outlined below. The regional centers will be increased in size and service level; the

branches will in some cases be decreased in size and in all cases revitalized as *neighborhood* or *community* institutions. Staffing patterns will differ in the two kinds of agencies, and each will have a separate administrative organization.

Additional regional centers and branches

Extension units must extend to the point where people will use them and where they will be within reasonable reach of all Chicagoans. Regional centers must exist within three miles of all residential sections of the city. Branches may be a little more than one mile from users in outlying areas where travel patterns and the availability of automobiles carry people greater distances, but in high-density areas—the ghetto, older concentrations of blue-collar families, high-rise apartment areas—smaller, special-purpose branches close to potential users should be provided. The result will be ten, rather than three regional centers, and up to 100 nearby, locally identified, neighborhood branches.

Shift of construction emphasis to regional centers

Chicago has been caught in a cycle of constructing local library buildings. If this is continued, every community in the City will want such a facility, at an eventual cost in excess of twenty million dollars. The resulting buildings are suited to some areas but not to others, and in any case are subject to change in the next twenty to thirty years as alteration in community composition and the use of new electronic communication with central resources will probably reduce the scope of what needs to be housed locally. Priority would better be given to building regional centers, to benefit more Chicagoans more rapidly, provide long-range fixed points in the city-wide extension plan, and open the way for much greater variety and immediate usefulness of library provision within localities. Two regional centers should be built annually, at a cost of one million dollars each, so that these anchor points may be completed by 1975.

New staffing pattern

The regional centers will need professional staffs for reference, bibliographic, guidance, and educational service, as at present, but increased in quantity as well as quality. The branches, on the other hand, will be staffed by indigenous technicians rather than professionals, except in the case of the 15 to 20 largest branches, which will have one librarian-administrator in charge. Professional staff will be brought into community service, not as minor administrators absorbed in the operation of smaller agencies, but as full-time service coordinators and field workers organized into regional *task forces* attuned to distinctive sections of Chicago. The task forces will work with and through a technician staff that is to be recruited locally.

Extraordinary effort in the ghetto

Effective methods for reaching people in the disorganized sections of the city are not fully known. Certain principles are clear enough—greater physical accessibility, close planning and working relationships with local residents, flexibility in resources and methods, use of nonprint media, protection of users within the library and while traveling to and from the library. These principles are to be applied rigorously and continuously. The Chicago Public Library in the past year has tried several innovative approaches, some of which are promising. This effort should be regularized and funded as a continuing activity, rather than kept on a short-term and special-project basis. Wide diversity must mark ghetto programs; some

branches in these areas may be primarily information centers, others cultural centers built around predominant local interests, and others media centers to introduce people to the world of communication.

Unification of administrative control

Each kind of decentralized unit, the large regional centers stressing subject scope and the small local branches stressing neighborhood identification and diversity, needs unified city-wide administration. There should be an Assistant Librarian for the ten regional centers, and another Assistant Librarian in charge of branch and related extension programs. Within the branch-extension division, four regional subunits defined by community type as well as by geographical area will apply, with task force staffs to revitalize, diversify, and guide branch service within the regions. Under this plan quite different, and at times competing, kinds of service will not be grouped into one office.

Integration of geographical and functional extension

Geographical extension (branches and bookmobiles) and functional extension (deposit collections) are related means for accomplishing the same end. Both seek to bring a part of total library service to a defined clientele. Both are devices for making library resources convenient for people who do not often travel to a large central collection, and both afford opportunity for fresh and unconventional ways of reaching people, free of the restrictions of standard organization that must apply to a large collection. The two forms of extension should therefore fit into the same administrative group, with a unified two-front plan for serving the city, and both drawing on a single large materials reservoir.

Regional Library Centers

It is suggested that these units be called *centers* rather than *branches*. The term "branch" implies a small, local, and fragmentary agency. The proposed regional units will be libraries of substantial size serving 300,000 or more people living in several adjacent communities and thus should be termed *regional library centers*.

FUNCTIONS

Provide book resources for adults with developed interests

These will be libraries for the wide range of interests—whether in a region of the world, a historical period, a social problem, a technological development, a hobby interest, a type of literature—developed by people today. The regional centers will be marked by both breadth and depth of holdings, in both the range of subjects covered and the variety of material within each subject. The local resident will turn to his nearby branch for the most popular current-interest publications and for materials of wide interest in his locality (for example, gardening in some communities). But he will go to the regional center within two to three miles for interests beyond the most general (following up on the gardening example, he will turn to the regional level when his interest develops in the growing of roses or iris as specialties). These will be the library agencies for a mounting population of educated adults with a rich range of avenues of self-development, short of the advanced and near-research resources to be held in the Central Library. *Strong libraries for contemporary living.*

Provide book resources for students going beyond their school and college libraries

Working libraries of 25,000 volumes or more will increasingly be maintained within the schools. The city junior colleges and other community colleges are building up library resources. The regional library centers will be for advanced high school students when they prepare special assignments or engage in advanced and accelerated programs, and for college students in the first two years of higher education as they broaden their educational scope. Academic subjects from astronomy to zoology and from ancient history to Zola will be well represented. *The backstop library for the student going beyond resources available in the school or local college.*

Provide periodical and document resources for students and adults

The regional centers will provide both current and back files of many of the subject journals issued today, which are a prime resource both for students doing papers and for adults pursuing subject interests. Not only academic titles (*American Journal of Sociology, Antioch Review, Asian Survey,* and on through the alphabet) but also applied topics (*Advertising Age, Antiques, Aviation Engineering,* and the like) will be included. Similarly, selected publications of the federal, state, and local governments will be an integral part of the regional collections. *The center for printed materials in nonbook form.*

Provide newer media for an age of varied communication

Audio-visual materials will be an integral part of regional resources, not a supplementary or fringe commodity. Recordings of music and literature and languages, 16mm films for groups and 8mm films for home use, filmstrips, art reproductions and pictorial material will be available. There will be listening and viewing facilities in the regional centers. Students, individual adults, and families will increasingly turn to such resources in the next decade. *The regional multimedia center.*

Guide the use of resources for self-education

The regional centers will not be provision warehouses only. Information and reference service also will be provided at a high level. Bibliographic aid and reading guidance will be given. Resources will be arranged in related groupings of relevance to the seeker of knowledge. Programmed materials —in book form, for teaching machines, on learning consoles—will be featured. *The self-education center for a region of the city.*

Serve as a connecting link with central resources

The regional centers are to be connected by coaxial cable with the Central Library. They will have computer-produced records of the full holdings in Central. Increasingly technology will permit (1) facsimile reproduction of central resources in the regionals, and (2) in time, direct "on-line" viewing of materials. *The regional contact with resources anywhere in the Chicago area and beyond.*

Serve as a local branch outlet

This is the local branch function, to be fitted into the regional center building in order to avoid another nearby installation for the immediately adjacent community. Because of the extensive regional resources within the building, the extra provision for local service will amount to (1) a children's room and collection equivalent to that in local branches, and (2) a selected collection of recent and local-interest publications for adult browsing. *The local branch within the regional building.*

STANDARDS FOR REGIONAL RESOURCES

175,000 volumes; capacity over a 10-year period to move up to 200,000 volumes

6,000–7,000 new titles added per year (one-quarter the number to be acquired annually for the central collection)

Rigorous weeding of older publications (which will be kept by the Central Library)

400–500 periodical subscriptions (the Central Library will acquire 5,000–6,000)

Back files of most periodicals for 10 years, in microfilm wherever possible (the Central Library will maintain complete and permanent files of periodicals)

3,000 recordings in literature, language, and subject fields as well as in music

Selected acquisitions of government documents, avant-garde and underground magazines and newspapers, maps and realia

Microfilm and microfiche reader-printers

500 motion-picture films, divided between 8mm and 16mm and including short "single-purpose" films

Projectors for home use

2,000 filmstrips, on both school topics and self-education topics for adults

Programmed resources, in book and machine form, as these become available.

STANDARDS FOR REGIONAL STAFF

Minimum staff complement of 25 to 30 (full-time equivalent)

Composed one-half of librarian-technician teams

Remainder of staff in clerical ratings

One or more professional-technician teams devoted to

reference and bibliographical service

reading stimulation and guidance service

multimedia service

New professional position of "student librarian" (LII level) for maintaining contact with schools and colleges, helping build regional center collections for students, and aiding teachers and students in the center

Regional center head librarians at the LIV rating (actually LV in present salary level).

STANDARDS FOR REGIONAL BUILDINGS

35,000 square feet of service, book, stack, and work space

Main reference-subject service on one level of 20,000 square feet

On plot of 25,000–30,000 square feet

Located at major intersection, but not necessarily in large shopping area (Cultural-Educational Centers are possible sites)

With both off-street parking and public transportation in two directions

Within three miles of every Chicago resident.

LOCATIONS FOR REGIONAL CENTERS

Ten regional library centers are proposed, distributed as shown in figure 13:

1. Present Hild Regional—partially remodeled in interior, service to blind located elsewhere, adjacent off-street parking space acquired

2. Present Legler Regional—partially remodeled in interior, Deposits Department located elsewhere, adjacent parking space acquired (Note: rehabilitation at Legler to occur when neighborhood becomes stabilized and travel to the center is resumed)

3. New near-northwest regional—1600–2000 north, near Lincoln Park, perhaps in proposed Waller educational park

4. New far-northwest regional—in vicinity of 5600 west and 4800 north (site owned for Jefferson Park Branch suitable if adjacent property can be acquired)

5. Mid-northwest regional—in vicinity of 4800 west and 2400 north

6. New south regional (Woodlawn is not large enough to serve this function and cannot readily be extended)—4700–5500 south, 800 east

7. New far-south regional—in vicinity of 8700 south and 1600 east (site owned for Avalon Park Branch suitable if adjacent property can be acquired)

8. New near-southwest regional—in vicinity of 5500 south and 4000 west

9. New mid-southwest regional—in vicinity of 7100 south and 2400 west

10. New far-southwest regional—in vicinity of 9500 south and 800 west.

Branch Libraries

No formal distinction is made here between regular branches and subbranches. Some installations will be larger than others, depending on materials used locally, and some will be in separate library buildings, depending on stability of local areas; but all communities need local library service at the full potential that will be utilized, and all should be developed as libraries for their particular neighborhoods. Even the limited group of common functions listed below should be varied as circumstances suggest and leads open.

FUNCTIONS

Provision of reading materials for younger children

The local branch is to provide resources for children as they first enter the world of

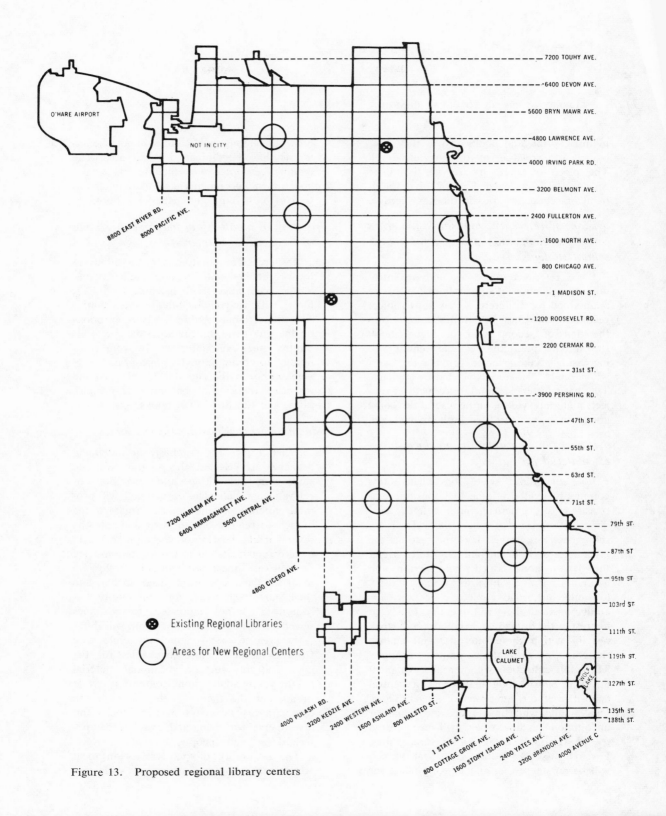

O'HARE AIRPORT

NOT IN CITY

8800 EAST RIVER RD.

8000 PACIFIC AVE.

7200 HARLEM AVE.

6400 NARRAGANSETT AVE.

5600 CENTRAL AVE.

4800 CICERO AVE.

⊗ Existing Regional Libraries

◯ Areas for New Regional Centers

4000 PULASKI RD.

3200 KEDZIE AVE.

2400 WESTERN AVE.

1600 ASHLAND AVE.

800 HALSTED ST.

1 STATE ST.

800 COTTAGE GROVE AVE.

1600 STONY ISLAND AVE.

2400 YATES AVE.

3200 BRANDON AVE.

4000 AVENUE C

LAKE CALUMET

WOLF LAKE

7200 TOUHY AVE.

6400 DEVON AVE.

5600 BRYN MAWR AVE.

4800 LAWRENCE AVE.

4000 IRVING PARK RD.

3200 BELMONT AVE.

2400 FULLERTON AVE.

1600 NORTH AVE.

800 CHICAGO AVE.

1 MADISON ST.

1200 ROOSEVELT RD.

2200 CERMAK RD.

31st ST.

3900 PERSHING RD.

47th ST.

55th ST.

63rd ST.

71st ST.

79th ST.

87th ST.

95th ST.

103rd ST.

111th ST.

119th ST.

127th ST.

135th ST.

138th ST.

Figure 13. Proposed regional library centers

pictures, print, and books and as they later launch into reading at the juvenile level. The place of children's service is to be reviewed in 1980, in the light of the development of school libraries in the next decade.

Provision of reference and study materials for upper elementary and beginning high school students

Basic reference resources and an introductory collection of subject books are to be maintained for children as they start subject reading in the 4th or 5th grades and on up to the first or second year of high school. Beyond this point the regional centers will increasingly take over to provide the ever-wider range of materials needed by students. The basic reference and introductory subject materials will also be useful in some communities for adults of limited education.

Provision of current-interest and local-interest material for adults

Localities differ widely in what adults commonly read. In some locations the emphasis is on practical, home-related, mechanical interests. In others the stress is on sports, hobbies, travel. In some sections the great interest is in current publications and the newest book issued, both fiction and nonfiction. Branch libraries would not try to build up broad subject collections for adults; instead they will identify topics of interest in the immediate neighborhood, stock heavily within these interests, and change the emphasis when the community changes. The adult collection will not be permanent but will be on long loan from a central deposit reservoir, for a year or longer. Those local adults who have more individual or uncommon reading tastes will be referred to the regional center within three miles. For out-of-school adults the local branch will be an interesting and alluring place for

browsing among publications about the interests that predominate in their area. The reading resources will include magazines, government documents and pamphlets, as well as hardbound and paperback books.

Provision of audio-visual materials on topics of frequent local interest

Resources for children and for adults in local branches will include pictorial materials, recordings (with listening facilities), films (with viewing facilities), and exhibits. The proportional relationship between books on the one hand and audio-visual materials on the other will differ widely from community to community. In some branches in neighborhoods that do not readily respond to print there may be more recordings, films, and filmstrips than books.

Educational programs in selected topics

When topics for emphasis in individual branches are selected, the program will not stop with acquisition and provision of relevant materials. The library staff will promote interest in the topics, organize the branch to feature one or several, relate the several media bearing on the topic, bring in local or outside talent to talk or demonstrate or answer questions, provide follow-up leads for those who want to go further, and then start fresh when the community has responded (or not responded) to the topics selected for emphasis. These again will differ from area to area—elementary child care for the mothers, basic mechanics for the men, and introductory vocational material for the young adults in one community, while in another the theme might be more the contemporary novel for women, stocks and investments for men, and avant-garde materials for young people.

The possibility of rich variety in local educational programs opens up with this approach, as in the Spanish-speaking community building up around the Toman Branch, or in the book-oriented section around Northtown Branch, or in the young-family, lower-middle-class area around Scottsdale Branch, or in the struggling section around Douglas Branch where the library is already probing for a distinctive program suited to this special neighborhood. Instead of standard-subject collections in each branch·that try but fail to serve the widening subject needs and interests of students and adults, these will be changing educational programs. Branches will in time be equipped with closed-circuit television, on which selected educational programs on video tape will be run on request from a central source—once again, programs selected to further designated educational or special-interest themes.

Individual personalized service

All persons coming into neighborhood branches should be contacted at some time during their visit to see what help is needed. In some cases the patron will indicate his preference for browsing or making his own search. In other instances brief locational information will suffice. But some users, young and old, will need more extensive guidance. The technician in the local branch will know his immediate collection and will have basic training in information and advisory techniques, and he will have direct access to the task force team for special cases beyond his experience. Local branch libraries in Chicago should be more neighborhood stores providing individual attention than distant supermarkets with large stocks and little personal help.

Information tie-in to the Central Information Service

Local branches will have small collections of standard information sources, and trained technician staffs for handling these resources, and will therefore provide answers to quick-information questions from their own shelves. But prominent in each branch will be a no-charge tie-line telephone to the Information-Bibliographic Center (see in chapter 4, page 67). Patrons may use the direct line while in the branch, and after doing so would be likely to seek information by telephone directly from the central unit in the future. This link to a powerful central source will at once provide better service and avoid duplication of ever-larger information units in each branch.

STANDARDS FOR BRANCH RESOURCES

Precise standards cannot be set down for materials needed in all branches to achieve the functions outlined. Variety of resources must follow variety of program. The guidelines here will give some indication of the size and scope of the branches as conceived:

Book collections up to 25,000 volumes, one-third for younger children, one-third in introductory subject materials, one-third on selected topics for adults

One thousand reference volumes (300–400 titles)

Forty to 50 magazine subscriptions, in some communities with selected titles duplicated; no back issues kept

Four hundred to 500 recordings, with varying selections depending on community

Films and filmstrips on long loan to support education programs adopted.

STANDARDS FOR BRANCH STAFF

Branches will typically be headed by a Technician III, and have a TII first assistant and a TII children's assistant (for a period extra-large branches with over 200,000 circulation will be headed by an LIII). Total staff complement in a branch is to be determined not by circulation but by need and potential response.

Four task forces composed of professionals and operating out of regional administrative offices are to be set up, two from an inner city office and one each from a north-northwest and a south-southwest office; each task force is to consist of a minimum of nine staff members:

> Task group coordinator
> Children's specialists (two or more)
> Young adult specialists (two or more)
> Adult community workers (two or more)
> Educational program specialist
> Audio-visual specialist
> Information specialist.

The coordinator will be at the LIII level (reporting to the Branch Coordinator) and the other members at LI and LII ratings. The task forces should be composed of both librarians and other professionally-trained personnel, as in adult education or audio-visual media. Their job will encompass planning, program design, field contacts, training of technician staff on the job, conducting pilot projects, and evaluating results.

STANDARDS FOR LOCATIONS AND BUILDINGS

The essential standard is to provide nearby outlets for people where they live, with priority given to convenience and adaptability rather than to half-million-dollar buildings.

Physical provision as follows:

> Specially designed and constructed buildings in areas of long-term stability

Multipurpose commercial buildings designed specifically for branch use, constructed by private builders, and leased to the Library for ten years with renewal option, in areas that may become transitional or disorganized

Rented storefront quarters in areas of transition, two-year or three-year leases, carefully reviewed when they are in prospect of terminating

Small target installations in apartment complexes and portable units.

Square footage of 7,000–8,000 square feet, on one level, in library-built or commercially-built structures, and of at least 4,000 square feet (double-front store) in rented quarters

Within one mile of all residents in outer areas and one-half mile in transitional areas

To meet location criteria of being within (not just outside of) shopping center or shopping strip, on main thoroughfare, near major intersection, and adjacent to public transportation and parking

Adherence to these distance and location standards will increase the number of local branches in the city from 59 at present to approximately 100, including the local-service divisions in the 10 regional centers.

Exact locations for the various additional branches cannot be specified, because these must be worked out with respect to the actual availability of rental space, vacant lots for the placement of portable units, and space within large housing projects. However, several obvious sections and locations come immediately to mind. There is first the area of considerable size in the inner city, extending from Halsted to Damen and from Chicago Avenue south almost to Roosevelt Road, immediately to the west of the Loop. Chicago and Ashland Avenues and Madison and Ashland Avenues are natural centers in this section. There are similar gaps immediately to the south—Halsted between 18th Street and Cermak Road, and the Chinese neighborhood south of Cermak Road and Wentworth Avenue. In the almost continuous row of housing projects on State Street from 22nd to 55th Streets, within which the Library has opened one "apartment" library, there should be at least three such units, spaced out at 25th, 39th, and 51st Streets. Forty-seventh and Halsted Streets, and 35th Street and Damen Avenue should be considered for storefront installations. Further south, in a section in transition, 71st Street and Cottage Grove Avenue, and 71st Street and Stony Island Avenue are both possibilities for small neighborhood agencies. To the west, in another transition area, Madison Street and Cicero Avenue, and Central Avenue south of Madison both need local libraries. Well beyond the inner city, such communities as Edison Park and Beverly should have small branches in place of bookmobile stops (each of the latter two outlying areas will also be within reach of large regional centers, Edison Park with a center at Lawrence and Central Avenues, Beverly with a center at 95th and Halsted Streets).

A Unified Extension Program

With 10 regional centers and 100 community branches as the base, library service is also to be carried to special groups for special purposes by means of (1) mobile units, (2) functional collections, and (3) the unit for the blind and physically handicapped. The whole concept of extending library service applies to the visually and physically handicapped who, like other readers, need some materials immediately at hand (present delivery is by mail) and also broad resources in centers that they can reach (which are now entirely lacking in Chicago). All should be conceived as part of a total program, varying from the largest fixed-point branch to the smallest temporary case of books in a meeting room. Communication and coordination should unite them in common cause, and in turn link them with the strength of the Central Library. The extension agencies have a high mission—to bring the many forms of communication close to people, and then to make them meaningful to the great diversity which is Chicago.

6 Personnel for the Future

A vital problem in any public service organization is that of recruiting and keeping a competent staff. This applies with full force to the Chicago Public Library. The 1938 survey of the Library contained a sentence which has not lost its validity today: "Books there must be in a library system, but a collection of books is not a library without a competent staff" (p.161).

Size of Staff

As of 1 January 1969, the total library staff numbered 1,671 persons, both full-time and part-time. Clerks numbered 563 (33.7 percent) library aides and pages, most of whom work on a part-time basis, 615 (36.8 percent); the maintenance staff, including guards and drivers, 154 (9.2 percent); there were 220 librarians (13.2 percent), 31 library trainees (1.8 percent), and 88 technicians (5.3 percent).

When compared to other large cities the Chicago Public Library is trying to serve more people per staff member—in fact, on the average almost twice as many. The figures in

---

Sources of information included personnel records of the Library, questionnaires to all professional and subprofessional staff members and a sample of clerical personnel, and interviews with approximately 140 staff members, including entrance and exit interviews with professional and subprofessional staff entering and leaving the service of the Library from 1 June through 21 December 1968.

table 28 are for 1967; Chicago would be even lower today, because the number of professional librarians has decreased in the past year.

Table 28
AVERAGE POPULATION SERVED PER STAFF MEMBER*—SELECTED CITIES, 1967†

City	Average population served
Cleveland	1,113
Boston	1,209
Baltimore	1,606
Saint Louis	2,006
Philadelphia	2,528
Detroit	2,581
Los Angeles	2,946
Chicago	3,329

*Excluding maintenance personnel.

†New York is excluded as not comparable because library service in that city is divided into three autonomous systems, and the central unit of the New York Public Library is a highly specialized research agency.

Professional Staff

As of 1 January 1969, the Chicago Public Library employed 220 professional staff members (15.4 percent of total personnel, when figures for all staff members are reduced to full-time equivalent). The usual percentage accepted as a standard is one-third of staff at the professional and subprofessional levels.[1]

---

[1]American Library Assn., *Minimum Standards for Public Library Systems, 1966.* (Chicago: the Association, 1967), p.50.

Interpreting Chicago's librarians, trainees (part-time appointees attending library school) and technicians (college graduates assigned to sub-professional duties) as falling in these categories, the system has 339 individuals in the professional and subprofessional group, 22.9 percent of the total.

This low proportion of professionals means that each professional staff member is trying to serve an extra-large group of Chicago readers. Compared with other selected cities, Chicago rates last in the average population served per librarian, as shown in table 29. Baltimore, Boston, and Cleveland have more than three times the number of librarians per population served than Chicago. This is a little as though a city were to provide one teacher for each 75–90 students rather than one for 25–30 class members.

Table 29
AVERAGE POPULATION SERVED PER
LIBRARIAN—SELECTED CITIES, 1967

Boston	4,638
Baltimore	4,810
Cleveland	4,892
Saint Louis	5,653
Detroit	6,073
Los Angeles	8,579
Philadelphia	8,680
Chicago	15,448

The staffing situation for professionals is not improving. There were more librarians on the staff twenty years ago than there are today (table 30). Since 1955 there has been a steady decrease in the number of professional librarians employed by the Chicago Public Library, from 300 down to 220. Since 1963 there has been a 12 percent decline in the professional staff complement.

It is difficult to ascertain the number of professional vacancies that exist at any one time.

Table 30
NUMBER OF LIBRARIANS EMPLOYED BY THE
CHICAGO PUBLIC LIBRARY

1948	1950	1955	1960	1963	1968
266	262	300	267	250	220

Partly this is due to the fact that staff allocations made several years ago have not been revised to reflect changing needs. Another reason is that no allocations have been established for the Librarian Trainee and Library Technician classifications. As a result, staff members within these classes are replacing librarians (although unofficially) in many agencies. For example, it has become common to find a technician providing all of the children's service in a branch library.

In view of these conditions, the number of vacancies in authorized professional positions can only be approximately stated. As of 1 January 1969, a conservative estimate would be 100 vacancies. However, if the 31 Librarian Trainees (college graduates presently enrolled in library schools) are counted as professionals, then the number of vacancies is reduced to 69.

Closely related to the decline in the number of professional staff is the question of staff turnover. In the ten-year period 1958–1967, of the 195 professional librarians appointed, only 60 are still with the Library. Between January 1963, and December 1967, 111 beginning professionals were appointed to the staff, and of these, only 37 (33.3 percent) remained in 1968. These losses might have been absorbed, if recruitment had kept pace with resignations, but this did not occur. In fact, since 1962 resignations have exceeded appointments in professional staff, as shown in table 31.

Some of the turnover is due to retirement and is expected. What is not so easily explained, however, is the Library's failure to hold younger, career-oriented staff members. Some remain

Table 31
APPOINTMENTS AND RESIGNATIONS OF
PROFESSIONAL STAFF

Year	Appointments	Resignations
1962	2	19
1963	25	20
1964	12	16
1965	25	19
1966	18	27
1967	31	35
1968	29	26
Total	142	162

only a short time and leave, while others remain a few years—sometimes reaching senior positions—and then suddenly resign. This pattern manifests itself in the very low number of moderately experienced staff, those with five, ten, or fifteen years' experience who comprise the group from which the Library draws its middle managers and senior administrators (table 32). Less than 10 percent of the present professional staff has between six and fifteen years' experience with the Library. Fewer staff members are in this middle range than are in the "over forty years' experience" category. Over 30 percent of the professional staff has been with the Library for more than thirty years.

Table 32
EXPERIENCE OF PROFESSIONAL STAFF WITH
THE CHICAGO PUBLIC LIBRARY

Experience	Number	Percent
0–5 years	63	28.6
6–10 years	11	5.0
11–20 years	16	7.3
21–30 years	60	27.3
31 years or more	71	31.8
	220	100.0

Some specific measures which would hold professional staff come immediately to mind, but the problem is pervasive and deep-seated and is not likely to yield to single and isolated adjustments. Some could be retained if the Library adopted more flexible assignment patterns and sought out ways to capitalize on special capacities and interests. Others might stay if there were opportunities for them to move above the second professional level (Librarian II) within a reasonable period of time. It would be a mistake to assume, however, that the failure to retain and develop staff has been solely due to official policies. An obviously important consideration is the sense of effectiveness and the professional milieu in which the new appointee finds himself, a milieu which is largely determined by the attitudes and values of the administration and the staff itself. Exit interviews with resigning young professionals brought out more concern about program and direction of the institution than dissatisfaction because of personal grievances.

Perhaps the most obvious social characteristic of the professional staff is its age distribution. More than half of the professional group is over 50 years of age, while less than one librarian in five is under age 30. In fact, there are considerably more librarians over age 60 than there are under age 30 (figure 14). Moreover, there are relatively few professional staff members in the 30 to 40 age group (25 at present), a group that will increasingly be called upon to assume senior positions in the next period.

Still another but no less obvious characteristic is that less than 10 percent of the professional staff members are males. In the 41 professionally-staffed branch libraries, there is only one male librarian.

Somewhat related to the age and long tenure of the majority of the professional staff is the fact that relatively few librarians (22.3 percent) have worked in libraries other than the Chicago Public Library. Almost half of those reporting such experience indicated that it did not exceed two years (table 33). Too few librarians have had any extended experience or exposure to the techniques and programs of other libraries which might be applicable to the Chicago Public Library.

Table 33
EXPERIENCE OF PROFESSIONAL STAFF AT OTHER LIBRARIES

Experience	Number	Percent
1–2 years	24	49.0
3–5 years	16	32.7
6–10 years	7	14.3
11 years or more	2	4.0
	49	100.0

In general, the education level of the professional staff (Librarian I and above) is low. Almost 40 percent have not graduated from college (table 34). An additional 22 percent hold academic degrees in subjects other than librarianship. Thus, almost two-thirds of the professional staff lack formal professional education. It should be noted, furthermore, that there are more librarians without college degrees than there are with graduate degrees in librarianship.

Table 34
EDUCATIONAL ACHIEVEMENT OF PROFESSIONAL STAFF

Educational level	Number	Percent
Some college	86	39.6
College degree	31	14.1
plus some graduate work	14	6.4
plus graduate degree	5	1.7
Master's degree in librarianship	59	26.8
plus additional graduate work	11	5.0
plus another graduate degree	14	6.4
	220	100.0

An obvious question arises: if applicants for professional positions are now required to hold master's degrees in librarianship, how can there be such wide variation in education among professional staff? The explanation is that at an earlier period, until 1952, it was possible for staff members lacking college and professional education to progress by promotion into professional grades. Many of these staff members are still employed by the Library. Several have continued their careers and now hold administrative positions. Their qualifications lie chiefly in their long years of experience with the Li-

Figure 14. Distribution of professional staff, by age

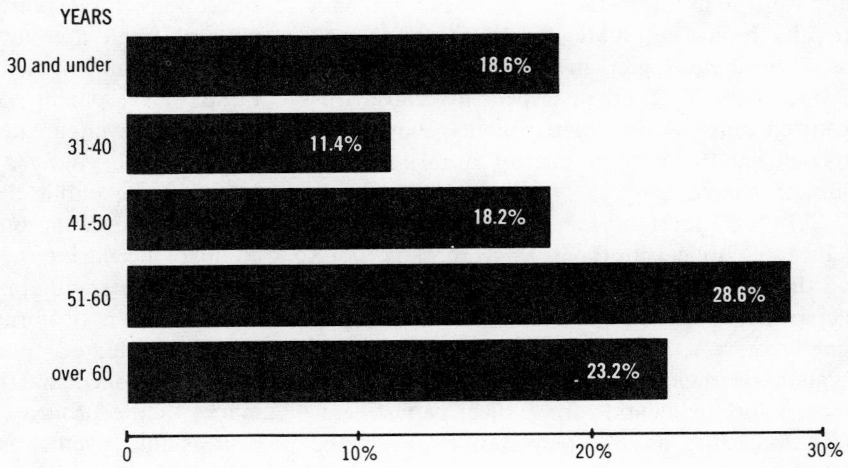

YEARS

30 and under   18.6%
31-40   11.4%
41-50   18.2%
51-60   28.6%
over 60   23.2%

0   10%   20%   30%

brary, and their unflagging devotion to their work. One effect of such staffing practice has been that the overall level of educational achievement among the professional staff has been depressed, despite the fact that since 1952 all newly employed librarians were required to have at least a bachelor's degree in librarianship.

Those staff members who have attended accredited schools of librarianship represent 21 colleges and universities. In the past, the University of Chicago was the chief source of librarians for the Library, but more recently this distinction has passed to Rosary College. Since 1965, Rosary College has supplied just over 50 percent of the librarians hired by the Chicago Public Library. Undue emphasis on local schools reflects a provincial recruitment policy. Recruitment must be expanded and intensified beyond the metropolitan area, indeed beyond midwestern universities, to attract the top graduates of library schools throughout the country.

In an age characterized by increasing specialization, the master's degree in librarianship no longer constitutes sufficient education for some types of library service. Many research and university libraries with subject strength require both a graduate library degree as well as a graduate degree in an academic subject. Large public libraries, especially those organized into subject departments, have also recognized the need to recruit librarians with subject competence.

The high level of service proposed for the Chicago Public Library in this report is based on the assumption that Central Library subject departments will provide service which is distinctly more specialized than that provided by branch or regional libraries. Such service, in fact, is the justification for subject departmentalization. Just as the patron coming to the Central Library expects to find broader, deeper, and generally more specialized collections than in branch libraries, he also expects that the librarians staffing these collections will have greater competence and background. At the present time, however, only 8 percent of the professional staff hold graduate degrees in subjects other than librarianship, and about one-third of these are assigned to branch libraries.

Public library service to children has long been one of the Library's more effective services. There has been and there exists today in the Chicago Public Library a strong tradition of serving children. But at the same time, perhaps no other type of service has been so hard hit with staff shortages. At present there are only 35 children's librarians available (including supervisors) to staff the Central Library and 62 branch libraries. An earlier chapter (chapter 5) on branch libraries indicates that children account for more than half of the use made of these agencies, yet there is only one children's librarian for every two branch outlets. Children's librarians comprise about 15 percent of the total professional staff. This shortage is not due primarily to conditions within the Chicago Public Library but more to two general considerations. First, recruits interested in working with children are not being attracted to the profession in sufficient numbers. Second, the rapid development of school libraries has caused an even greater demand for librarians to work with younger readers, many of whom have left the public library to accept positions with schools. While public libraries can usually compete in salaries, they cannot readily compete with the hours and appealing working schedules offered by school libraries.

Closely related to educational achievement and subject specialization, which are traditional marks of the professional, are participation in professional events and activities. Librarians employed by the Chicago Public Library are not well represented in any of the professional associations. Less than half belong to the American Library Association. Approximately one-third are members of the Illinois Library Association, and just over one-fourth belong to the Chicago Library Club. Only five librarians in the Central Library reported membership in the Special Libraries Association. This is an extremely poor showing, since Central Library subject departments should function to an extent as special libraries.

A few staff members have contributed articles to professional journals and several have had book reviews published. Attendance at professional conferences is quite high when they are held in the Chicago area, but trips to more distant meetings are limited. For many years only a few administrators attended conferences on library funds, but in early 1969 the Board of Directors took action to liberalize travel and expense allowances for staff members.

There has recently appeared a measure of upward mobility within the professional ranks. Promotions during 1968 were almost twice the number for any of the years 1962 to 1965, as shown in table 35. Despite the average age of the staff and their relatively long tenure with the Library, over 50 percent have held their present grade levels for less than five years. Twenty-seven percent have been at their present grade levels for more than ten years.

For staff members now in the professional ranks, the average elapsed time in the past in moving from Librarian I to Librarian II has been 7.3 years, and from Librarian II to Librarian III, 8.1 years. The substantially smaller group who have gone on to Librarian IV have waited an additional 6.0 years on the average. This relatively slow rate of promotion reflects the characteristics of professional staff members which were described earlier. In recent years, however, the picture has changed dramatically. The rate of promotion for presently employed librarians hired during the period 1958–1967 is considerably faster. Between the grades of Librarian I and Librarian II there has been a time lapse of only 2.2 years, and between Librarian II and III approximately 3 years. The prospect of moving from Librarian I to Librarian III within a half-dozen years or so, and into a salary range of $10,056–$14,148 at present rates, opens a promising career prospect for young, professional recruits to the Chicago Public Library.

The data in table 35 show that it is now relatively easy to advance from a Librarian I to a Librarian II position. Generally this is due to the fact that the Librarian II position is not an administrative one (except for Librarian IIs who head smaller branch libraries). However, the next step, Librarian III, is an administrative position, as are those above it. Librarian IIIs are often branch administrators, and a few Central Library departments are headed by librarians at this level. Because these positions are administrative, librarians can only be promoted to positions at the Librarian III level or above as specific vacancies occur.

Positions classified as Librarian IV and V comprise senior administrative levels character-

Table 35
PROMOTIONAL APPOINTMENTS BY GRADE, 1962–68

Year	LII	LIII	LIV	LV
1962	11	3	—	—
1963	9	2	1	—
1964	11	3	—	—
1965	11	2	2	—
1966	14	6	1	1
1967	13	4	1	—
1968	18	10	2	—
Total	87	30	7	1

ized by increased responsibilities. Because there are three levels, not including the chief librarian, which are administrative and only two which are nonadministrative, there is an irregularly shaped pyramid of career opportunity (figure 15). For a large proportion of staff, the Library II position is a crowded watershed, without an exit unless openings occur in positions above it. At present there are more Librarian IIs than there are Librarian Is, and twice as many as there are librarians holding positions above this level.

The personnel program in this report calls for three primarily service grades for profes-

sionals (Librarians I–III) and three administrative levels (Librarians IV–VI). This opens the opportunity for a redistribution of staff in the professional ranks, as set forth in figure 16. The career prospect for persons not taking on distinct management responsibility extends up through three levels. The beginning grade of Librarian I becomes essentially an orientation and proving period, from which the young professional would be expected to move in two to three years to the second level and in time into the sizable group at Librarian III. At the same time, this distribution also enlarges and strengthens the administrative ranks, utilizing

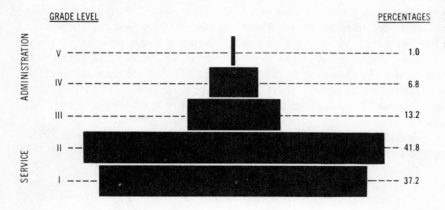

Figure 15. Present distribution of professional staff, by grade

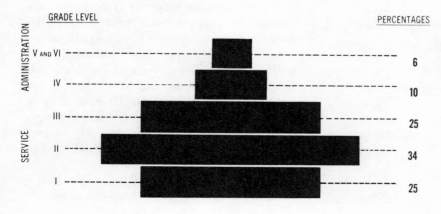

Figure 16. Proposed distribution of professional staff, by grade

Grade VI (now without any appointees) for this purpose.

One area in which the Chicago Public Library has kept abreast of and even excelled comparable metropolitan libraries is salaries. The new salary schedule adopted in 1969 will make positions with the Library more attractive. Of eight large public library systems, Chicago offers beginning professional librarians the highest starting salary (table 36).

Table 36
SALARY RANGES FOR BEGINNING
LIBRARIANS—SELECTED CITIES, 1969

Chicago	$8,268–$11,100
Philadelphia	8,098– 8,411
Los Angeles	7,908– 9,312
Detroit	7,749– 7,981
Cleveland	7,447– 9,078
Baltimore	7,335– 8,916
Boston	7,000– 8,200
Saint Louis	6,751– 7,101

Although the salary for entering librarians is attractive, salaries above this level are not. Stated differently, compensation is not commensurate with responsibility, either professional or administrative. There is insufficient differentiation in compensation among the various classifications or grades. The high degree of overlap between scales is illustrated in table 37. For grades I through IV, only about $1,000 separates the entering salary for each grade from the next higher grade. In fact, the salary range for Librarian I extends to the entering step of the Librarian IV grade, so that a new appointee recruited as a senior administrative officer in the latter classification might receive no more compensation than a person still at the beginning professional level with many years of service. Only at grade V does a clear salary differential occur. The scale favors longevity of service over progressing to assignments of higher responsibility. If the junior librarian is

disposed to relax in his job, and to avoid additional assignments, he does almost as well financially as the individual who takes promotional examinations and accepts more demanding job assignments.

Table 37
CHICAGO PUBLIC LIBRARY SALARY RANGES, 1969

Classification	Range
Librarian I	$8,268–$11,100
Librarian II	9,120– 12,240
Librarian III	10,056– 14,148
Librarian IV	11,100– 15,600
Librarian V	14,856– 20,928

Table 38 indicates the number of librarians at each salary level for Librarian I through IV. It should be noted that the largest concentrations are at the lower and upper salary steps for Librarians I and II, reflecting the ambivalence of staff concentrated more at the lower and upper levels in age and length of service. Within a year or two, over half of the incumbents in the first two levels will be at the maximum salaries for their grades.

Table 38
NUMBER OF LIBRARIANS (GRADES I THROUGH IV) PER SALARY STEP

Salary	I	II	III	IV
$ 8,268	31			
8,688	8			
9,120	5	17		
9,564	2	5		
10,056	12	7	3	
10,560	24	9	2	
11,100	0	21	1	1
11,652		27	9	2
12,240		5	6	5
12,840			2	1
13,476			7	3
14,181			0	2

As was noted earlier, Librarian I and II positions are not administrative, whereas Librarian III positions and above are. Yet 27 Librarian IIs at an annual salary of $11,652 earn at least as much as 40 percent of all Librarians III and IV. The result is that administrators may earn less than the staff members whom they supervise. Not only does this have an adverse effect on morale, it also tends to stifle initiative and career motivation.

These various data demonstrate the limited success of the Chicago Public Library to date in building professional staff. Insufficient numbers, rapid turnover, high age level, almost two-thirds of the professional incumbents without formal professional education, limited career opportunities—the picture is filled with negatives. Small wonder that when sample users sought professional help from the Library they either did not gain access to a qualified person or too often obtained deficient service when they did. At the same time, to keep the record in balance, it must be recognized that a seasoned band of librarians is the nucleus of the service staff, and they have been joined recently by a cadre of young professionals.

Librarian Trainees

A total of 31 Librarian Trainees were employed by the Chicago Public Library in 1968. These are college graduates who are enrolled on a part-time basis in programs leading to the master's degree in librarianship. The plan as developed by the Library is an advanced work-study program. Trainees typically work 18 or more hours per week, depending on their academic schedules. Several libraries throughout the country have developed similar programs. Some require that the trainee obligate himself to work for the sponsoring library for a certain period—usually one to two years— after acquiring his degree. Despite the fact that the Chicago Public Library does not im-

pose any such stipulation, 16 librarians presently employed by the Library began their careers as Librarian Trainees, out of a total of 168 who have been in this special program since its inception.

The trainee program was initiated in 1959. At first, response to it was quite limited, but over the years the number of staff members enrolled in the program has increased almost every year. Most trainees (87 percent) are under 30 years of age. The majority (60 percent) hold degrees in the humanities, a smaller percentage in the social sciences, and less than 20 percent in the sciences. Approximately one-third are male.

In the course of this study, entrance interviews were conducted with 16 trainees. A few admitted that the program offered a relatively painless way to acquire a master's degree. The majority, however, had made a clear career decision and were quite sanguine about their commitment to become librarians. Many also were optimistic about the program itself.

The starting salary for Librarian Trainees is $6,480 per annum, with a higher starting level if some library courses have been completed. Since many trainees work only part time, their salaries are prorated according to the hours worked. Annual increments are included in the salary scale.

Librarian Trainees are not offered a formal program of in-service training. They do receive some orientation, usually in the form of a tour of the Central Library. Along with professional staff members, they are also invited to attend lectures arranged by the Personnel Office. For all practical purposes, however, a systematic program of in-service training for trainees does not exist.

Both questionnaire and interview returns indicated that the Chicago Public Library is not consistent in utilization of trainees. The official job description states that trainees will practice those techniques and skills required in the performance of professional library work, under immediate professional guidance. In actual practice, however, some trainees are assigned semiadministrative tasks quite apart from any professional guidance, while others are assigned duties which are clearly clerical in nature. In fact, almost half (47.8 percent) of the trainees responding to the questionnaire indicated that the major part of the work they do is clerical.

Although the function of the Librarian Trainee requires further definition and clarification, the evidence suggests that trainees are making a substantive contribution to the service program of the Chicago Public Library. They perform basic professional tasks if given the opportunity to do so, and some remain in the service of the Library after they have acquired their degrees. The Librarian Trainee position should be further reinforced and utilized as a source of professional personnel.

Library Technicians

The Chicago Public Library currently employs 88 Library Technicians. Technicians are college graduates who are assigned duties which are above clerical routine but which do not require formal professional competence, such as assisting readers in the use of the library, assisting with program activities, and bibliographic checking.

The technician class was inaugurated in 1966 for the purpose of alleviating somewhat the critical staff shortage at the professional level. After a brief period of orientation and in-service training, several technicians have assumed responsible positions such as providing children's service, staffing reference and information desks, and conducting film and

record programs. Others, in contrast, are not being utilized to their capacities. Technicians, until recent salary adjustments, did not have monetary incentives to continue employment with the Library, and there is still no career prospect for advancement in grade classification for them.

Of the 88 technicians now employed, 78 completed questionnaires and almost two-thirds were interviewed. Most (69 percent) are under 30 years of age. Approximately 15 percent, however, are 40 years of age or older. Over 75 percent hold degrees in the social sciences or humanities, with history and English predominating. Only 17 percent are male.

The program has attracted a miscellaneous group of college graduates. Some are mothers who, after raising their children, seek intellectually stimulating work. Several are the wives of husbands who are completing graduate degrees at universities in the area, and who look on their positions with the Library as temporary. A still larger group is composed of humanities majors who, lacking graduate degrees, find it difficult to find employment in keeping with their interests. For this group the technician program is especially attractive, because to a certain extent it offers intellectual challenge and an opportunity to find "the right job." And, of course, there are those who are interested in establishing a career for themselves in library work.

Partly because of the type of graduate that the program attracts, and partly because the program itself lacks focus, there is a very high turnover rate among staff at this grade level. In the past two years, 192 technicians were employed by the Library; less than 50 percent remain. In the six-month period 1 July–31 December 1968, exit interviews were held with 20 technicians. Those reasons for leaving cited most often included boredom associated with assignments, general lack of challenge, and limited career opportunity.

Every technician employed by the Library is given in-service training. This training is conducted during the last week in each month for those who have been appointed during the month. Training sessions are conducted by various department chiefs and library administrators, and each focuses on a type of library operation or service. For example, there are sessions on circulation procedures, the cataloging system, assisting readers in the use of library collections, and an introduction to basic reference tools. A written examination is given after each session.

Once this initial training period is over, the technician must learn while on the job. Theoretically a professional staff member is always nearby to answer questions and handle any problems, but in actual practice the individual is frequently on his own. Technicians completing questionnaires were almost unanimous in requesting additional orientation and training sessions.

The entering salary for Library Technicians was recently raised from $5,748 to $6,180 annually. This is also the salary paid Principal Library Clerks at the first step within that classification. Although this does not occur frequently, it is possible for an entering junior clerk to be promoted to principal clerk within three years. At this point a high school graduate with three years' experience earns as much as an entering college graduate. Furthermore, a technician who wants to establish a career with the Library can only look forward to a top salary of $9,120, and this only if he stays at this same level for 25 years.

The technician class, despite its limited career prospects, has opened a source of much-needed personnel. For all the high turnover and lack of consistent policies in job assign-ments, various library agencies would be sorely handicapped if employees in this group were lacking. Technicians are also a potential source of professional librarians, for they lack only a year of professional training, and the Librarian Trainee opportunity provides a stepping stone in this direction. In the face of the total staff problem, broader and better utilization should be made of Library Technicians in the future.

Extension of this intermediate class both upward and downward should also be considered. Chicago is one of the cities in the United States with a well-developed junior college program. The nine junior colleges are now turning out some 1,500 graduates annually, and several offer courses in library routines. Yet under present library employment policies there is no way for the Chicago Public Library to capitalize on this manpower. A junior college graduate, regardless of whether or not he majored in library technology, can only be offered a position as junior clerk, the entering clerical grade. The Library should tap this supply, at once helping to meet its own personnel needs and providing opportunity for increasing numbers of partially trained and semiskilled persons.

Clerical Staff

The clerical staff of the Chicago Public Library comprises by far the largest single group of full-time employees. They are essential in the work of the Library, not only at beginning routine tasks but also in handling complicated record-keeping, giving direct service to the public, and at the upper grades in the supervision of staff. Such persons are neither easily recruited nor easily replaced.

The total number of clerical staff members has varied from year to year, as has the professional staff. Between 1963 and 1967 the number remained fairly stable and then turned upward in 1968, as shown in table 39.

Table 39
CLERICAL STAFF COMPLEMENT, 1963–68

1963	1964	1965	1966	1967	1968
556	508	525	500	499	541

The Library does not recruit staff at the clerical level, although some contact is made with high schools. Recruiting is primarily the responsibility of the Civil Service Commission. As vacancies occur, the Personnel Office requests candidates to fill openings. These appointees are selected from civil service lists. If no candidates are available, the Library may either request that an examination be scheduled to fill vacant positions, hire on a temporary basis pending qualification by examination, or wait until the next regularly scheduled examination.

The Library does not conduct its own in-service training program for clerks. Occasionally classes are offered—for example, Bell Telephone was invited to give a class on telephone courtesy—but such classes are not part of a regular training program. To a certain extent this training gap is filled by programs organized by the Civil Service Commission, such as typing classes which are offered free of charge to interested employees.

Table 40
EDUCATIONAL ACHIEVEMENT OF CLERICAL STAFF

Education	Percentage of staff
Some high school	8.1
High school graduate	28.1
Some college/business school	60.1
College degree	3.7
	100.0

An important characteristic of the Library's clerical staff is its rather high level of educational achievement. Most staff members have completed high school and almost two-thirds have attended or are presently enrolled in colleges or business schools (table 40).

The clerical sequence is grouped into four levels, as shown in table 41. The beginning level is described in the official Civil Service announcement as "a trainee position," yet almost half of the clerks are at this beginning or "vestibule" level, and the large majority of them (71.3 percent) have been with the Library one year or less. If this is a vestibule stage, not very many are progressing beyond this point to become career clerks in the Chicago Public Library.

Table 41
DISTRIBUTION AND SALARIES OF CLERICAL STAFF, 1968

Classification	Percentage of total in grade	Salary range	Average annual salary
Junior Library Clerk	48.1	$4,624– 7,152	$4,812
Senior Library Clerk	31.6	5,088– 7,872	5,760
Principal Library Clerk	18.0	6,180– 9,564	7,116
Head Library Clerk	2.3	7,152–11,100	7,944

Those who do elect to stay have in the past progressed only slowly up through the several grades. On the average, 3.7 years have elapsed in moving from junior to senior, and 6.4 years up to the next grade—in other words, 10 years from Junior Clerk to Principal Clerk. The average experience of Senior Library Clerks with the Library is 9.7 years, at an average salary now of $5,760. The comparable figures for Principal Library Clerks are 16.3 years of experience and $7,116 in annual income. Very few progress beyond the Principal level because there are only 13 Head Library Clerk positions in the system.

The salary scale for clerical workers, like that for professionals, favors longevity of service over promotion to greater responsibility. The total range from $4,624 to $11,100 is attractive, if one stays long enough. But the differential between grades is small and the overlap between them is large. As a result, relatively few clericals actually receive the higher amounts, as shown in table 41 by the average salaries currently received, which for each level are near the bottom of the range. The typical incumbent in the third grade of Principal Clerk, after ten years of service, is earning less than the top of the range for the first grade.

Promotional mobility has recently increased in the clerical ranks. Almost 21 percent of Senior Library Clerks have been promoted to this grade within the past year. Just over one-fourth of the staff at the next higher level, that of Principal Library Clerk, have reached this grade during the same period.

Despite these recent improvements, the career opportunity offered to clerks by the Li-

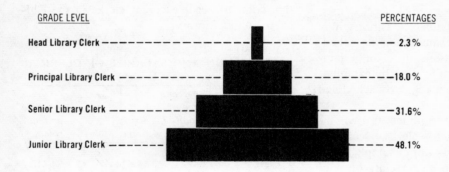

Figure 17. Present distribution of clerical staff, by grade

GRADE LEVEL	PERCENTAGES
Head Library Clerk	2.3%
Principal Library Clerk	18.0%
Senior Library Clerk	31.6%
Junior Library Clerk	48.1%

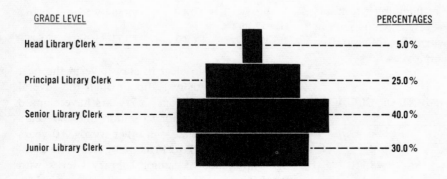

Figure 18. Proposed distribution of clerical staff, by grade

GRADE LEVEL	PERCENTAGES
Head Library Clerk	5.0%
Principal Library Clerk	25.0%
Senior Library Clerk	40.0%
Junior Library Clerk	30.0%

brary is not attractive. Figure 17 shows the preponderance of positions in the first or trainee level and the limited number at higher levels. This structure does not permit sufficient advancement, and consequently does not provide adequate incentive. Figure 18 pictures a sounder distribution, with the first level reduced in number of positions and a larger number of opportunities at the second level, so that young clerks who prove competent and productive can be quickly promoted. Similarly, the proposed distribution shows more jobs in the upper two clerical grades, 30 percent of the total rather than the present 20 percent. These advanced clerical positions are needed to handle present work—in large circulation units (regional library centers, for example), in the acquisition and cataloging divisions, and in business and financial records. As automation of record-keeping progresses in these next few years, trained and experienced clerks will be increasingly needed, especially those with computer, accounting, auditing, and bookkeeping skills.

Other Staff

In addition to the staff members already discussed, there are 154 maintenance personnel. Approximately two-thirds of these employees are janitors who are responsible for maintaining the Central Library and 62 branch libraries. The remaining third is composed of engineers, guards, drivers, and skilled laborers.

Several branches, in addition to the Central Library, are staffed by uniformed library guards. Often the mere presence of a guard will have a quieting influence on teen-agers. The maintenance of order, the security of library buildings, and patron safety are the chief functions of guards. They are not required to inspect the briefcases or packages of patrons when they leave the Library, nor to check on whether library materials are properly charged.

Guards receive no formal training. They are informed of general duties and learn routines while on the job. To a certain extent, new guards work closely with senior guards; however, there is no "captain" of the guards. Guards are not bonded; they are not armed nor are they authorized to make arrests. Their annual salary is $6,708, with no longevity increases; senior men earn the same as newly appointed guards.

Although the maintenance staff taken aggregately have the lowest rate of turnover within the Library (only ten resigned during 1968), there are limitations within this group also. Only four engineers are available to maintain heating, air conditioning, plumbing, and electrical equipment throughout the entire Chicago Public Library system. Only three carpenters are available to make building and equipment repairs in the main library and 62 branches. These limitations are reflected in long delays in needed repairs throughout the Library.

Over one-third (615) of the total number of library employees are part-time library aides and pages. Pages (males) number 251; library aides (females) 364. Many aides and pages are high school and college students. Usually these employees are assigned routine tasks such as shelving books, typing, charging and discharging books, and tracing lost or missing items.

Salaries are based on the number of hours worked per week, the rates in 1969 being $1.65 to $1.80 per hour. As many as one-third of the aides and pages are sponsored by the Board of Education's Cooperative Work Training Program or its Office Occupations Program. Students in the latter program have consistently performed above library expectations, and several will be joining the library staff on a full-time basis. Every opportunity should be taken to encourage these young people to consider careers in the library field, whether as clerks, technicians, or eventually as professional librarians.

Library aides and pages are assigned to Central Library departments and branch libraries as needed. Those assigned to branches are usually supervised by an experienced clerk or by a professional staff member. In the Central Library, however, problems of supervision and control arise. Partly this is due to the layout of the central building, which necessitates housing a large segment of the various subject collections in closed stack areas. It is quite easy, therefore, to lose track of pages in these large and separated areas. Another reason for poor supervision is the decentralized departmental control of page staff. Each department is responsible for supervising the aides and pages assigned to it. Weak and undefined administrative controls lead to a substantial degree of inefficiency. The appointment of a stack supervisor for the Central Library should be considered as one means of improving this situation, the supervisor to be a high-level clerk or library technician.

Personnel Administration and Related Functions

As originally defined, a position of Associate Librarian carried responsibility for personnel administration. This position, a step above the assistant librarian level (Librarian V), was eliminated in 1966 when the incumbent in that office retired. The position was then reclassified as Assistant Librarian for Personnel, corresponding to other assistant librarian positions at the Librarian V level. The post remained vacant from 1966 to 1969.

In the interval the responsibilities of the Personnel Office have been carried on by two personnel assistants (Librarian IIIs), who share the duties. These fall into two broad categories: record maintenance and control, and professional recruitment and placement, with one assistant taking responsibility for each set of activities.

Record maintenance includes the control of salary increases, vacations, absences, overtime, transfers, and service ratings. This work is not streamlined. All record keeping is manually performed. Until very recently, the professional personnel assistant for record control had to manually calculate average scores on service ratings for over 1,000 employees semiannually. There are three major files for employees currently employed, in addition to several minor ones. Records are also maintained on former employees, regardless of rank or tenure. Given this dispersal of file information, it is difficult for the Personnel Office to generate anything but rudimentary information for either the Business Office or the Chief Librarian's Office, or for policy planning, evaluation, and budgeting.

Professional recruitment and placement—the general responsibilities of the second Personnel Assistant—include the selection of professional librarians as well as subprofessional librarian trainees and library technicians. Recruitment of professional staff is conducted by means of job announcement packets mailed to all accredited library schools, and through annual visits to several midwestern schools. If there is sufficient response to the mailed recruitment information from a more distant school, it is also visited. Librarians who respond to these recruitment efforts are invited to Chicago to discuss possible assignments and the interests of the prospective employee. However, the candidate must make the trip at his own expense. Those candidates who come to the Library for interviews, moreover, may not be afforded the contacts and amenities which a professional person would typically expect. For example, they often are not introduced to library officers or interviewed by heads of departments or agencies in which there are vacancies. Such arrangements would not only provide the applicant with the information he came for but also would build his image of the Library.

Librarian trainees and library technicians are usually recruited by means of information packets mailed to various colleges in the area, and by advertising these programs in the Central Library and all branches. In addition, the Illinois State Employment Service sometimes refers candidates to these programs. In view of future dependence on both librarian trainees and library technicians in the staffing plan presented below for the Chicago Public Library, recruiting must also be intensified at these levels.

Related responsibilities of the second personnel assistant include provision of in-service training, and the formulation and scoring of professional examinations for the Civil Service Commission. These duties, along with recruitment and placement, place an undue burden on one person, and they are responsibilities that cannot be delegated to clerical assistants.

Promotional civil service examinations are usually held once a year for each grade level and type of position for which openings exist. The Library may request that additional examinations be scheduled if the need arises. Professional examinations are composed of several essay questions, the answers to which are written. There is no oral interview in promotional tests. The final examination score is based on three elements: written examination, 70 percent; service ratings of performance, 20 percent; seniority, 10 percent. Thus, the career prospects of a graduate librarian in Chicago with some years of demonstrated performance depend heavily on written exercises.

With regard to entering Librarian I positions, the Civil Service Commission maintains a continuous register whereby qualified Librarian I applicants are given temporary appointments with the Library. There is no written examination for this grade. A score is assigned, however, on the basis of the applicant's education and professional experience.

Recruitment of nonprofessional employees is the responsibility of the Civil Service Commission. Entering examinations for junior library clerks are scheduled semimonthly. Promotional examinations are scheduled several times a year, and are usually based on a combination of factors. For example, a promotional examination might be made up of a written test (50 percent), a typing test (20 percent), service rating (20 percent), and seniority (10 percent).

According to civil service regulations, each staff member employed by the Library must undergo a six-month period of probation. If he does not perform adequately during this period, he may be dismissed upon recommendation of his supervisor. Once he has completed his probationary period, however, he receives civil service appointment, with job security. If the employee fails to fulfill his responsibilities after this point, his dismissal becomes much more difficult, requiring a listing of specific charges by his supervisor, and action by the Personnel Office and the Library's Board of Directors. The employee may request a hearing before the Civil Service Commission, which then rules whether or not he may be discharged.

Some employees, notably at the clerical level, have used civil service protection to their own advantage. During the probationary period they perform as model employees. Once this period is over, however, several have become so unproductive and careless as to demoralize other staff. Some staff members are consistently tardy by more than one hour a day, and others are consistently absent. This kind of behavior and the attitudes which it reflects continue unchecked in several departments and branches of the Chicago Public Library. Obviously this not only diminishes the productivity of the individuals involved but it has an adverse effect on the morale of conscientious employees.

From the Library's point of view, the amount of red tape involved in the dismissal of a civil service appointee frequently deters action from being initiated against an employee. Despite these constraints, if the Chicago Public Library is to become an effective service agency, it must rid itself of uncooperative, unproductive, and incompetent employees, regardless of their rank or tenure. Any organization is only as effective as the employees who staff it.

By and large the Civil Service Commission and its staff have in recent years proven responsive to service and personnel needs of the Library while maintaining the requirements of a merit system. All regular positions in the Library are filled by determination of merit rather than by political patronage. Requested examinations are held promptly. Position classifications can be reviewed. Constructive suggestions on personnel practices are made by the Commission staff. A current example of flexible and cooperative effort is an announced examination for an Assistant Chief Librarian in charge of Personnel, a position which has been made original rather than promotional (and thus is open to experienced people outside the Library as well as qualified individuals within), is open to nonresidents of Chicago, and also is open to personnel specialists as well as to experienced librarians. Nonetheless, problems remain, such as the excessive weight given to the written portion of promotional examinations as against proven performance on the job. Closer informal contact and communication between the Personnel Office of the Library and the Commission offices would facilitate working relations and clarify policies and practices about which

there seems to be some misunderstanding on both sides—it would be worth a day's time of senior people in both offices to go over and find out just what the others do.

Allocation and deployment of staff are functions of the Acting Librarian, senior officers, and the Personnel Office. Allocation of staff consists of assigning a certain number of positions at various grade levels to library departments and agencies. Such allotments are based essentially on the size and the amount of use of the agency or department. Physical layout is also taken into account; departments which occupy several rooms require more staff than others. However, due to a variety of circumstances, the present staff allocations (which have not been revised since 1965) are used not as precise indicators for staffing, but only as general guidelines. Shortage of personnel in professional positions has forced a thin allocation and frequent transfers at this strategic level throughout the system. To help meet the situation the Library Technician classification was introduced in 1966, but no allocations have ever been established for this group. The rapidity with which branch usage has fluctuated in transitional neighborhoods has often resulted in a decrease in staff in less-used branches and an increase in more heavily-used agencies. Most recently this draining of staff from lesser-used outlets has been partially reversed as special grant programs were set up in several ghetto areas. The placement of staff, therefore, appears to be based more on reaction to shortages or staffing problems than on defined policies and tangible management standards.

Employees are consulted as to what type of agency—central or branch—they prefer, but the Personnel Office does not guarantee preferred placement. Professional employees must also designate what type of library service they prefer to give. An entering Librarian I, for example, specifies one of four types of service: adult, children's, foreign languages, or technical processes. Librarian Is seeking promotion must register with the Civil Service Commission for examinations not only by type of service, but sometimes for either Central Library or branch library assignment, depending on the examination announcement specifications—thus further narrowing career prospects into restricting channels. Beyond the Library II level it is quite difficult to transfer from assignments in the Central Library to branches and vice versa. Thus the Library, already severely handicapped by a shortage of professional staff, is further restricted in full utilization of skilled manpower by division and deployment of limited human resources into exclusive categories.

A factor affecting staff allocations is the ratio between professional and nonprofessional personnel. Earlier the point was made that Chicago has an unusually small proportion of graduate librarians and that subprofessional employees (technicians and trainees) are serving in place of librarians in various agencies and departments. Both in its percentage of professional staff and in the ratio of librarians to other staff members, Chicago ranks lowest among eight metropolitan library systems (table 42).

Table 42
RATIO OF NONPROFESSIONAL TO
PROFESSIONAL STAFF—
SELECTED CITIES, 1968

City	Nonprofessional to professional staff	Percent professional staff
Detroit	1.9 to 1	34.5
Los Angeles	2.3 to 1	30.2
Saint Louis	2.3 to 1	30.1
Baltimore	2.6 to 1	27.5
Philadelphia	2.9 to 1	25.3
Boston	3.0 to 1	24.8
Cleveland	4.4 to 1	18.4
Chicago	5.6 to 1	15.4

The function of a Personnel Office is not only to maintain records, apply existing practices, and utilize what staff resources there are, but also to review present policies and to help meet personnel needs and problems. There has for some years been limited change in employee programs and practices in the Chicago Public Library. The underlying standard has been "business as usual," despite shortages in numbers of staff members attracted and problems of performance and morale once they join the agency. For three years the established position of Assistant Librarian in charge of Personnel has been allowed to stand vacant. The two senior assistants carrying the load have been severely overburdened—one with voluminous records (of an outmoded system) and clerical staff allocations (a complex problem), the other with professional recruiting (requiring special effort), in-service training (a need throughout the system), and promotional examinations (critical in the professional career structure within the Library). An exception to "business as usual" was the establishment in 1966 of a new class of workers, Library Technicians, which illustrates the value of fresh approaches, because the technicians have been an asset to the Library during a time of acute shortage.

Staff Morale

Staff morale necessarily varies in an organization the size of the Chicago Public Library. Some staff members are highly motivated and enthusiastic about their work. Others have lost spirit over the years, but their loyalty remains and they help keep the Library going. But indications of distinctly low morale, too many for the health and vitality of the organization, turned up at several points and levels during the survey.

Exit interviews brought to light the relative apathy of some older staff members. New recruits, on the other hand, have emphasized the resistance to new ideas which pervades some departments and agencies. Many young professionals admitted to being restless with their assignments and watching for other employment possibilities.

Low morale is evident at higher levels also. Several senior staff members have resigned recently to take positions elsewhere. Among the frequently cited reasons for leaving are excessive "red tape" and the restricting procedures which surround both large and small decisions. The feeling that the Library lacks a dynamic program was also characteristic of this group.

The lack of a clearly defined level of responsibility is a primary reason for low morale among subprofessional staff. In some departments and agencies, for example, technicians are given responsibilities of at least a semi-professional nature, while in others they are assigned routine clerical duties as a matter of course.

The morale of some clerical staff members poses a particular problem. The most common complaint of many department heads and supervisors has to do with lack of competence of clerks and their poor attitudes. There are two sides to this, and the blame must be shared both by the staff members who are not performing and by the management of the Library.

Some clerical employees are disinterested, careless, and occasionally rude. Records were found of chronic tardiness and absence. Some individuals do not respond to even the most thoughtful and constructive supervision.

But for many clerks in the lower classifications there is not much that the Library does positively that they can respond to. No general orientation or in-service introduction is given to junior clerks, and no effort is made to impress them with the service standards of the agency and each employee's individual importance in providing service. The recruit is put into a job without understanding his place in the organization. He sees others who get away with shoddy performance. Shortly he realizes that it will probably be a considerable time before he gains promotion to the senior clerk rank, no matter how hard he works. And when he does move up, he will see that further opportunities are very limited because the pyramid of the clerical career structure narrows fast. An added strike against the morale of some experienced clerks has appeared with the creation of the Library Technician class and failure to assign all these recruits to professional supervisors. Clerks of some years' service often find themselves instructing a new technician who is making almost as much money.

Finally, but most importantly, the Library must make special efforts to recruit and develop black as well as white staff members for supervisory positions. A natural starting point for developing supervisory capacity is within the group of Senior Library Clerks (numbering 175 at present and to be increased to 240 by more rapid promotion of qualified individuals now in the junior grade), who should have an opportunity to study basic supervisory methods after they are at the senior level for two years. Instruction should be provided by outside experts, paid for by the Library, and with time off given to enable staff to attend. By this means the Library will develop a pool of much-needed supervisors, opportunity will open before the staff worker, and even if he is not promoted immediately he will gain insight into his own performance. While no organization has room for a large number of generals, one the size of the Chicago Public Library has the need for a goodly complement of staff sergeants, who are not being trained at present.

An effective grievance procedure can also improve morale. At the present time such a procedure does not formally exist in the Library. Both the Staff Association and the American Federation of State, County and Municipal Employees (Local 1215) attempt to fill this gap and serve as mechanisms through which the staff can voice its problems and concerns. But the fact remains that the Staff Manual does not outline concrete procedures. This manual should be revised to include specific grievance procedures—from immediate supervisory levels through final arbitration.

Perhaps the most obvious and pervasive cause of low morale lies with poor working conditions. The Central Library and most branch libraries are not air-conditioned or properly ventilated. In summer, parts of the Central Library are veritable sweatshops while in winter the antiquated heating system and stale pockets of air have an equally deleterious effect on the employee's attitude towards his job. In the central building, lighting is inadequate in most public service departments, sometimes causing eye strain among patrons and staff alike. Electric typewriters are a rarity in the Chicago Public Library, as is other modern equipment. It is not very productive to tell an employee that his job is important and that he should work hard, and then belie these fine words by not providing suitable working conditions and tools.

Working space in the Central Library is extremely crowded, with aisles between desks frequently filled with trucks of books. In technical service departments, employees are stationed side by side in small work spaces. Public-service professionals seldom have their own work areas for examining publications and preparing lists and reports. Some department heads do not even have a desk of their own.

Both clerical and professional staff members refer critically to working schedules and hours of work. The Library is open at times when other city agencies are closed, and open also on some holidays. Many employees work two evenings a week and some also work on Saturday. To compensate for this difference, the lower ranks of nonprofessional service are given three-week vacation periods after one year, instead of the customary two weeks. Professional employees are given four weeks' vacation, as are Principal and Head Library Clerks. Vacations must be taken in the year earned. It is not permissible for any staff member to accumulate vacation. This inflexible policy is unfortunate in that it does not permit an employee to accumulate vacation time even for the purpose of attending summer school, when he could continue his college or professional education.

There is little in these vacation provisions that really balances evening, Saturday, and holiday work. The four weeks' vacation for professionals, for example, is actually less than the full month that applies in most libraries. In the future certain of the divisions of the Central Library—the Contemporary Media Center, the Family Materials Center, and the Information-Bibliographic Center, for example—should be open on Sunday afternoons. It is proposed that staff members who work more than five hours per week outside the 9:00 A.M.–6:00 P.M. work period receive either a 5 percent increment in salary or a reduction in the work week from 37½ to 35 hours.

No one factor makes or breaks morale. The starting point is the sense of purpose and mission that should pervade the whole institution. Each employee must be shown that he is important, and each must have an opportunity to develop on the job. There must be reasonable career prospects for the person of ability who applies himself. And, at the most mundane level, the worker must have space in which to work, light to see, and ventilation to keep him comfortable. The Chicago Public Library falls short on all these points.

Personnel Organizations

Two organizations directly serve employees of the Chicago Public Library: the Staff Association and the American Federation of State, County and Municipal Employees (Local 1215). Membership in both is voluntary and each has the welfare of its membership as its objective.

The Staff Association was organized almost 50 years ago to foster the professional and economic interests of the staff and to promote communication and understanding between staff and administration. In view of these objectives, a representative of the Staff Association attends all meetings of the Library Board. Occasionally this provides a means through which the will of the staff is made known to the administration. The Staff Association also publishes a monthly newsletter which is sent to all departments and agencies within the library system. The organization schedules several social events each year —for example, attendance at a play or concert and architectural tours of Chicago. Generally these events are not well attended. Over 500 employees are members of the Association, with professional as well as nonprofessional employees represented.

The Staff Association serves a useful role as a communications link among staff and between staff and administration. However, its attempts to expand its functions or to determine what additional contributions it might make have not been successful. It does not have a personnel program, nor does it regularly press for specific benefits for the staff. In fact, were it not for the dedication of its officers, the Association would probably wither due to the indifference of many of the members.

The union, the American Federation of State, County and Municipal Employees (Local 1215), was established for Chicago Public Library employees in 1937. Since that time it has taken various forms, and has gone through several periods of growth and decline. Since 1958 it has been a local of the AFL-CIO. The number of library employees holding membership in the union has not been disclosed, and the group has not asked for an election to determine whether it has a majority for bargaining purposes. However, there are indications that membership in the union, which includes professional staff, has been increasing to some extent in recent years.

The union has developed a series of personnel goals growing from direct concern of its membership. The organization has pressed for specific benefits, some of which are currently under consideration by the Library Board. Relations between the library administration and the union have improved to the point where they are able to talk and to some extent to work together.

The voice of the employee must be heard, for the good of the Library as well as for his own welfare. Both the Association and the union provide a channel for this purpose; both should be encouraged as such by the library administration and both should be treated equally. Although there is some overlap in personnel between the two, each has a viewpoint and a somewhat distinct membership, and each can contribute to the dialogue that should go on between management and staff. While there is a natural tendency for each organization to view the other competitively, the library staff would be best served if both could work cooperatively on projects of mutual interest.

Recommendations

The personnel problem is clear. Staff resources must be substantially built, not from the ground up, but at many and various points in both number and quality. New and promising staff members must be recruited, and career prospects provided for them. Fresh manpower sources must be tapped, particularly by building a new technician class of employees. Both salaries and number of workers must be in-increased. As a first step, the central Personnel Office must be strengthened so that it can take the initiative in building staff for the future. All plans for better library service in Chicago and for reaching more people will be so much idle talk unless the troops and the commanders needed to press the campaign are obtained. Proposed here is a five-year plan for building the staff of the Chicago Public Library.

In the period 1970–1975 the clerical-technical-professional staff of the Library should be expanded according to the following schedule:

Levels of staff	Number of present staff	Needed by 1972	Needed by 1975
Clerical service	563	650	750
Technician service	88	200	325
Professional trainees	31	50	50
Professional service	220	350	400
	902	1250	1525

Overall this is an increase of two-thirds in staff. Chicago still will not have as high a staff-to-population ratio as various other large cities, but it will have the human power to carry out the program proposed in this report. The resulting division in staff will be approximately one-half clerical, one-quarter technical and trainee, and one-quarter professional. In the clerical ranks a moderate and steady increase is called for. In the professional ranks the increase should be rapid at the outset and then taper off. The largest and steadiest increase is prescribed for a new technician sequence of positions.

The professional class in this plan will carry only duties and responsibilities calling for graduate education and judgment in evaluating publications and guiding users.

The 400 professionals will not be an "all-purpose" staff as at present, performing some professional tasks, handling minor management details, performing technical operations, helping with clerical tasks if necessary. The professional will be hired as a professional, and will perform as such. Technical aides and trained clerks will handle the other duties now performed in part by librarians. Most professionals will have a technician assigned to them, for whose training they will be responsible. Inevitably the Chicago Public Library will be short of graduate professionals—maximum use must be made of every one who is recruited.

Salaries of professionals are to match responsibilities, providing (at 1969 price levels) $9,000–$15,000 for professional service without substantial management duties, and $15,000–$18,000 when management is added.

The proposed scale represents less than a 10 percent increase over prevailing salaries, except at the Librarian IV level, where the increase is about 20 percent. Application of this scale to the present professional group would cost no more than $250,000 in a $10,000,000 budget, yet it would put Chicago definitely out in front in attracting top-quality librarians. The sequence as shown below would also provide sharper distinction than at present between grades, so that there would be less reward simply for staying at the junior levels.

Librarian I	$ 9,000–$11,000
Librarian II	$10,500–$13,000
Librarian III	$12,500–$15,000

Through the Librarian III level, duties would be essentially professional rather than administrative. At the next and distinctly administrative level, the range would be $15,000–$18,000. Assistant Chief Librarians would then be in the $20,000-plus level.

The professional service (Librarians I–III) should be open to professional specialists other than librarians, such as persons holding graduate degrees in adult education, audio-visual resources, social relations, and the communication arts.

While these nonlibrary-trained professionals will not constitute a large portion of the staff, some are needed in the Library's growing programs in community relations, ghetto service, and nonbook media. They will at once enrich and enlarge the professional group. The proposed $9,000–$15,000 salary range provides a sufficient career prospect for such specialists to contribute their expertise to the library program, and those who have administrative talent could compete for Librarian IV positions.

Examinations for advanced levels in the professional service (Librarians II and III) to be original as well as promotional.

To bolster the thin ranks of professional staff, experienced librarians from elsewhere should be recruited to advanced positions, rather than depending solely on promotion from within. For Librarian II, three years of experience subsequent to the professional degree would be required to register for the examination, and eight years for the Librar-

ian III level. Professional incumbents within the library system would be protected by the feature of original promotional examinations that calls for appointment first of those who qualify on a promotional basis. Opening of advanced professional assignments to outsiders will help to round out the professional ranks within the next few years, which is preferable to a wait of ten years to bring beginning professionals up to senior capacity.

As another means of getting maximum return from professional manpower, the separation and channeling of librarians into restricted career categories should be abandoned.

At present a professional in the Chicago Public Library becomes a children's librarian or a branch worker or a subject librarian or a technical processes specialist. Then when a senior position opens, only persons in a given channel are eligible. Promotional examinations follow the same categories. As a result an advanced position may stand vacant because a less experienced but qualified person is in the wrong channel, or a second-best person may be appointed because he is the one in the right channel. There is no reason why a branch librarian, if qualified, should not become a subject department head, or a children's worker become a branch librarian, or a subject librarian a senior reference assistant in a regional library center, or a cataloger a senior subject librarian. Examinations would simply be given for Librarian II, III and IV, each as a single category. Optional questions might well be provided for those who have been working in one or another aspect of service. In any case the decreased weight to be given to the written examination would put less emphasis upon narrowly defined professional problems. This plan would require more flexibility in assigning personnel, but it would provide more promotional opportunity to staff members and enable the Library to use every experienced professional to the fullest.

The technician program should be developed into a third career sequence within the Library, between the clerical and the professional levels, by establishing the civil service positions of Technician I, II, and III:

Technician I to be junior college graduates, with a salary range of $6,000–$7,500

Technician II to be a Technician I eligible for promotion by examination after two years, or an original appointee with a four-year college degree, with the salary range of $7,000–$8,500

Technician III to be promotional from Technician II by examination, with a salary range of $8,000–$10,000.

Development of this intermediate group is a key element in building the staff for the future. Relative success to date with a single Technician class indicates the potentialities at this level. A lower beginning grade requiring junior college graduation is to be established, as is a senior grade for experienced technicians, providing a three-step sequence and a $6,000–$10,000 income range. Further, the shift by technicians to the professional sequence is to be facilitated; this will not be a large step upward for technicians who are college graduates. New technicians will be given a period of in-service training and then a period on the job directly under a professional. They will be able to handle a wide range of assignments involving complex operations, they will man both children's and reference desks in branches, and Technician IIIs will be in charge of all except the largest neighborhood branches. In thinking of the capacity of technicians to provide direct public service, after appropriate in-service training, it must

be remembered that many will be college graduates and therefore have as much general and subject background as graduate librarians. Finally, the enlarged technician group will make it possible to hire personnel from within local neighborhoods, particularly in ghetto areas, for staffing of the varying and differentiated programs to be provided in such localities.

The Librarian Trainee group is to be expanded somewhat in size and made more attractive financially, in return for a commitment to remain for two years as a professional with the Library.

The present group of 31 trainees is to be increased to 50. Within the program will be a favorable option beneficial to both Library and recruit: full salary for service of 27 hours per week (allowing completion of the graduate library degree in three years or less), with those electing this option committing themselves to serve for two years in the professional service. Subsequent to completing requirements for the professional degree in two to three years, and after another year as Librarian I, such trainees would be eligible to take the Librarian II examination. Trainees should, after a period, be providing almost one-half of new professional recruits for the Library.

The clerical career structure in the Chicago Public Library is to be made more attractive by treating the Junior Library Clerk as a training position and by increasing the portion of clerical positions above this base.

Junior clerks should normally move up to the senior level within two years (the present average is 3.7 years), and should be given definite learning opportunities at the junior level. Positions at the Senior Clerk level will constitute 40 percent of the jobs in this classification, providing ample room for young clerks who perform to move up. Above this grade, positions at the Principal Clerk level should be increased in number by 25 percent, and those at the Head Clerk level should be doubled in number. The 170 Principal and Head Clerk positions, increasing to 225 by 1975, will constitute a key resource for carrying out the ongoing business of the library.

Opportunities for self-development of staff should be provided in all classifications (professional, technical, and clerical) by means of financial aid and free time for formal education.

At the professional level a fellowship program should be provided for five graduate librarians each year to pursue graduate subject study, continuing full salary for half-time service for two years if fellowship holders register for nine credit hours per semester. The trainee program will be available for technicians who choose to advance to professional study. For technical and clerical workers, those matriculated in a college-degree program should be granted three hours off with pay each week to attend one such class. Another and important means of employee development is attendance at professional meetings; the Library should provide expenses for 20 staff members each year to go to the annual meeting of the American Library Association, and for an equal number to attend the annual state convention.

At the same time, standards of performance are to be established and enforced for employees of the Chicago Public Library, in a tightening all along the line.

In substance this will affect only the minority who have been unproductive, recalcitrant, or rude to the public. Standards of personal performance should be clearly formulated, set down in the Staff Manual, and explicitly conveyed to each staff member. Violators should be promptly and impersonally reprimanded. The probationary period before gaining civil service tenure should be increased from six months to one year. If performance deleterious to the service of the Library persists on the part of individuals who have gained civil service status, selected cases should be prepared for the Civil Service Commission in support of dismissal. Consistent and impartial application of a firm policy for a year or two will go a long way to deter those who seek to take advantage of tenure and do injury to the service for which the Library is maintained.

More weight is to be given to proven performance on the job in promotional examinations, and less weight to a specific written test.

Obviously the opportunity for promotion is important to all staff members. At present in most cases the decision on whether or not an individual will qualify depends 70 percent on a brief written examination. Past performance counts 20 percent, and seniority up to 15 years 10 percent. There are not only isolated but repeated examples of staff members who consistently perform at a high level for years, taking on additional responsibility in the process, and then fail on written answers to several essay questions which results in their being denied promotion. For promotion the proportions that should prevail are approximately 40 percent of credit for the examination, 50 percent for past performance as shown by service ratings, and 10 percent for seniority. At the upper levels for both professional and clerical service (Librarian IV and Head Library Clerk) the examination should be both written and oral. Seniority credit should be extended from 15 to 20 years.

The service rating form and procedures for evaluating job performance also need review and revision.

The form itself is unnecessarily lengthy and complex. Qualities to be evaluated are not clearly defined. Supervisors should know the numerical values of the ratings they assign. Service ratings should be discussed with employees at least annually. The scope of review of the staff committee now examining service rating procedures should be widened to include the rating form and the criteria for employee evaluation. There is a dual aim here: not just to get a score to apply to promotional examinations but also to establish supervisor-employee relations that foster constructive appraisal of job performance and the mutual setting of goals for higher achievement.

An extensive and ongoing program of in-service training should be developed to release the maximum potential of staff at all levels.

It is proposed that a third senior position be established in the Personnel Office, specifically to plan, direct and, in part, to conduct a program of in-service training (this at the same time would open an existing position primarily for recruiting). Funds should be provided to hire specialized teachers for specific topics. The instruction will range from orientation of junior recruits to acquainting experienced personnel with computer techniques, from training of technicians in basic service methods to improving management skills of administrators. Two areas requiring special attention are basic training of technicians and instruction for Senior Library Clerks aspiring to supervisory assignments. From its present status of being a fringe and part-time activity, in-service training should become an integral part of staff growth at all levels.

Special developmental opportunities should be fostered for younger professionals who constitute the primary source of senior personnel and the future middle and general managers of the Chicago Public Library.

Approximately 50 of the Library's 220 professionals are under 35 years of age, and the number will increase with more aggressive recruiting. This is a group whose members uniformly have graduate professional education, and who have been trained in the newer theories and methods. They also are the individuals who have been leaving the Library after a short period of service. Young professionals have a special contribution to make, and in the process they themselves gain experience and seasoning for wider responsibilities. It is proposed that a Council of Young Librarians be fostered in the Chicago Public Library, to function under its own leadership in studying library service and proposing new projects. These younger members should appear on most committees—for example, the group developing selection policies and the one reviewing service ratings. Some funds should be earmarked each year for representatives of this group to go to the national convention of the American Library Association. Young professionals can be used in a stepped-up recruiting campaign—the Librarian I or Librarian II a few years with the Library can relate to young people in library school and can bring back a fresh judgment of the prospects. Even as the strength of the Library today resides in a core of older staff members, so its hope for tomorrow exists in the younger group not now being fully challenged or utilized.

An extraordinary recruiting campaign must be waged to move the Chicago staff up to requisite strength and quality.

Salaries are now competitive in the Chicago Public Library, and recommendations made here will strengthen them further. This report sets forth a service program that will attract attention and recruits. An intensive nation-wide campaign will pull in professionals from library schools and libraries, and an equally intensive campaign in the Chicago area will attract trainees and technicians. Every means should be used for the purpose—more effective recruiting folders, distribution of an annual report that tells of the work of the Library, even an economical pictorial record of the newer projects being undertaken. Given the staff shortages of the Chicago Public Library, at least during a five-year period of buildup, recruiting should be a full-time job.

Control for the launching of a revitalized personnel program will be in the hands of the Assistant Chief Librarian for Personnel. The salary for the position as recently announced is low, and should be raised (along with the compensation of other Assistant Chief Librarians) in 1970. The test is whether an individual can be attracted who will have the inventiveness, the force, and the human sensitivity and judgment to capitalize upon the desperate need and the golden opportunity for building the staff of the Chicago Public Library.

7 Technical Services

This chapter deals with the preparatory units of the Chicago Public Library, which acquire materials to build collections, and prepare and catalog these materials to facilitate use by readers. Within the Division are the following operational departments: Accessions, Cataloging, and Binding and Processing. Procedures for selecting materials are also reviewed here, although staff members outside the technical service departments also participate in this process.

The Division

The several preparatory units in the Chicago Public Library are properly organized into a single Technical Services Division. The operations of the various units are necessarily interrelated and sometimes continuous; books and other acquisitions must flow through them as along an assembly line, and the same records can often be used for more than one operation.

This unified structure should be retained, and the vacant position of Assistant Librarian for Technical Services filled in the immediate future. This is necessary to bring the several

operations back into close working relationship, to institute changes in present procedures recommended in this chapter, and to move toward implementation of computerized operations recommended in chapter 8.

The Assistant Chief Librarian for Technical Services should have responsibility for the following:

Definition of policies for the several preparatory activities

General supervision and assignment of responsibility for technical service operations

Coordination among the several units

Effective relations between technical services and the direct public service divisions of the Library, both in the central building and in branches

Planning for development and change in technical operations, including automation

Appraisal of results in the form of usefulness of records and catalogs, the speed with which resources become available, and the cost efficiency of operations

Maintenance of standards in public catalogs, including those in subject departments and in branches

Interrelations and coordinated operations among the several staff groups participating in book selection.

The person appointed to the position should be rich in professional background (collection building, bibliography, cataloging, uses of resources), administrative skill (work organiza-

---

Sources of data included interviews with staff members, tracing of operations, analysis of flow charts and of such manuals and working memoranda as existed, a questionnaire to each member of the technical processing units to identify individual job descriptions, and counts of time lags for both books and finished catalog cards in a sample of twelve branches.

tion, maintenance of production, budgets and budgeting), and understanding of new technology (data processing, computerization, information storage and retrieval).

The present organization of technical services is represented in figure 19. Accessions, Catalog, and Binding are the current major units. Selection and serials are subdivisions of the Accessions Department, and processing and preparation of materials for use are a unit within the Binding Department.

The program of development proposed in this report calls for a Central Library to serve at a distinctly more specialized level than at present, for a series of regional library centers throughout the city, and for a system of branches and extension agencies flexibly related to the communities and groups served. This program of service in turn prescribes the supporting technical functions outlined in figure 20. The proposed reorganization provides distinct units devoted to functions which will grow in size and complexity as the Library develops in the next decade, and thus will facilitate proper development of staff groups with the necessary capacity and authority.

A separate Selection Department is proposed to handle not only records of titles under consideration, as at present, but also to administer selection policies and to coordinate selection among the various agencies of the Library. Decisions on materials to be acquired will still be made by subject department heads (with the assistance of subject bibliographers), regional center librarians, and coordinators responsible for the extension outlets. The head of the Selection Department would be the Library's overall promoter and coordinator of collection building, operating under the Assistant Chief Librarian for Technical Services. He would also handle gifts and exchanges for the whole system. Selection properly involves staff from the

several major divisions of the Library; at some point, not identified with any one of the service units, the selection process must be brought together into a coherent plan for the whole system.

An administrative unit is proposed for Photographic Reproduction. In the future, multiple duplication of materials will play a role in building collections. The Library in a sense will become printer and issue publications in short runs, these to be derived either from already published items (duplication of a valuable pamphlet no longer available from the original source, for example) or from manuscript prepared within the Library (one-page information sheets about such practical matters as job training, tenant rights, and child care for low-education neighborhoods, for example). The necessary duplicating equipment and skill should be provided; there also will be complex questions of copyright and the need to work out special arrangements with publishers. The Chicago Public Library, in carrying out the flexible, community-oriented, and individualized program recommended in this report, should function as a small-scale and special-purpose publisher and printer; but it would do well not to engage in large-scale printing operations, which are best left to commercial printers.

The future Technical Services Division must be closely related to a system-wide Communications-Computer Center. Automation of parts of the preparatory operations is a priority requirement, the computerization and programming aspects of which will be handled by the system-wide center. Once automation is installed in the Technical Services Division, there must be continuing joint endeavor with that Center to correlate computerized technical operations with circulation and other record-keeping operations, which are also to be machine-controlled.

Selection of Materials

Collection building is to library service what architecture is to a finished building. Even as the architect determines the shape and scope and height and depth, which together result in function and use, so the selector of materials for a library determines its reach and limits. At no other point do library purposes, responses to users, and standards of evaluation come together so precisely.

The Chicago Public Library does not have a written acquisitional policy, such as exists in other library systems. The Library is examining its selection policies currently, seeking to de-

Figure 19.   Present organization of Technical Services Division

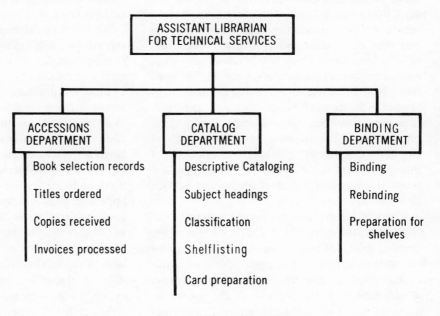

Figure 20.   Proposed organization of Technical Services Division

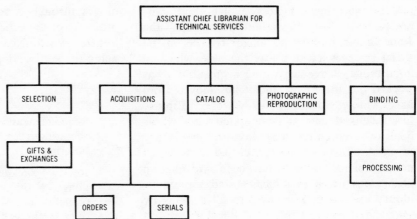

velop a written statement. The fourth edition (1968) of *How Baltimore Chooses: Selection Policies of the Enoch Pratt Free Library* provides a starting set of suggestions for Chicago.

The task at hand has two distinct dimensions. One is to clarify the standards that are reflected in the present selection of the broad middle range of materials that characterizes the existing Chicago collections. The other is to venture into new fields beyond the middle range, on the one side into a level and specialty of resources now lacking except in a few isolated subtopics, and on the other into simplified and in part non-book printed materials of value to people of limited education. Policies also are uncertain regarding provision of materials for the Library's single largest user group, high school and college students. The recommendations of this report for these several clienteles are set down in chapter 3, "User Groups and Service Policies."

The starting point again is urban change, the city today and tomorrow. That Chicago is the home of 600,000 people who are trying to enter the economic system and contemporary culture is clear enough. Equally certain is the extension of specialization, for the city is the source of technological and artistic change. Even institutional and legal factors evolve, and cannot be assumed to be set and permanent—the John Crerar Library no longer collects in the social sciences (which was the case when an interlibrary agreement on acquisitons was worked out in 1897), and it has moved from its downtown location; the Newberry Library has redefined and at some points limited its fields of research responsibility; and the library of the Art Institute recently closed its doors to nonmembers. The gap has been widening in library resources in Chicago, and the public library has made little effort to fill it. Now by state mandate the Chicago Public Library has been designated as the Research and Reference Center for northern Illinois. Those who are to compile the statement of selection policies would do well to look out to the City rather than look in to existing Library holdings; the initial question is not present standards and the solving of immediate problems but the kind of central collection needed by Chicago and the metropolitan area.

The policy statement on book selection should go well beyond general and unexceptional principles. The range of responsibility for reader groups, large and small, must be defined, as must the depth of resources to prevail in different subject areas. Policies for duplication must be stated, and the scope and standards for audio-visual resources set. Selection of foreign-language publications needs fresh formulation. For example, the present Spanish-language sections in branches are limited in scope, dull in appearance, and lacking even the bright paper-back publications in Spanish which one can see in drugstores down the street from such branches. At a very different level the acquisition of foreign-language books in subjects outside of humanistic publications is most fragmentary and requires broadening.

Selection in the Chicago Public Library moves through a sequence of five steps, the initiators of the process and the primary determiners of acquisitions for the whole system being the subject department heads:

1. Initial selection for the central collection by central subject department heads

2. Recommendations for regional and branch acquisitions by these same central subject librarians

3. Review by regional librarians of the designations of the department heads for the branches, occasionally eliminating or adding titles for branch consideration

4. Selection by branch librarians from among the designated titles, for their own agency and for any subbranches for which they are responsible

5. Final review by regional librarians of the branch choices, sometimes making adjustments.

Selection depends primarily on the recognized sources of information and evaluation which reflect more popular and student publications: *Publishers' Weekly, Kirkus Service, Library Journal, Book Buyer's Guide, Saturday Review,* and the several newspapers such as the *New York Times, Chicago Tribune, Chicago Sun-Times, Chicago Daily News* and the *London Times Literary Supplement.* Subject journals and specialized sources of reviews, to the extent they are used, are consulted at the early stage of original evaluation by subject department heads. Even such a useful and relevant aid as *Choice* is not consulted with any regularity by those responsible for original selection; the Library has only one subscription to this periodical that should be studied soon after it is issued by every department head, and indeed by all other staff members participating in the selection of central resources.

The jobber from whom books are purchased, A. C. McClurg and Co., is required by contract to "supply, for examination before purchase, one copy of all new books as currently listed in *Publishers' Weekly.*" The Library also has standing orders for all the publications of 17 publishers, mostly university presses. The approval copies from the jobber and the standing orders are intended to facilitate the selection process.

Various questions arise from this plan and procedure for building collections. At the point of original selection, attention is almost exclusively to current publications, with only occasional retrospective selection despite the many gaps in the central collection. The focus is primarily upon general-interest rather than specialized titles. There is virtually no buying of out-of-print titles to fill gaps in the collections; only two want lists of older titles have been prepared in the last six years, and these primarily dealt with the humanities. Concentration of the original selection in department heads alone, with relatively little participation by other subject librarians, limits the time and attention that can be given to subject journals and other sources of specialized listings and reviews. Seeking out of British and important foreign-language publications in subject areas is most spotty at this initial selection point.

Dependence on one general jobber for approval copies has not in practice provided access to a majority of annual titles published despite the contract provision, as is shown in table 43. Approval-copy provision has improved in the last few years but is still not

Table 43

APPROVAL TITLES SUPPLIED BY LIBRARY JOBBER

Year	New titles published*	Approvals supplied	Percent of total
1963	25,784	6,540	25.3
1964	28,451	6,052	21.3
1965	28,595	4,680	16.4
1966	30,050	11,202	37.2
1967	28,762	13,055	45.4

The Bowker Annual

even to the half-way mark. The effect is particularly restrictive in the scientific and technological fields, which the jobber apparently handles on a selective basis because more titles in these fields are supplied by publishers on short discount. Standing orders with only 17 presses is a small number for a library with any pretentions to depth in its subject holdings.

The original selections by the department heads, and their designations for branch titles, determine the limits of what is considered for the branches. An argument in favor of this plan is that the subject librarians know more about the content of books. On the other hand, few subject department heads have had branch experience—in fact, the position classification plan militates against transfers and promotions between branches and the headquarters units. Communications between the subject department heads and the branch librarians is very limited, so that there is little if any feedback from users over the city. For example, no one consciously seeks out titles for adults at a relatively easy reading level—which accounts for the small holdings noted on page 89 in chapter 5 of titles on the American Library Association list of "Books for Adults Beginning to Read." Obviously the purposes and user audiences of central subject departments and of branch libraries differ and this will be increasingly true under the plan proposed in this report. The determining role of subject department heads in branch selection must be reassessed.

Each branch is allocated a sum of money annually to spend for books. This sum is divided by 22, the number of book-order sessions. At each order meeting, the branch librarian is allowed to spend only 1/22 of the annual book budget. This system does not recognize the seasonal nature of publishing. The same amount of money must be spent in May (a low point in publishing) as in November (a peak month in book production).

Present procedures call for examination of titles for branches by three persons: the subject department head, the regional librarian, and the branch librarian. The first serves more to restrict than to enrich branch book selection; this is not a criticism of the subject department heads as individuals but of the concept that subject specialists are to determine the limits of what will go into local neighborhoods. Rather than asking, "Of the titles currently being published, which are particularly suited to the purposes and programs of distinctly different branches?" the subject librarian essentially asks, "Of the books I am buying for the large central collection, which are nonspecialized enough to be considered for branch collections?" The regional librarian checks this judgment to be sure that no limited-audience materials have slipped through. Selection until this point is more negative and protective than positive and constructive. Then the branch librarians are permitted to choose from among the items that have been proved unexceptionable. They have not seen beforehand the lists of books to be considered, so they can make no direct comparison with their present holdings. They have had little incentive to survey the scope of current publication themselves, because they know that a selected and typical menu will be set before them. In the course of a few hours, they scan 50 or more books and look through several reviews for each; some of the reviews are those that readers in the local community also consult, but for many localities in this city of transitional and workingmen's neighborhoods neither the subject titles nor the reviews deal with the topics and problems of greater local concern. Rather than improve judgments, this restrictive and cumbersome selection procedure militates against collections adapted to the needs and interests of varying communities, and in the end, as was documented in chapter 5, produces bland and standardized branch collections.

Branch selection occurs in the book selection unit of the Accessions Department. The unit assembles inspection copies and inserts reviews from standard sources. The selection unit maintains the following records: (1) the "current order" file, which includes items selected during the last two years; (2) the "new purchase" file, which includes items considered but not ordered during the same period; (3) the "old possible purchase" file, which goes back twenty years; (4) the "gone-through" file, which contains data on items purchased during the last fifteen years; and (5) the "reject" file for fiction, which is intended to be complete for several decades. Files are kept of reviews in popular reviewing media for the past year. The original order slip for each item is also retained.

Unless it can be demonstrated very clearly that these records are essential in their present form, they should either be eliminated completely or reduced to files of much smaller proportion. The "reject" file for fiction may be useful as a record of the basis of decisions in the last two years, but its value as a complete retrospective record is not clear. The "old possible purchase" file contains many items which are now out of print. The "gone-through" file of 120 drawers is of very limited value. The retention of *Kirkus* reviews is questionable, because the value of this service is the fact that reviews appear before publication, not in the quality of the reviews themselves. In any case, records of past selection and nonselection on the part of the Library will become increasingly invalid as the scope and level of the central collection is increased. The Chicago Public Library must reject fewer titles in the future, and therefore it will not need such extensive records of what has not been purchased.

The selection staff at one time reported on orders that were not filled, but this is not done in detail at the present time. There is no central system for identifying old orders that have not been filled. Branch librarians keep records of their orders and make claims directly for items not received.

Given the present method and standards of selection, and its assigned task, the selection unit operates with internal efficiency. All the records it maintains are not essential. The more basic problems go back to the lack of a clear selection policy on the part of the Chicago Public Library, its failure to define the publics it will serve and at what levels, and the limitations in book and reader knowledge on the part of the several echelons of librarians who select the books.

Accessions Department

Besides selection record control, this Department places orders, receives and records materials, and authorizes payment of filled orders. The staff, other than the four members working on selection, consists of the head of the department (at the Librarian IV level), and 26 full-time people plus 6 part-time workers.

Counting all pieces, the Library acquired over 500,000 items during 1968, for central, regional, and branch collections. Different new titles purchased numbered only 14,249, plus an almost equal number of recently published titles which were reordered. This volume of flow of materials has been characteristic of the last several years, since substantial state financial aid beginning in 1966 was received. The Accessions Department orders not only books and periodicals, but also music scores (over 500 pieces per year), recordings (20,000 discs per year), pamphlets (almost 20,000 annually), microfilm (over 1,000 reels), and motion picture films and filmstrips (300 annually). Memberships, business and governmental services, and subscription books are also ordered through the Accessions Department. Foreign books are ordered by the Foreign Language Division, using Hachette in Paris as agent.

Orders come into the Accessions Department

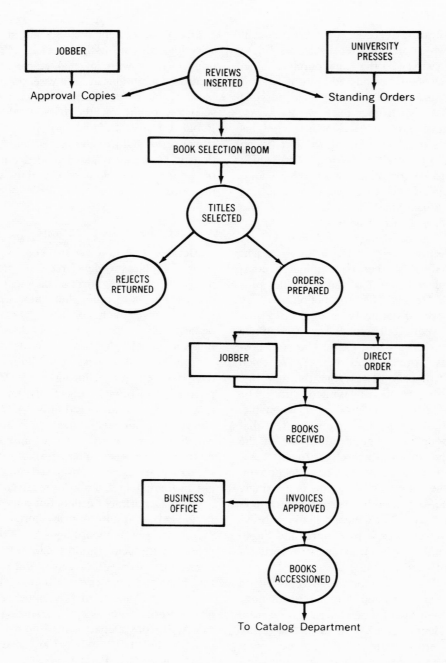

Figure 21. Procedure for receiving books

on standard order cards. At this point a detailed, laborious, and time-consuming sequence of record-making and handling goes into effect. This occurs within a complex structure of operations and relationships, as shown in figure 21.

A typist first prepares a list entitled "Current Order Sheets" from the order cards. This is a new title list which includes branch numbers and is prepared semimonthly. The order slips are stamped with the authorization date. Current fiction, nonfiction, and extra copies are identified. One copy goes to the jobber, one to the outstanding order file, and one is kept in the selection unit. The jobber reports on the orders filled, and the bills are sent to the library with the order slips and the invoices which are in sequential order. The cards are then pulled from the outstanding file and attached to the duplicate invoices. The order slips then are matched with the library outstanding file and with the invoices. Thus, there is a three-way matching of slips, invoices, and books to prevent errors, and to keep the purchases free of complications. The library acquires such a large quantity of materials that it is not surprising that there arise such problems as receipt of damaged books, improperly bound publications, oversupplies, missing items, unauthorized orders, and wrong editions.

Upon receipt and checking, books are sent to the Catalog or Bindery Department, and finally to the Shelf Unit. Approval copies are sent to the Catalog Department when branch orders amount to more than 25 copies. After invoices are cleared and any difficulties straightened out with the supplier, the invoices go to the bookkeeper, who keeps a record of the individual volumes purchased and of the money involved. Upon clearance, the invoices are then sent to the Business Office for payment. Allotment cards of expenditures are kept by the branch librarians.

Although some orders go directly to publishers, McClurg is used for 90 percent of acquisitions. As a rule relations with McClurg permit the acquisition of new titles prior to publication. Since February 1968, the library has been using EBSCO of Birmingham, Alabama, for periodicals through a bid arrangement. In the early stages there was some difficulty in speed of acquisitions, but this has been reduced significantly. Every effort is made to retain jobbers, as a change causes problems and delays, but this should not be the governing factor when a supplier is not doing his job.

When books are reported to be out of print, it has been the policy of the library to cancel them automatically. Out-of-print books may be reauthorized later, and sought in the secondhand market, but such activity is very limited for a library of this size. If titles are reported out of stock, jobbers are asked to keep the orders on hand.

Although an effort is made to synchronize orders between different divisions and branches, this procedure has not been successful. There are many orders for single copies of books which come in after the basic multicopy orders have been placed. This creates a problem for both the Accessions and the Catalog Departments, and counteracts the advantage of processing all copies of a given title at once. Although single-copy orders cannot be eliminated entirely, it is important to set up a program for synchronizing orders on the basis of scheduled date periods. This is a problem that should be examined carefully by the regional and branch librarians.

An acquisition unit is measured, among other criteria, by the extent of unintentional duplication. A study of the titles which were ordered unintentionally by the Accessions Department reveals that they amount to somewhat less than one percent of the total. This is normal and is indeed quite good since the staff is working under pressure to meet deadlines.

The Library maintains a file of continuations for which separate volumes or issues arrive at intervals. In order to claim systematically, a signal system involving a book of dates is kept. Assuming that the present system for recording continuations is retained, a modern visible file would be useful. More basic and efficient would be to apply to continuations the automated acquisitions procedure outlined in chapter 8.

The serials unit within the Accessions Department handles periodicals, government publications sent to the Library as a partial depository, and various microfilm reels of periodicals and other serials. The whole system receives the relatively small number of 2,631 different periodical titles. With duplicates for the various agencies and branches, 7,754 subscriptions are maintained. The issues themselves are received directly by the agencies, although the major record is maintained at Central. Claims for material not received are sent to the Central Library.

In general, there has been little change of periodical and serials titles over the years. Here again the Chicago Public Library must greatly increase its holdings in the future if it is to be a reference and specialized library of any real scope. As more periodicals and serials are received, automation of record keeping should be adopted.

The bookkeeping procedures are fairly simple. The Accessions Department maintains a running account of expenditures. Four copies of the order form are made for each title ordered. The second of these forms is sent to the book dealer, and a letter usually accompanies each batch of orders. General directions concerning the relationship of the Library with the dealer are established when the contract is made. Invoices are checked by the Business Office after verification and confirmation of orders have been made in the order unit.

The procedures for handling materials after their receipt are shown in figure 22. This diagram provides information concerning the forwarding of books for both the Central Library and the various branches.

Gifts are received and handled by the Humanities Department in the Main Library. This does not apply to all gifts, for those received at branches do not go through this procedure but are discarded without being seen by subject librarians; and some gifts also go through departments other than Humanities. The procedure now followed is not systematic. In the future a unit within the proposed Selection Department of the Technical Services Division should handle gifts to the Library received at any point in the system.

In addition to multiple order forms which are used to acquire items from dealers, the Accessions Department has developed a series of special forms for communicating between the department and the various subject rooms and the branches. These include forms related to book selection, approval, return of books to dealers, discounts, and orders for special materials. Routing slips for sending material to the Catalog Department have also been developed.

The various forms have appeared at intervals over a long period of time, as one or another department head or staff member (many now no longer with the Library) thought they might be useful, and once started they have been continued. Forms and records should be examined carefully for relevance to the reorganization of units and the introduction of mechanized or computer approaches. Oddly enough, some records are not made on multiple forms and therefore must be separately duplicated at additional cost and expenditure of time.

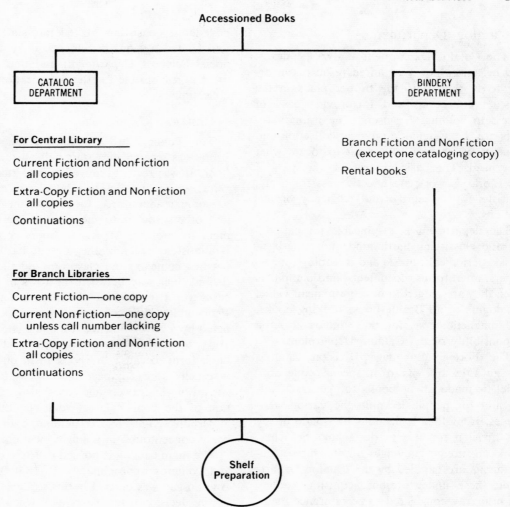

Accessioned Books

CATALOG DEPARTMENT

BINDERY DEPARTMENT

For Central Library

Current Fiction and Nonfiction
all copies

Extra-Copy Fiction and Nonfiction
all copies

Continuations

For Branch Libraries

Current Fiction—one copy

Current Nonfiction—one copy
unless call number lacking

Extra-Copy Fiction and Nonfiction
all copies

Continuations

Branch Fiction and Nonfiction
(except one cataloging copy)

Rental books

Shelf Preparation

Figure 22.   Procedure for processing books

The Accessions Department does not provide the catalogers with Library of Congress numbers for ordering printed cards. It takes no responsibility for establishing entries. This means that one unit of the Library carries searching and verification work as far as necessary for its own operation, then drops the process; the next unit then must start over again, duplicating part of the work already done. It is recommended that coordinated searching procedures be established by the Accessions Department to provide entry and catalog card information data for the Catalog Department.

Catalog Department

The Catalog Department analyzes, indexes, and organizes newly acquired resources in order to fit them into the proper place in the existing collections and to provide ease of access to holdings for users. The primary results are the systematic physical collection and catalogs which readers consult to locate what they need. The basic criteria for this part of the Library's work are effectiveness for users, consistency of records, and efficiency of operations.

The department is responsible for cataloging and classifying hardbound and paperback books, periodicals, music and recordings, newspapers, microforms, documents, and pamphlets when they are judged to have permanent value. Cataloging of all Braille books, talking books, and magnetic tapes for the blind is also the responsibility of the Catalog Department.

The Foreign Language Division catalogs foreign titles for its own special collection, which is made up of books for general reading and for people learning the various languages. Long-loan collections are made up by this division for use in designated branches. Books in foreign languages for the subject departments are handled by the Catalog Department; these under present acquisition policy are primarily considered to be reference materials. Inasmuch as the Library has not received any quantity of foreign books, cataloging in this area has not presented a problem in the past.

The Chicago Public Library is a federal depository of documents, and handles these government publications in various ways. In some departments they are kept as separate collections and not cataloged. In other departments documents are treated as books and receive complete cataloging. The bulk of the document collection, consisting of federal, state, local, and United Nations documents, is kept in the Social Sciences Department, and that department is responsible for the organization of the collection.

CENTRAL CATALOGS

The Public Card Catalog in the Central Library is located in a stair hall on the fourth floor. It was recently moved from a main corridor, which at times was hopelessly crowded as some readers tried to consult the catalog and others sought to move from one department to another. At certain hours congestion is almost as great in the present location, as patrons come off the elevators and then seek to find their way between the rows of catalog cases to get to the Social Sciences Department. Incidentally, this congestion would be eliminated by the recommendation made later (page 164) for a computerized printed catalog in book form, because the book form of catalog is much more compact than separate cards spread out in drawers and cases; also, consultation of the book catalog would be dispersed at various points in the building rather than being concentrated in a single location.

The main catalog is housed in 1,656 drawers and contains approximately 1,018,000 cards. An odd gap was opened in this strategic record by the decision a few years ago, when the departmental catalog for the History and Travel Department was made, to remove many of the history subject entries from the main catalog for inclusion in the departmental record to avoid duplicating the cards. Theoretically the Public Card Catalog is complete, except for this gap in history entries.

A simple inspection showed 80 percent of the cards in the main catalog to be in good or fairly good shape, but the remainder need replacement because of heavy soil and broken edges; this applies in particular to entries for classical and well-known authors and for school topics in regular demand. Here again the computerized book catalog would eliminate the problem because the catalog will be automatically reprinted at intervals, as are new issues of telephone directories. Many titles that are lost or stolen have not been officially cancelled; consequently the main catalog contains entries for items no longer in the collection.

Fourteen departmental catalogs are maintained in the central building in addition to the comprehensive Public Card Catalog. Table 44 on pages 156 and 157 summarizes their scope and condition. The departmental catalogs vary in condition and need for rehabilitation from very good (Natural Science and Useful Arts) to very poor (Music Scores). Maintenance of these fourteen catalogs involves a major and continuing outlay of time and money. The printed book catalog would eliminate most of these separate catalogs, because the single and complete listing would be available in all departments, with titles in the individual department identified by their call numbers.

In addition to the fourteen official catalogs, each subject division maintains a variety of special-purpose files and catalogs. Eighty-two such special and supplementary files were located. They range from a dance index to a career file, from an index to pictures of musical instruments to a file of small industries, from an index to monologues by dialect to a file of mystery stories comprising 42 trays. Some of these catalogs are virtually inactive (and their existence is not even known by younger staff members), some have occasional utility, and a few are essential bibliographical tools. A record of how frequently each is consulted should be made for a sample period with an eye to the elimination of at least half of these supplementary catalogs.

BRANCH CATALOGS

The Catalog Department is responsible for preparing full catalog entries for books acquired by the branches. Due to the delay in card preparation, the books are received in branches without cards. In a special check of a sample of 12 branches made for this study, it was found that 62 percent of recently acquired books had been waiting two months or more for cards, and 41 percent had been waiting six months. The branch units do not withhold the books from the public during this period but proceed to make their own catalog entries which duplicates work already done in the Catalog Department. The branch-made cards are inserted temporarily into the catalog file and removed when the regular cards are received. This is clearly a gross duplication of work which substantially increases the cost of cataloging and preparation of branch books in the Chicago Public Library. When the permanent cards from the Catalog Department arrive, the branch staff must add subject headings and call numbers which requires an additional expenditure of time.

There is no question but that the goal should be the prompt preparation of all catalog entries, in complete form, to go out with the books to the branches. In a conservative estimate the elimination of duplicate work in the branches would save $70,000 per year in the Chicago Public Library. To accomplish this it will be necessary for the Catalog Department to have more space which cannot be obtained in the present quarters, and appropriate equipment. In place of the present Minigraph machine for card duplicating the department should have Xerox equipment for short runs and Multilith for longer runs.

In general the branch catalogs are maintained in reasonable physical condition. How-

Table 44

DEPARTMENTAL CATALOGS IN THE CHICAGO PUBLIC LIBRARY

Name & location	No. of trays	Estimated no. of cards	Condition of cards	Condition of guides	Condition of labels	Remarks
Applied Science and Technology Department	70	74,300	Good except Chemistry & Electronics	Good	Replacement needed	Additional trays requested years ago not received
Art Department	74	59,324	Good	Good	Good	Art Department keeps catalog in sound condition
Education Department	54	49,680	Good	Good	Accurate, but replacement needed	Catalog equipment is in poor condition and in need of repair or replacement
Music Department Catalog	20	21,600	Soiled	Soiled, bent	Too small, soiled	One of the older departmental catalogs, new equipment is needed
Music Department Recordings Catalog	56	54,435	Soiled and worn	Worn, but still readable	Not attractive, but readable	No subject entries and the various methods of cataloging are obvious and confusing
Music Department Score Catalog	83	83,620	Poor, soiled from age and wear	Some broken and unevenly placed	Too small, soiled, hard to read	Various methods of cataloging are evident

ever, some units are behind in getting entries into the public record, and others are not replacing badly soiled cards. If the provision of separate card catalogs in branches continues, the Central Catalog Department should be given authority and responsibility for maintaining standards in the various catalogs over the City, plus periodic inspection and consultations with branch librarians.

The "Union Catalog" of the Chicago Public Library is not, as its name might imply, a complete listing of all holdings in the institution, but provides, in the central building, cata-

loging and shelflist information about branch holdings. This catalog includes tracings so that a set of cards can be prepared for a branch which is receiving a title for the first time. It shows which branches have copies of the book but it does not indicate how many copies each branch has. Records are removed for books which no longer are in the various branches, but there exists a huge backlog of such withdrawal records which has not been processed (approximately 50,000 items cancelled by branches but file record not corrected). The Union Catalog is used regularly for adding

Table 44 *continued*

Name & location	No. of trays	Estimated no. of cards	Condition of cards	Condition of guides	Condition of labels	Remarks
History and Travel Department	180	140,000	Good	Good	Good	This is the newest subject department catalog
Humanities Department	180	102,500	Mostly fair, some very poor	Poor	Poor	A complete catalog of the Humanities collection is in preparation
Natural Sciences and Useful Arts Department	89	62,000	Good	Good	Good	Cards for cancelled books are regularly removed and catalog is up to date.
Popular Library	24	22,488	Fair	Good	Adequate but soiled	An author, title and biography file; no subject entries
Social Sciences and Business Department	180	160,200	Soiled	Location and number inadequate	Some inaccuracies; poor typing job	Guides and labels suffer from too much shifting
Training Class Catalog	15	7,500	Good	Need Mylar guides	Good, but require cleaning	The Library's "professional collection"
Visual Materials Center	3	2,200	Soiled	Soiled and broken	Requires new labels	Catalog of books only
Young Adult Collection	15	12,000	10 percent are soiled	Good	Slightly soiled	

extra copies and for answering staff and patron questions concerning which branch has a copy of a book. Because this catalog is not up to date, the information it provides is sometimes inaccurate. It would seem sensible to have a crash program using summer employees, for one or two summers, to eliminate this backlog, rather than allow the situation to remain chronic.

CATALOGING PRACTICES

Within the catalogs themselves, the primary elements are (1) identification of entry, (2)

descriptive cataloging, (3) assignment of subject headings, and (4) classification for shelf location.

The Chicago Public Library in general follows rules of entry which are consistent with those established by the Library of Congress, and are included in the 1967 *Anglo-American Cataloging Rules* issued by the American Library Association. This means that there is an effort to include sufficient information concerning a title and its authors without excessive details. It would be advisable for the department to stay as close as possible to the practices of the Library of Congress for descriptive cataloging.

The Library normally uses subject headings which are on Library of Congress printed cards. Deviations have occurred in the cataloging of Chicagoana, and various areas in the social sciences, particularly political science, as well as in the arts and the humanities. Since the Cataloging Department is now engaged in preparing a new catalog for the Humanities Department, an effort is being made to bring as many of the humanities subject entries into agreement with the Library of Congress as possible.

In the interest of improving production, the Library would be well advised to follow as closely as possible the Library of Congress assignment for subject headings. This does not prevent some alteration and addition of headings which fit the local situation in Chicago. The basic rule, however, should be adherence to the *Library of Congress List of Subject Headings*.

Descriptive cataloging and subject headings are for the most part handled effectively from the standpoint both of facilitating use by readers and of economy of operation. Compatibility of practices in the Chicago Public Library with nationwide designations appearing on Library of Congress cards is relatively close, so that LC cards can be used without time-consuming and expensive review. Such compatibility will continue under the national automated MARC (machine-readable cataloging) project now moving out of the developmental stage.

However, an essentially noncompatible situation exists in the classification of books (the numbering system used to locate titles and to bring related books together on the shelves). The Library uses a Dewey Decimal classification plan which over the years has been modified and customized for Chicago to the point where it is in substance a unique classification plan. This applies not just to such special fields as local history but is also widespread throughout the various subject areas.

As a result, the Chicago Public Library is not able to make use of the Library of Congress assignments of Dewey numbers without careful and costly review and adjustment. In a sample count made for this study between 3 June and 18 July 1968, it was found that of 1,247 titles for which Library of Congress proof slips or cards were available and processed during this period, 995 (79 percent) had changes in the classification numbers on the cards made locally. The remaining 21 percent required professional review to determine that the number did not have to be adjusted.

Thus each and every title acquired needs professional attention for processing, even though all cataloging and classification information has already been prepared and appears on LC cards. It therefore is not possible to have most of the cataloging processing done by experienced clerks, as is the case in many large public libraries. As a result the Chicago Public Library has more cataloger-classifiers than are normally needed for its present scope of title acquisitions, and books are delayed in getting to the public because four out of five titles require this review and adjustment of classification numbers.

This is the present situation. It is not just a temporary problem but one that has been building up over the years. Looking into the future, the problem will increase at a greater rate, with the Library spending more and more money that could better go into additional books and services. One reason that the volume of classification adjustment will increase is that the Chicago Public Library must buy more different titles annually if its central collection is to meet the needs of a large city and the obligations of a state reference and research center. Where some 10,000 changes in classification from the numbers assigned on LC cards are made at present, in the near future this will be 20,000 per year.

In fact the acceleration in extra classification work will be at an even greater rate, because as more specialized titles are acquired, an increasing proportion of the LC cards will lack Dewey numbers entirely. Of 120,000 titles cataloged annually by the Library of Congress, only one-third receive Dewey assignments. Chicago in the past, with its modest conception of what a central collection should be, has purchased mainly within the range with Dewey assignments, but it must start selecting from among the other two-thirds; the Library will then have to make its own original classification. This extra work is burdensome enough under a manual system, but it will be more so under the computerized MARC system, because titles without Dewey numbers as well as titles for which Dewey adjustments must be made will have to be removed at least in part from standardized processing channels. Once a computerized sequence is interrupted in mid-process to insert manual work, much of its advantage is lost.

Three alternatives therefore open before the Chicago Public Library. One is to accept the present and increasing drain on efficiency and speed to avoid a more basic adjustment. A second alternative is to arbitrarily start accepting the LC assignments of Dewey numbers without adjustment. This would separate newly acquired titles in many instances by locating them in the collections away from previously acquired publications on the same subject. This in itself may be tolerable, for in time the national numbers and groupings would apply to the many recently added titles, which are the items most frequently consulted by users; the newer acquisitions would be under one number and the older issues under another.

However, at this point a further complication enters the picture because each new edition of the Dewey Decimal schedules involves many changes in existing numbers, in order to stretch the plan to cover emerging and changing topics. Libraries using Dewey face this problem of modification with the appearance of each new edition of the schedules. If they want to retain the systematic subject arrangement of titles and maintain the integrity of the catalog, it is necessary that relocations be made and that relevant catalog entries be revised. In other words, as revised and expanded Dewey schedules appear at intervals of some years, large libraries to be entirely consistent must double back and review and in some cases change previously made assignments, and then also change the numbers on the books and on the corresponding catalog cards.

Some large libraries using the Dewey Classification, rather than make the necessary modifications, have accepted the varying numbers provided in each edition of the classification schedules. Since the Library of Congress printed cards contain Dewey numbers from new editions of Dewey schedules as soon as they appear, and since it is more economical to use catalog copy from this central agency, these libraries follow the standard assignments. This practice leads to repeated scattering of books dealing with the same or similar subjects. In libraries where the classification and the catalog call numbers are not revised to meet relocations in schedules, the primary purpose of locating similar materials together on the shelves is in time defeated.

The scattering of subject publications as the Dewey schedules are modified from edition to edition is not particularly noticeable in a small or moderate-sized collection, nor does it occur all at once, but in a larger collection the sense and usefulness of the classification scheme is compromised step by step. This will occur in the Chicago Public Library if this second alternative is adopted. The Library must make an adjustment because the present plan is draining away money, year by year, and is also delaying the processing of books. As long as some change is necessary, it would be wise to go to a completely different scheme of classification to provide a workable system for the future.

This leads to the third and more fundamental alternative—to shift to the Library of Congress classification system. In the short run this will be costly and confusing, but the Chicago Public Library will be in existence for a long time. Once this step is achieved, adjustments in numbers assigned by the Library of Congress will seldom be necessary, and most titles acquired will not have to be reviewed by professional catalogers. More specialized and foreign-language publications—those that usually are not given Dewey numbers in the national cataloging system—will also have their assigned numbers. Later adjustments due to changed classification schedules seldom will be necessary, because the LC classification scheme has proven itself adaptable to expanding and changing subject fields without extensive restructuring. Finally, full compatibility with the forthcoming national computerized cataloging system will be assured, athough it must be noted that MARC input can be used with Dewey numbers with adjustment and some loss in automation.

The decision to reclassify according to the Library of Congress scheme cannot be made casually. At the same time various public libraries, after reviewing factors similar to those presented here, have made the decision in the interest of long-range economy and to achieve the most rapid possible preparation of books for readers. These include the public libraries of Baltimore, Boston, Buffalo, Hawaii, Providence and Saint Paul, and other large public libraries are considering the step. University libraries with much larger collections in terms of number of titles than Chicago's have also made the change, among them Columbia University, Massachusetts Institute of Technology, and Stanford University. The view that the LC system may suitably apply to university collections but not to a public library does not hold when the public agency is to have the scope of collection specified for the Central Library in Chicago in this report.

To reclassify over 2 million volumes would be a traumatic experience. But this is not what is being proposed. Even if all present holdings were reclassified, which is not recommended, the number of changes would be not much over 200,000, the estimated number of different titles in the Chicago collection. Most libraries making the change do so by selective reclassification. They do not go back and alter all present titles; they do not change all existing catalog cards. Rather they start by applying the new classification to currently acquired publications. Then actual reclassification would normally include the reference collections, serials, editions, and other portions of the collection which are identified as vital for integration with current acquisitions. This results in a considerable period of transition, with two systems applying, but after a few years this works out so that the materials consulted most frequently are in the new system and the collections build forward from that point.

A shift from a manual card catalog to a computerized book catalog, as recommended later in this chapter (see page 164), affords a further strategic opportunity to change classification schemes. The book catalog, like reclassification, would not be retrospective for the whole collection but also would start with current acquisitions. Thus the new classification base and the new book catalog could start together. In this case, MARC tapes would be the source for most of the cataloging input, and the greatest possible future automation of technical services can be anticipated.

One additional concern that may arise is that the Library of Congress classification scheme, no matter how desirable for the large main collection, is not appropriate for branches. However, there is no evidence that users understand or remember Dewey numbers any better than LC numbers. What the reader wants is for related books to be shelved together and some guide (a catalog) to be available to tell him what number or numbers he should consult. The Dewey Decimal system is no more suitable for the new, flexible, locally sensitive service programs being proposed in the neighborhood branches than is the LC system. What arrangement of resources is effective in a small library in the heart of the ghetto, what arrangement suitable in a small branch in the middle of a high-rise, cosmopolitan section? No single standardized plan fits both communities and the many other variations found in Chicago. If the local program proposed in this report is to be achieved, fresh and varying arrangements of materials must be worked out in the different localities under the guidance of community task force teams.

As to regional library centers in the years ahead, much the same arguments concerning the advantages of the LC scheme over Dewey can be made for collections of 200,000 as for 2 million. Further, eight of the ten regional center collections are yet to be acquired and classified, so that purely from the standpoint of speed and economy of processing it would be preferable to use the LC classification.

MANUALS

The Catalog Department has not developed a complete procedures manual. The importance of uniformity and consistency in the work of a catalog department suggests the desirability of setting down general policies and specific routines in one or more staff manuals. The manuals should include the policies of the several units, as well as the routines for specific processes or groups of processes, such as descriptive and subject cataloging, the handling of titles for which printed cards are and are not available, special procedures in recataloging and reclassification, and routines for replacements and withdrawals. Such manuals would reduce to a minimum the need to repeat detailed directions, facilitate the training of new personnel, and make available to the administrator and other staff members a systematic statement of policy and procedure. Recording these operations and procedures in detail will not only assist in training but may also lead to the modification of some phases of the work.

For several years the Catalog Department has been engaged in preparing a revised typing manual for use in the department and in the various agencies where cards are completed or retyped and where guides and labels are prepared. The *Branch Catalog Card Form and Typing Manual* has been completed, and was sent to the various agencies in December 1967. Since this is primarily for branch cards and catalogs, a supplement is in process for the Central Library.

Rules for Filing Cards in CPL Catalogs has been compiled by the Catalog Department and is intended to provide a guide for the filing of cards in all Chicago Public Library catalogs. As the need arises, filers in large catalogs such as the Central Library Public Card Catalog or in subject department catalogs with a concentration of material in difficult areas will find it necessary to consult the *ALA Rules For Filing Catalog Cards*.

SERIALS AND PUBLICATIONS

The handling of serial publications (magazines, titles issued in parts at intervals, continuations) is not consistent. When serials are purchased for the book collection, they are classified and handled as monographs. When they are purchased for the serial collection, they are unclassified and handled as serials. The serial collection consists primarily of magazines. When the *Union List of Serials* is checked against the Chicago serial shelflist, many titles in the collection are missed because the Catalog Department does not handle them as serials.

The Catalog Department maintains a complete shelflist record of all bound volumes in all departments of the Central Library and provides each subject department with the initial shelflist card for every title added to its collection. Thereafter the subject department maintains a complete record of all the periodicals in its collection, noting the specific locations of titles and volumes as necessary. When a periodical changes title, ceases publication, subscription is dropped, or binding is discontinued, the subject department notifies the Cataloging Department so that the records can be adjusted.

The Reference Department maintains on visible file equipment a location record which gives title holdings and location by department of all the bound periodicals in the Central Library. The Catalog Department provides the necessary information about new titles in the subject departments for this file, and notifies the Reference Department when bound titles are discontinued so that accurate notation of holdings can be kept.

The information which the Catalog Department is able to provide is sometimes inaccurate and does not always reveal what the Library has for the following reasons:

The Catalog Department may not receive all volumes of a periodical as bound, and cannot record items which are not received

The notation "to date" on the record does not always actually mean up-to-date, because the Catalog Department is sometimes not informed when a subscription is dropped or when a periodical ceases publication; as a result, cards now exist in the catalogs which read "to date," for periodicals to which no new volumes have been added for some years

Unbound portions of a serial publication are never recorded, so the library user could interpret the record to mean that the library has nothing beyond the date noted on the catalog cards, when various additional issues actually have been acquired.

The head of the Catalog Department has proposed a record form for all periodicals currently received which would simplify the cataloging of serials and at the same time help to maintain accurate and current records. The proposed form would show the main title; the subtitle would be shown only when there are two or more periodicals with the same title, or when the subtitle includes the name of an organization for which an added entry has been made; plus necessary bibliographic notes; and then a general statement to the user such as "For holdings, consult periodical record in _____Department." In addition to its simplicity and the facilitation of accuracy, this plan would eliminate the need for any but new or changed or discontinued titles to come to the Catalog Department; periodicals could therefore be returned to their respective departments more quickly.

With the likelihood of a substantial increase in serial acquisitions on the part of the Chicago Public Library in the future, as it moves into its necessary role as an advanced and specialized library, it is important that certain changes be made in the handling of these materials:

As the number of titles increases, computer controls should be used as a simplified means of recording serial material received

The Library should use LC cards for the cataloging of all new serials

Communication between the several departments of the Central Library and the Cataloging Department should be regularized so that accurate records are kept and provided for the user

The practice of acquiring periodicals on microfilm or other microform to conserve shelving space and to reduce cost of binding should be extended.

PRODUCTION OF CATALOG DEPARTMENT

The Catalog Department now catalogs approximately 15,000 new titles annually. Figures for new and recataloged items in recent years are shown in table 45. The number of volumes shelflisted is about 225,000 annually. The remaining 275,000 volumes acquired by the

Table 45
ITEMS CATALOGED, RECATALOGED, AND RECLASSIFIED

Year	Total number
1958	7,683
1959	9,867
1960	12,118
1961	12,208
1962	12,658
1963	14,742
1964	16,344
1965	14,885
1966	14,838
1967	15,347

Library, such as multiple copies in paperback form, do not require cataloging and shelflisting.

The staff of the department is made up of 13 professionals (including the head of the unit), one trainee, and 36 clerical workers. This is a larger staff than is needed for the work load, if quarters, personnel, and procedures were suitable. Actually the physical space is not adequate nor efficient for the volume of materials handled, and working conditions in terms of heat and humidity are not conducive to full productivity either in midsummer or in midwinter. Clerical staff does not appear to be well trained nor well motivated. Turnover in the clerical group is high; for example, of 18 authorized positions of Junior Clerk, only two had one incumbent during the full year of 1967; three were promoted to senior rank, and the other 13 resigned.

Assignment of responsibilities must be reviewed to determine whether staff members are utilized most efficiently. Catalogers devote time to the classification of Accessions Department bills, the purpose of which is questioned. Catalogers spend over 1,000 hours per year at Information Desks, the manhours of one person for 27 weeks. Whereas other departments usually send technicians and clerks, the Catalog Department does not use technicians, and only a few clerks in the Department have been accepted for Information Desk service.

Book-ordering practices are responsible for delays in the Catalog Department. The same title may be ordered at different times by various agencies, and even by the same agency. If most copies could be ordered at once, the technical process departments could operate more efficiently. The Catalog Department especially suffers because of this practice as their records are in process when additional copies arrive. If such copies are received as new books, they may inadvertently be cataloged over again.

Should they be recognized as extra copies, the records either have to be located or the books held until the records are completed and filed. Both conditions create problems and delays. All of this additional work is time-consuming and expensive; extra delays result because books that are retained unnecessarily also occupy space needed for other books which must be processed.

One important step to reduce the time and cost of processing materials would be maximum use of the information and classification numbers on Library of Congress cards. This is not a matter to be decided unilaterally in the Cataloging Department, but must be worked out with the various public service units because uniform adoption of LC information would involve a change in the location of some materials. At the present time there is no machinery for presenting such questions and getting a decision which would permit maximum use of the national cataloging network.

BOOK CATALOGS

For some time library practice has favored the catalog in card form. The card catalog has the distinct advantage of interfiling, so that new additions and necessary withdrawals can be made readily.

However, new computer methods now make interfiling possible by machine and the automatic production of catalogs in book form. These open new prospects, both in service and convenience for the user and in cutting through the mounting costs of hand maintenance of the 76 separate and ever-increasing card catalogs in the Chicago Public Library.

Twelve advantages of the catalog in book form are as follows:

1. Multiple copies are produced so that the catalog can be consulted at various places in the building, in the branches and other agencies throughout the system, and in libraries throughout the metropolitan area.

2. Book catalogs are mobile—patrons can be comfortably seated while consulting the catalog; reference librarians can have a copy within reach on their desks; volumes of the book catalog may be placed in the stack area so that users can consult them in the immediate vicinity of the books; the patron can photocopy any section of the book catalog and carry it home with him.

3. The book catalog is easy to scan. A full sweep of the holdings on a subject can be seen at a glance, whereas in a card catalog only one title is seen at a time, and the catalog must be consulted within a narrowly defined area.

4. A number of simultaneous users can be accommodated at once; it is awkward for many persons to use a card catalog at the same time.

5. Book catalogs strengthen coordinated library systems by providing full cataloging information in branches; no matter in which branch the user is located, he can learn about any book in the total collection without having to travel to a regional center or the main library to consult card catalogs.

6. Branch card catalogs can be eliminated as an unnecessary expense, and a separate catalog will not have to be made each time a new branch is opened.

7. The book catalog is compact, occupying less floor space than that taken up by a bulky card catalog, a particular advantage in the crowded central building.

8. Numerous problems relating to the maintenance of the card catalog, such as the continuous cost of hand filing, are avoided.

9. Because catalog information is controlled at one point, the book catalog encourages uniform cataloging, classification, and subject headings throughout the system.

10. A new catalog can be produced in book form rather than changing the old one in situations where significant changes in cataloging are undertaken to remove inconsistencies and update headings.

11. With an automated catalog it is possible to produce many more approaches to the holdings of the library and increase the number of access points to the collection for both user and staff than is feasible with a card catalog system.

12. The use of the book catalog may be easily taught to patrons; children use the catalog in this form as readily as on cards.

The book catalog is not a panacea. The printed document is incomplete and out of date as soon as issued, because it lacks the titles added to the collection after copy goes to press. This in turn leads to supplementary issues, which means that the searcher must look in more than one volume. Frequent cumulations and reissuing of the complete updated record reduce this inconvenience but add to costs.

Several characteristics of the Chicago Public Library lead to the recommendation that the shift be made to the computerized book catalog in the near future. This is a large system with various departments and branches and many separate card catalogs. The cost of manually maintaining these many records is high, and each catalog lists only the local resources. The book catalog pays off economically to the extent that multiple units use it. Further, the collection in the Chicago Public Library, while large in number of volumes, including duplicates in all the branches, does not have nearly as many different titles for entering in the catalog as does a large research library. Once the shift to computerization is made, and as the Chicago Public Library steps up the number of titles it acquires in the future, the computerized system can grow with the increasing load.

The time is strategic for the changeover, for the experiments that have been going on elsewhere for several years have identified the best procedures and eliminated the mistakes (The Free Library of Philadelphia now uses book catalogs throughout the system and the Enoch Pratt Library in Baltimore is well along in the change), and the availability of new equipment makes additional applications feasible.

A system plan for computer production of a book catalog for the Chicago Public Library is outlined in the next chapter (chapter 8). The plan does not call for conversion of the existing card catalog into book form, but for the initial application of the proposed system to new acquisitions. Much of the original copy would be obtained by a tie-in with the national MARC system from the Library of Congress. Two versions of the catalog are proposed—a longer one for the Central Library and regional centers and a shorter one for branches and other extension outlets. The shift to the book catalog will not be easy or problem-free, but the handwriting on the wall is clear; this is the time for the Chicago Public Library to make a fresh start.

Bindery Department

The Bindery Department of the Library is responsible for the binding of new books (when necessary), the rebinding of older works, pamphlet binding, the handling of paperbacks, and the repair and physical maintenance of the collections. The department also has major preparational responsibility for the processing of new materials for the use of clientele; this includes insertion of pockets, book plates, and plastic jackets for certain types of books. In addition, the department handles the processing of music scores, albums and recordings, as well as Braille books (see figure 23 on page 166).

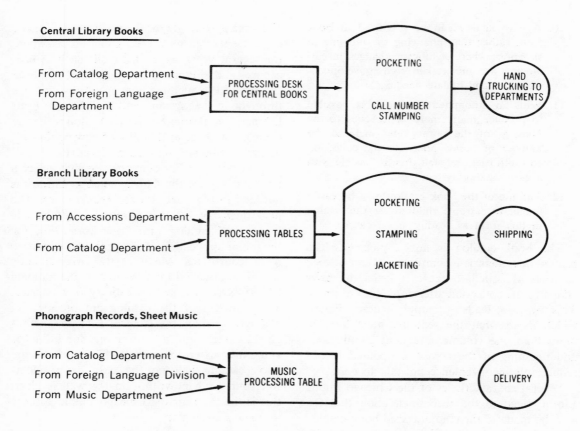

Central Library Books

From Catalog Department →
From Foreign Language → PROCESSING DESK FOR CENTRAL BOOKS → POCKETING / CALL NUMBER STAMPING → HAND TRUCKING TO DEPARTMENTS
Department

Branch Library Books

From Accessions Department →
From Catalog Department → PROCESSING TABLES → POCKETING / STAMPING / JACKETING → SHIPPING

Phonograph Records, Sheet Music

From Catalog Department →
From Foreign Language Division → MUSIC PROCESSING TABLE → DELIVERY
From Music Department →

Figure 23. Preparation of materials for shelves

The responsibilities of the Head of the Bindery Department involve administering, training, and supervising a staff of 25 full-time members and 4 part-time pages in two separate units, one of which is located in the Central Library, the other at the Hild Regional Branch. She sets standards of job performance and spot-checks work performed. She is responsible for the scheduling and assigning of materials to five commercial binders, and for the distribution of rebound books to all library agencies. She is also responsible for the restoration of valuable library materials and training of the staff in the operation of various machines.

The Bindery Department performs a miscellany of extra tasks in maintaining materials for the public service departments. These include work on paperback books and on periodicals which need special binding, the preparation of dummy books for displays, and the repair of books which ranges from routine mending to highly skilled restoration work. Plastic covers are added to some books to retain and protect the bright-colored dust jacket with which most books arrive; but these attractive jackets are usually discarded with the result that the collections in the Chicago Public Library look duller and less attractive than is customary in public libraries.

The overcrowded conditions under which work is performed in the Bindery Department present many difficulties and problems. Worktables are too close together for staff to function in any degree of comfort and efficiency. The aisles, lined with book trucks, are too narrow for the flat trucks on which packed cartons must be brought into and out of the department. The bins into which books are sorted for shipment to branches are too small for the amount of work that goes through the department, and shelf space also is insufficient. Poor ventilation and lack of temperature control aggravate the situation.

Here, as in other sections of the technical services operations, staff quality and staff control fall short of reasonable standards. Productivity is not high. Turnover among staff is above normal. Morale is low, as judged by the attitude of employees toward supervisors and toward each other, and by application and effort at work stations. Overtime service is used heavily because of backlogs; as a regular practice this is subject to criticism, because some staff members who become accustomed to the extra income have little incentive to maintain productivity during regular hours.

The routing of materials is relatively simple and direct. Channels for insertion of pockets, call number stamping, jacketing, sorting, packing, and delivery to the Shipping Room are recognized and flow smoothly. Variations in routing of work, such as multiple copies of branch books which come directly to the preparations unit rather than go through cataloging, are made where relevant.

While routing is simple and sensible, the same cannot be said for internal handling and operations. There is an excessive number of physical moves of items within the department; these require staff time for the shifts and make for the likelihood of pile-ups at one or another work station in the sequence. An assembly line and conveyor system is much needed to facilitate the handling of the several hundred thousand units that go through this department annually.

In the specific operations of inserting and stamping, basic principles of scientific management have not been applied. Hand motions of workers are not simplified and regularized. Often one hand remains idle when it could further the operation. Holding devices are not used so that both hands of the worker can be freed and made productive. Because operations are not standardized, production quotas cannot be set and worker productivity varies widely.

Recommendations

Various specific steps for improving technical services in the Chicago Public Library have been suggested in the course of this chapter. The larger and more significant recommendations are summarized here. Rather drastic steps are proposed; these will cost money and create problems in transition, but the present system is not effective now and will be less so in the future. The Chicago Public Library faces the same prospect that confronts a manufacturer who must modernize his production methods. Fortunately for the Library the result will both save money in the long run and increase service, the more so if the changes are achieved and tied in with the emerging automated network of national bibliographical information.

The Technical Services Division is to be re-located in a Processing Center outside the Central Building, a step that should be taken even if a new central structure is not started in the immediate future.

Limitations in the present space prevent efficient and productive technical processing; in addition, this space is needed to relieve pressure on various other central work units that must remain in the central building. Technical operations—acquisition through cataloging and shelf preparation of books —not only can be detached from the central structure but would definitely gain in the process. Location in a single-story industrial building outside the Loop would open the way for an assembly-line plan of processing and the delivery and movement of several hundred thousand volumes annually with less cost and delay. Since preparatory work requires mostly nonprofessional staff, it is suggested that the Processing Center be located in a low-income area and employ and train recruits from the local area.

Computerization is to be introduced in the acquisition, recording, cataloging, and shelf preparation of books and serials.

A design for computerization that encompasses ordering procedures, receipt, voucher approval, shelflisting, cataloging, classification, and preparation of books for use is presented in the chapter on new technology which follows. Book and serial processing should be the first application of automation in the Library. However, all unnecessary records and procedures should be eliminated before automation, as recommended below. Also before conversion to a new data-processing system is undertaken, a period of experimentation and testing will be required to ensure that the proposed system will be workable and to identify procedures that need adjustment in operation.

An automatically-produced printed book catalog is to be adopted in place of the many card catalogs now maintained in the Chicago Public Library.

The computerized processing system either can produce cards for the present system or tape for the automatic typesetting of a comprehensive catalog in book form. Multiple copies of a printed book catalog would have many service advantages for users and staff, and would eliminate the laborious and time-consuming procedures now followed. Such a duplicated record of holdings would also help to relate the Chicago Public Library to libraries throughout the metropolitan area. Two versions will be required: the complete record for central and regionals, and a selected, topically-arranged record for branches. The book catalog is one of the most important service recommendations in this report.

The Library should convert to the Library of Congress classification scheme for current acquisitions and selectively reclassify older materials that are closely related to new purchases.

This step is necessary to keep costs down over the long run and to benefit fully from the automated national network. Computerization, the printed catalog in book form, and the shift to the LC classification scheme go hand in hand and should be adopted simultaneously for new acquisitions. Once this combination is working, after an appropriate trial and testing period of two years, Chicago will have a processing system suitable for the period ahead.

Systematic review, elimination, and simplification of records and forms should occur throughout the technical services activities.

The starting point is the elaborate records going back 15 and 20 years that are kept of books previously purchased and those not purchased. Both records and forms of doubtful value also continue to apply in accessions work. In cataloging the many supplementary indexes and catalogs maintained in the subject departments are other examples. Where it can be demonstrated that such records are distinctively useful and regularly used, they can be retained; but hard-headed assessment is needed to identify and eliminate hangers-on in the elaborate battery of records maintained by the Library, and thus to free staff time and energy for those jobs that remain undone.

Along with simplification in records and forms should go systematic application of scientific management principles to the various manual operations in the technical services.

One way to accomplish this would be to call in an operations specialist for an intensive study. However, this would impose methods from the outside, these new methods would not accrue naturally from staff experience, and they would apply only to present procedures. Instead it is proposed that two supervising clerks on the staff be sent out for training in scientific management principles after which they are to come back and utilize their training to revise work operations with the present staff. Once these principles are understood by supervisors, they can also be applied to new procedures under a computerized system.

A general cataloging manual is needed to set forth policies, rules, and practices both for internal cataloging operations and for the system as a whole.

Among matters to be covered in the manual are the following: consistent practices for

handling pamphlets, government documents, and serials; a reduction in the number of delayed and nonsynchronized orders for single copies of orders after the main order has gone through; closer and coordinated relations between accessioning and cataloging operations; and prompt preparation of catalog cards to be placed in the pockets of books going to the branches. Questions and problems of this type involve not only the technical services departments but public service units as well in both the Central Library and the branches. Technical services staff should (1) describe these problem areas in brief reports, (2) propose appropriate solutions, and (3) take these matters to service department and branch heads for review and adjustment if necessary. Policies will then be ready for inclusion in a system-wide manual.

Additional book jobbers should be used, rather than the current practice of depending on one source that does not provide a full range of approval copies of titles.

It should be possible to accomplish this under existing city purchasing regulations by separating out certain categories of publications—scientific and technological titles, for example—and obtaining these from a specialized dealer. If this is not the case the regulations should be modified as they apply to the Library (in accord with state statutes which specify that the Library Board shall have control over expenditure of money provided for library purposes); certainly the present system is not getting a full range of publications to the people of Chicago. Greater use should be made of foreign book dealers, in England as well as on the continent. The point is to open a wider and more varied flow of publications into the collections of the Chicago Public Library.

Completion of the statement of book selection policy for the Library should be a priority project, to prepare for the new era of acquisitions and collection building in the near future.

This project has been progressing slowly, in part because an overall sense of direction has been lacking and in part because attention has been given to detailed problems within present aims and practices. The policy statement must in the end come down to specifics, but first it should define the responsibility of the Library to widely divergent reader groups, such as subject specialists, students, and adults of limited education. Formulation of selection policies represents a first step for the library staff in applying the recommendations in this report.

Another early step is organization and reorganization within the Technical Services Division.

The position of Assistant Librarian for Technical Services should be filled promptly by recruiting at the Librarian VI level and by providing a salary starting at $20,000. Not only the systematic improvements within technical operations but also the major recommendations for modernization, such as the book catalog, computerization, and reclassification, depend on the presence and leadership of this coordinating officer. Within the Technical Services Division, separate departments are needed for Selection (not only to maintain records but also to develop and coordinate policy) and for Photographic Reproduction (to enable the Library to broaden and intensify its service to varying reader groups). These two new units, plus the modernizing recommended for existing departments and procedures, will prepare the Chicago Public Library for the efficient and effective handling of resources that are required—first, to catch up with Chicago's current needs, and second, to remain ahead of user demands in the future.

8 New Technology and the Chicago Public Library

Computer control and electronic communication will apply to the Chicago Public Library in the near future and in time will significantly transform the institution.

However, it is an oversimplification to assume that the push-button library or the library-in-a-computer is just around the corner. No matter how far one looks down the road of new communication technology there will still be a central source, collection, or information-resource bank (i.e., a library), and somewhere an individual reader, viewer, receiver (i.e., a library user). Eventually the user may not come to the library but will have electronic access to the central resource directly from his home, office, and classroom. The prospect was put neatly in a newspaper series on the 21st Century: "From his carrel the pupil will call on electronic information sources in the campus library, the Chicago Public Library, and the Library of Congress in Washington" (*Chicago Tribune,* 12 January 1969). At that stage, still many years in the future, the branch program will be distinctly modified, but a central resource will still have to be maintained.

One source of confusion in thinking about computers and libraries is to equate specific information with systematic reading. It is one thing to program isolated bits of information into a machine for later retrieval, but something very different to computerize the complex sequence of searching a library and then of reading a hundred or a thousand pages. For this essential library purpose the book remains a remarkable invention.

The proper course is neither to expect miracles from technology nor to reject it as somehow alien to or improper for libraries. The Chicago Public Library must start now to apply available techniques to its present operations and recordkeeping, as outlined below. It must also begin experimentation with new prospects, starting with facsimile transmission and information and bibliographic control. A Computer-Communications Center is proposed within the Library for the purpose.

The Library has already taken a first step with a teletype installation, used to obtain and distribute interlibrary loan information rapidly. The connection is with the three other official reference and research libraries in Illinois and with library systems in the suburban areas. At this stage the installation is used only as a substitute for the mails; it has not affected the interloan procedure at other points.

Stages of Technological Application

No one can exactly predict the form and timing of new inventions or equipment improvement that will facilitate both information retrieval and transmission. Developments on

---

The tentative system designs in this chapter were prepared by Theodore Stein, data processing specialist, after detailed analysis of the present acquisition-cataloging and registration-circulation procedures of the Chicago Public Library.

the horizon may have profound effects—millimeter waves through buried waveguides, for example, or coherent light waves from lasers. But a possible and partial sequence of nine applications can be predicted for planning purposes:

1. Computer control of publications acquired —specifically the ordering and accessioning of books (now in excess of 400,000 items annually in the Chicago Public Library) and the receipt of issues of magazines and serials (some 100,000 items per year currently, probably doubling in number within a few years)

2. Computer assistance in bibliographic control of holdings—specifically the production of a uniform book catalog of collections, to be printed in multiple copies for use in many locations in the Central Library, in the branches, and in libraries throughout the metropolitan area

3. Computerized communication with bibliographic information about library resources outside the Chicago area—initially through the MARC (Machine-Readable Cataloging) system of the Library of Congress, which will be used as a source of copy for the book catalog

4. Computer control of records of library use —specifically of registration and circulation information (close to 10 million transactions per year)

5. Facsimile transmission within the Chicago system (i.e., electronic reproduction of printed pages at a distance)—specifically contact between the Central Library and the regional centers throughout the city

6. Facsimile contact outside the Chicago system, initially with selected libraries and library systems in the Chicago region and with the designated and state-aided "reference and research" libraries in the Illinois program

7. Closed-circuit TV to provide individual or group showing of films and video tapes from a central bank and available on demand in local branch libraries

8. Computer storage and retrieval of specific factual information, probably starting with data in frequent demand within circumscribed fields, such as certain kinds of business information and information in out-of-town telephone directories

9. Picturephone contact within and beyond the Chicago Public Library—eventually for direct reading at local terminals of books located at a distance, with automatic paging and print-out control on demand.

This establishes a priority list for the next decade. Beyond this sequence responsible predictions cannot be made because entirely unforeseen devices and systems are likely to enter the picture. It may be that certain computer utilizations and communication connections will first function *within* the Chicago Public Library—for example, on-line pictorial contact through TV terminals—and then in time much the same system may be extended *outside* to direct access from homes and offices, but this goes beyond the next decade.

When and if such direct individual access to extensive resources at a distance becomes a reality, the whole concept of the branch program in Chicago will have to be reconsidered. In the interval library resources must be made available in local communities, but in quarters and buildings that can be shifted to other purposes if and as library service becomes directly available from a central source.

At any rate, coaxial cable connections must be built into new and permanent structures for the Library, specifically a new central building and a series of regional library centers. These units of the Chicago library system must be able to communicate with each other in all media and also must be able to tie into networks beyond the local system, out into the metropolitan area, the midwest region, and the country as a whole.

Systems designs are presented below for the first four steps in the sequence of computer applications. One combines the three initial steps under an integrated systems design for acquisition and cataloging. The other deals with circulation control and registration of users.

The acquisitions-cataloging design is more firm and finished, and is recommended for first action. A half-dozen installations of computerized book catalogs in the country can be studied (Philadelphia Free Library and Baltimore County, Maryland, are examples) and some idea of costs under different systems obtained. The registration-circulation control proposal needs further review, to determine how costs compare with those of the present photographic and transaction card system, before concrete action is taken.

Computer-Communications Center

The Chicago Public Library now has the opportunity for technological applications and improvements. Taking advantage of this opportunity should be one of the priority goals in the years immediately ahead.

It will take informed background and concentrated attention to realize these complex systems prospects. Ready-made packages cannot be purchased on the market. Software systems must be individually designed and then modified as application proceeds. One series of adjustments will result from the particular equipment that is available for use, either in the municipal government or in commercial

service agencies; the Library is advised against obtaining a large computer installation of its own because this requires special physical quarters and probably would not be used to capacity. Whatever systems are adopted must first be programmed, a laborious process. Before plunging completely, pilot projects must be tested out—computerized acquisitions for two large branches as an initial step, for example. Once new systems are installed, present personnel must be instructed in how to use them.

For all these reasons a new office or center for computer and communications development is recommended within the Chicago Public Library. It should be attached to the Chief Librarian, as one of his specialized agencies for moving the Library into the future. The director of the Center would be a data-processing specialist, at a level equivalent to that of Librarian V. He would call on outside experts to help design and refine systems and would commission detailed programming. But he would be on the scene, within the Library, getting early steps started, testing pilot runs, relating technological change to existing methods and personnel, studying new prospects, and over a period of time moving the Chicago Public Library toward the technetronic age step by step. Establishment of a Computer-Communications Center within the Library is an essential early step in developing the new Chicago Public Library.

Computer System for Acquisition and Cataloging

A systems design is presented here for automation of various steps and records in the technical processes of ordering, receiving, shelf-listing, cataloging, and preparing books for use in the Chicago Public Library. This is a unified and integrated system; i.e., a computer record is made for each title when selected for purchase, and this same record serves throughout subsequent steps. For cataloging input, the Library would subscribe to MARC (machine-readable cataloging service of the Library of Congress). The advantages of the whole MARC system are economy (such as complete elimination of shelflisting and of the shelflist staff unit, elimination of the branch-catalog staff unit, and the like), speed of operations, and conformity to national catalog data.

The end product can be either catalog cards to continue the present plan of a central catalog, departmental catalogs and branch catalogs (some 76 separate catalogs), or a unified book catalog issued in one or more versions, varying by completeness of coverage, for the main library and the branches.

As the system is presented here, certain steps are identified in present practices which could be eliminated without going over to a computer. These adjustments would effect minor economies in the present manual system, but realization of the larger advantages of the proposed machine system depends upon computerization.

SELECTION

The computer system will have no effect upon the various review files currently maintained for selection purposes. If these files are to be eliminated, they can be eliminated equally well with or without a computer system.

1. In making selections, the subject departments would proceed as they do presently. That is, a slip would be typed for each title to be selected. Because of the changed function of this slip, it will be called a selection slip here, rather than an order slip.

2. One copy of the selection slip, or a machine-readable by-product of selection slip typing,

would immediately be forwarded for entry into the computer system. The subject department would keep one copy of the selection slip. The method of entry to the computer system is a detail for later investigation. It might be desirable to originally type in machine-readable type font, or it might be desirable to have a punched paper tape by-product of selection slip typing, or it might be advisable to do a retyping, in order to produce punched cards for machine entry.

3. At the time selection slips are entered into the computer system, the computer would check to see if the title had been previously placed on order. If so, a notification to the subject department would be produced.

4. From the selection slips entered, the computer would produce selection lists. These lists would go to branch librarians in advance of the order cycle to give them a preview of books that would be available for ordering. Copies of these lists also go to the subject departments. After the subject department staff checks the retained copy of the selection slip against the selection list, and verifies that computer entry was properly made, the retained selection slips can be discarded.

5. After the selection slip is used for entry to the computer system, it goes to the Book Selection Room, where it now becomes a requisition slip.

ORDERING

1. In the usual fashion, branch librarians will mark their orders on the requisition slips. The results of this marking will be entered into the computer system, as shown in figure 24.

2. The computer will compute total volumes ordered on each requisition slip, make vendor assignments where possible, and prepare order slips for the vendor.

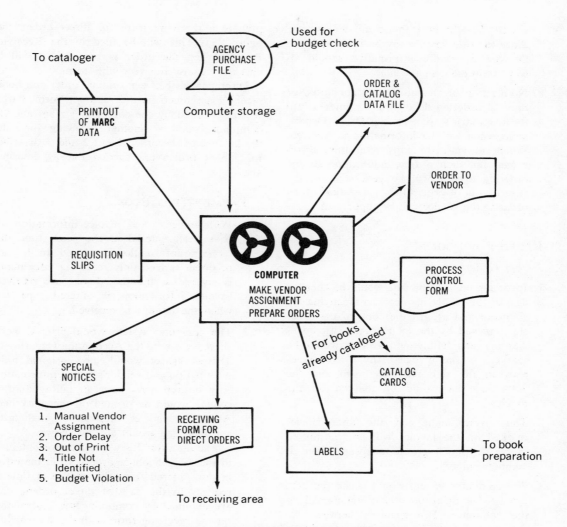

Figure 24. Automated book ordering system

3. Vendor assignment is made in those cases where the title can be assigned to a vendor on the basis of type of material and publisher. In other cases, an exception list is printed out. The Accessions Department reviews the exceptions list and assigns vendors. These assignments are entered into the computer system and the preparation of order slips is completed.

4. The order slips are sent to the vendor. The computer system has complete information about all orders placed. No external open order file need be maintained.

5. Extra copy requisitions are in all cases pro-

cessed directly into the computer system. Since the title has already been entered into the system, vendor information should always be present in the file.

6. Notification of an out-of-print condition, or unusual ordering delay, will be entered into the computer system by the Order Department whenever the information is received. Whenever an extra copy requisition is received for such a title, notification to the ordering agency will be generated. In the case of out-of-print titles, generation of an order to the vendor will be suppressed.

RECEIPT OF BOOKS

Jobber Orders

1. Incoming book shipments would be checked against the jobber invoice accompanying the shipment and against the copy of the order slip returned by the jobber. Any discrepancies between billing and receipt would be marked on the invoice. Any discrepancies between the returned order slip and the book received would be marked on the invoice.

2. The invoice data and the discrepancies marked on the invoice will be transmitted to the keypunch group for preparation of computer input.

3. The computer system would check the data against the open order file maintained in the computer. Discrepancies between receiving and ordering information would be printed out for attention by the Order Department.

Direct Orders

The general procedure for direct orders would be similar to that for jobber orders with one exception. Since it cannot be assumed that each shipment of books received on direct order will be accompanied by an invoice, the computer will prepare a receiving form for direct orders (see figure 25). This will be filed in the Receiving Room. When the order is received, it will be checked against the receiving form.

Discrepancies between original order and books received are noted on the receiving form. Partial receipt is noted by the computer system and the computer produces another receiving form for the balance of the order. Steps 2 and 3 described for jobber orders are carried out as described above.

PAYMENT FOR BOOKS

1. With jobber orders, invoice information will have been entered at the same time that receiving information is entered. In the case of direct orders, only receiving information is entered at the time books are received. Invoice information is entered separately when the invoice is received.

2. The computer system would print a worksheet for use by the Accounting Department. The worksheet would show original order information and vendor's billing information. Any discrepancies between billing and receiving would be printed on the worksheet. Any discrepancies between original order and receiving would also be shown.

   The data for this worksheet are obtained, in the case of jobber orders, from the information entered from the invoice at time of receipt. In the case of direct orders, data are obtained by combining the information on the receiving form with the information entered from the invoice.

3. The invoices themselves would be immediately retired to a chronological file and kept for reference purposes only. All further financial work would be based upon computer-supplied information. Reference would be made to original invoices only to resolve problems.

   To assure that all invoices have been entered into the computer system, an in-

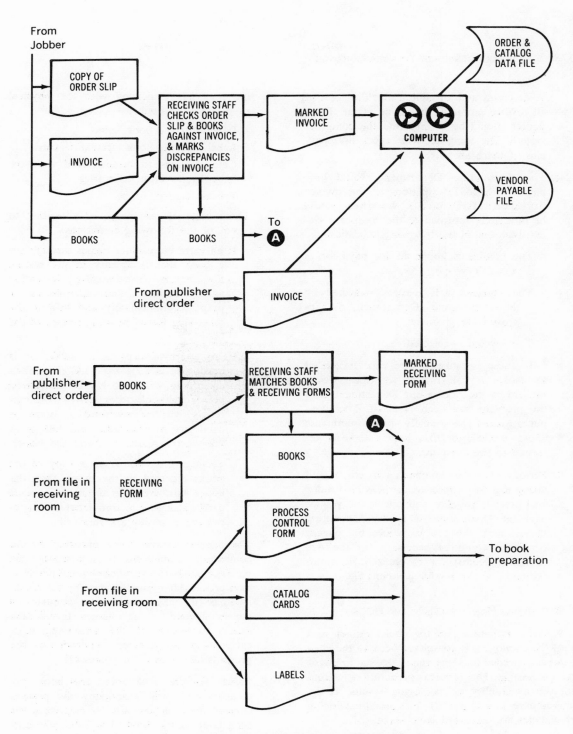

Figure 25. Automated book receiving system

voice count and an adding machine total of all invoice amounts should be taken. These figures should be entered into the computer system. The computer will report discrepancies, if there are any.

4. The Accounting Department would base payment upon information on the invoice worksheets. Each invoice worksheet would be ultimately returned to the computer system with one of the following indications:

The invoice is approved for payment as it stands

The invoice, with changes indicated by the Accounting Department, is approved for payment

The invoice is rejected.

In those instances where time is needed to resolve a problem, the worksheet would be held by the Accounting Department until the problem had been resolved. The computer would periodically print reminders about worksheets that had not been returned to the computer.

5. Periodically, the computer system would group together approved invoices by vendor and print a voucher and check for vendor payment. Upon approval by the Accounting Department, the checks would be mailed. Provision would be necessary for the Accounting Department to enter various adjustments to the vendor payment file.

PHYSICAL PREPARATION OF BOOKS

Physical preparation of the books cannot start until the cataloging is completed because the class number is needed on some materials used in physical processing. The physical preparation, assuming the availability of cataloging results, is described here (see figure 26). The actual cataloging procedures are described later (page 181).

1. The computer system will prepare the following materials associated with the physical preparation of books:

Labels for the book spine

Labels for the book circulation card

Catalog cards to be delivered with the books for branch libraries

Process control form.

These materials are prepared according to one of the following conditions:

If an extra copy order comes through for a book that is already in the system files, then all the cataloging information will be available. The materials will be prepared immediately and held in the Receiving Room pending receipt of the books.

If an approval copy is available, or if cataloging is done from LC copy, then cataloging will probably be completed before the book order arrives. The materials will be prepared as soon as cataloging is completed and will go to the receiving area to await the books.

If cataloging is done from a copy of the books received in the order, then the books will be held in the receiving area until cataloging is completed, and processing materials are received.

2. The process control form, prepared by the computer, is intended to accompany the batch of books through the physical preparation process. It serves to identify the books and has full information about numbers of copies intended for each agency. It will have spaces to check off the processing steps carried out and serve as a control over the progress of the physical processing.

3. Labels for the book spine and book circulation card will accompany the process control form. There will be one label for each copy of the book. The label will contain copy number and agency identification.

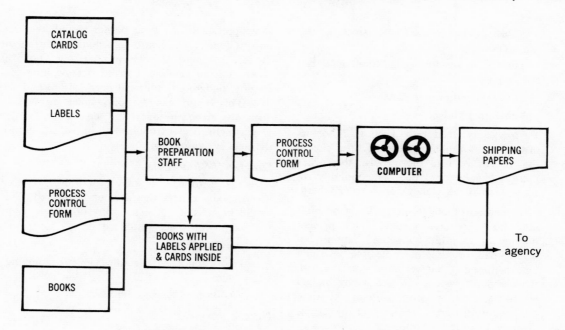

Figure 26.   Automated book preparation system

Thus, the work of writing copy numbers into the books by the shelflister would be eliminated. If it appears desirable to have the copy number and class number actually written in the book, then it would be most efficient for the person who pastes the labels to do this at the time the label is pasted; the information would be copied from the label.

4. Catalog cards will be printed at the time the labels are printed and will be present in the receiving area, along with the labels. Thus, the cards can be sent out with the book when preparation of the book is completed. If book catalogs are extensively used, then the preparation of catalog cards should not be necessary.

5. When the physical preparation of the books is completed, the process control form will be returned to the Computer Department. If there is any discrepancy between the number of copies indicated on the sheet and the

number of copies finally processed, this will be marked on the process control form. Such discrepancies may result from the discovery of imperfect copies.

SHIPMENT OF BOOKS AND MAINTENANCE OF AGENCY BUDGET

1. On receipt of the process control forms, which signal completion of physical processing, the computer will prepare shipping lists indicating which books are to be sent to the agencies. The lists will be used in the shipping room to control distribution of the books. One copy will accompany the books to allow the receiving agencies to check the accuracy of the shipment.

2. Each month each agency will receive a report which shows the following:

   Books ordered by the agency but not yet shipped to the agency

Books shipped to the agency since the last report

Total increase in expenditure since last report

Total expenditure to date

Remaining budget.

3. Each agency need only keep track of its orders between monthly reports. After checking orders against the report, the order records can be discarded. The monthly reports serve as the agency's open order record.

4. Any method of budget control can be built into the computer system. The present method of monthly budget allocations can be retained, or some more flexible basis can be established. Whatever basis is established, the computer system can detect any budget violations, print a notification at the time the requisitions are received, and reject requisitions in excess of budget.

EXCEPTION REPORTS

The computer system can be programmed to monitor the procedures and prepare reports of any condition that requires attention. The following reports should be prepared at a minimum:

Late Receipt from Vendor

Orders outstanding in excess of some preestablished time period would be listed on this report. Listing would continue until one of the following actions occurred:

The order is received

The order is cancelled

The order department enters an input indicating either out-of-print or excessive order delay.

In the third instance, the computer system would record the out-of-print or delay condition and treat subsequent orders accordingly.

Late Delivery to Agency

Orders outstanding from an agency longer than some preestablished time period would be listed on this report. The status information relevant to the order would also be printed, e.g., not yet received from vendor, received but awaiting cataloging, undergoing physical preparation, and the like. This report would supply quick answers to questions from agencies and enable the Order Department to spot troubles and investigate before the agency complains.

Orders Not Placeable

A report to each agency would be prepared showing any orders that cannot be placed. This would be relevant to extra copy orders. Reasons for inability to place would be:

Out-of-print

Title cannot be identified in the computer files

Violation of budget limits.

Unpaid Invoices

Invoices that have been in the files for longer than some preestablished time period and have not yet been paid would appear on this listing.

OTHER COMPUTER OUTPUTS RELATED TO BOOK ORDERING

New Acquisitions Listings

A new acquisitions listing in the format of the present book bulletin could be prepared. Bulletin slips would be sent to the computer center for direct entry into the computer. Preparation of the book bulletin would then be an entirely automatic procedure.

Complete new acquisitions listings, by agency, without annotation could automatically be prepared by the computer from order information.

Miscellaneous Order Listings

The need for order listings that correspond to certain currently maintained Order Department files is doubtful. However, to the extent they are required, they can be prepared entirely by computer from the basic order information. Thus, a complete listing of all titles ordered on each order cycle can be prepared, and a list of titles received in any time period can be prepared.

In general, however, exceptions listings of titles which require some action would be more useful in the computer system.

Statistics

All statistical reports should be computer-prepared. The order inputs would provide the basis for almost all statistics needed.

CATALOGING

Cataloging of New Titles

1. The library would subscribe to the MARC (machine-readable cataloging) information service of the Library of Congress. The first step in the cataloging procedure would be a search by the computer system for MARC cataloging data. This search would be initiated by one of the following actions:

   At the time the order slip is entered into the computer, a search for MARC copy will be carried out. The copy, if found, will be printed and transmitted to the Catalog Department. If an approval book is available, the approval book and MARC copy will go to the Catalog Department. If no approval book is available, the cataloger will receive MARC copy only.

   If no approval book is available, the cataloger can exercise the option to catalog from MARC copy only. If he chooses not to do this, he will return the MARC copy to the computer system. Re-entry of an identifying number on this MARC proof sheet will signal the computer system that proof copy should be produced once again, upon receipt of the order, when a copy of the book is available.

   If MARC copy is not available, the computer system will record the request for copy, and if at any later time MARC copy is received, it will be printed out

for the cataloger. The library can establish procedures according to its own requirements. A waiting period can be established during which cataloging will be delayed in the expectation that MARC copy will arrive, or original cataloging can proceed immediately. In any event, the computer system will print the MARC copy when received, even if original cataloging has already been completed. This allows a change in the Library of Congress cataloging at a later time, if this is desired.

2. If MARC copy is found, no preliminary investigation of subjects and names by clerical staff is necessary. The subject and names used in the MARC copy will be matched against a machine-maintained copy of the Chicago Public Library's authority file. Any discrepancies will be recorded on the MARC copy proof sheet that is printed by the computer for the cataloger.

3. If no MARC copy is found, a catalog worksheet is printed by the computer. Information available from the order is printed on the proof sheet.

4. Whether or not MARC copy is found, a cataloging slip is printed by the computer if the MARC search was initiated by an order for a title for which an approval copy is available, or if the MARC search was initiated by receiving information. The catalog slip and either the MARC proof copy or the computer-produced catalog worksheet are matched against the books. The book is sent to the cataloger along with MARC proof, or a worksheet. The catalog slip goes to the computer to signal receipt of the book by Cataloging.

5. If MARC copy is available, the cataloger will mark modifications on the proof sheet prepared by the computer. He may resubmit the proof sheet unmodified. If no MARC

copy is available, the computer will print a worksheet for the cataloger, and on the worksheet it will print the information that is available from the ordering process, e.g., author, title, publisher, place, date, edition. The author information will have been checked against the authority file. The cataloger will change any of this information as needed and will add original cataloging information.

6. After completion of cataloging, the data goes directly to the Computer Department for entry into the computer system. Only changes made by the cataloger or information added by the cataloger are entered into the computer system. Any information which was printed by the computer and not changed need not be reentered.

7. If any changes or additions to MARC copy have been made by the cataloger, or if there was no MARC copy, proof copy is produced by the computer. Any changes that involve the use of established forms are checked against the authority file. Errors are flagged on the proof copy.

8. If proof copy is produced, it is reviewed by a proofreader or a reviser, depending upon library policy.

9. If changes are made to the proof copy, new copy is produced. This is continued until no further changes are submitted.

10. The computer system will regard the catalog information as firm under either of the following circumstances:

   A proof sheet is returned unchanged, or

   Three days elapse without submission of changes.

11. When the computer system recognizes catalog data as firm, it will produce all of the outputs which require catalog data, i.e.,

   catalog cards

   labels for book spine

   circulation card.

At the same time, the process control form for physical preparation will be printed. The computer system has all of the information needed to determine how many labels and cards should be produced and to put copy numbers and library identification on these items (figure 27).

WORK OF OTHER UNITS

Most of the work of the units following would be eliminated by the proposed computer system. However, not all of the work reduction that follows is attributable to computerization.

Preparation Unit

The work of checking in the books and transmitting them to the catalogers will remain. It will also be necessary to match computer-produced proof sheets with books. However, the following functions will be eliminated or reduced in extent:

Maintenance of the in-process file will be eliminated. Computer-maintenance of the in-process file is described below

Catalog check for form of names and subjects is to be eliminated by computer look-up

Cutting and filing of LC proof slips and search for LC proof slips is to be eliminated by use of MARC tapes

Filing of catalog cards will be greatly reduced because the computer can produce pre-alphabetized cards, numbered in a way which correctly interfiles them with numbered cards that are already in the catalog. If a book catalog is used, filing is entirely eliminated.

The following functions would be eliminated by the computer system. However, these also would probably be eliminated by changes to the manual system:

Preparation and filing of multiple slips

Ordering and filing of LC cards.

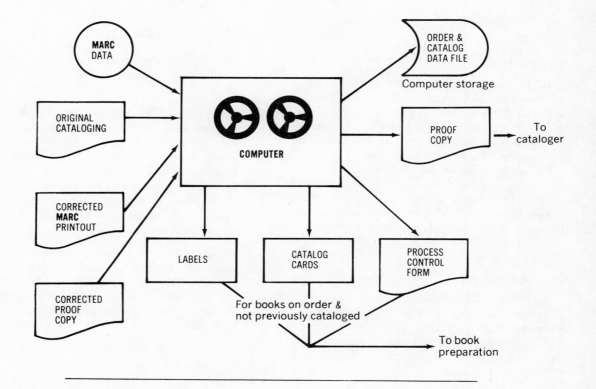

Further Step for Production of Catalog in Book Form

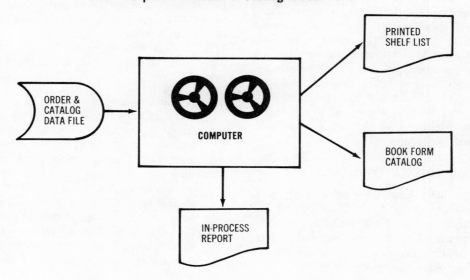

Figure 27.   Automated cataloging system

Shelflist Unit

All of the work of this unit would be eliminated by the computer system. The central shelflist and the union branch shelflist can both be replaced by computer listings which can be entirely produced from order information and cataloging information with no additional inputs. The marking of copy number and class number in the books should be rendered unnecessary by the presence of this information on the computer-prepared labels. However, if it is necessary to have this information in the book, it could be most efficiently copied from the label at the time the labels are pasted on.

Branch Catalog Unit

All of the work of this unit would be eliminated. However, such elimination is based upon the assumption that a uniform cataloging procedure will be adopted for Central and branches. This is not related to the introduction of computer methods.

Typing Unit

Most of the work of this unit is to be eliminated. Operation of duplicating equipment and the typing of headings and circulation cards will be completely eliminated. No typing of any kind is required when MARC copy is used unchanged. A small amount of typing would still be required to introduce changes. When original cataloging is done, keyboard work will be required to enter the data. This work is equivalent to the typing required to prepare a single master card under conventional procedures.

FORM OF THE CATALOG OUTPUTS

Once the basic cataloging information is in machine storage, the preparation of catalog outputs in either card or book form is a straightforward matter. The decision on which form should be used is a matter of cost and convenience of use. The following options are open:

1. Continuation of the card system. The computer would prepare cards for all agency catalogs and for all catalogs in the Central Library. It would also prepare shelflist cards.

2. Combination book and card catalog. At infrequent intervals, the computer would prepare a complete book catalog. In between issues of the book catalog, cards would be furnished. These would be filed in the usual fashion and would represent a cumulative supplement to the book catalog. At the next issuance of the book catalog, the cards would be discarded.

3. Book catalog. The catalog of the entire collection could be printed at infrequent intervals. Between these printings, cumulative supplement book catalogs could be printed at frequent intervals, probably once each month.

In considering the use of book catalogs, the possibility arises of showing holdings of a number of agencies in a single catalog. This must be considered, both because of increased value of this union feature of the catalog, and because of the very great decrease in printing costs which results if a book catalog is used in common by a number of agencies.

If catalogs entirely in book form are to be used, then the following approach should be considered:

1. A union catalog of all titles held by the Library, except juvenile titles, should be maintained. Automatically, because of library policy, this is a catalog of Central Library holdings. This catalog should carry coding to show the holdings of the regional libraries. A substantial number of copies of the catalog should be held at the Central Library to serve as the catalog of that library, and at the regional libraries to serve as their catalogs. Copies would also undoubtedly be in demand at locations outside of the library system.

2. All of the branches in the system should be

grouped into about five groups on a geographic basis. This will allow printing of a single union catalog for each grouping, and will allow use of symbols to indicate individual branch holdings without requiring too many symbols.

3. A restricted number of copies of a total holdings list would be prepared. This would be kept at Central and at regional libraries. It would be a single entry title only list and will show holdings of all branches. It would be prepared entirely on the computer printer and not require expensive offset printing.

4. Separate juvenile catalogs could be prepared. Presumably, the format and content would be different from that of the adult catalog. However, the organization into groups of union catalogs marked with holdings symbols might be a little difficult for juvenile readers. On the other hand, preparation of individual branch-by-branch catalogs would be too expensive.

Previous studies have shown that the approach described above, as far as the adult catalogs are concerned, is quite economical. The cost of preparing the union catalogs is offset by the fact that each union catalog replaces many card catalogs. The juvenile catalogs present a special problem.

IN-PROCESS REPORT

A unified in-process report would be produced for both acquisitions and cataloging. Periodically, all titles in active status will be printed on a status listing. The tabulation below shows the various types of status in which an item may be, and shows the event which causes the computer to recognize that the item has changed to the indicated status.

Event	*Status*
Receipt of selection notice	Selected
Receipt of order, no approval code	Books on order
Receipt of order, with approval code	Books on order, one copy en route to cataloging
Receipt of invoice input or receiving form	Books in receiving area
Receipt of invoice input or receiving form for title not cataloged	One copy en route to cataloging
Receipt of cataloging slip	Book in Cataloging Department
Receipt of catalog worksheet	Cataloging completed
Production of cards, labels, process control form	Physical preparation has started
Receipt of process control form	Physical preparation is completed
Preparation of shipping papers	Books are shipped

Computer System for Circulation and Registration

Computer systems for registration and for circulation have not been widely used in public libraries as have systems for acquisition and cataloging. Less experience and less hard cost data are therefore available. Computerized circulation has been applied successfully in college and university libraries, but conditions in such agencies differ from those in public libraries, and different kinds of circulation information are needed.

Because the plan outlined here for complete on-line circulation and registration control represents an innovation, it is proposed that the plan be reviewed with care before deciding on its adoption. There is no question of the technical feasibility of the system. What needs to be appraised first is the significance of the service improvements (the elimination of error in sending overdue notices, for example) and the by-product advantages for internal operations (such as for inventory, weeding, and selection). If these are judged to have little if any advantage, then the decision to go ahead or not should be made solely on the basis of comparative cost. Careful cost studies should be run, both for the present operation and for test runs under the computerized system.

The "on-line" feature is not essential to the proposed system; for the most part the whole operation would work if computer processing were done at the end of the service day. The "on-line" or direct communication feature will definitely add to cost of computer time. Here again the final judgment must be made after cost studies by the computer-communications staff as to the value of automatic calculation of fines and instantaneous identification of books on reserve.

It is the opinion of the survey staff, based upon observation of time now devoted to calculation of fines and to location of books to fill reserve requests, that the extra cost of on-line computer contact and communication is not justified, but that the advantages in cost, speed, and accuracy of registration and circulation control by off-line computer here outlined are significant and should be applied soon after computerization of acquisitions and cataloging occurs.

GENERAL DESCRIPTION OF THE SYSTEM

The system to be described is what is known in computer parlance as an on-line, or real-time, system. The book card and borrower's card will have punched holes which can be read by a special charging device. Physically the book card will be much like an ordinary punched card. The borrower's card will be of a special plastic for greater durability. The charging machine is a card-reading device which can interpret the punched holes in the book card and borrower's card and transmit the resulting information to a computer.

The computer that controls the system is directly connected, by means of telephone lines, to the charging machines at the Central Library and all branch libraries. The punched holes in the book cards and borrowers' cards represent unique identifying numbers for books and borrowers. Each time a book is borrowed, the charging machine transmits book number and borrower number to the computer. Each time a book is returned, the charging machine transmits the number of the returned book to the computer. In the computer files are the names and addresses corresponding to all borrower numbers and the bibliographic information corresponding to all book numbers. Thus, the computer has all of the information necessary for keeping track of books and detecting and reporting overdues.

Associated with the charging machine is a typewriter, which will be called the "book-charging typewriter." This typewriter is used to enter special information into the computer or it is actuated by the computer to print special information for the worker at the circulation station.

PROCEDURE FOR CHARGING BOOKS

1. The borrower presents the book and borrower's cards at the charging desk.

2. The worker inserts the borrower's card into the charging machine. At the time of insertion the computer system can, in exceptional circumstances, cause a special indication to be printed on the book charging typewriter. These exceptional conditions are discussed on page 192.

3. The worker inserts the book card into the charging machine.

4. The worker removes the book card from the charging machine and stamps the due date on the book card.

5. The worker returns the book card to the book pocket.

6. The above process is repeated for all books.

7. The borrower's card is returned to him.

It is not necessary to indicate the due date for the book to the computer. The computer programs have information about the standard loan period. In the computer master files is information about any deviation from the standard loan period for specific titles or specific classes of books. The computer system knows the date on which the book was charged out, and from this and the loan period it can calculate the due date (see figure 28 on page 188).

PROCEDURE FOR DISCHARGING BOOKS

1. The worker receives the books from the patron.

2. The worker removes the book card from the book pocket and inserts it into the charging machine which has been put into the discharge mode of operation.

3. If there is no response from the computer system, the worker returns the book card to the book pocket and sets the book aside.

4. Computer responses are obtained in the following instances:

    The book is overdue. In this case, the amount of the fine will be printed on the typewriter. If this occurs, the worker accepts the fine payment and depresses a special key to indicate payment of fine. If the fine is not paid at the time of the return of the book, the worker will not depress the key and the computer system will retain the record of fine due.

    The book is on reserve. The action taken in this case is described in the discussion of reserved books (see page 189).

    A replacement has been prepared for the book card. Periodically the computer system will prepare replacements for book cards. This is necessary because of card wear and because after a certain number of charges there will be no space for stamping the due date on the book card. When this indication appears on the typewriter, the worker discards the old card, obtains a replacement card from a file kept at the discharge desk, and inserts the new card into the book pocket. Rules are built into the computer program to call for card replacement after a stated number of charges. The computer retains a record of the number of charges that have occured for each book since the last card replacement. It checks this record each time the book is newly charged out. If it discovers that the maximum number of charges has been reached, it initiates the card replacement process and the replacement card is ready at the charge-out desk by the time the book is returned.

5. The above process is repeated for all books that are returned.

PROCEDURE FOR RENEWING BOOKS

Renewal is a discharge followed by a charge.

PROCEDURE WHEN CARD IS MISSING

If either or both the book card or the borrower's card is missing, the complete charging or discharging procedure described above can be carried out with the following changes:

1. If the borrower's card is missing, eligibility to borrow must be verified and the borrower number must be ascertained. The borrower number is then entered by the charging typewriter. The remainder of the charging procedure proceeds normally.

2. If the book card is missing, the book number must be ascertained. This can be accomplished by a search of the printed lists provided by the computer system. The book number is then entered via the charging

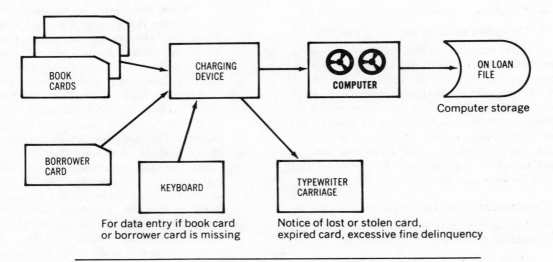

**For data entry if book card
or borrower card is missing**

**Notice of lost or stolen card,
expired card, excessive fine delinquency**

Book Discharging On-Line System

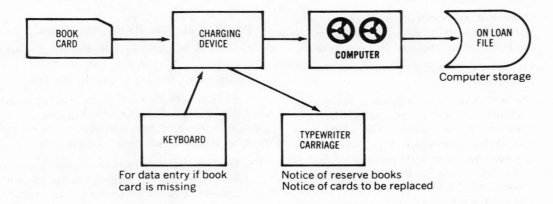

**For data entry if book
card is missing**

**Notice of reserve books
Notice of cards to be replaced**

If an off-line system were used, the direct connection from charging device
to computer would be replaced by locally prepared paper tape or punched
cards. These would be transported to the computer at the end of the day.
The notices prepared on the typewriter would be eliminated.

Figure 28.   Book charging and book discharging

typewriter. The due date is stamped on a temporary book card which is put into the book pocket. The worker depresses a special key which notifies the computer that the book card is missing. The computer will prepare a new book card which will be available at the desk when the book is returned. The remainder of the charging procedure proceeds normally.

3. If the book card is missing at the time of discharge, the book number is entered via the charging typewriter. A special key is depressed which will cause the computer to prepare a new book card. The book will be set aside pending availability of the book card. The rest of discharge procedure proceeds normally.

PROCEDURE FOR RESERVING BOOKS

1. The patron makes the reserve request.

2. The worker enters the book number at the charging typewriter to verify that the book is in circulation. If the book is in circulation, the date due back is printed on the typewriter.

3. The borrower's card is entered into the charging machine and the reserve key is depressed.

4. The borrower prepares a postcard for notification of availability of the reserved book. This is filed by the attendant at the desk.

When the book is returned and is available for circulation, the following occurs:

1. When the card is entered for discharging, the typewriter will indicate that this is a reserved book.

2. The book will be set aside, the postcard will be retrieved from the file and will be mailed.

PROCEDURE FOR DETECTING OVERDUES

No human work is required to detect overdues. The following is carried out by the machine:

1. As a result of the charging procedure described above, book numbers for books in circulation are entered into a circulation list maintained by the machine. As a result of the discharge procedure described above, book numbers of returned books are removed from the circulation list.

2. Each day the computer scans the circulation file for overdue books. For each overdue discovered, action described below is taken.

PROCEDURE FOR PREPARATION OF OVERDUE NOTICES

1. For each overdue book, the computer searches the master files for the book description corresponding to the book number and the borrower name and address corresponding to the borrower number (see figure 29 on page 190).

2. Overdue notices are printed on postcards by the computer printer. Each card is imprinted with the borrower name and address and the book description retrieved in step 1.

PROCEDURE FOR FOLLOW-UP ON OVERDUE NOTICES

1. The computer program can be arranged to provide second notices, third notices, or as many follow-up notices as are desired at stated predetermined intervals.

2. After a predetermined number of follow-up notices are printed, the computer will print a delinquent notice which goes to a member of the circulation staff. Full details, including the phone number, are given on the delinquent notice. The circulation staff member will continue follow-up by phone contact.

3. When a book for which a delinquent notice has been printed is returned, the computer system will print a notice to the circulation staff indicating that this book should be removed from the delinquent list.

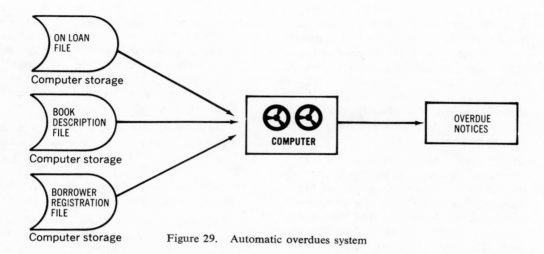

Figure 29. Automatic overdues system

PROCEDURE FOR RECORDING FINE PAYMENTS

1. If fine payment is made when the book is returned, then it is recorded as described on page 187 under "Book Discharging."

2. If fine payment is made after the book is returned, the borrower's card is entered into the machine, or the borrower's number is entered via the charging typewriter if the borrower's card is not present. The charging typewriter then prints the total amount of fines owed by that borrower. Payment is accepted and the key is depressed to indicate payment of the fines.

3. If necessary, the system can be programmed so that partial payment can be accepted and the amount of partial payment indicated.

PROCEDURES FOR REGISTRATION OF BORROWERS AND BORROWER REGISTRATION RECORDS

1. The borrower fills out an application form and signs it (figure 30).

2. A borrower number is assigned from a computer-prepared list of available numbers, which is kept at the registration desk.

3. A temporary borrower's card is issued to the borrower.

4. The application goes to the Computer Center for entry into the system.

5. At the Computer Center, the information about the borrower goes into the computer files. A permanent borrower's card is prepared and is transmitted to the library, where it will be picked up by the borrower. The original application form, with the borrower's signature, is filed chronologically by date of application.

6. Periodically, borrowers' lists are prepared by the computer. At infrequent intervals the total borrowers' list is printed and at frequent intervals cumulative supplements are printed. Lists are printed both in borrower's number sequence and in borrower's name sequence.

7. Borrowers are dropped from the computer files automatically after the registration period has expired. If desired, the system can be programmed to prepare a notice of pending expirations some time prior to termination of the registration period, properly addressed for mailing to the borrower. Periodically, lists of expired bor-

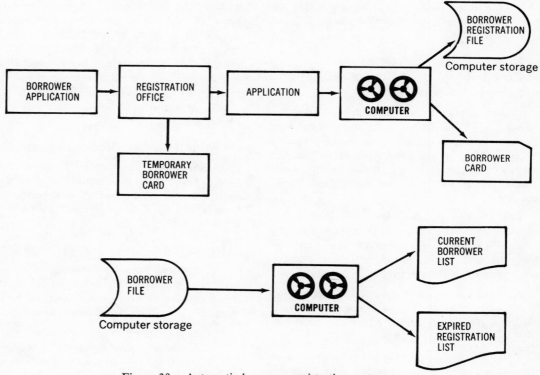

Figure 30. Automatic borrower registration system

rower records are printed for historical purposes and notices to the circulation department are prepared which will allow them to remove and destroy the original applications representing borrowers whose cards have expired.

8. The computer will maintain a file of delinquent borrowers. This file will be maintained after expiration of the registration period as long as the borrower remains delinquent. Notices will be printed to instruct the circulation department to save the original application forms belonging to such delinquent borrowers. When new applications are processed, the computer will do a name and address check against the delinquent file to avoid the possibility of issuance of a new card to a delinquent under a new number.

9. To eliminate keyboarding labor when cards are renewed, it would be possible to have the applicant fill out a new application, check it against his present card, and if the information had not changed, enter the old card into the charging machine, along with a code to indicate that the card was to be renewed. The user could continue to use the old card until a new one was prepared.

10. When a name or address change occurred, the new information would be entered into the computer. However, it would not be necessary to issue a new card. The information on the old card could be crossed out

and rewritten by the borrower. It is only the information in the computer file that is relevant in communicating with the borrower.

NOTIFICATION OF EXCEPTIONAL CONDITIONS WHEN BORROWER'S CARD IS INSERTED

Under certain circumstances, when the borrower's card is inserted into the charging machine, the computer system will cause special notices to be printed on the charging typewriter. These are intended to guard against misuse of borrowers' cards. Notices will be printed under the following conditions:

1. If the card has been lost or stolen, the card number will be kept in a computer file. When someone attempts to use that card, the fact that it has been reported lost or stolen will be typed out.

2. If the card number is invalid, a type-out will occur. Normally this would occur only under the circumstance that a formerly valid card number had expired.

3. If the card belongs to a borrower with delinquent fines in excess of some predetermined total, a type-out of this information will occur.

USE WITH THE RENTAL COLLECTION

The system as described is usable with the rental collection. The fines recording procedure is adapted for use in recording rental fees and all other procedures remain as stated.

INTERLIBRARY LOAN AND LOANS FROM THE CENTRAL LIBRARY TO BRANCHES

These loans are handled by the same mechanism that is set up for loans to library patrons. Each borrowing library is assigned a borrower's number. Each branch library is assigned a borrower's number. When books are charged out, the borrower's number assigned to the borrowing library or branch can be entered via the charging typewriter, or a borrower's card can be prepared for the library or branch and kept in a file at the desk where this type of charging occurs. For branches of the Chicago Public Library and for outside libraries to whom loans are frequently made, preparation of such a card would be convenient. The computer programs would allow for a different loan period for these types of borrowers. It might also be desirable to print overdue notices in a format different from that used for library patrons.

INQUIRIES ABOUT BOOKS IN CIRCULATION

At any time, the charging typewriter can be used to find out if a book should be present on the shelves or if it is out on loan to a borrower, to a branch of the Chicago Public Library, or to another library.

INVENTORY

The present continuous reading of shelves for inventory purposes would not be required with the circulation control system described here. The inventory procedure would be as follows:

1. Every year, or every two years, the computer system would prepare a listing of all books that had not circulated in the previous year or previous two years and are not currently in circulation.

2. The shelves would be searched for all books on this listing.

3. Any book on the listing that was not found on the shelves could be presumed to be missing.

WEEDING

The circulation control system can provide a valuable guide to weeding. Periodically, the computer system could prepare a printing of all books held at an agency, listing the books in order of circulation. At the head of the list would be those books which had not circulated at all in the period under consideration. Those books which had not circulated, or had circulated infrequently, could be sent to another agency, put into some convenient storage location, or discarded.

Reports of Fines and Rentals

The system will prepare all needed accounting reports relevant to income from fines and rentals and income due from fines and rentals. The reports can show totals by time period and breakdowns by agency.

Selection, Added Copy, and Replacement Guidance

The listing of titles in order of circulation, mentioned above for weeding purposes, can also be used for acquisition guidance. A library that is considering an older title might look at the circulation history of that title, as shown by the listings prepared for other agencies which did acquire the title, in order to decide upon acquisition. An agency could use the higher circulation end of its own listing as a guide to procurement of added copies. If a book is lost, then before replacing it the agency might want to look at the circulation history of that book.

9 Organization of the Library

In the broad sense, the organization of the Chicago Public Library extends from the formal legal authorization which brings it into existence to the informal internal communication which keeps it going. Strategic elements include the governing board, the chief librarian, and the structure of general and middle-management officers. Together these organizational factors, formal and informal, set the scope and limits of the institution and determine the direction in which it moves. In the end the measure is what occurs when user and library make contact and the skill and attitude of the staff member are put to the test; but back of service and staff are officers and organization, either leading and coordinating or limiting and frustrating the enterprise.

Legal Foundation

Four elements enter into the legal base of the Chicago Public Library: state statutes which apply specifically to libraries (those setting the form of library government, for example), general state legislation which includes libraries (those specifying civil service, for example), local municipal ordinances and practices (those regulating the handling of finances, for example), and actions of the Library Board itself (those formulating the rules and regulations for the agency, for example). There is yet another aspect to this picture; the Chicago Public Library has metropolitan and regional responsibilities, both by law and by actual service practice. It is the balance among these several legal and quasi-legal elements, and the

occasional conflict among them, that determines the governmental character of the Library.

The Chicago Public Library is a legal creation of the State of Illinois. Its governmental structure is prescribed in state law and the upper limits for its local financial support are specified in state legislation. Legally the Library is an educational arm of the State, although it is primarily administered and supported locally.

State statutes specify policy-making and administrative control of the Chicago Public Library by a lay board of nine directors appointed by the Mayor of Chicago. The authority and responsibilities of the Board are set forth at length and include such broad powers as ". . . exclusive control of the expenditure of all moneys collected for the library" and the authority ". . . to appoint a competent librarian and necessary assistants, to fix their compensation, to remove such appointees" (Illinois Revised Statutes, 1967, Chapter 81, Section 4–7). Other more general laws affect the Library along with other public bodies, in part limiting the broad powers specified in the library acts. Some of these are of major import (the application of civil service regulations to municipalities in hiring of employees, for example), and some are of a specific nature (Illinois Revised Statutes, 1967, Chapter 29, Section 36 provides that coal purchased for fuel purposes must be mined in Illinois if the cost is not more than 10 percent above that available elsewhere). From time to time the state-level legal prescription is extended or modified by the legislature, as in the application in 1961 to libraries of the provisions of the Illinois Code for the drawing of contracts and the letting of purchase orders. All public libraries in the state follow this pattern, but different and explicit limits are set on financial support for the Chicago Public Library —at a rate lower than that which applies to other cities.

In 1965 the state passed legislation for the "establishment and development of a network of public library systems," and provided financial aid for the purpose. In a declaration of policy in the act of 1965 (Illinois Revised Statutes, 1967, Chapter 81, Section 111), it is stated that "Since the state has a financial responsibility in promoting public education, and since the public library is a vital agency serving all parts of the educational process, it is hereby declared to be the policy of the state to encourage the improvement of free public libraries." Thus the State of Illinois not only authorizes local libraries but also is committed to their development and improvement.

Chicago qualifies as a library system in its own right under explicit terms of the law (Section 116), and as such receives state financial aid. The Chicago Public Library is also designated as one of four "research and reference centers" (Section 122), which together are to improve the level of resources and facilities available to all residents of Illinois. Under this law Chicago is responsible for resources and for interlibrary loans for northern Illinois. This state action in effect places an additional responsibility on the Chicago library and officially makes its resources available beyond the boundaries of the city. In the chapter of this report dealing with finance (chapter 10), the question is raised whether the state, having mandated reference and research service by the Chicago Public Library to northern Illinois, has provided funds adequate for the purpose.

The 1891 act (Section 30) authorizing construction of the central building of the Chicago Public Library on the present Dearborn Park site specified that the structure include ". . . a memorial hall to commemorate the patriotism and sacrifices of the Union soldiers and sailors of the late Civil War." This occurred because the Soldiers' Home of Chicago owned the northern one-quarter of the site. The original leasehold was for fifty years. In 1941 this was extended and at the same time the use expanded to ". . . other organizations of United States soldiers, sailors and marines of succeeding wars and expeditions of the United States, having their headquarters in Cook County." In 1949 the use of the rooms surrounding the Memorial Hall—the auditorium, the rotunda, the Visual Materials Center, and rooms devoted to conference and display purposes—passed by law to the Library, leaving only the Hall to the leaseholder, the Grand Army Hall and Memorial Association of Illinois.

The historical exhibit in the Hall commemorates Civil War events and the activities of Civil War participants from the Chicago area. This exhibit has remained static in content, and the use of the Hall has not changed or expanded since the revised legislation in 1941. The displays related to the Civil War have served their purpose on the present site and in the present quarters. Now this location, either in the existing library building or in a new library structure, is not favorable for an exhibit associated with the history of Chicago. It should be transferred to the Chicago Historical Society, where the artifacts and mementos would produce a stronger combined collection, where they would stand among other Chicago historical material and thus be related to earlier and later periods, and where the active educational program of the Society would bring them to the attention of Chicagoans, particularly young people who need greater knowledge of their heritage.

Removal of the Memorial Hall from the Library will require state legislation. The alternative is to plan quarters for the Hall in a new library building, but this cost hardly seems justified when the essential purpose of the exhibit can better be served by coordinated action with another and more closely related institution, the Chicago Historical Society.

Legal relations with the City of Chicago raise certain questions, deriving from the fact that both are formed under state law and have broad power by state statute over their respective affairs. Various matters are clear in the law or have been settled by court action. The Library is not a tax-levying or tax-collecting body. As to custody of tax money collected, in 1908 the courts held (*City of Chicago* v. *County of Cook,* 136 Illinois 120) that "The city and not the Library Board is the authority to which the library tax is payable. The library tax fund is the property of the city." The law regarding the authority of the municipality to reduce the appropriation or library tax determination of a library board is less clear and currently is under judicial review; a recent case (*Effertz* v. *Brozinski,* 234 NE 2386) holds that municipal bodies are not required to follow library board recommendations for taxation.

In dealing with the question of the applicability of civil service regulations to libraries, the court in 1940 (*Board of Library Directors of the City of Springfield* v. *Snigg,* 303 Illinois 340) made a general pronouncement on the relation of library boards to municipal authorities: "Under the statute authorizing the establishment and maintenance of a public library . . . the directors were appointed by the Mayor with the approval of the City Council. Reading the entire statute together we think its whole scope and intent is that the Library Board is part of the city government. Without the City Council the Library Board is . . . wholly unable

to effect the objects of its creation." This case in turn was based on the earlier *Johnson* v. *City of Chicago,* 258 Illinois 494, where the decision was rendered that the City of Chicago and not the Library was the proper party to sue for the negligence of a library employee. Similarly, as early as 1896, when suit was brought against the Board of Directors of the Chicago Public Library for breach of a building contract, the court dismissed the case on the ground that suit should have been brought against the City.

For the most part problems and conflicts do not arise or have been worked out in practice. The legal precedence of the municipality is recognized in most matters. The Library acts in accord with city ordinances, regulations, and procedures, functioning more as a department of the city than do either the school system or the park district. City officers in their turn tend to think of the Library as an integral part of municipal government, particularly in fiscal matters.

But potential issues remain, particularly in the sensitive area of finance. Two recent incidents illustrate the problem, one having to do with local fiscal practice and the other with control over the application for and expenditure of state and federal funds.

On February 3, 1969, the Office of City Comptroller notified the Library that it had sold $2,500,000 in tax warrants for library operations (such warrants must be sold because Chicago operates on funds in anticipation of taxes still to be collected). The Library Board had not requested the sale of the warrants, and the Library did not have immediate need for the funds. The interest rate for the issue was 5¼ percent. The city could realize only part of this cost by short-loan investment of the money not being used, and in any case would credit the Library with only part of the earnings, as evidenced by the fact that the record of earnings on Library balances in 1968 amounted to less than 2 percent. The Library therefore had to carry extra and unnecessary interest payments amounting to over $10,000. Such unilateral action by a city office, placing unnecessary interest charges on library funds, does not accord with the statute specifying that the Library Board shall have ". . . exclusive control of the expenditures of all moneys collected for the Library." Separate from the legal question of whether the imposition of an unnecessary interest charge on the Library does or does not constitute interference in the "expenditures" of funds, it would seem to be prudent management on the part of the city not to sell tax warrants and start incurring interest charges until the money is actually needed. It is natural for a city fiscal agency to seek full control over the funds which it handles, but in the case of the Library specific state law prevents any such take-over.

The second recent instance of potential conflict is a directive of 25 April 1969 from the city to "Department Heads" concerning the handling of state and federal aid. The City Comptroller's Office is given responsibility for review and approval of all budgets and financial plans relating to projects funded by the state or federal governments; for preparation of grant fund requisitions; and for accounting, auditing, and preparation of financial reports. It is sensible for a municipality to seek to coordinate and control such outside projects. However, the application of the order to the Library Board raises legal questions both of appropriate procedure and of legitimate control. Detailed state law and regulations of the Secretary of State prescribe the various conditions for financial grants to "library systems" in the case of per capita aid and to the "Chicago Public Library" for research and reference service, both presumably meaning the Board of Library Directors as

recipient of the funds. These legal requirements at the state level will have to be reconciled with the local directive. Similarly, federal funds coming through the state to the Library are authorized in a national Library Service and Construction Act, also supplemented by regulations on requisition and control of funds appropriated under this act. In this instance municipal, state, *and* federal practices must be in step.

It is worth noting that these problems are not isolated instances that once resolved will not occur in some other form. In terms of actual patron use, an agency such as the Chicago Public Library is more than a municipal institution. In terms of law, it is more than local because of its mandated responsibility outside the city. In terms of financial support the Library already receives 15 percent of its total money from nonlocal sources, and this proportion may well increase as further progress is made toward national, state, and regional networks of library service, with the Chicago Public Library playing its proper role in such intergovernmental systems. A library of this scope and strategic strength cannot be viewed solely as a local department of a single municipality. Legislation in the period ahead will increasingly define the Library's role as a public educational and informational resource beyond Chicago.

Resolution of these potential legal conflicts is in the interest of both the City of Chicago and of the Chicago Public Library. In the end, service to the people will be increased and costs shared equitably. These goals are not incompatible with close relations with the city government, but they should not be lost sight of in devising mechanisms for internal control within the municipality. To keep the relationship on a smooth and productive basis calls for adaptability on the part of the Library on the one side and also calls for recognition of the legal prerogatives and the extracity service responsibilities of the Library Board on the part of city authorities. It would be wise to review and clarify city-library relationships together in the light of these several considerations. On this cooperative basis, adjudication in the courts of the respective powers of the municipality and of the Library Board will not become necessary.

Board of Directors

The function of the Board is to set policy and impart direction and improvement to the Library. It can do this in various ways and at many points—in the selection of administrative officers with the best professional qualifications, in program evaluation, in budget review, in establishing personnel standards and salaries, and by promoting the library cause in civic and other groups. A lay board is at its best and most constructive when it is in active interplay with the professional administration, bringing initiative, judgment, and community review to the service program developed by the professional staff and officers. There are dangers on either side of such board-administrative balance —either an apathetic Board that holds the Library back, or an overzealous Board that instigates fragments of a library program through a "captive" Chief Librarian.

The Chicago Public Library has a relatively "new" Board, in that five of nine members have served for three years or less. One of the recent appointees functions as President. There is a veteran member with over forty years of service, and the remaining three have served for periods from seven to ten years.

The group represents a variety of viewpoints and backgrounds. There is a specialist in Lincoln material and fine books, an engineer, a clergyman, a labor official, an optometrist, a newspaper publisher, and a university professor. Two women members are active in the affairs of distinct groups in the city. Two members are Negroes. In age distribution the majority are in the middle years, with two older members and one who is relatively young. As vacancies occur it would be wise to seek out additional young members and individuals active in community affairs at the local level.

A comparison of Board minutes for 1963 and 1968 reveals some improvement in attendance on the part of trustees. In the former year, two members did not attend any meetings. In 1968, while no such flagrant neglect of library business was evident, two members missed more sessions than they attended, and two more missed five or more meetings. A question should be raised about bimonthly sessions; meetings once a month would suffice to discharge board business, the attendance record would be better, and there would be suitable time in the intervals between meetings for preparation by the Chief Librarian of data and recommendations for consideration by the Board.

Procedures of the Board have recently been streamlined. The several committees criticized in the 1938 study have been reduced to two, one for administration and one for buildings. Lengthy readings of lists of appointees and of purchases have been eliminated; these details now appear in the minutes of Board meetings. Time is thus freed for consideration of policy and program. Topics dealt with during 1968 by the Board included salary scales, building policies, and legislative needs. The Acting Librarian has brought in staff members to describe aspects of the Library's work and inform the trustees of what the Library actually does.

However, the Board of Directors and the professional administrators have not yet worked out joint procedures for consecutive planning and sustained review of policies. Topics are brought before the Board without prior notice or supporting data. Members themselves raise questions which are discussed briefly and then dropped without further analysis. The Board does not enter into the budget-making process until the finished request is ready for transmittal to city authorities, at which time basic policy review is no longer feasible. In short, this is a Board that reaches decisions with relatively little staff work to inform its actions, and a Board that approves or modifies policy on the basis of only cursory study.

This is also an "activist" Board, often anxious to act quickly. Specific program proposals are made and pushed for immediate adoption by individual members in the course of meetings, without review or analysis. It is quite proper for lay board members to suggest projects and lines of development. These should then be referred to the administrative staff for planning and detailed proposals. Normally recommendations for action should originate with the staff and officers, then the proposals reviewed from a policy standpoint by the Board. The Board of Directors, in its zeal to improve the Library, tends to propose and then authorize specific projects; its greater contribution would be to study and recommend policies and set goals and directions within which the administrative officers would design action programs. Unless Board and staff each recognize what its role is and should be, the program of the Library will become disjointed and out of balance, and the resentment and frustration of the strongest and ablest of senior staff members will continue to grow. There are the coaches and the players; both sides must remember their roles.

Finally, the Board of Directors of the Chicago Public Library faces some difficult public decisions in the next year or two—about a new central building as this relates to some public sentiment for the present structure, about demands for new branch buildings, and about the need for new and continuing service programs. Resolution as well as tact will be needed and criticism as well as praise will result. The test is whether the Board will make the hard decisions required or whether those conditions which curtail and hinder service will be allowed to prevail. There has been a period of review and study; now attention should shift to priorities and action.

In the course of the survey Board minutes and reports of the past five years were reviewed, Board meetings were attended in 1968 and early 1969, and most Board members were interviewed. A sense of purpose and direction is emerging. Every member has better service as a goal, and each approaches this from a special viewpoint which contributes to total planning. But this interest and variety must be harnessed and systematically directed to underlying policies and standards, rather than expended on immediate and isolated projects, for it is at the roots that self-renewal of the Library must be nurtured.

General Administrative Officers

The administrative structure of the Chicago Public Library has atrophied at the upper level in recent years. Never strong in general officers, the Library's senior group was further reduced as vacancies occurred. The positions of Assistant Librarian in charge of Branches and of Supervisor of Children's Service were eliminated earlier. When the former Assistant Librarian for Personnel retired in 1966, the vacated position was downgraded in rank (from Librarian VI to Librarian V), and has gone unfilled; although a civil service examination for this position was set recently, the downgrading has the practical effect that now the Library is trying to recruit at a relatively low salary of

$14,856 for this key position responsible for rebuilding staff in a professional and service enterprise of 1600 employees. The position of Assistant Librarian for Technical Services (acquisitions, cataloging, book preparation, and binding) has stood vacant since mid-1967, when the incumbent was designated Acting Librarian.

In recent years the organization had become highly centralized and dependent on one individual. There were very few senior officers to help carry the institutional load, and no "cabinet" group to share the responsibilities and enrich the review of policies and the making of plans. All depended on the Chief Librarian. When that individual resigned in 1967, a vacuum was created. Just when the Library faced a crisis in public esteem, its top administrative team was at its weakest.

There is one Assistant Librarian for the Central Library but no comparable officer for the branch and extension program. There is a business officer but not a personnel officer. Clearly designated coordinators are lacking for children's service and for young adult service. There is no associate or deputy librarian with system-wide responsibilities. The person directing the whole system is designated as Acting Librarian. The one Assistant Librarian and the three regional branch librarians find themselves loaded with functions and details beyond their formal assignments. The result is that the Library does not have an administrative group with time and strength to plan in any depth, to lead the agency in change and innovation, to carry out programs thoroughly, to supervise and inspire middle-level managers, and to evaluate what has been accomplished.

The strain has become more marked in the last year as the Acting Librarian has taken steps to get the agency moving. Only a few senior people are available to take up the cause; they are on the one hand stimulated by the new prospects but on the other feel even more burdened. New projects take on a hasty and even desperate quality under these circumstances, and run the risk of failing or fading out when close and continuing care might have nurtured them into healthy maturity. At the same time little attention can be given to the strengthening of basic and ongoing service, from book selection policies to staff attitudes toward the public, from branch-central communication to recruiting and training of new personnel. Together these various gaps and vacancies make for an emasculated and harassed top administrative team, the members of which deserve public acclaim for their complete dedication.

But the existence of these same gaps and vacancies creates an opportunity. Strong appointments at the top levels would quickly bring force and direction to the total program, even as weak appointments will retard the Library for many years.

The officers lacking are of several types: overall responsibility for system-wide programs and problems (such as an Associate or Deputy Librarian), direct-line officers handling broad areas of operation (such as branches and technical operations), auxiliary officers (as for personnel), and planning-coordinating officers (such as a coordinator of children's service). Figure 31 shows the proposed structure of general and middle management in the Chicago Public Library.

The broad division of responsibility among the several senior officers is important, so that each supplements and reinforces the others and together they provide the leadership and coordination which the Library needs. The Chief Librarian will of course be the administrative officer responsible for the total enterprise. In particular, as conceived here, the Chief Li-

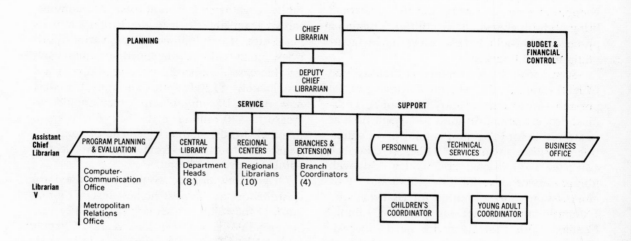

Figure 31. Proposed organization of general officers and middle managers

brarian would devote himself to planning, external relations, and the direction of development of the agency. He would prepare the budget (as the financial plan for future development) and prepare policy proposals for the Board (as the steps in future growth). He would evaluate progress and performance. He would actively represent the Library in civic, educational, and library affairs of the city and the metropolitan area. The Chief Librarian would essentially plot the course, inspire the staff, and judge progress—that is, he is to be the leader.

To direct the myriad operations there should be a Deputy Chief Librarian. He would be the officer on deck, steering the course that has been set. His responsibilities would not be limited to part of the library operation but would extend across the board. All Assistant Chief Librarians with line responsibilities would report to him. His job would be to see that the various divisions of the Library get their tasks done, and that they do so jointly and in coordination. At the same time, the Deputy Chief Librarian would function as a member of the Librarian's inner cabinet, along with an Assistant Librarian for Planning and Evaluation and the Business Manager, calling on such of the other assistant librarians and coordinators as needed for particular purposes.

Allied with the Chief Librarian and helping him with planning should be both the present Business Manager and a new officer serving as Assistant Librarian in charge of Program Planning and Evaluation. The business officer would participate in planning sessions as the agency's fiscal expert, knowing what funds are available, how they are used, and how they might be reallocated. The new Assistant Librarian would be the Chief's research arm, handling matters as specific as an exact new branch location and as general as the evaluation of collections for subject specialists. As new experimental programs are authorized, this office would gather data to determine results. A young and vigorous person in this post would bring both timeliness and depth to the planning process and would be a key person in facilitating needed change.

Seven positions are proposed at the Assistant Chief Librarian level. Four of these exist at present—for Central Library, Personnel, Technical Processes, and Business Management. The new position for Program Planning and Evaluation has been mentioned. Then, as described (on page 107) in chapter 5, which deals with library service over the city, there should be an Assistant Chief Librarian for Branches and Extension and another for Regional Library Centers. Both these activities need city-wide direction and coordination, and each is both large enough (one to have some 600 employees and the other 300) and different enough (one to deal with collections averaging 25,000 volumes in size and the other with collections of 175,000–200,000 volumes) to require its own director. The Assistant Librarians should be classified and compensated at the Librarian VI level; the Chief Librarian and the Deputy Chief Librarian both are to be exempted from civil service and serve at the pleasure of the Board, with salaries of $35,000 and $30,000 respectively.

Thus the Chicago Public Library, now with a very few officers carrying general responsibility, would have nine senior administrators at or above $20,000 in salary. They would be of distinctly different types and capacities, and together would constitute the planners, directors, and controllers of the system. Because the ranks of middle managers at the next lower level are also thin at present, civil service examinations for Assistant Chief Librarian should be original, thus opening competition both to senior staff now in the Library and to strong

administrators from outside. Here is the opportunity to gather a fresh and balanced administrative team able to lead the Library into its next stage of development. These various positions, along with recommended substantial salary increases applying to them, will add approximately $120,000 to an annual budget now over $10 million and which should increase to $20 million in the next few years—in other words, under 1 percent of total expenditures to change from weak to effective administrative direction.

Of great importance would be two age-level coordinators at the next highest level (Librarian V), for children's service (to age 12) and young adult service (the teen years). Chapter 5, in which service programs were discussed, stressed the point that public library service to younger readers of this generation should be revitalized, with a review scheduled for 1980 to determine the degree of development of school libraries by that time. In substance the various middle managers—central department heads, regional center librarians, and particularly branch coordinators—plan for service to older students and to adults. The Children's and Young Adult Coordinators will be concerned with facilities, materials, personnel, and programs for younger users, functioning in a staff relationship to the various departmental, regional center, and branch managers.

Two additional new officers at the Librarian V level are needed for emerging aspects of library service. One would direct the Communications-Computer Center recommended in chapter 8, which describes the new technology. The other would serve as the liaison officer for metropolitan relations with other libraries and with schools. Both are to report directly to the Chief Librarian, functioning as his senior staff officers in the areas of enlarging responsibilities and opportunities for the period ahead. In time it is likely that the new technology and a metropolitan network of liaison services may have as profound an effect on the Chicago Public Library as any changes and improvements in internal operations and service.

The ranks of middle management in the Chicago Public Library, below the general officers, have also been limited. The proposed organizational plan calls for 22 positions at this level, and classified as Librarian V. Five central subject department heads are specified, for Art and Music, History and Travel, Humanities, Social Science, and Science. Each of these departments would also have one or more Librarian IV positions, such as for education and for business in the Social Science Department. Three intensified service units that cut across subject lines also need high-level middle managers: the Information-Bibliographic Center, the Contemporary Media Center, and the Family Materials Center.

Then there are to be ten heads of regional library centers spread out as strong points over the city. The reorganized community branch program calls for four task-force coordinators for neighborhood service in separate parts of the city, and a fifth officer (at the Librarian IV level) as head of functional extension to groups. These proposals substantially increase the number of upper-level supervisors and coordinators, who together with the seven Assistant Chief Librarians will bring administrative strength and leadership to the Library.

The proposed organization for branches constitutes a distinct change from the present structure. At present the three regional librarians each carry administrative responsibility for part of the branches. They have become bogged down in management details and the branches lack effective program guidance and stimula-

tion. A basic recommendation of this report is that the branches depart from the present stereotyped provision and activities that prevail over the city, each adapting itself completely to its neighborhood. This fundamental change will require steady and sensitive direction and guidance.

The proposal here is that the present regional librarians become service and coordinating rather than management officers, working closely with branch librarians and developing fresh services and resource patterns. Administrative direction of the complete branch system will come from a central branch office, to which these Branch Coordinators will report. Thus they will be able to concentrate on service, and they will have the immediate assistance of a professional task force of eight to ten persons for the purpose. There will be four such Branch Coordinators and task forces, two for the inner city (the West Side including the near-northwest Cabrini Homes section, and the South Side), and two for the north-northwest areas and the south-southwest areas. The proposed structure of branch administration is shown in figure 32. Along with the Branch Coordinators will be a Director of Group Collections, to build an expanded program for groups and organizations on the base of the present Deposits Department. The branches and the group collections together will comprise a two-dimensional extension activity, geographical and functional.

Middle-level management and coordination were found to be particularly blurred and uncertain among such auxiliary functions as purchasing, shipping, supplies, and mailroom. On inquiry the Business Office expressed the view that the Personnel Office has responsibility for shipping and delivery; Personnel in turn said that it belonged to Business; and the head of

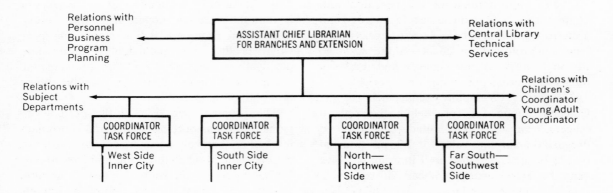

Figure 32.   Branch organization

shipping was of the opinion that he answers directly to the Chief Librarian. The formal organization chart of the Library shows shipping under the Personnel Department, an odd location evidently carrying over from an interest of the Assistant Librarian who retired in 1966. These auxiliary functions need to be pulled together, authority established, and standards of performance set. An administrative assistant under the Business Manager is needed for the purpose.

The combination of Chief Librarian and Deputy Chief Librarian positions, both now vacant, open up alternative possibilities for getting top leadership for the Library. One alternative is to seek out a nationally qualified person of middle years to assume direction of the institution for the next two decades or more, with an older and experienced administrator serving in the Deputy position. Or, if the right Chief Librarian is not located, another alternative is to confirm the present Acting Librarian in the post, and to seek out a highly promising younger administrator who would serve as Deputy for a period and then if qualified move into the top job. Either way

the agency would have the benefit both of experienced management and of fresh direction. It is proposed that a search be instituted among library administrators in the country with these alternatives in mind, the decision on the alternative adopted to depend on the applicants who come forward.

In any case, directorship of the Chicago Public Library is one of the two or three top public-library positions in the country, and at this stage may be the most challenging. The job calls for a remarkable combination of qualities, of which seven are set down here as a guide in seeking the new director.

1. Ability to plan for the future, to see beyond present problems and take a macroscopic view, to think in metropolitan and cosmopolitan terms

2. Ability to communicate at all levels: with the city's decision-makers, with the Board, with community leaders, with the educational community, with ghetto and blue-collar neighborhoods, and ethnic groups

3. Capacity to crystallize the aspirations of the staff, inspiring purpose and generating enthusiasm

4. Ability to get work done through others, leading and coordinating strong middle managers

5. Capacity to make hard and fair decisions and then stick by them, particularly in rebuilding staff

6. Quality of constructive skepticism backed up by objective evaluation of performance and progress

7. Sensitivity to the variety of people, the complexity of problems, and the prospect of a better urban life, all of which characterizes Chicago today.

Such leadership—at once constructive, sensitive and tough—will release the capacity that is imprisoned within the Chicago Public Library.

Communication

Communication between management and staff, among staff members, and across departmental and branch lines is an elusive but essential ingredient in holding a far-flung organization together. If individuals get the information they need to do their jobs, work gets done, and the load of supervision is reduced. If at the same time, in the course of communication, staff members get a sense of an efficient and effective agency standing behind them, morale receives a definite boost.

The Chicago Public Library is organized into just under 100 units—branches, departments, divisions, and offices. At best, communication in this scattered organization would be difficult. Interviews with staff, questions testing their degree of information, analysis of communication media, and observation in the field all suggest that the flow of information is sporadic and that at certain points psychological barriers inhibit communication.

The first requirement is the recording of practices and decisions. The *Staff Manual* seeks to convey basic matters of wide application, both of policy and of procedure. It contains 1198 numbered paragraphs and is in looseleaf form to facilitate revision. Its length precludes ready communication of broad purposes and policies, so that it is more a procedures manual for initial study of a process or for later review of details. The problem is to keep the *Staff Manual* up to date. Revised sheets are slow to arrive. In general, it conveys a sense of inflexible routines in service matters and leaves little room for judgment in meeting special situations. Users complain that the index is inadequate.

It is suggested that the several distinct functions of the *Staff Manual* be identified, and separate sections be issued for the different purposes. Some sections could be retained in looseleaf form for ease of regular revision, but others could better be in more compact printed form, done economically and reissued at intervals. The *Staff Handbook* now being compiled, to contain information about personnel practices and benefits, is an example of what is proposed for the *Staff Manual*.

The staff member who seeks to keep up with official developments and problems of the Library has two vehicles for the purpose: the *Proceedings* of Board meetings and a monthly *Bulletin* from the Office of the Librarian. The former are routine and institutionalized, stressing the details of purchases, construction authorizations and personnel appointments, and compressing into cryptic summaries the occasional discussion of policy, program, and personnel matters by the Board. The *Bulletin* is informative and describes new projects and staff activities, but it is retrospective; staff members often hear first about new library activities and policies through the public press. The *Bulletin* by its nature has an official or "establishment" attitude, presenting matters from the standpoint of the front office. The *Staff News* of the Staff Association, which could deal with library matters from the standpoint of the staff, is primarily devoted to personnel notes and notices of social affairs.

Many matters of policy and practice are not set down in any form. This starts with book selection standards, on which a staff group is currently working. Manuals are lacking for acquisition and cataloging activities, procedures for which are carried in the heads of one or a few supervisors. It is not common for records to be made of occasional staff meetings that are held. Department heads and branch librarians get precise information about the amounts of their book budgets, but are not informed about and have only the most general notion of what the total budgets for their units may be.

Staff meetings occur infrequently throughout the system. At the Central Library, prior to a series of sessions recently held on selection policies, meetings of department heads evidently occurred at intervals of several months. When sessions do occur, persons who could contribute and who in any case should be informed—the business manager, the public relations officer, a representative of the Personnel Office—are usually not included. Practices differ from branch to branch, but those staff meetings occurring during the course of the survey tended to deal usually with concrete "problem" matters and seldom with prospects for service or professional trends. On the other hand, the branch children's librarians do get together at regular intervals, and discuss materials and services as well as procedures. Meetings of either all of the staff or of representatives of the various agencies occur only at the widest intervals, so that there is no direct personal channel for communication between central administration and individual worker.

Annual reports are prepared by service departments and by branches but are not shared, so that administrators do not get a sense of the accomplishments and problems of other divisions of the Library.

The pragmatic test is whether staff members serving the public are informed about what they need to know to give successful service. No inclusive judgment can be offered on this point, but members of the panel of users in some cases brought back surprising reports. A branch reference librarian had not been informed about extended hours of central subject departments. A Central Library subject librarian was misinformed about the scope of resources of the Newberry Library. Branch librarians tell the public that reference books cannot be obtained on short-loan among agencies, although the *Staff Manual* states that such books may be borrowed for three days. These may be isolated instances, but they raise a warning signal.

More pervasive is the attitude of staff members in seeking information about other parts of the Library. Individuals may not only know little about other service departments, but they are prone to think that they do not need to know. A communications barrier seems to exist between the Central Library and the branches. Branch librarians in some cases say that they hesitate to call central subject departments with difficult subject questions because they anticipate an inhospitable response. Department librarians complain of the inadequate information given on short-loan requests from branches, and the branches return the compliment by complaining of slow and inappropriate responses from Central to these requests. The branch librarians in particular express the feeling that they are on the outside and not cognizant with what is going on throughout the system.

A recent suggestion contest prompted a favorable staff response, probably as much because it was an expression of interest in staff opinion as for the nominal prizes provided. The winning suggestions have tended to be concrete and practical in nature, such as a change in a printed form in one instance. This device of a suggestion contest would have a fresh appeal if awards were given for the most original as well as for the most immediately useful ideas.

Communication is not just a one-way street, with information and directives passed down from superior to subordinate. Staff members themselves have relevant information to report, as well as opinions and ideas to contribute to policy-making and problem-solving. Because staff meetings are infrequent and other channels unavailable, junior professionals in particular feel left out. More than once, after survey team members had interviews with younger staff members, the individuals were moved to write warm notes of thanks, saying the interview had been their first chance to express their views. Actually some of the ideas expressed by such persons were among the most original and practical of those put forth by staff at any level. Perhaps as much as any other single ingredient the Chicago Public Library needs young ideas; actually it has a reservoir within its own ranks that it is not tapping. From the employee's standpoint, consideration of his views goes far toward giving him a sense of place and effectiveness in the organization. This is a period of participating democracy in administration as well as in politics, and both service institutions and government in general can benefit from the trend.

A clogging and blurring of communication both ways is not exceptional in a large and decentralized organization. But staff members in the Chicago Public Library have drifted apart, first into separate work units and then into individual jobs, as a consequence of a period of administration by fiat. There was limited occasion for individual judgment and therefore limited need to communicate, at least up the line. This heritage remains and has progressed to the point where some staff members now feel not only isolated but alienated from the institution. They see fresh stirring in the Library, but in circumscribed spots and at a distance. A new effort to communicate is needed, not just to inform staff but to bring them into the organization. This is the function of every administrator, from the general officer to the supervisor responsible for one subordinate.

Short-Loan Service

A concrete example of interagency coordination and communication is in the loan and exchange of books and other resources among the various branches and the Central Library of the Chicago system (as distinguished from "interlibrary" loan between the Chicago Public Library and other cities and libraries). Short-loan is important in the total service design, because it theoretically makes available on request in every part of the Library any material held anywhere in the system. It also has implications for building and maintaining branch collections; if special titles can be obtained as requested, there is little reason for keeping infrequently used books on the branch shelves.

How much is this interagency service used; how well does it work; how long does it take to get requested materials?

Approximately 32,000 requests are originated annually in the branches.[1] Of these some

---

[1] Only partial statistics are kept by the Library on short-loan, and no reliable record on the total number of requests filled and unfilled. The data here are based in part on available statistics and in part on information collected for this study in a sample group of branches.

20 percent are never filled, others are not filled to the satisfaction of the inquirer, and some are so delayed in being filled that the inquirer no longer wants or needs the material. The overall success rate is therefore somewhere between 60 and 65 percent of the requests registered. This means about 20,000 volumes circulated annually through short-loan, approximately two-tenths of 1 percent of the total circulation of the Library. The volume of materials moving through interagency channels is small, but for those users who can get desired material promptly, it is a valuable service.

The short-loan privilege is not announced or advertised in the branches. The user must take the initiative, or a staff member may suggest it to him. Branch librarians give widely varying answers to the question of whether short-loan is available to high school students. Requests for material from other branches or Central cannot be made by telephone—the user must come into the branch to place his request even if he knows that the material he wants is not in the local collection. Some branch librarians were frank to say that they do not push short-loan because it takes so long on the average or the request may not be filled at all; in the end the reader may be more frustrated than if the procedure were never started. Instead, the branch librarian may go out of the way to call the regional and other branches to see if a desired title is on the shelves, and then advise the inquirer to go directly and get it.

Oddly enough, the short-loan requests that cannot be filled from the collection of the Chicago Public Library are not turned over to the interlibrary loan system so that the desired material can be obtained from another library in or outside Chicago. If the material is not in the city collection, the inquirer is so informed. If he still wants to get it, he must make a trip to the Central Library to place his request for

further action. Thus the Chicago Public Library regularly furnishes interlibrary loan service to other libraries, but it does not customarily request the reciprocal privilege for its own users.

The requests initially go from the local branch to the nearby regional library. Hild Regional is able to fill 56 percent of title requests and 50 percent of subject requests coming to it, and for the other two regionals the figures are 46 percent of title requests and 36 percent of subject requests. These relatively low rates are another indication of the limitations of the regional collections. Overall more than 50 percent of the requests received at the first referral level must then be redirected to the Central Library, increasing the delay to the reader and adding to staff handling time.

Materials requested through short-loan tend to be adult nonfiction titles at an intermediate level. Not many student requests for study materials are handled in this way; the time delay would not meet student deadlines and students are sometimes discouraged from using this special service. Not many specialized sources are requested through short-loan; the more specialized reader evidently prefers to go directly to a larger collection.

The delivery system contributes to delays in getting short-loan materials into the hands of the inquirer. Even if titles are in the regional collection as the first point of search, they are not transported directly back to the requesting branch but are taken into the Central Library and resorted for separate truck runs. For sample books traced through as part of this study, the total delivery time averaged three to four days to transport items a relatively few miles from regional collection to local branches.

The various steps, procedures, and problems result in time delays as shown in table 46. While a small percentage of short-loan requests are filled within one week, 40 percent require more than three weeks, and 16 percent more than five weeks. The average time is 10 to 12 days.

Table 46
TIME REQUIRED TO FILL SHORT-LOAN REQUESTS

Time period	Percent of sample requests
One week or less	12
One to two weeks	47
Three to five weeks	24
Six weeks to three months	8
Three months or more	8

No information is sent back to requesting branches about delayed materials. The branch must institute a "tracer," which is done at an interval ranging from one month to three months after the request is received, depending on the branch. In the interval both the staff and the user are in the dark as to what may be happening. A check in the file of one branch showed that 14 percent of items on loan request required a tracer, and that for almost one-third of these tracers no reply had been received from the regional branch or the Central Library (usually Central) after a lapse of three months. Evidently of every ten interagency loans requested by readers, one cannot be filled from Chicago Public Library resources, another remains lost or unfilled somewhere in the pipeline, and two more arrive only after a delay of six weeks or more.

Interagency loan of materials between units of the Library is a promising plan for getting the full strength of the institution out to its farthest outpost. The service is not promoted nor heavily used. In practice it is marked by delays and uncertainties. In this useful joint service that directly reaches users, the several parts of the Library are not well coordinated and effective. Short-loan service provides a con-crete example of the need for better organization and coordination at the working level in the Chicago Public Library.

Recommendations

A priority need of the Chicago Public Library is a top-flight management team. Even before new programs are launched, standards of collection and staff raised, and existing services made more flexible and responsive to the people served, a half-dozen general officers must be enlisted. Other organizational changes —in government, structure, and communication—can either follow or proceed apace, but responsible human hands are necessary to mold these as well as any other developments.

The legal relationship of the Chicago Public Library to the City of Chicago under state law should be clarified so that both parties will be sure where they stand.

This does not mean deviation by the Library from municipal practices that are not in conflict with library service requirements, nor does it mean duplication of functions that can economically be carried out in City Hall. But proper utilization and disposition of funds is the responsibility of the Library Board under law, and should be so recognized by municipal fiscal offices. Similarly, the Board has an obligation, again under law, to build an effective staff, working within civil service principles and merit-system aims, but not necessarily following all past detailed practices of the Civil Service Commission. It is proposed that the Library retain legal counsel to help in this process, the clarification to come by means of an exchange of official memoranda. It would be best to spell out relationships objectively and at leisure rather than under the pressure of an issue.

As future vacancies occur on the Board of Directors of the Library, appointments should be of relatively young individuals and persons experienced in local community life.

The users of the Library are predominantly a young group, two-thirds being under 25 years of age. One or even two Board members relatively close to this age level could represent the needs of this dominant user group in Board deliberations, and indeed with their fresh outlook would invigorate policy consideration and decisions. A local community viewpoint, and actual experience in neighborhood groups, as contrasted with membership in city-wide and professional agencies, would also help to strengthen the Library's local roots.

Membership on the Library Board should by practice be limited to three terms of three years each.

The nine-year period would provide ample time for appointees to learn library policies and problems, make a contribution, and stay with developments long enough to get results. Individuals whom the Board wished to serve as officers would have several years of service in this capacity. A city such as Chicago has many citizens who could add to library counsels, bringing fresh ideas and concerns as turnover occurred, to say nothing of new energy. Particularly since members of this agency are appointed rather than being directly elected by the people they represent, it would be wise to avoid having the Library Board become an ingrown and semipermanent group.

Board deliberations need more careful staff work to provide the background, data, and alternatives required for the complex

social planning and public decisions for which the Board has responsibility and which affect so many people.

A Chief Librarian giving primary attention to the next stages of development will be in a position to provide such staff work for the Board, and he will have an office for program planning and evaluation to gather necessary data. The Board should expect documentation for matters on the agenda, should receive the information prior to meetings, and should base its decisions on such relevant intelligence material. Action should not be taken on the spur of the moment or in response to the enthusiasm of one or a few members. Both from the trustee and administration sides, the Library should gain that steady course and those criteria for best use of public money that come from a program-planning approach to policy-making and budgeting.

A committee of experts familiar with the historical record of Chicago and with collections and displays of mementos of the Civil War period should be appointed to review the desirability of transferring the exhibit in the Grand Army Memorial Hall to the Chicago Historical Society.

The present historical exhibit, as it stands, is not where the public in general and young people in particular benefit from it. The representation of this period of Chicago history would be better presented in the City's eminent historical museum. This is a matter for review by specialists who can evaluate these resources. If it is deemed in the public interest that the exhibit remain separate, then funds will have to be found to provide space for it in a new library building. The time has come to judge the question from the standpoint of value and best availability of the Civil War record.

A Citizens' Committee for the Chicago Public Library should be established to advise with the Library Board and to help relate the Library to the many aspects and organizations of Chicago.

A Board of nine members, no matter how constituted, cannot directly represent the multitudinous interests and groups of a large city. To engender wider public participation, the Chicago Public Library in the past had a Friends of the Library group. This organization for several years has been virtually inactive. It is proposed that the Friends group join forces with the Citizens' Committee of 140 individuals that advised on the present survey, to form a newly constituted organization to promote the interests of library service in Chicago. Its first major project might well be the furthering of the recommendations of this report.

A national search must be instituted immediately for a Chief Librarian.

This key officer should be exempt from civil service. He is to be the planner and manager of the Library for the Board of Directors and must work effectively with this group. His tenure will derive from the leadership he exerts rather than from civil service regulations. The Chief Librarian must be a man or woman who can plan for and carry through a multidimensional service program, inspire purpose and generate enthusiasm in the staff, take his place among educational and cultural leaders in Chicago, and make those firm yet sensitive decisions that are called for at times of crisis. He must have a definite metropolitan/state interest and a place in the national library profession. A salary of $35,000 will be necessary to attract such a person.

A position of Deputy Chief Librarian for overall internal administration of the Li-

brary system is to be created, thereby enabling the Chief Librarian to concentrate more on planning and external relations.

The Chicago Public Library is a large organization, in number of employees, variety of purposes, diversity of people served, and number of service outlets over the City. The director must be free to lead the institution into the period ahead. The Deputy Chief Librarian, working closely with him, is to be the executive officer, directing, coordinating, adjusting throughout the system, and solving specific problems as they arise. He would also be in charge in the Chief Librarian's absence, and would be ready to take over the Chief's duties if necessary. This officer, like the Chief Librarian, should be exempt from civil service.

The Chicago Public Library needs seven Assistant Chief Librarians to carry out the total program, four of which exist as positions at present (central library, technical services, personnel, and business) and three of which should be created (branches and extension, regional library centers, and program planning and evaluation).

The branch-extension administrator is needed to give unified direction and coordination to the far-flung program of local community service. The regional libraries, which have been thought of as branches in the past, will be separate intermediate libraries in the future, and should be grouped under their own Assistant Librarian. The program planning and evaluation director, to be attached directly to the Chief Librarian, is to research and clear the way for new developments; he is also to be an independent officer who will evaluate existing and fresh activities and ventures, his findings and results to feed back into the planning process. The vacancy in the Assistant Librarian position devoted to technical processes should also be filled promptly. This need for four additional Assistant Chief Librarians affords an opportunity for a combined national search for persons qualified at this level. However, the present starting salary of $14,856 for Assistant Librarians will not attract the capacity that is needed. It is proposed as an initial step that the position of Assistant Chief Librarian be reclassified from Librarian V to Librarian VI, with a starting salary up to the midpoint of that level. Civil service examinations for these positions should be original and open to all United States residents.

The responsibilities of the present Regional Librarians will be modified under this plan, from line administration to staff and coordinating functions for their respective sections of the City.

These officers should be called Branch Coordinators rather than regional librarians, which is confusing in view of the regional library centers. They would not carry the details of management which now absorb their time and energy and prevent them from concentrating on service improvement and development. Personnel, statistical, and similar work will be handled once in the central branch and extension office. The coordinators for sections of the City will continue to guide and direct book selection for the branches, and in fact will designate materials for more and more of the branches not headed by professional personnel. The "task force" groups, serving as the functional personnel in planning, installing, improving of service programs, and in the training of local staff in the branches, would be under the coordinators. The Branch Coordinators will report to the Assistant Librarian in charge of branches and extension. Four coordinators and four task forces are rec-

ommended, two for the inner city (one for the West Side and one for the South Side) and two for the outlying sections to the north-northwest and the south-southwest. They are to be at the Librarian V level (along with central department heads), at a revised salary range of $18,000–$20,000 for this grade.

Two high-level system-wide coordinators are to be appointed, one for children's service (preschool and elementary-school years) and the other for young adult service (teen years).

These staff officers would plan, initiate, guide, stimulate, evaluate, and modify service programs at their respective age levels. They will be the Library's specialists on reading and other library materials for younger readers. Both the Children's Coordinator and the Young Adult Coordinator will work with central library department heads, regional center librarians, Branch Coordinators and their task forces, and individual branches. Their closest relationship will be with the Assistant Chief Librarian for Branches and Extension. They are to be at the Librarian V level, below the rank of Assistant Chief Librarian. Related to them, and serving in the task forces in the several sections of the City, will be field coordinators for both young children and teen-agers.

Administrative specialists are to be designated for two new offices having to do with applications of new technology within the Library and with its relations with other libraries and educational agencies.

The first will be the director of a Communications-Computer Center. He is to be a specialist in data processing and an individual able to build and adjust computer system designs for library operations. The second specialist will head a Metropolitan Relations Office, to maintain communications and build joint activities with suburban libraries and suburban library systems, with the Newberry and Crerar Libraries, with college and university libraries, and with public, parochial, and private school systems. Both these officers would answer directly to the Chief Librarian and act as his agents for these two innovative dimensions of library service. They are to be classed at the Librarian V level, with salaries in the $18,000–$20,000 range.

The scope of duties and authority of the Business Manager are to be reaffirmed, so that the budgeting, financial, purchasing, supply and delivery functions of the Library operate as a unit.

This incumbency does not primarily require reorganization and new authority so much as clarification of existing structure and the forceful exercise of specified responsibilities. The Business Manager should gather full data for budget-making and function as the Chief Librarian's senior assistant in building the budget. He should take responsibility not only for the processing of payments and the accounting for expenditures, but also for those purchases other than selection of books and related materials for the collections. His office should generate financial information showing the functions and purposes for which funds are spent.

The Business Manager's responsibility for business affairs, such as purchasing, supply, and delivery, should be reaffirmed, set down in writing, and applied. The Library needs aggressive business administration to pull together its varied business and financial activities and to relieve the Chief Librarian of business details. The Business Department

should be more than an accounting unit, and should function also as a budget office, a controller's office, and a business management office, operating under the general direction of the Chief Librarian. There will have to be administrative help within the office to accomplish this.

Short-loan requests are to be filled within 48–72 hours, and requests that cannot be filled within the Chicago Public Library are to be transferred to the outside interlibrary loan system for fulfillment.

This rate of speed is entirely feasible at the present time, for the most part with the use of existing facilities. Requests should be telephoned in from branches to the regional center, thus saving a day. As soon as printed book catalogs showing when the regional center does not hold a title are available in the branches, the call will go direct to Central, thus saving two to three days at the outset. The regional centers should have teletype terminals connected with the TWX unit now in the Central Library, so that requests can be referred immediately to the main collection. When material is available at the first step of the regional center, it should not go on the circuitous delivery route first to the main building and then on another truck back out to a nearby branch. Frequent delays in the delivery process can be avoided by closer supervision.

Within five years new and more direct electronic communication should be installed to link regional centers visually with the Central Library, but until then the short-loan service should be speeded up with the facilities now at hand. One day is time enough to transmit the request, plus one day to locate the book and one day to deliver it—and in many instances even this time span can be telescoped.

Communication at all levels, formal and informal, official and unofficial, should be consciously fostered to pull the staff members of the Library together and have them function as members of a system.

There is no one means or device or publication that will fully meet the purpose. Actually the starting point is recognition of the need for communication. This applies both to concrete information about library affairs and discussion of new challenges facing the Library. Practices should be systematically recorded, starting with cataloging. Policies should be clarified and set down, starting with book selection. The *Staff Manual* needs revision. The *Staff News* of the Staff Association needs revitalization as the voice of the employees. For this purpose it is proposed that a young technician be given one-third time to serve as editor, the choice of the individual to be made by the Staff Association.

Parallel to a flow of communication should be an exchange of views and ideas and concerns between the administration and staff members old and young, professional and nonprofessional.

The busy administrator may see discussion of program and policies with staff members on any scale as a diversion from his appointed task of getting things done. But if he takes the time he will find the exchange rewarding. In this day and age he has no choice but to find the time, if he wants to carry his staff with him. Exchange does not mean communication solely between the Chief Librarian and representatives of the staff but discussion all along the line between supervisor and individual worker. Too many staff members of the Chicago Public Library are standing on the sidelines and watching; they need to be brought into the game of improving the institution; everyone has a contribution to make.

The process of change in response to the developing urban scene is to be consciously facilitated within the Library to enable the institution to modify programs, rearrange priorities, and, if necessary, alter direction in the period ahead.

The capacity for self-renewal exists within the Chicago Public Library. Measures should be taken to release this potential, rather than exhaust all energies on the continuance of present programs. These are to start at the level of the Board of Directors, which should be adopting goals for the Library five and ten years hence, rather than sponsoring specific projects. The Chief Librarian's position should be one of planning and innovation. For internal management, there should be a Deputy Chief Librarian. To strengthen the Chief Librarian's hand in identifying and initiating needed change, there should be an Assistant Librarian for Program Planning and Evaluation. The several proposed branch task forces (combining library and nonlibrary professionals) are to be instruments for innovation, not managers of existing units. The communication process proposed above will foster change; providing a voice to younger staff members will produce new ideas. Significant and enduring response to urban needs will come more from a continuously responsive organization and staff and less from formal and static reports.

10 Financial Support and Administration

Any criticism of the Chicago Public Library, and any proposals for its future, come back to the question of money. Some needed improvements do not necessarily wait upon dollars—for example, pure service-mindedness on the part of staff. But even here a shortage of financial support can have a direct and depressing effect. Where total staff is short in numbers, where general officers are lacking and thus leadership weakened, where working conditions are deficient—all of which has been true of the Chicago Public Library for the past twenty years—staff performance inevitably is affected. By any recognized financial standard the Chicago Public Library is poor, and it is therefore not surprising that its service leaves something to be desired.

Sources of Support

The bulk of support of the Chicago Public Library comes from local municipal taxes, up to a limit of $9 million established by the state legislature. Since 1966 state financial aid, primarily from the Library Development Fund, has assumed a significant place in library support. The Library has only very modest endowment funds, which in 1968 returned $17,978, about .2 of 1 percent of total income. The other larger items under "Miscellaneous Receipts" in table 47 are earnings on cash balances held (primarily building funds not spent) and income from rental of books.

The Library requests an amount of tax

Table 47
LIBRARY OPERATING INCOME, 1968

Income sources	Amount	Percent
Local Tax Income	$8,882,033	83.4
State Aid	1,650,969	15.5
Miscellaneous Receipts	111,644	1.1
Total	$10,654,696	100.0

income from the city, which, when approved, is added to the total municipal tax levy. The library appropriation therefore does not compete directly with the requests of other departments of government. The Library does not receive the face amount of the tax levied for library purposes, but only that portion actually collected, after tax delinquency and taxpayer protests. Chicago operates on borrowed funds in anticipation of tax collections; tax anticipation warrants are sold for library as for other expenses, which incurs interest expense for the borrowed funds, currently at over 6 percent. Taken together, the various losses and charges mean that no more than 80 percent of the appropriation is actually available for cash payments.

For construction purposes, a separate levy is authorized by state statute, pegged currently at $800,000 annually. The Library uses this money to carry out its branch building program and for major alterations and repairs. Federal funds, under Title II of the Library Services and Construction Act and amounting to $53,909 in 1968, also help in branch construction. Thus a pay-as-you-go policy is maintained for capital improvements and bonded indebtedness is avoided.

The Library has recently been resourceful in seeking out grants for special projects for the urban poor. Federal money supports an experimental program in the west side Lawndale area, based on the Douglas Branch, and private funds have been obtained to convert part of the Woodlawn Branch into a children's library center.

Approximately 67,000 residents of Cook County outside of Chicago use the Chicago Public Library directly, but the county does not participate in financial support of the city library. This figure for users is built up from 59,000 card holders who live in the county plus at least 8,000 reference users (primarily of the Central Library) who do not hold cards; the latter number is projected from the use study made in early December 1968. To a small extent this out-of-city use is counterbalanced by Chicagoans who turn to such well established suburban libraries as those in Evanston, Skokie, and Oak Park. But the balance is still tipped heavily toward Cook County residents who receive their library service from the Chicago institution. Of the Cook County residents who are Chicago card holders, 14.9 percent live in communities that do not provide any local public library service, so that Chicago in these instances is not only supplementing local facilities but actually providing library service without any local tax provision for the purpose. The nonresident load naturally falls unequally on different units of the Chicago Public Library —the largest group uses the Central Library; among branches, Northtown on the far north side shows 15 percent of users as nonresidents, West Addison on the far northwest side 8.9 percent, and Mt. Greenwood on the far southwest the unusually high percentage of 37.1 of registrants who are residents of such Cook

County communities as Evergreen Park, Oak Lawn, and Alsip. The per-user cost of Chicago Public Library service runs close to $12 annually. A rendering of a balance sheet would show some $750,000 of direct library service provided to residents of Cook County by Chicago; this service is separate from interlibrary loan under state legislation and for which the Chicago Public Library receives a state grant.

Illinois was slow to adopt a state-wide library plan and to provide state funds to improve service over the state. At an earlier stage, relief funds were provided on an emergency basis during the depression and terminated in 1937. Then in 1966 legislation for a "network of public library systems" was passed and state funds appropriated. In the legislation (Revised Statutes, Chapter 81, Section III) a noteworthy policy is set forth: "Since the state has a financial responsibility in promoting public education, and since the public library is a vital agency serving all levels of the educational process, it is hereby declared to be the policy of the state to encourage the improvement of free public libraries. In keeping with this policy, provision is hereby made for a program of state grants designed to aid in the establishment and development of a network of public library systems covering the entire state." The relationship of state to municipality in the maintenance of library service is further clarified later in the act (Section 113) in these terms: ". . . promote the full utilization of local pride, responsibility, initiative and support of library service and at the same time employ state aid as a supplement to local support." Thus state and municipality must assume a partnership in financing libraries even as they jointly provide for the schools, with the base of support resting in the municipality.

Chicago qualifies for state financial aid both as a library "system" and as one of four "Research and Reference Centers" in the state. Grants to the Chicago Public Library as a Research and Reference Center started in 1965 and as a system in 1966. The Library Development Fund provides in excess of $1,400,000 annually to Chicago under a formula calling for 40 cents per capita and $5 per square mile of service territory. The grant for specialized service to northern Illinois has varied from $75,000 to $92,000 annually, depending on funds available.

The state money came to the Chicago Public Library at a crucial time, when the existing pegged levy imposed a ceiling on local support, and when public criticism of the institution was mounting. The state funds saved the day. It is only from outside sources that it has been possible to replenish the book stock, make needed adjustments in salaries, and mobilize special programs for disadvantaged areas.

National standards do not exist for *state* support of public libraries and no definite percentage or per-capita figure can be set down with authority. Similarly, comparisons between states are not particularly helpful because of differing policies and tax structures. At present the state provides 15.5 percent of public library expenditures in Chicago, less than half the proportion carried for schools. A balanced partnership might well call for at least one-quarter of library funds from the state.

Designation as the Research and Reference Center for northern Illinois places an extra burden upon the Chicago Public Library. In this capacity the Library is to maintain collections at an advanced level and make resources available for direct consultation by nonresidents and also locally in the surrounding area by means of interlibrary loan. Even if the Chicago Public Library had resources at the "research and reference" level, which it does not in any consistent sense, the present

grants would hardly compensate for their provision to some 4,000,000 people outside the city. Unless more adequate financing is provided to help build a specialized collection equal to the state mandate, the Chicago unit will be a weak link in the state-wide plan at this level, and—given the plan which opens Chicago resources to the larger metropolitan area—expenditures by Chicago for the purpose will constitute a benefaction by the beleaguered city to the more affluent suburbs.

Chicago has not actively sought private benefactions for the support of the Library. The agency in the past was the recipient of several modest bequests which together return .2 of 1 percent of current income. This source can hardly be expected to maintain or take over regular services, but at least two potentialities should be aggressively explored—foundation money for experimental programs (as for the urban poor), and private gifts for the building of special research resources (such as a collection of Negro literature and culture).

Amount of Income

Among larger cities, Chicago was at the bottom in per-capita support of its public library at the time of the 1938 study, and it continues at the bottom today. As compared with such cities as Baltimore, Boston, and Cleveland, the Chicago rate of library expenditures is less than half as much. The figures for 1967 (the latest year for which comparable data are available) are given in table 48. Chicago expenditures increased in 1968, but this is also true of other cities, so that Chicago remains the straggler.

The second column in the table, showing the rate of actual appropriation for library purposes by local municipal governments, puts Chicago a little further in the rear. On this basis the differential between the top city and

Table 48
PER CAPITA LIBRARY SUPPORT, 1967*—
Chicago and Eight Benchmark Cities

City	Library expenditures	Local library appropriation
Cleveland	7.23	7.18
Boston	6.98	6.14
Baltimore	5.90	5.02
New York†	4.23	3.17
Detroit	4.07	3.44
Saint Louis	4.05	3.53
Philadelphia	3.98	2.91
Los Angeles	3.88	3.54
Chicago	2.73	2.26

*Source: Summary issued by Enoch Pratt Free Library, Baltimore, December 1968.
†For New York Public Library branch system only; privately supported Reference Department expenditures would add $1.04 per capita.

Chicago at the bottom becomes three to one. The difference between expenditures and local appropriations is due primarily to state financial aid, which for some cities runs as high as 16 percent of the total (New York City is one) and for some as low as 1 percent (Los Angeles, for example). Chicago is in the upper range, with 15.9 percent of its 1967 expenditures having come from state aid, and a similar proportion in 1968.

In general Chicago has been losing rather than gaining financial support for library service compared with other large cities. Table 49 shows support figures for four cities that happened to be very close to the same starting line of $2 per capita in 1960, one of the four being Chicago. The other three cities have on the average almost doubled their operating expenditures since 1960. Chicago in contrast has increased its operating expenditures by only a little more than one-third, hardly enough to keep up with inflation in the interval. This very modest showing on the part of Chicago has occurred despite the fact that it has obtained

substantially more state aid than the others. Counting local tax appropriations alone, Los Angeles increased in seven years from $2 to $3.54 per capita, Philadelphia from $1.92 to $2.91, Saint Louis from $2.28 to $3.53, and Chicago from $1.98 to $2.26.

Table 49
PER CAPITA LIBRARY SUPPORT, 1960 AND 1967—Chicago and Three Benchmark Cities

City	1960	1967	Percent increase
Chicago	1.98	2.73	37.9
Los Angeles	2.00	3.88	94.0
Philadelphia	1.92	3.98	104.2
Saint Louis	2.28	4.05	77.6

In other words, Chicago's low support of public library service must be placed directly on the doorstep of the city. While the Library does not have as much state aid as is justified by its role in the state educational system, it does fare as well as other large city libraries in this respect. It was the municipal appropriation that did not keep pace.

At this point the division of responsibility in Illinois for determining amount of library support as between city and state enters the picture. By any calculation of need or comparison with established standards, Chicago is derelict in the amount of its library appropriation. But the total that the city may designate is established by the state legislature in the form of a pegged levy. This provides a ready-made situation for passing the buck from city to state. Chicago is behind in library support, but the state legislature must act before the city can increase its appropriation. The body to which the buck is passed, the state legislature, is confronted with a host of state-wide problems, and in any case knows little about library needs within Chicago. Library service is caught somewhere between.

In state library law in Illinois (Revised

Statutes, Chapter 81, Section 3–3) there is a provision for direct referendum for raising the library appropriation above pegged amounts. As applied to Chicago, the library tax may be increased at any single referendum in an amount not to exceed $1 million, the maximum to be attained in successive years not to exceed $15 million. This introduces the new factor of direct voter action to increase library support. In practice it has not been used because of the cost and effort in mounting a campaign to inform the electorate, not once but in successive years.

The $9 million limit for local library appropriation for Chicago works out to .75 mills on each dollar of assessed valuation in the city. For other municipalities in Illinois the statutes specify 1.2 mills, a rate over 50 percent higher. Thus the amount of local support that the city may provide for its public library is not only limited by state action, but also at a rate which discriminates against the large city. The distinction in the law is created by means of the euphemism of legislation for "cities over 500,000," of which there is only one in the state.

Whatever the amount or rate, a pegged levy raises various problems of government finance. No real appraisal of library needs and budget requirements occurs on the part of city officials, because their hands are tied. The public has difficulty in making its will known. And with the levy fixed as a dollar amount even the natural increase of return from a specific rate, as assessed valuation goes up, is lost. A prescribed dollar levy provides a protective floor in time of severe economic depression (which was the occasion for incorporating the concept into state law), but the effect in time of economic prosperity and inflation is more that of a rigid fixed-price ceiling.

From time to time, at intervals of several years, the Library Board goes to the state legislature to get the pegged levy raised. Usually this occurs when revenues fall seriously behind, and the legislature in its wisdom makes the decision as to how much money the library in Chicago should have. Thus a new plateau is established and remains until the situation becomes intolerable, when the trip again is made to Springfield.

The net effect is not only that the Chicago Public Library does not get enough money to maintain standards, but within municipal revenues the library share keeps slipping. On its current plateau of $9 million, the local library tax rate decreased from .76 to .74 mills in the 1965–1968 period; back in 1938 the tax rate worked out to 1.02 mills. By the same token, the percentage of local government operating funds going to the library has slowly but steadily decreased since the early 1950s. School funds in Chicago, certainly no model for educational support, nonetheless increased by 150 percent from 1950 to 1968, while library funds increased by 100 percent; the schools in 1969 are moving a definite step forward with an increase in the base for calculating state school aid from $400 to $550 per pupil.

Thus library progress in Chicago depends on adequate financial support. In the end the shortcomings in library service come back not only to administration and staff but also to local government officials and the people of Chicago. For what they have paid, Chicagoans have received reasonably full return. But there is no magic by which Chicago can get quality library service for a fraction of what it costs elsewhere.

Library Expenditures

The operating expenditures of the Chicago Public Library passed the $10 million mark in

1968 for the first time. This constitutes an increase in outlay of 62 percent from 1960, due primarily to an increase in the pegged levy and the introduction of substantial state aid in the interval. The total and the distribution for 1968 are shown in table 50.

Table 50
LIBRARY OPERATING EXPENDITURES, 1968

Category	Amount	Percent
Salaries	$ 7,295,204	68.8
Library materials	1,871,716	17.6
Binding	248,100	2.3
Rent, heat, light	292,331	2.8
Other operating	895,410	8.5
Total	$10,602,761	100.0

Salary expenditures in the Chicago Public Library consistently ran over 70 percent of total operating expenditures during the 1950s and into the 1960s (72.7 percent in 1960, 70.1 percent in 1965). Expenditures for books, periodicals, and related materials ran about 10 percent in the 1950s and then moved a little higher in the early 1960s (up to 14.1 percent by 1965). These two proportions—70 percent or more for staff and little more than 10 percent for books—are characteristic of public library budgets when funds are seriously short; an effort is made to hold on to staff and in the process book purchases are sacrificed. Other operational costs—for supplies, telephone, postage, repairs—also tend to be a higher proportion of expenditures when funds are limited, because to some extent they are fixed costs.

With the advent of state money to the extent of nearly $1,500,000 per year, beginning in 1966, the Library budget moved out of an unbalanced stage. By 1968 personnel expenditures, despite increases in salary scales, decreased below 70 percent and towards a healthy two-thirds of total outlays, library materials including binding and rebinding increased almost to 20 percent, and other operating costs fell below 12 percent. The index numbers in table 51 present this shift in quantitative terms, using 1960 as a base, then 1964 as the year before state aid was received, and 1968 as the most recent year.

Table 51
CHANGE IN DISTRIBUTION OF LIBRARY EXPENDITURES, 1960–68 (1960 = 100)

Category	1960	1964	1968
Salaries	100	116	153
Materials and binding	100	101	228
Other expenditures	100	123	138

The significant change is in expenditures for library materials (books, films, recordings) which more than doubled from 1960 to 1968. The figures for 1964 demonstrate the unbalanced situation that previously prevailed. As total funds went up some from 1960 to 1964, on a limited base, it was salaries and other expenditures that benefitted, while books gained little if at all. But with substantial outside financial assistance, library materials became the major benefactor. This use of the extra money is to be commended, although pragmatically it was also the easiest policy; additional books can be ordered more readily than additional staff can be found, and adjustments are not quite as overwhelming if state grants are decreased. However, it must be noted that the book budget in Chicago was shortchanged for twenty years after the end of World War II, with resulting gaps and weaknesses in the collection reported in chapter 4. The lesson here is that part of the added book funds now available should be used, particularly in the central collection, for the titles of continuing worth that were missed from 1946 to 1965. Further, unless additional funds for library support are shortly found, the recent salary raises and the continuing inflation in cost of supplies and services will put the squeeze on book and material funds, the former pressures will come into play once more, and the lifeblood of the library will again be constricted.

Maintenance costs were analyzed separately, combining salaries, materials, and services, to determine if Chicago's older central plant might be unduly draining funds. In an "unbalanced" year, such as 1960, 19.4 percent of Chicago library expenditures went into building maintenance (for both central unit and branches), a substantially higher proportion than in any other large city library system. Under the normal distribution now prevailing, the percentage is down to 13.8. This is still on the high side (the two other city libraries serving more than 2 million people, Los Angeles and Philadelphia, spend 10.9 and 13.2 percent of their funds on maintenance), but in general Chicago's maintenance costs seem to be in line.

Chapter 6, dealing with personnel, indicated that the Chicago Public Library is severely short-staffed, so that more money will have to go into this category. At the same time more funds must be available for books, periodicals, and the much-expanded audio-visual materials, to say nothing of building seven additional regional collections. As but one comparison, Chicago is still spending only $52,000 a year for magazines and journals, while much smaller cities such as Cleveland and Buffalo (with Erie County) are spending $89,400 and $129,300 respectively. The last few years have seen a little relief in the Chicago Library budget, but, unless additional funds are found promptly, the old pressures and expenditure imbalance will shortly return.

Financial Administration

Certain essentials of responsible financial administration prevail in the Chicago Public Library. Final authority for fiscal planning and control, under the Library Board, is centralized in the chief administrative officer rather than being divided between the Librarian and a financial officer also reporting directly to the Board, as was formerly the case. The chief business officer functions under the Librarian, with responsibility for estimating revenues, gathering budget data, authorizing purchases, and controlling expenditures—that is, as fiscal controller within a centrally directed enterprise. Accounts are kept meticulously within the business office, and a sense of economy prevails throughout the organization.

But other essentials are lacking. Budgeting is a partial and rudimentary process. Prudent financial controls are missing. Recordkeeping is cumbersome and inefficient. And staff provision for fiscal operations is inadequate for proper financial control and administration.

BUDGETING

The budget represents in dollars and cents the plan for operating the Library within an anticipated amount of income. Families which have made their financial plans and carried them out by means of budget controls know the mechanics of budget making—the simplicity of the idea and the practical difficulties attending its operation.

Underlying any budget, whether expressly stated or not, are a set of goals and a plan of work to be done. Too often both purposes and activities are determined by what was done the previous year; budget making becomes a mere forward projection of previous figures, with adjustments for emergencies and contingencies that have come to light. As this process continues year after year, rigidity is built into the program of action, and bureaucracy becomes entrenched. Any new challenges are met only with money that is "left over," and any redirection of program falters and dies for lack of sustenance. Budget making should start—long before the budget as such is "due"—with a long-range plan of goals and activities. In a certain sense the complete present report is an initial step in effective budget planning for the Chicago Public Library.

Against the background of a long-range plan, specific steps in budget making can be taken. Staff on a wide scale should be involved; the process should grow from "needs up" and not from "available money down." This does not mean that all the funds requested will be obtained, but if cuts in requests are made it is only against a program plan rooted in service needs that wise adjustments and compromises can be reached. Without this guide the hard decisions are usually made on the basis of "commitments," which relate more to what the agency has been in the past than to what it should be in the future.

Ideally the ten steps in budget making from this point on would encompass the following:

1. Preliminary consultation with general officers, department heads, and branch librarians for direction and emphasis needed to meet service aims and obligations

2. Adoption of general policies by Board and Chief Librarian, that is, determination of immediate objectives for the next year within the long-range plan of development

3. Preparation and provision by the business office of cost figures and financial analyses, first by departments and branches and then by services (cataloging, circulation, and reference)

4. Detailed planning by senior officers and staff of work units to be accomplished, so that budget proposals, department by department, will result

5. Consolidation of proposals and design of budget request by the Chief Librarian, with the assistance of the Assistant Librarian in charge of Program Planning and Evaluation and the Assistant Librarian in charge of Business and Finance

6. Estimate of anticipated revenues by the business office and calculation of appropriations necessary

7. Review of the tentative budget request by the Board of Directors

8. Preparation by the business office of the budget request in the form prescribed by the City of Chicago

9. Budget hearings before the City Council

10. If necessary, adjustments and reductions in budget, involving the Board, administrative officers, and senior staff members.

In actual practice budget preparation by the Chicago Public Library is a circumscribed operation with relatively few individuals participating. The process is initiated by receipt of a letter from the budgetary division of the Mayor's Office requesting that the Chicago Public Library, along with other city agencies and departments, submit a preliminary budget estimate for the coming year. Enclosed with the letter is a standard form on which the Library is requested to provide data on which the preliminary request is based.

Upon receipt of the letter from the Mayor's Office, the Librarian requests the Regional Librarians and the Assistant Librarian-Central Library to estimate their needs for books and binding for the coming year. Each of the Regional Librarians meets with the branch librarians under her supervision and requests them to estimate their needs. The Regional Librarian then summarizes the data and sends the summary to the Librarian's office. The Assistant Librarian-Central Library requests the subject department heads to estimate their needs for books and binding, and she then collates and summarizes their requests on a worksheet and sends this to the Librarian's office. The Business Manager also prepares a budget estimate based on the current year's operations and estimates of revenue for the coming year and submits this to the Librarian's office.

At this point, the Librarian has estimates before him of the needs for books and binding from the branches and subject departments of the Central Library, estimates of revenue to be available, and estimates of overall expenses. He has no estimates from the Personnel Department or the agencies of what their staffing requirements will be and therefore no way to determine what budget request should be made for wages and salaries. Nevertheless, calculations are made for nonsubject departments (e.g., maintenance, technical services, engineering, circulation, registry) and for personnel requirements of all agencies.

Actually, what happens is that an estimate is made of the amount of revenue to be received and this amount is distributed over the various accounts to conform with city requirements. These estimates are summarized and posted to the proper line on the Preliminary Budget Estimate form and submitted to the Budgetary Division of the Mayor's Office by the first Monday in July. Discussions then ensue between the Library and the Budgetary Division until the budget request is more or less finalized, usually about Labor Day. During September and October (and sometimes into November) hearings are held by the City Council Finance Committee to pass on budgetary requests of all city agencies, including

the Library. For the Library these hearings are normally handled by the President of the Board and the Chief Librarian. When approval of the Finance Committee is more or less certain, the Business Manager prepares budget worksheets for inclusion in the Mayor's Budget.

At about this time (usually in November) the budget figures are presented to the Library Board of Directors for their approval. This, of necessity, becomes merely a pro-forma approval, because the figures are submitted so late in the budget process.

Following approval by the Board of Directors and the City Council, the overall figures for books and other materials, based on the initial requests and adjustments thereto, are broken down by agency. Each department and branch is required (by Library rules, not city regulations) to spend within 50 cents, either way, of 1/22 of its appropriation for books, periodicals and binding in each of 22 periods (twice monthly except monthly in July and December).

Several shortcomings in financial planning are apparent in the procedure as outlined. No basic plan of service development exists to guide budget planning. Policies which will prevail in any given year are assumed rather than formulated; no statement is composed or discussed concerning what services will be maintained, strengthened, and deemphasized. Administrative staff participate in studying needs for books and related materials (which account for less than one-fifth of expenditures) but not in reviewing staff needs (which account for over two-thirds of expenditures). Similarly, control over book expenditures is rigid, to the point where no adjustment is permitted for seasonal changes in rate of publication, although no parallel controls exist over personnel and other expenditures. Department heads and branch librarians do not have a general allocation within which they operate. If adjustments become necessary because full requests are not granted, they are made unilaterally in a central office. The Board of Directors, the governmental body responsible for the Library, serves more as a rubber stamp than as a participant in budget-making.

City practices require budget requests to be submitted by "organizational activities" and by "performance data," as well as by object of expenditure. The organizational groupings used are administration, central service, extension service, processing of materials, operation of buildings, and loss and cost in collecting taxes. The Library does not keep its own accounts under such headings, but at the time of submitting the budget request informally allocates present and anticipated expenditures among the several required headings. If the allocations were taken at face value, serious questions would have to be raised. For example, the organization allocation shows $1,017,060 for acquisition and processing of materials in 1968, separate from the purchase cost of the books and other materials themselves. This would mean close to $2 to handle each piece acquired, including more than 200,000 items such as paperback books and government pamphlets which were not considered worth shelflisting, and most of which have a purchase price well under $2.

Performance units are supplied, as required by city practice, under such headings as books circulated and reference questions answered, but cost figures are lacking so that the work units play a very marginal role in budget-making, analysis, and defense. Here also the figures must be taken with a considerable grain of skepticism. For instance, the Central Library is credited with 1,690,700 "items circulated" and then with 3,381,400 "items returned,"

although the branch breakdown includes no separate work unit for "return." The figure of 805,000 borrower's cards carried in budget material for 1968 does not check with the departmental count of 697,802. The Library cannot be said to have a functioning performance budget, related to work actually done, much less a program and planning budget, related to the work that should be done.

Once adopted, the budget has import for its total but not for its various subdivisions. Thus the budgeted amount for salaries in 1968 was underspent by 18 percent and that for books and materials overspent by 17 percent. The $1,500,000 of state aid is used where needed, backing up short accounts, getting new projects started, going into books if not required elsewhere—a kind of supercontingency fund. In 1969, with an increased salary scale to meet but very little more in city appropriations to carry the increase (that $9 million pegged levy again), a significant part of the state money will go into salaries rather than into books—a step back from the sound balance between salaries and materials that has existed since the advent of state aid. The large state contingency fund can be a decided convenience to the administrator, but one of this size makes for loose expenditure control. The state funds should be built into the working budget and controlled as for any planned expenditure.

ACCOUNTING

Accounts are kept under object of expenditure, using categories built up by the Library and not corresponding entirely to those used by the City. An unusually large line for undesignated "other expenditures" has been allowed, amounting to $70,924 in 1968. Records appear to be kept accurately and are audited annually, although there is no internal audit. The standard posting procedure provides monthly and accumulated expenditures under object categories, although the monthly statements usually require three weeks to prepare.

Beyond this, little if any analysis and interpretation of financial information is done for management purposes. Neither Board members nor administrative officers request additional information, and the manual method of accounting would make it difficult to supply in any case. As previously indicated, neither budgets nor expenditure accounts are kept for departments or branches; if the question arises as to how much is spent for a particular unit, there is a scurrying about to assemble figures, and some items are likely to be left out. No unit cost figures for circulation of materials or registration of borrowers or handling of new books are attempted. At budget time no analysis of trends in expenditures over a period of years or increases in costs (for example, changes in the average prices of books) are asked for or produced. For the expenditure item on which close control is maintained, semimonthly book allocations for departments and branches, the individual units keep their own running balances. It is not too strong a statement to say that the Chicago Public Library really does not know where its money is going.

Standard and prudent internal controls are lacking at several points in financial and related operations. Checks and balances of course are not aimed at any individual or group, but are approved practice when funds of any size are handled or authorized for payment; these constitute a preventive measure against human frailty. Starting at the top, the Business Manager also serves as financial officer, and in this dual capacity often alone authorizes both purchases and payments, and reconciles balances. This is not in accord with the principle of sharing responsibility for monetary disbursements. As another example, over a quarter-million dollars in fines are taken in annually, at several score stations and under varying staffing conditions, with no control over collection and transmission, other than a handwritten notation for each transaction on a "cash sheet" by the individual collecting the money. Cash registers would not be suitable to the library atmosphere, but there are recording devices, visible to the payee as well as to the receiving staff member, and these have the added advantage of automatically totaling what the intake should be; some such device should at least be installed in the Central Library and the larger branches. Once cash is received in the business office, tight controls are exercised, and a "Manual for Validation Procedures" guides operations. The materials-receiving function (excluding receipt of books) is also subject to limited controls, with individual agency heads counting and verifying the condition of deliveries. In a far-flung organization this lack of control opens the possibility of misconduct either by the individual alone or in collusion with a vendor. It also adds another housekeeping job to the duties of professional administrators, as against having deliveries examined in a central unit and then quickly double-checked in the operating agency. Accounting for fixed assets, physical plant and property inventories is most spotty and not current. No evidence was found of collusion or misuse of funds, but the principle of internal controls and checks, if in no other form than in the division of responsibility between two individuals without family connections, should still be applied.

Handling of payroll presents a particular problem of workload in the Business Office. The whole process is most complicated and involves (1) daily timesheets for individuals in each agency, (2) tabulation and verification by branch librarians and department heads at the end of each pay period (another record-keeping task for the professional administrator), (3) noting of changes in status of employees by the Personnel Department, (4) checking for accuracy and preparation of the official payroll register by the Business Office, (5) approval of the register by the Civil Service Commission, (6) preparation of payment checks by the Data Processing Center of the city, and (7) final verification by the Library Business Office before checks are released; a diagram of the detailed steps covers several pages. All this must occur within a few days, so that employees can be paid promptly, and the brunt of the work falls on the business and accounting office. The total staff of the office must pitch in to get the job done. Rather than the present laborious processing of time sheets through central offices within a few days at the end of each payroll period, the process should be simplified by depending only on exception notices for which the department head or branch librarian would be responsible, such exception notices to be processed daily rather than cumulated to the end of the period. Any changes that might occur would then be recorded on a continuous basis, thus preventing the bottleneck that now develops.

The financial recording methods used by the Library are archaic. Most work is manual, with use of a bookkeeping machine suitable to a disbursement load much smaller than the present $10 million plus budget. Vouchers move through a procedure requiring (1) coding as to fund and account, (2) posting on individual ledger cards by means of the bookkeeping machine, (3) typing of city invoices for payment, (4) another typing for schedule of bills to be approved by the Board, and (5) totaling and verification for dollar amounts—

each a manual operation. Procedures for these operations are set down in a staff manual in detail, showing a proliferation of tasks and regulations; these procedures have not been reviewed and no attempts have been made at simplification. Some papers are rehandled several times—duplicate files are maintained—most documents are filed "forever." Original records are kept and not transferred to microfilm for reduced storage and easy access. Some effort has been made toward automating of records, but this affects only a small part of the operation and costs $900 per month at a service bureau. The business record, payroll, and accounting operations of the Chicago Public Library are conducted responsibly by a few dedicated employees, but these operations cannot be given a passing mark for efficiency.

The Library functions financially as a division of the City: the budget is processed through city offices, control accounts are kept there, invoices move through the municipal purchasing department, payrolls are verified and checks prepared centrally. Yet working relations between the Library and City Hall are neither close nor smooth. Library financial officers report a lack of understanding of library needs in the municipal offices, and these offices in turn express concern about library practices. The situation is further complicated by the nature of financial administration in Chicago, with a distinct variation between "appropriation" and "cash" budgets. The Library in substance must maintain an unofficial internal cash budget, while the legal budget is based on the amount of money available for appropriation.

The staff conducting financial, payroll and accounting operations in the Chicago Public Library is inordinately small. The Business Manager supervises work within the department, serves as fiscal officer as well as business agent of the Library, and is designated Secretary of the Board of Directors. One accounting officer handles recordkeeping for all accounts, and he is the only individual in the department other than the Business Manager with a formal accounting background. A head library clerk supervises clerical personnel in the unit and functions as administrative assistant to both the Business Manager and the Library Accounting Clerk. Seven clerical assistants help carry out the work, and there is considerable turnover in this group. A comparison can be made with the Municipal Tuberculosis Sanitarium of the City of Chicago, which has just over 1,000 employees compared with the Library's more than 1,600, and an operating budget three-quarters that of the Library. The Municipal Tuberculosis Sanitarium has a thirteen-person accounting section under a comptroller, a seven-person payroll section, and a four-man cost and inventory control unit. The Chicago Public Library will not have adequate internal financial control and necessary financial data for effective management review and planning until its business and accounting staff is strengthened; if it should lose one or two of the present key people in the department the Library would be crippled.

Recommendations

Library support constitutes a minute portion of municipal expenditures. Yet the service provided—a combination of education, functional information, specialized background, and pure cultural enjoyment—reaches to every part of the city and is available to all its residents. The public library is a mirror or measure of a community, reflecting the quality of its life and demonstrating whether those in power really want to help the people help themselves. Chicago has provided only a fraction of the money needed by its public library; it is not surprising that the institution has reached only a fraction of its constituents with a service program short of contemporary standards.

In the next five years, from 1970 to 1975, the operating budget of the Chicago Public Library should increase by $2 million per year, from its present level of just over $10 million to at least $20 million.

A breakdown of additional dollar needs, year by year, is presented in table 52. A step-up in central collection building should start immediately, and then continue at a steady pace. At the same time central staff and service must be strengthened, in subject departments, information provision, contemporary publication units, and audiovisual materials. Experimental inner-city efforts beyond the recent limited projects should be launched and continued at a moderate level for two years while these efforts are evaluated, after which wide-scale mobilization is needed. Improvement in branches in the more stable parts of the city and the opening of a few additional branches already scheduled in these areas should proceed steadily. Costs for additional regional library centers will be small in the first year or two, while centers are being built, but then will accelerate and by 1975 will be one of the largest additional items in the budget. For a few years extra funds are needed for the automation of book processing and the preliminary work to produce a printed book catalog, and for selective reclassification, but this added cost will then disappear. Metropolitan service—bibliographic control, information provision, subject reference, interlibrary loan—should build up steadily to a level well beyond the present rudimentary state. Salaries of present staff will of course not stand still (new staff salaries are included in the preceding items), and 5 percent per year is specified for this purpose.

Table 52
ADDITIONAL FUNDING NEEDED TO FINANCE RECOMMENDED PROGRAMS—
in addition to 1969 operating budget

Program	1970	1971	1972	1973	1974
Strengthening Central collections (research, subject, audio-visual)	$250,000	$350,000	$500,000	$600,000	$600,000
Strengthening Central Services (bibliographic, information, subject centers, media centers)	300,000	400,000	500,000	600,000	700,000
Intensification of inner-city service	600,000	900,000	1,000,000	1,600,000	1,700,000
Extending and improving service to outer city	200,000	400,000	600,000	800,000	900,000
Regional centers (collections and staffs)	100,000	600,000	1,300,000	2,000,000	2,700,000
Automation and reclassification in Technical Processes	75,000	270,000	250,000	75,000	————
Metropolitan services (bibliographic, information, reference, interlibrary loan)	75,000	150,000	300,000	400,000	500,000
Salary increases for present staff	400,000	800,000	1,300,000	1,800,000	2,300,000
Strengthening management team	90,000	175,000	200,000	225,000	250,000
Total over and above 1969 base	$2,090,000	$3,975,000	$5,950,000	$8,000,000	$9,650,000

Listed last, but actually needing priority action, is the strengthening of the very limited group of general officers and central coordinators. Unless the Chicago Public Library keeps close to this schedule of $2 million added per year for the first half of the next decade, it will not be able to eliminate the weaknesses in its present service and it will not reach any portion of the 2,500,000 Chicagoans who do not now use it.

State and locality in Illinois should develop a genuine sharing of financial support for public libraries, in line with state responsibilities for education and the policy concerning libraries set forth in state statutes (Revised Statutes, Chapter 81, Section 111).

The time has come to recognize that the public library is an integral and essential branch of education. It does not teach the child to read, but it provides educational reading materials for him not only as a child but also as an adult, and increasingly it also supplies him with the newer educational media throughout his life. Even as the inspiration of a teacher in school may change a youngster's life, so also may the guidance of a librarian set him on the road to self-development. For libraries as for schools, the state should establish a foundation of minimum adequate support, which at present must be at least $5 per capita. Each municipality, Chicago included, would be expected to levy a one-mill tax for library purposes, with the state then making up the difference between the return on this levy and an amount equivalent to $5 per capita. In the case of Chicago, $5 per capita would be in the range of $18 million for library support, up toward what we have seen is required to meet program needs.

The return from a one-mill local tax would be $11,500,000, which would then call for $6,500,000 of state funds to complete the support base. It has taken considerable time and experience to work out equitable school financing along this line, and it would be wise to go to such a base promptly for library service to provide the needed information sources and educational materials for all the people. The state would then be discharging its constitutional obligations for the education of its people. It would at the same time have a proper formula for the sharing of tax revenues with those parts of the state that have financial difficulty in maintaining adequate public services, starting with the hard-pressed and threatened city. Many suggestions are made as to how the state with its broader tax base can help in the urban crisis; a logical starting point, actually in accord with existing policy, would be to participate significantly in the financial underpinning of the educational agency for lifelong self-development.

In the interval, and until a long-term partnership is developed, the state limitation on local library support should be eliminated, or at the least be set at some such flexible rate as 2 mills on the dollar of assessed valuation, so that the people of Chicago and their Mayor and Council can themselves decide what they want to spend for library service.

As a first interim step, Chicago should be put on the same 1.2 mill basis as other public libraries in the state. This will permit appropriations covering the first two increases of $2 million. But then a new crisis will arise unless the city is able to determine whether it wishes to go further with an institution which by then will be having a visible effect on basic city problems. The state may properly establish a minimum on library support, so that the library

segment of the educational program is not neglected, and also to ensure full return from whatever state money goes to libraries, but establishing a maximum imposes a limitation which is better set by the people themselves and their local government.

The state share in public library support should be continued and enlarged as the state and the municipality together maintain library service.

When the operating budget of the Library reaches the required $20 million by 1975, the state should be carrying at least $4 million (20 percent) and more properly $5 million (25 percent) of the total. The base figure for state aid under the Illinois Library Development Fund might well move up to $1 per capita. For research and reference service to northern Illinois, the cost projected in table 52 (which see) continues upward to $500,000 in 1974. This should be furnished from Springfield, from tax income provided by all the people of northern Illinois, and not by the Chicago taxpayers alone; for this part of the state program a per-capita base of 10 cents would represent a bargain rate for bringing advanced library service to the residents of suburbs and detached centers.

Both the county at the local level and the federal government at the national level have a stake in the service program of the Chicago Public Library, and should contribute to its support.

Federal policy in supporting library service will gravitate toward one of several alternatives: a decline in national commitment to education (the indication as of this writing), support of experimental and demonstration programs (the recent policy), direct participation in financing of a basic minimum of service for all citizens, or return of lump aid sums to the states for them to allocate, presumably with education as a priority consideration. The sound national policy would appear to be not just a benign concern about schools and libraries but a direct and ongoing commitment to their support. An added factor is that an agency with the potential of the Chicago Public Library will increasingly take its place in a national library network. As to Cook County, the residents of which are receiving local service on a considerable scale from the Chicago Public Library, policies will have to be worked out by means of governmental consultation. Both sides would gain by financial support from the county for the city library, the county by receiving service for some of its people who either do not have facilities or who prefer to use those of the city, and the city and its library by not having to consider refusing service to nonresidents who do not contribute to the Library's support. Both federal and county funds, at their different levels, would help to meet the unpredictable demands of these next few years, over and above the projected $20 million figure.

The designated capital improvements income should be increased to a .2 mill rate, thus producing some $2,250,000 annually, and used for a period to build two regional library centers a year.

This report recommends that building funds no longer be allocated for constructing branch structures, because communities will change, the relation between the public library and local school libraries is uncertain, and the new technology will alter the future character of branch library service. Actually much of local service may eventually derive electronically from fixed regional centers. Such centers will be necessary, even in a new pattern of service, because sources of centralized materials and sources of automated information must form the foundation

of a new system. With the Chicago building fund at the rate of .2 mills, it will be possible to construct two of these regional centers a year, and thus have the foundation built by 1975.

The recordkeeping, voucher processing and payroll handling operations of the Business Office need internal review and simplification and then computerization.

These two steps of streamlining and automation go hand in hand. For the internal review of procedures, a consultant should be hired to guide the analysis and suggest alternative methods, but the actual review should be done by a regular staff group. This would include the Business Manager, the Library Accounting Clerk, the Head Library Clerk, and a representative from the comptroller's office at City Hall, along with an additional accountant to be hired for the library staff, who as a new appointee would initially devote full time to this review, acting for the internal review committee. With streamlined procedures should go computerization, both of voucher processing and of payroll records. This is not a highly complex application of automation, such as is recommended elsewhere in this report for book processing and for circulation records, but rather an operation that has become standard in business and government. The tie-in would be direct with the Data Processing Center of the city. An additional tie-in will occur when book processing in the Library is controlled by computer records, specifically in the handling of invoices for payment of materials purchases. Input for the computer will still have to be prepared, but once done, automatic production can occur of purchase orders, lists of bills, monthly expenditure reports, and expenditure breakdowns by departments and branches. A parallel application could apply to payroll processing. The actual computer work would be done at the city Data Processing Center or at a service bureau. In the review of procedures, appropriate internal control and accountability should be established; this is to include sharing of authorization and countersigning procedures for all disbursements of any size.

The staff group devoted to financial and related activities needs reorganization and strengthening.

The Business Manager of the Library should be designated as Assistant Librarian for Business and Finance, with the position at the Librarian VI level. The position calls for an officer of high caliber to direct the substantial and varied business functions of the Library (accounting, financial analysis, payroll, and purchases and receiving) and to bring business judgment into the central planning and review councils of the institution. He properly serves under the Chief Librarian. His designation as Secretary of the Board is to be retained, as a channel of communication and a means for financial recording, and in this capacity the Secretary can function with the Chief Librarian in approving major bills for payment. Within the department there should be three sections —accounting, payroll, and purchasing—each

with a section head in charge. The present Library Accounting Clerk should be named head of the accounting section, at a Grade 15 level, and a second accountant's position created in the section. In total the number of positions in the department should be increased by at least four, not only to handle the present workload but also to provide financial information now not compiled.

Formerly the business and secretary's office of the Library prepared budgets, controlled expenditures, set personnel quotas, and, in general, managed the agency separate from materials selection and service programs. At present the office keeps accounts, supplies limited financial information, and maintains contact with the fiscal offices in City Hall. From a program control unit at one extreme, it has swung over to a recording office at the other. The appropriate and constructive function is somewhere between the two, not, on the one hand, to make decisions that affect the total service program, but, on the other hand, to participate in the fiscal planning of the Library and control expenditures through the year. The Chicago Public Library needs a streamlined fiscal office even as it needs service-oriented public departments.

11 Metropolitan Library Relations

Libraries appear in response to need and tradition. They spring up in municipalities large and small, in schools and colleges and universities, in modest professional associations and great commercial enterprises. Either one or both of two assumptions is back of each new arrival—the belief that at least some needed library resources are not available elsewhere in the area, and the calculation that those resources that do exist are neither conveniently and legally accessible nor functionally organized for the purpose in hand.

Proliferation of libraries is accelerated in a metropolitan region such as the greater Chicago area, with its complexity of endeavor and multiplicity of private and governmental units. No recent inventory has been taken of Chicago-area libraries, but the number now exceeds 1,500 (twice the total recorded in the 1945 *Directory of Libraries of the Chicago Area*). Numerically the almost 1,000 school libraries are the largest group; then there are some 300 "special" libraries varying from a few thousand volumes to world-renowned collections, 94 college and university libraries (substantially more if departmental units and separate collections within universities are counted), and finally 144 public libraries in the six counties comprising the standard metropolitan statistical area.

As libraries proliferate, a kind of pattern in the web or fabric emerges. Each library seeks to fill a gap in the pattern, for a more or less distinct group of users with somewhat different purposes and circumscribed by a locale defined geographically or functionally. Rather than web or pattern, the better descriptive image would be that of a constellation of libraries, associated by forces not consciously planned, marked by gaps and overlaps, yet related in an impersonal sense.

The Chicago Public Library is the largest of the libraries in the region, on the basis of number of volumes or size of staff or multiplicity of branches. But this does not mean that it is necessarily the brightest star in the constellation. Others have greater depth or closer immediacy of service or more specialization of staff. We must seek first to "place" the Chicago Public Library among the 1,500 agencies of this kind in the metropolitan area.

The Chicago Public Library in the Metropolis

There are several ways to describe and relate the many libraries in a metropolitan region. One is by sheer size of collection. On this basis the Chicago Public Library, with its 4 million items, is the largest, followed by the University of Chicago with a little under 3 million and Northwestern University with a little under 2 million. Among public libraries the collection next largest to Chicago is that in the Evanston Public Library with 234,000 volumes, about the size recommended for the ten regional centers within Chicago.

But if some standard of depth or uniqueness

of holdings is used, relationships change drastically. The University of Chicago has almost ten times as many *titles* as the Chicago Public Library. The city library subscribes to 2,600 journals in all subject fields; the John Crerar Library receives 11,000 journals in the science and technology fields alone. The Newberry Library has two thousand incunabula; the Chicago Public Library has none. Even the collections in a hospital or an advertising firm or a publishing house may have items not found in the huge stacks of the city agency. In terms of specialization of holdings, the Chicago Public Library, despite its bulk, is one among many.

Another way to look at libraries in the Chicago area is politically and geographically. The base becomes almost 200 municipalities, of which 144 maintain their own libraries. Most restrict use to their own residents and taxpayers and build little fences around communication, in sharp contrast with the area-wide scope of television and radio and newspapers and the national scope of the very books and magazines which constitute the collections of the local libraries. From this perspective the Chicago Public Library serves the largest piece of territory on the map—the piece in the center. It is worth noting that there is no fence around this large central unit; the Chicago Public Library issues cards to any resident of the metropolitan area without payment of fee.

The municipal libraries, including the Chicago Public Library, are "general" libraries in purpose and holdings and clientele. Most of the others exist for fairly specific purposes—the media requirements of the Evanston Township High School, the information needs of the First National Bank, the resources requirements of students and faculty at De Paul University, the reference inquiries received from the members of the American College of Surgeons. The public library is multipurpose in character and multipublic in clientele. It serves many of those with their own institutional libraries, and besides has its own distinct patron group. Just over half (51.9 percent) of the users of the Chicago Public Library also use other libraries, while for the remaining group, some 370,000 individuals (10 percent of the population), the city library is the primary institutional source of recorded knowledge.

Another way to place the Chicago Public Library among the many libraries of the Chicago area is to think in terms of a spectrum of exclusiveness and inclusiveness of persons permitted to use an agency. At one extreme there is the internal information system within a corporate research laboratory, essentially a collection holding the output of a series of researchers and expressly prohibiting any outside consultation because of industrial competition. There are libraries built up for the workers in an individual enterprise that on request admit outsiders. Then there is the special library that may welcome and encourage outside use, as do some insurance companies and professional associations. College and university libraries which are maintained for the students and faculties of their respective institutions, regularly receive requests for use from persons not associated with the campus and often find themselves perplexed by just what their policy should be toward such demands. School libraries have not commonly experienced requests for use by individuals not connected with the school, but this could change as their collections grow and become attractive to a wider group, and if the school library were to become the all-purpose community source for children that presumably would include local youngsters attending institutions other than the public schools. Such an agency as the Municipal Reference Library, while built primarily for use by government employees, is maintained by public funds and welcomes anyone who has a legitimate claim on its resources. At the end of the spectrum is the public library, maintained by all, ostensibly built for all, and open to all.

One way to describe the role of the public library in this metropolitan complex is that it does what is left over to do. Those who can have their own library, be it in their school, in their business or industry, in their home. Others must take second-best and make a trip to the general library. Following this line of thought, in time, if enough special libraries existed, no general library would be needed.

Such a view unduly diminishes the role of the general public library and discounts its capacity to change. When the very considerable use of the public library by special librarians themselves, as reported below is noted, perspective is regained. But as applied to the Chicago Public Library, this principle of diminishing function has a measure of truth. The agency presumably functions as a local community library for people who have no other institutional source for books and journals and recordings and films, yet it does not adapt to the needs of differing communities. The Library serves many students but does not maintain close relations with the schools; in any case this clientele will decrease as school libraries become stronger. The Central Library offers special subject service, but at a level below that needed by specialists. In the past, for lack of adequate resources elsewhere in the Chicago area, the public library has been used moderately if not extensively. In the future, unless the Library clarifies its purposes, strengthens its capacities, and heightens its impact, it could be superseded as new means of disseminating information, recorded knowledge, and visual communication are developed.

But the Library has been resilient in the past, adjusting to change and demand. It may be expected to do so again in the future, specifically in response to urban change. In essence this report is an exercise in suggesting directions of adjustment and intensification. The direction indicated is away from a middle range of resources, which are increasingly available elsewhere and toward a series of special programs within the general framework of service—for the unaffiliated specialist and amateur scholar, the information seeker, the cosmopolitan family, the ghetto neighborhood.

That new business, professional, and technical libraries are appearing is laudable—but there are many people who do not work for large corporations and are not members of organized professions. It is essential that school and college libraries continue to improve, but students even from the stronger institutions fall back on the public library, whether for reasons of necessity or convenience. There is a future for the public library, but it is not necessarily the same as its role in the past when general reading was hard to come by and special collections were few and far between. Currently the tendency is to equate the urban environment with problems and poverty and deterioration; actually the urban setting, in the sweep of history, is variety, intensification, and affluence. While the Chicago Public Library must mobilize to help meet the current urban crisis, essentially it will function for the rest of the century in a developing urban environment, serving persons with ever-higher education. Specialization and depth of service, rather than the general provision of a middle-range collection handled by nonspecialized librarians, increasingly will be called for in these years.

The user does not look at the many libraries within Chicago and over the region in the same way as the librarian. The latter thinks first of a single organization, his own, and only secondarily of how his agency relates to the others.

The user on the other hand simply asks, "Where can I get what I need?" For each individual the answer is different. To some the company or institution or school library is the center of the library universe, and they seldom if ever turn to the municipal agency. To others the immediate "special" collection is the more frequently used, with the large public library a second line of supply when more comprehensive materials are needed. To some 10 percent of Chicagoans the public library is the beginning and end of their library outlook, although they are likely to purchase some resources or borrow from friends. Each reader works out his own "system" of libraries, picking and choosing among those to which he can gain admission. The user's common sense area-wide viewpoint, looking on all collections as integral parts of a total social resource, is to be commended to professionals and planners. At the same time the planner should be cautioned against the other extreme, the setting up of a neat interlibrary structure, for the ways that people use libraries are many and wondrous to behold.

To a limited extent the Chicago Public Library has sought to find a proper and constructive place among the many libraries of the Chicago region. This grows naturally out of its size, its public nature, and its location in the economic-cultural center. Part of the relationship goes back seventy years to the joint agreement involving the Chicago Public Library, the John Crerar Library, and the Newberry Library. Part has since been built up in response to pressure and opportunity.

USE BY NONRESIDENTS

Chicago-area users themselves have tended to make the Chicago Public Library a metropolitan institution. Twenty-two percent of the patrons of the Central Library do not live in Chicago—some of these are commuters to the Loop and adjacent sections, some are shoppers in the nearby retail district, some are college students who attend institutions in the city but live outside, and a small percentage come into the city primarily to use the central collection. In branches near the city boundaries, nonresident use goes as high as one-third (Greenwood Park is an example). Harwood Heights and Norridge, two small municipalities entirely surrounded by Chicago, do not maintain their own libraries; in a 1966 count there were 888 residents of the former "village" with Chicago cards, and 2,368 from the latter jurisdiction. The same is true for such partially enclosed governmental units as Lincolnwood in the north (2,109 Chicago registrants in 1966) and Alsip (740 Chicago residents) in the south. These outlying localities are getting a free ride and do not put up any money for library service for themselves. In fact the 1966 count identified almost 10,000 registrants of the Chicago library who live in 27 municipalities that provide no library service of their own.

The Chicago Public Library has received the non-residents with open arms. It offers full borrowing privileges without fee, and 70,000 suburbanites have taken advantage of the opportunity. This liberal policy contrasts with that of the suburban public libraries, most of which impose a nonresident fee for a library card for persons living outside the municipality. In many cases the fee is $10 or more (Evanston, Oak Park, Skokie, Glencoe, Highland Park, Park Ridge, Wheaton, Elmhurst, Berwyn, for example). Four North Shore suburbs (Glenview, Lake Forest, Wilmette, and Winnetka) set the figure at $20. Residents of all of these communities not only can but do use the Chicago Public Library without charge, but the privilege is not reciprocal. As examples from the list above, 2,220 Berwyn residents had Chicago cards in 1966, 2,479 from Evanston, 814 from Glenview, 3,626 from Oak Park, 1,480 from Park Ridge, and 3,071 from Skokie. If a Chicagoan seeks to reverse the process, he must pay from $10 to $20.

In other metropolitan centers it is usually the larger and older libraries that throw up barriers by means of nonresident fees, for fear of being inundated by outsiders who would gravitate to the stronger facilities, while the smaller places favor free reciprocal access in the belief that they get the better of the bargain. In the Chicago area the situation is reversed, with the metropolitan library opening its doors and smaller agencies imposing a fee. The present unequal balance is not likely to prevail permanently; either a reciprocal exchange will be achieved, with both large and small municipalities benefiting, or pressures will appear to exact a fee for borrowing privileges from the Chicago Public Library, thus penalizing readers.

RESEARCH AND REFERENCE CENTER

As this study reveals, the Chicago Public Library is *de facto* a metropolitan library, with its central building and branches used by nonresidents both for reference and for borrowing purposes. Designation of the library by state legislation as one of four Research and Reference Centers in the state in a sense recognized an existing situation and provided some money to help meet its cost. The question was raised earlier in this report apropos the present capacity of the Chicago Public Library to serve at advanced reference and research levels for its own people, much less for twice the population in northern Illinois.

The Central Library has for many years also supplied books for short periods to other agencies in the Chicago area on interlibrary loan. Until recently this was a steady but modest demand amounting to some 2,000–3,000 requests per year (2,934 in 1967). The volume remained modest not because potential demand was lacking but because smaller libraries hesitate to request help constantly from a large center. Then designation of the Chicago Public Library as a Research and Reference Center included responsibility for handling interlibrary loan requests. Local libraries now look on the interlibrary service from the big city as a right rather than a benefaction. The number of requests from northern Illinois in 1968, the first full year of operation, rose to 14,136 (plus 553 requests from other areas) and in the first months of 1969 was again running ahead of the previous year.

The interlibrary service is being organized on a businesslike basis. Requests properly come not directly from each small local library but first through a regional system, so that resources within a coordinated group of libraries are called upon before the large central library in Chicago is turned to. For nearby suburban systems, delivery is speeded by carrying books on Chicago trucks to outlying branches, where they are in turn picked up by system trucks. Teletypewriter is being installed to connect the suburban systems with the main building in Chicago, and that in turn with the three other Research and Reference Centers in the state (Illinois State Library, University of Illinois Library at Urbana, and Southern Illinois University at Carbondale) to locate titles not available in the Chicago collection.

Of the 14,136 interlibrary loan requests received by the Chicago Public Library from northern Illinois library systems in 1968, 42.7 percent were filled from the Chicago collection, 26.8 percent were referred to other libraries, and 30.5 percent were returned unfilled to the requesting libraries. In the early months of 1969 the success rate rose slightly to 44 percent. In both years the fulfillment percentages were distinctly lower than the 66.7 percent rate found in a 1967 study which included Chicago.[1] Thus the performance score has gone down with the recent increase in the number of requests. Certainly the findings in chapter 4 describing the Central Library collection indicate that a high level of fulfillment cannot be expected at present from this source if the material sought approaches the level required for research.

Actually many of the requests are for nonspecialized titles that one would expect to find in a strong suburban library. These include publications about home repairs and hobbies, elementary business and medical books, even sports and general self-help items. This local-suburban systems-city library hierarchy for interlibrary loans cannot be expected to function at an advanced level until two basic conditions are met: the metropolitan library systems must develop their own collections to intermediate strength so that they can fill more routine requests from among holdings of their own members, and the Chicago Public Library must develop a level of specialized resource which it does not now possess.

Other potential attributes of the research and reference program have thus far been realized only to a limited extent if at all. No plan exists for the coordinated building of resources among the four centers. Very little "reference" or bibliographic service is requested or given. The referral service has moved some requests along to appropriate collections, but this occurs primarily within the channel

[1]Terry L. Weech, *The Illinois Research and Reference Center Program: an Evaluation* (Urbana: Library Research Center, Univ. of Illinois, 1968), p.81.

of the four designated centers and cannot be said to draw systematically and consistently on the total library resources of the 1,500 Chicago-area libraries. The present program represents only one step or phase in the emergence of the Chicago Public Library as a genuine metropolitan center.

Library Development in the Chicago Area

Before the future possibilities and responsibilities of the Chicago Public Library in the metropolitan region can be assessed, some sense of present library resources and structure in the area must be recorded. Some units are within the city and others in the burgeoning suburban and exurban districts. Also involved are questions of relations between the Chicago Public Library and such agencies as the city school system, the academic libraries in the area, the many special libraries, and the new coordinated systems of suburban libraries currently developing. Provided here is a most selective and general overview of library resources in the metropolitan region; these should be studied in depth to identify both strengths and weaknesses.

SCHOOL LIBRARIES

The development of libraries in the public schools of Chicago has been a long and deliberate process, with progress clearly evident if wide enough intervals of assessment are used; but a look at the current situation shows that Chicago still lags markedly behind national standards. High school libraries first appeared in 1918; by 1934 there were 33 central collections at this level, and 44 by 1947. Currently each of the 57 public high schools has a centralized library, with 136 librarians assigned. Libraries at the elementary level were established during the 1920s, were in 319 schools by 1947, and today are available in all 458 elementary schools, which are staffed by 394 school librarians.

The school librarians are primarily teachers who have obtained the required 15 credits in library science or beyond that the master's degree, usually at Chicago State College (formerly Chicago Teacher's College). The professional staff complement works out to one librarian to each 1,080 students, as compared to one to 250 students in the national standards.[2] These calculations do not include 157 additional librarian positions authorized in 1968, evidently provided when the elementary teachers won a free period each school day, with this to be achieved by assigning classes to the library during such periods.

A high school library typically has 15,000–18,000 volumes, with a few as large as 25,000 volumes. The elementary collections average 5,000 volumes. Audio-visual materials are provided only to a limited extent; a separate Division of Visual Education handles films, filmstrips, and related materials, for the most part from a central reservoir. The per-pupil appropriation for printed library materials is $1 at the elementary level and $1.50 at the secondary level, plus a small reallocation of some 10–15 cents per pupil from the Division of Visual Education for audio-visual materials to be located within the libraries. This contrasts with the nationally recommended figure of over $4 per pupil for annual acquisitions in the several media.[3]

This is the situation today. It must be concluded that the school libraries are hard pressed to meet needs for immediate instructional ma-

terials. It is clear that Chicago is unlikely to be in the vanguard of school library development in the next decade.

But less tangible positive elements must also be recorded. At the level of concept or purpose of school library service, the goal in Chicago is stated to be provision of instructional materials in all media, provision of general reading beyond the curriculum, instruction in the use of libraries, and reading guidance —in other words, comprehensive service related to the young person's total educational experience. Plans for libraries in prospective high schools now on the drawing boards call for 10,000–14,000 square feet (more space than in branch library buildings), book collections of 25,000 volumes, provision for viewing and listening stations, a photographic laboratory, substantial numbers of individual carrels, and a section for magazines and journals. Tentative plans for the first of a series of cluster schools encompassing both elementary and secondary levels, on the near West Side, allocate 28,000 square feet to an instructional materials center.

Not all positive factors are in the future. The Chicago school libraries have provided after school service hours in 25 inner-city schools since 1960, with both a librarian and a "homework teacher" on duty; the number of such "extended day" programs went up to 229 schools with federal grants, but since has dropped back when the outside funds were terminated. Summer library programs operate in 95 schools, with a school librarian on duty in each. A comprehensive publication, *Curriculum Guide for Library Sciences: Kindergarten, Grades 1–8*,[4] outlines systematic and class-

[2]*Standards for School Media Programs* (Chicago: American Library Assn., and Washington, D.C.: National Education Assn., 1969), p.12.

[3]Ibid., p.35

[4]Published in 1968 by the Board of Education of the City of Chicago. This publication was formerly known as *Developmental Concepts for Instruction in the Use of the Library and its Resources*.

room-integrated instruction in library skills. When federal ESEA money was received recently, much of it went into audio-visual materials for the libraries, thus demonstrating commitment to the concept of the school library as a media center.

The point is that forward-looking plans have been made and are applied as funds permit. In time the school libraries in Chicago will be multipurpose materials centers for the children and young people of the city. At the same time, given the rate of progress in the past and current financial prospects, it would be overly sanguine to assume that these goals will be achieved in Chicago to any significant degree in the next few years and unrealistic to design a children's and young people's library materials and service delivery system in the immediate future on the basis of this assumption.

In earlier years relations between the school system and the public library were close, both structurally and functionally. The first high school libraries were provided entirely by the public library; this included supervision, staff, materials, and centralized cataloging. Step by step the Board of Education took over this provision, first taking responsibility for the cost of personnel (1923) and later of materials (1931). In 1948 administration passed from the Chicago Public Library to the Division of Libraries then established in the school system. This was logical as the school libraries increasingly became an integral part of the instructional programs of the schools, and inevitable as policy differences concerning the aim and nature of school library service opened between the two institutions.

The first elementary "libraries" were classroom deposit collections furnished by the public library. At the peak, in 1932, 3,364 such classroom collections were maintained; these classroom deposits accounted for two-thirds of the 300,000 juvenile volumes then held by the Chicago Public Library. Thereafter, as elementary school libraries were established and grew, the school deposits went into a long and steady decline, down to 433 in 1958, and almost disappearing (30 classroom deposits in the public schools) by 1968. Clearly a cycle has been completed.

The sequence is worth repeating. First there was little provision in the schools beyond the textbook. Then the public library, from its own funds, provided materials within the schools. Later the two agencies jointly handled this service. In the last 20 years sole responsibility for library provision within the schools has rested with the Board of Education, and for library provision outside of school for the same individuals with the Library Board.

Relations today between the school system and the public library are cordial but lacking in substance and continuity. Classes come to the community library, and a recent experiment by the public library provides bus transportation from the schools to a branch library in one section of the city. Teachers turn to the Education Department in the Central Library, and students use all agencies of the public library in substantial numbers. But no systematic exchange of information, consultation, or joint planning occurs between the two educational institutions serving the same clientele for closely related purposes. No interagency committee exists. Contacts at the administrative levels are sporadic and then usually general rather than concrete. Both the schools and the public library proceed with plans for new buildings without knowing what the other contemplates. No guidelines exist to indicate where the services of one leave off and those of the other begin. In only a few branch libraries has branch personnel been in the school libraries in the neighborhood in the past year, and in most cases the branch librarian could give only the most sketchy information about the school library down the street, much less about the school curriculum and what was going on in the classrooms. Indeed, even at the day-to-day level, channels of communication are clogged; the most common complaint of branch librarians is that whole class groups are sent to the public library for resources on a specific topic without prior warning.

The roads once were united and then later they were parallel. Now they are separate, with few official crossovers between the two, although students cut across from one to the other constantly.

A similar story could be told for the parochial schools, except that there was no earlier period of close relations. Libraries in these schools were slow to develop but now show a pattern of growth. The number of classroom deposits in parochial schools from the public library has leveled off and remains fairly constant at around 150 collections. But official contacts, communication of needs and problems, and planning for joint action are if anything less than with the public schools.

COLLEGE AND UNIVERSITY LIBRARIES

The 94 colleges and universities in the Chicago area vary from world-renowned institutions to community colleges only recently opened. Their libraries have a similar range, some filling requests for specialized resources from over the country, others being grossly inadequate for their everyday needs—which means that some constitute an important part of the research holdings of the area while others are really no more than weak school collections. Some of the new colleges frankly depend on the public library and other outside resources to meet their library resource needs.

The enrollment in the 94 institutions was 200,618 in 1968.[5] Table 53 shows the distribution of enrollments between city (roughly two-thirds) and suburbs (roughly one-third). The additional information in the table indicates the overall balance of library resources in colleges and universities between Chicago and the part of the standard metropolitan area outside the city, with the two-thirds to one-third distribution holding fairly even. In resources per student and book expenditures, rough measures of library effort, the city institutions on the average and the outside institutions are at approximately equal levels.

Table 53
HIGHER EDUCATION ENROLLMENT AND LIBRARY RESOURCES
(Chicago and Metropolitan Area, 1968)

	Chicago	Metropolitan area outside Chicago
Number of colleges and universities	49	45
Enrollment	130,300	70,318
Volumes in libraries	5,124,000	2,750,000
Volumes per student	39	39
Book and periodical expenditures	$2,610,000	$1,160,000
Materials expenditures per student	$20	$17

In the city proper, as shown in table 54, enrollment between the public and the private schools is now about evenly divided. The public institutions are expanding more rapidly and will move out ahead in the 1970s. The total enrollment in higher education in the city alone will approach 200,000 by 1975, close to six percent of the total population; by 1980 the students in institutions of higher education

[5] G. J. Froehlich, *Enrollment in Institutions of Higher Education in Illinois, 1968* (Urbana: Univ. of Illinois Bureau of Institutional Research, 1968), p.105.

combined with staff providing the education and those conducting related research will constitute almost 20 percent of the adult work force of Chicago, thus becoming one of its major "industries."

Breaking down the figures for library resources among kinds of academic institutions within the city brings several significant variations to light. The private colleges and universities hold over three times as many volumes per student as the public institutions and reflect the long period over which these collections have been built and the preeminent strength of the University of Chicago in particular. On the other hand, the book budgets per student of the public four-year and graduate colleges and universities are now on the average higher than for the private schools, as a result in part of substantial expenditures at the Chicago Circle unit of the University of Illinois. The public institutions are making an effort to catch up.

The junior colleges stand at a distinctly lower level. Resources of the scope necessary in four-year and graduate schools are of course not required in these two-year institutions, but in many cases their holdings are meager by any standard; college collections of under 20,000 volumes (Bogen, Fenger, Loop, and Southeast City Junior Colleges) are actually below the size now being installed in high schools in the city.

Commuting students constitute almost 100,-000 of the 130,000 total enrollees. They turn to the public library in part because branch units are often closer to where they live and in part because the libraries in some of the commuting colleges are among the most limited in the city.

Relations between the Chicago Public Library and the colleges and universities of the area are even more casual and fragmentary than are those with the schools. The Metropolitan Library Council, which met at intervals in the 1940s and 1950s and provided a means of contact and channel of communication, has been inactive for several years. Even informal and professional-social exchanges among the senior staffs of the two types of libraries are infrequent. Yet here again some of the same readers use both the academic collections and the public library, sometimes for the same topic, and college students constitute a sizeable and growing contingent of public library users. They raise even more complex issues than do high school students in building collections in the Chicago Public Library, because a title purchased in a branch for a high school history

Table 54
LIBRARY RESOURCES OF CHICAGO COLLEGES AND UNIVERSITIES

	Private colleges and universities	*Professional schools*	*Public colleges and universities*	*Public junior colleges*
Enrollment, 1968	50,500	16,500	29,300	35,000
Library volumes	3,700,000	627,000	607,000	190,000
Volumes per student	68	37	21	6
Material expenditures	$1,400,000	Not available	$990,000	$220,000
Materials expenditures per student	$28	Not available	$34	$7

or literature or social science class is often also of interest to adult general readers, but this is less true for science treatises or readings in economics or technical books in psychology and sociology called for by college enrollees. At one time the Chicago Public Library actually maintained reserve shelves in the Central Library with materials on college reading lists, but this has long since dropped out of the picture. Both for internal administration within the various libraries and for adequate provision for the students themselves, guidelines and interagency agreements are needed between the Chicago Public Library and the various academic institutions to determine how the responsibility can best be shared and what the student can expect from each type of source.

RESEARCH LIBRARIES

Actually the base of research library resources in the Chicago area rests as much in a few universities as in separate special collections. Besides the University of Chicago with its broad scope and depth, Northwestern University has research holdings of distinction in various fields, of which Africana, modern novelists, and recent American political history are only a few examples. Loyola University continues to build resources in Jesuitica and Napoleonica. Smaller academic collections also contribute to total specialized holdings of the Chicago area—Irish literature at De Paul, philosophy at Circle Campus, down to programmed learning material at Felician College and Scandinavian literature at North Park College.

The great special collections in Chicago are those in the John Crerar and Newberry libraries. Although privately supported, they are functionally "public" libraries, maintained for the public and operating to an extent within a cooperative agreement with the Chicago Public Library.

Understanding of this agreement is prerequisite to comprehending both the structure of public library service in Chicago today and the historical development of the Chicago Public Library. The agreement went into effect in 1897, the year the present central building opened. In substance the Crerar Library agreed to provide advanced and research materials in the scientific and technological fields, and Newberry in literature and history. The social sciences at the advanced level of ". . . expensive monographs, long sets of periodicals and material of historical interest"[6] were divided between the two. The city agency would play the less illustrious role of supplying ". . . all wholesomely entertaining and generally instructive books, especially such as are desired by the citizens for general home use." The three institutions together would constitute a total public library program of the kind encompassed within one library system in New York and Boston.

While this pattern has determined library service in Chicago to this day, modifications and variations—put more bluntly, gaps and limitations in the tripartite program—have opened in the neat plan over the years. In the sciences Crerar has held firm to course, including its outstanding holdings in medicine. It started to build in its part of the social sciences, but then in the late 1940s officially relinquished this commitment and disposed of the considerable resources that had been acquired in economics. Newberry never did get started in its part of the social sciences, such as political science. It has built up rare and research holdings in aspects of the humanities—those de-

[6]Quotation from the 1896 signed agreement.

termined in the main by valuable collections of older material that have come on the market. As time has passed Newberry has also ceased acquiring in selected fields such as Asian and African history and literature, Scandinavian and Slavic materials, and contemporary Latin America in which a start was made. The public library, for its part, interpreted its mandate as stopping short of advanced and specialized materials, so that no one of the three libraries has systematically purchased over the years at the level above popular and student subject resources but below the research level in any rigorous sense.

Thus, seventy years later, there are gaps in subject fields, most notably the social sciences which in the interval have come to occupy a wide band in the spectrum of publishing. Also a segment of resources has not been acquired systematically, the segment related to that advanced level of publication needed by an increasingly educated and specialized society. These are comments on how the three-way agreement has worked out in practice, not criticisms of the libraries as such, for both Crerar and Newberry have built strength and depth in selected fields and within the funds available to them.

Crerar Library today is a possibly unique combination of scientific library and university library and in addition has special connections with industry. In 1962 it moved from its downtown location to a new building on land furnished by the Illinois Institute of Technology, the cost of the new structure being shared by the Institute and Crerar. Here it operates not only the Crerar collection but also administers the Institute collection, thus serving as a university library. Its connections with the scientific world and industry beyond the campus have not only been maintained but expanded.

On a fee basis Crerar offers advanced reference service in science, translation facilities, "current awareness" service to individual industries, and abstracting functions in such forms as *Leukemia Abstracts* and *Metals Abstracts*. The foundation for all these services is the extensive older and current holdings in science and engineering, both monographic and serial in form.

The Newberry Library has developed along different lines. It should not be thought of as a library that systematically buys current publications in fields of the humanities and history. Rather it acquires older and unique collections as these become available, then fills in and builds around these acquisitions, thereby assembling distinctive research collections in the process. Its holdings in such diverse fields as printing and typography, the history of music, the Renaissance, British and Western European history and literature, the American Indian and Midwestern American history and literature are exceptional. Rather than coordinating acquisitions with the Chicago Public Library, it is more likely to consult with the University of Chicago, Northwestern University, or the Art Institute. Admission is now by card, a device adopted to limit use to persons actually needing rare and research resources.

The 1896 agreement stands in the background and has shaped the contemporary pattern of library service in Chicago. But like an old building it shows cracks and it does not accommodate various contemporary resources or needs.

Relations between the Chicago Public Library and the John Crerar Library were fairly regular when both were located in the Loop. Readers could be directed across the street to consult advanced reference publications in Crerar or to borrow elementary science books from the public library. With the shift of Crerar to the campus of the Illinois Institute of Technology, contacts are infrequent, both in staff consultation and referral of users. When Crerar gave up its substantial economics materials in the late 1940s, the public library did not take advantage of the opportunity to extend its holdings in this field.

Contact and consultation between the Chicago Public Library and Newberry were meager from the outset. Currently when Newberry informally discusses acquisitions with other Chicago-area libraries, the public library is not included. Only one Central Library department head was known by Newberry officials to have visited the library in recent years. Neither reference librarians nor book selectors in the city agency are well informed about the time spans and limitations of Newberry resources, and the appropriate central departments do not even have copies of the published catalogs of such renowned Newberry holdings as the Ayer and Wing collections. The 1896 agreement was clearly the product of men who sat long around the conference table, considered the common good as well as their own needs, and worked out a design at once visionary and practical; today contacts are limited to an exchange of greetings at professional meetings.

SPECIAL LIBRARIES

The 300 or more special libraries in the Chicago area constitute a genuine resource both for the particular clienteles served and for the region as a whole. Typically these libraries do not try to assemble broad and comprehensive collections, but turn to the public library for this wider background. They do acquire special subject resources, often in sufficient depth to extend what can be found anywhere in the area. To the extent that such special collections can be tapped as needed, the metropolitan district

is the richer. Examples of larger special libraries come immediately to mind, such as the Joint Reference Library in public administration, the Municipal Reference Library, and the library of the Chicago Historical Society. Beyond these, a host of special units exist—in industries and industrial research centers, in banks and insurance companies and advertising agencies, in public utilities, in newspaper offices and publishing houses, and in professional associations, many of which have their national headquarters in Chicago.

In view of the demand on the Chicago Public Library from special libraries, a questionnaire was sent to a sample of 41 such agencies representing the various types. Thirty-six replies were received, often with copious notes and comments. Ten of the special libraries turn almost weekly to the public library, 19 are regular although not as frequent users, and 7 rarely if ever do so. A little more than half of the demand is for materials not held in the smaller special collections and somewhat less than half is made up of reference questions, which are usually handled by telephone. The heaviest call is on the Social Science and Business Department and the next heaviest on the two science departments. Of the special librarians who make fairly regular use of the Chicago Public Library, 20 rated the service as generally satisfactory and 9 as generally unsatisfactory.

These special library respondents are, of course, a group particularly knowledgeable of what library service can and should be, and they have high expectations due in part to the standards usually required in a business or industrial library. Their main criticism was that staff is usually not qualified to handle inquiries; another criticism was that resources they would expect to find in a large public library are not in the collection. To a general question concerning "improvement or deterioration" of public library service in recent years, the following is a typical reply: "For many years there was a gradual deterioration in service and collection. Since the recent change in administration, the morale is obviously better and there is more of a service attitude expressed. But there are also more staff members who are less skilled in giving service and using the collections."

Across the country the local chapters of the Special Libraries Association have been active in drawing special librarians together and affording an opportunity for public librarians in subject fields—who in a sense are special librarians—to make professional contact with this aspect of the library world. Only one department head in the Chicago Public Library is a member of SLA and attends its functions; very few other members of the public library staff participate. This contrasts with such suburban libraries as those in Evanston and Skokie, where staff are members of the Special Libraries Association and the libraries also hold institutional memberships in the organization. Special librarians are one important user group of the public library. "Special" users—meaning by this readers pursuing subject lines of inquiry—constitute a significant segment of Central Library patrons. Yet here again, as in the case of student users and community users, the staff of the Chicago Public Library stands apart, neither communicating with the agencies and organizations from which inquiries originate, nor participating in the professional groups seeking to understand special users and improve service to them.

SUBURBAN LIBRARY SYSTEMS

Beginning in 1966, a new and significant element entered the metropolitan library scene in the form of six library "systems." These are voluntary associations of public libraries which jointly seek to improve service by cooperative and coordinating projects. Another way to describe them is as libraries for libraries, wholesale centers for the direct outlets. Government of the systems is by trustee representatives of the member libraries, administration by a small professional staff, and funds come from state aid. These are exclusively public library associations, without school or academic or special members, so that orientation is toward general rather than student or specialized or research service. It is regrettable that such systems, when they appear, so often are limited to public libraries; if a new and coordinating element is introduced into the library mix, there is a golden opportunity to look at library resources from the interagency standpoint of users rather than along organizational lines and confined to one type of agency. The systems plan is ordained in state legislation.

Two of the systems (Suburban and North Suburban) completely surround Chicago—one on the north and northwest, the other on the west and southwest. Two more (DuPage and Bur Oak) are in a ring further to the west and southwest, extending to and beyond the formal boundary of the standard metropolitan statistical area. Three additional systems (Northern Illinois, Starved Rock, and River Bend) extend west across northern Illinois to the Mississippi River. In the 23 counties of northern Illinois, with a total of 249 public libraries (other than the Chicago Public Library), 196 libraries are members of the seven systems. Among the 144 public libraries in the metropolitan area proper, 128 are members of systems. The holdouts are a few larger libraries, such as Aurora and Highland Park, and several small agencies.

In their brief life spans, the systems first engaged in review, planning, and exploratory activities and have recently moved on to cooperative service programs. Interlibrary loan has to a degree been systematized and speeded up. Headquarters or central libraries have been designated. A centralized processing unit for acquisition and cataloging of books has been set up in the Oak Park Public Library, and is used by libraries in several systems. Additional books are being purchased. An intersystem feasibility study is underway on development of a bibliographic bank or center to facilitate resource sharing among system members. Less tangible but potentially of import is expert consultation from systems staff in analyzing local library problems. Some progress has been made in filling gaps where service was not available.

At the same time the Illinois systems are in an embryonic stage. In the metropolitan area the user has thus far only indirectly felt their impact. Reciprocal borrowing privileges have not been instituted, so that a user does not have direct access to any more library resources than before. Some headquarters libraries do not have collections equal to their assigned tasks, and only limited funds have gone into building them up. The user does not see the mutually advantageous projects that librarians devise. From his standpoint the essentials of a library "system" are clear and simple—nearby libraries that he can use interchangeably and a central collection and staff within reach that can take over where the local facilities leave off. Reference service between libraries, one helping the other with difficult questions, has hardly started. Finally, the fact that the federations are confined to public libraries, most of them of modest size, restricts the depth and variety that can be marshalled; thus a plan for "sharing resources" is limited from the begining if it draws only on a series of general and to a considerable extent similar collections. Smaller libraries have been the main beneficiaries of systems services thus

far; the larger and stronger suburban libraries report relatively little impact.

The Chicago Public Library is also a "system," although of a unified rather than a federated type. To this point it has not participated in the planning activities of the suburban combines. Potentially these new systems units are of importance in moving toward a planned metropolitan library program, with the individual systems pulling together local and often relatively small libraries, and then the systems together joining with the large city library for a region-wide approach. The time has come when the Chicago Public Library can extend its metropolitan role in a feasible and equitable arrangement. From the standpoint of long-range planning, for its own well-being as well as that of the region, the Library has no choice but to participate in the emerging metropolitan supersystem, indeed taking the initiative where its resources place it in the front of the parade.

Conclusions and Recommendations

In total the region of which Chicago is the center will pass the 10 million mark in population early in the 1970s. This includes almost 7 million currently in the Standard Metropolitan Statistical Area, close to a half million in northern Illinois outside the formal metropolitan area, 600,000 in the district immediately adjacent in northwestern Indiana, and close to a million and a half in southeastern Wisconsin. The 1970 census will show approximately 9,500,000 people in the tri-state metropolitan region in the broader sense.

Chicago is the single largest and most populous piece in the metropolitan jigsaw puzzle. Yet it contains only one-third of the total population of the region. As the largest center, it has a contribution to make to the entire region, in library as in other affairs, but at the same time, as a minority part of the growing region, it has much to gain by making this contribution, at once adding to and sharing in the strength of the whole.

A policy of consideration and planning for the total region so that the proper initiative can be taken to provide needed library services for the metropolis is therefore recommended for the Chicago Public Library. As this study indicates, the Library has much to accomplish for the residents of the city. But it also has a role in the metropolitan area, which if handled properly will strengthen the total institution and open fresh sources of financial support to carry the added load.

This does not mean a single inclusive structure dominated by the city library. Comprehensive regional centralization and consolidation across municipal boundaries for selected public services has occurred where two conditions hold: (1) use and interdependence across governmental lines is self-evident, and (2) personal or community attachment to the service in question is not strong (examples are highways, mass transport, bridges, and sewage disposal). Libraries are not among these services; to the local resident the need for area-wide coordination is not self-evident ("We have a good library in our town"), and people do feel attached ("and it's our library").

Local governments have proven almost indestructible in the face of repeated criticisms by political scientists and planners and, in one form or another, will relate to library service in the future. The beginning of realism and planning wisdom is to accept their existence. But this does not mean that coordinated metropolitan library service is either impossible or even revolutionary.

The heart of the problem is for library officers to find a constructive and working balance between regional centralization on the one hand and local control on the other. The former strengthens the service base; the latter promotes flexibility and individuality. The recommendations that follow do not present any finished and rigid plan for a metropolitan library program but rather some promising starting points for joint action of mutual benefit. A grand design for the future will have to be worked out by the many libraries together. These proposals are designed to release and deploy the potential of the Chicago Public Library's contribution in a way that will augment rather than dissipate what power the agency has.

The recommendations deal first with internal steps that the Chicago Public Library can take, then with the points of city-metropolitan interface where improved services on its part would contribute to the region as well as the city, and finally with the obvious need for contact, communication, and planning among the libraries of the Chicago region.

As a start toward reaching out to other libraries, professional staff members of the Chicago Public Library should become informed about and consciously and systematically relate themselves to the total library resources of the region.

First, this means in-service training in the scope, limitations, and policies of other libraries, to be followed by visits to the most important of them. In the process, explicit identification should be made of a contact person in each major agency—and on its side the Chicago Public Library should designate a senior staff member in the Humanities Department for regular liaison with Newberry, the Natural Science Department for contact with Crerar, the Social Science Department for contact with the Municipal Reference Library and the Joint Reference Library, and others as needed. This also means greater participation by Chicago Public Library staff members in the affairs of the Chicago Library Club and the Chicago chapter of the Special Libraries Association. Such steps do not require creation of any new structures or finding of fresh sources of funds. Contact can be made immediately, the flow of useful information to the service desks of the public library will be constant, and, in time, the exchange will become a two-way route to the benefit of total library service in the Chicago area.

As another early step, the Chicago Public Library should identify its research-type holdings which are not now being used and open negotiations with nearby libraries which may need the material.

At times over the years, the Chicago Public Library has acquired unusual material of special value; at an earlier stage there was a scholarly dimension to acquisitions. Of course, if this material will continue to fit the future development of the collection, it should be retained. But some runs of 19th-century periodicals, certain historical series, older newspapers, and various highly specialized bibliographies are, in a sense, lost in the municipal collection and would be of greater value and use in another location. Materials retired to the warehouse should be particularly scrutinized in this regard. At one and the same time, the transfer of such materials would strengthen another more appropriate collection and open needed shelf space in the Chicago Public Library. In the process, departmental staffs would learn afresh about some of the exceptional holdings within the Library. The exchange might work both ways; other libraries may locate materials that would be better situated in the Chicago Public Library. Here

again no elaborate structure is needed; the materials would simply be identified, reviewed, and, if better located elsewhere, offered to the most likely library, thus opening still another flow of communication.

The book catalog of Chicago Public Library holdings is to be made available to libraries in the metropolitan areas as a finding list and source for interlibrary loan requests.

The computerized catalog in bound printed form is recommended for the Chicago Public Library itself; the catalog will be available to both staff and readers throughout the central subject departments and the branch system. The same tool would be a prime bibliographic source in libraries over the metropolitan area. High school, college, and special librarians would find it of frequent use in locating titles for their patrons. In suburban public libraries, including the relatively small outlets, the catalog would be there to be consulted as though the user were in the central building on Michigan Avenue, and he could then select needed items to be obtained by interlibrary loan. For headquarters libraries in the suburban systems, the catalog would be an aid as they build up their collections, because quick reference would show what titles and subject areas are already well provided in the central city collection. For interlibrary requests, the book catalog would facilitate the verification of bibliographic data, and where the catalog shows that the Chicago Public Library does not contain items, requests might go directly to other libraries rather than unnecessarily moving through the Chicago office. A source of this kind, showing what is in the region's Research and Reference Center, will be a valuable asset in the emerging metropolitan program.

The interlibrary loan program of the Chicago Public Library as the Research and Reference Center for northern Illinois should be systematically moved upward to more advanced and specialized resources.

This will depend on greater depth and scope in the Chicago collection. It also waits upon greater strength in the headquarters collections of the suburban library systems. But over the next few years this raising of sights will be feasible. In the long run, the Chicago area will benefit most if its Research and Reference Center functions not at an intermediate level that can be handled by a collection of a few hundred thousand volumes but at an advanced level distinctive in Illinois and the Midwest, which is its true destiny. When interlibrary loan service at this level becomes possible, every effort should be made to draw in college and special libraries as users, and not have this become solely an exchange of resources among public libraries.

The research and reference service is also to develop as a bibliographic unit, a nerve center through which requests from the Chicago area for unusual materials clear.

The Chicago Public Library needs such a center for its own users, and, in its role as an interlibrary agency, to identify resources not brought to light by the regular catalogs and then to locate collections where such identified materials are held. As recommended in chapter 4, the Information-Bibliographic Center with a staff of subject bibliographers, is the unit proposed to discharge this function. If this is operating for the city library, it would seem sensible to extend the service to all types of libraries in the region. Automated means for recording holdings will increasingly become practicable. The suburban library systems, which have instituted a feasibility study along this

line, may want to join forces with the Chicago Public Library in this endeavor to avoid creating a duplicate facility that lacks the strength possible in the central city.

Advanced information and reference service, like interlibrary loan and bibliographic facilities, are best built on a central foundation such as the Chicago Public Library and then made available across boundaries to the whole metropolitan area.

This is contemplated in the state legislation designating the Chicago Public Library as Research and Reference Center for the region. Thus far this designation has primarily affected interlibrary loan but not interlibrary reference service. Actually there may be as much value to the patron in having a channel to which his local library can turn for the answer to a complex question as for the use of an unusual book—and as to technical means for the purpose, this is as close as the telephone. As in the case of bibliographic service, this should encompass the several types of libraries, both as the originators of advanced information inquiries and as the source of answers to which the Chicago Public Library can turn if necessary. The concept is not so much that of the large city library serving as the deepest well with all conceivably needed material in one collection, but more that of the nerve center mobilizing, opening channels, and providing access to the complete resources of a region. The proposed Information-Bibliographic Center in the Chicago Public Library would be the locus of this advanced reference service.

The no-fee policy for use of the Chicago Public Library should be used as a step toward a single public library card for the metropolitan region.

The most difficult hurdle has already been taken by the removal of restrictions in use of the Chicago Public Library. The same problem that it faced—the prospect of heavy use from the outside without reciprocal privileges or other balancing compensation—will in turn be faced by the stronger suburban libraries. The way in which this problem should be met is not that of having the larger libraries absorb the extra cost, but rather of providing a means to determine where the balance is unequal (sample use-checks at intervals, for example) and then compensating the libraries giving more than they receive. One possible source of funds for the purpose is augmented state aid to the systems which, in turn, would redress the unbalance. Or grants might properly come from Cook County to the three systems now covering the total county area—the Chicago Public Library, the Suburban Library System, and the North Suburban Library System. The beneficiaries of a single card to be honored in all libraries primarily would be residents of Cook County. The outlay from the county to correct unequal balances of interlibrary use would buy a substantial amount of educational service for its residents at modest cost.

As the Chicago Public Library moves toward a computerized system for acquiring, cataloging, and processing books, linked to the national MARC (machine-readable cataloging) program, this system should be made available to libraries throughout the Chicago area on a unit-cost basis.

Once cataloging moves out of the local library to a detached center, as has occurred in part in the new suburban library systems, the prospect is open for developing the optimum unit for the purpose. What limited evidence exists on costs of centralized cataloging suggests that a few libraries together can realize moderate savings and a large combine of libraries can realize substantial savings, although groups of intermediate or moderate size may not achieve much clear advantage.[7] The few together get the benefit of eliminating duplicate work, and the large combines go on to gain economies from large-scale mechanized operations; the intermediate groups appear to encounter extra costs and delays without being able to apply and fully utilize computer capacity. These considerations relate to centralized and mechanized book processing in the Chicago area. The Chicago Public Library must in any case move toward computer control and must tie into the MARC program. This can be done solely for the city library, but it would seem wise to plan for multiple library linkage from the beginning. There are of course large programming, start-up and debugging costs in getting a plan of this kind underway. The advantages to libraries joining an established network are saving in initial costs, increased efficiency as the system becomes larger, and verified feasibility along the way.

Formal and regular contacts, hopefully leading to systematic planning and joint projects, should be opened between the Chicago Public Library and the three distinct groups of libraries in the Chicago area—research libraries, school libraries, and the suburban library systems.

Separate channels of communication are proposed, rather than a single overall agency, because of the marked differences in relationships between the large city library and these three distinct types of agencies. In relation to research libraries, the problem is to determine what modest place the Chicago Public Library has among the various scholarly collections in the area; in the

[7]Nelson Associates, *Centralized Processing for the Public Libraries of New York State* (A survey conducted for the New York State Library, 1966), p.3.

case of school libraries, the need is to define and maintain a sharing of responsibilities to students while anticipating that an increased share will be carried by the schools; and with reference to the suburban systems there should be built up a joint program which at once defines the role of the big city and makes available to the suburbs a level of service not possible among groups of libraries of small and intermediate size. It is to be doubted whether one "metro" organization can function effectively in these three dimensions. There was a single Metropolitan Library Council in the Chicago area, but it withered and died. Actually the three-way plan proposed here may well result in three distinct organizations, but this is not necessarily undesirable. The senior position at the Librarian V level proposed in chapter 9 (pages 202 and 212) will carry the immediate responsibility and detail in maintaining these relationships for the Chicago Public Library.

Research Libraries. The starting point here is to reopen contact with the Crerar and Newberry Libraries. This is all the more important as the Chicago Public Library raises the level of its holdings; a "fit" with these research libraries will close the gap in resources that has existed in the Chicago area, and by so doing will reanimate the grand design of the agreement among the three made seventy years ago. Certain specifics call for early attention—just how the public library and the Crerar patent collections relate, is one example; another is the possibility of shifting the geneological collection to the public library which has been suggested by Newberry, along with an offer of financial help from Newberry in getting it established. Discussion of such concrete prospects may serve to open the channels of communication. The University of Chicago and Northwestern University should soon be parties to such consultations.

If the five libraries were to plan and build acquisitions together, the total region would benefit. In this partnership the Chicago Public Library will be a junior member, seeking out the particular topics in which it should itself acquire research holdings, and determining just what level it should achieve in order to meet the specialized and near-research demands not covered by Crerar, Newberry, and the university libraries.

School Libraries. A formal interagency committee should be established, with representatives of the Chicago Public Library, the public schools, and the archdiocesan schools as members. This committee should be a high-level planning group, preferably with representation from the respective boards and membership on the parts of the Superintendents of Schools and the Chief Librarian; it is not merely to be a consulting group for information purposes and occasional projects. At the same time a subunit related to the committee should maintain regular communication and liaison on immediate needs. The larger responsibilities of the group will be to foster experiments in combined facilities, and, as the school libraries develop in the next ten years, to plan for formal school commitment and public library pullback in meeting the resource needs of children and young people. It is this interagency committee that should commission a study of library service to younger users in Chicago in 1980.

Suburban Library Systems. The potential is great for developing public library service over the whole metropolitan region by means of the several systems and the Chicago Public Library. The suburban systems directors already consult regularly; the city system should become part of this group. Once again the senior officer in the Chicago Public Library for metropolitan library relations would carry the direct responsibility and would initiate those activities in which the large library should take the lead. Several of these have previously been mentioned: intersystem loan, intersystem reference, and bibliographic service. Moving toward reciprocal borrowing privileges and a single library card for the region has many complications which will require persistent joint effort. Additional prospects open for the future, such as coordinated planning for regional library centers within the city and headquarters centers over the area so that in substance they become one network of intermediate-level service. Together the several systems can build a service structure of greater strength than is possible for any one, including the Chicago Public Library, to achieve alone.

Thus there are various steps, large and small, some by the Library alone and some in concert with others, which the Chicago Public Library could and should take in the interest of improved library service over the region. But no library can be expected to expand in these several directions by drawing off funds from its regular budget, especially a city library that already is not doing what it should for its own poor people on the one hand and for its specialists on the other. The proposal here is not that Chicago proceed to become the benefactor of the suburban districts by building up a unique metropolitan program from its own funds.

Rather a means for sharing costs must be found. Unless this occurs, progress will be delayed in starting and aborted when it arrives. The principle to apply is that those districts and organizations that benefit must help to carry the cost. This is not a matter of deciding which single unit or level of government is to take on the total burden, but of involving every level together.

Financing of library service starts at the local level. Every locality should carry its share; rather than imposing a maximum rate of public library support the state would more effectively further the library cause by specifying a minimum rate of support, at least at the one-mill level. Individual localities that do not support library service at all—of which there are still a score or more in the metropolitan area—should not be given a free ride in the form of access to facilities supported by taxpayers in other jurisdictions. Smaller municipalities may properly depend on other nearby libraries for service rather than establishing their own separate facilities, but in this case they should be prepared to put up money like anybody else, and either (1) work out services with the suburban library system in their area, (2) enter into a contract with a nearby library, or (3) pay on a per-user basis for such of their own residents who elect to go to outside libraries.

Businesses and industries that call intensively on the larger municipal libraries, particularly on the Chicago Public Library, should carry their share of costs. A publishing firm, for example, that makes almost daily use of the central collection and that has been granted direct stack privileges might well "buy" this special service even as it commissions writing or editing or printing services. An organization of "Business Sponsors" of the Chicago Public Library should be created. If the 100 or more enterprises that make concentrated use of the library were each to contribute a modest $1,000 annually for the service, and the larger number which make regular but less concentrated use each contribute perhaps $500, some $200,000–$250,000 would be forthcoming annually to help maintain and strengthen this aspect of the program of the metropolitan library center.

The county is another source of funds that

should not be overlooked. The Chicago Public Library is today serving at least 67,000 out-of-city county residents, most of whom have full borrowing privileges. At the prevailing non-resident rate of $10, almost $700,000 of service is involved annually. The point seems clear and logical; for whatever reasons, large numbers of nonresidents seek out the services of the Chicago Public Library—this is to be encouraged in the interest of an informed and educated populace—but it can hardly be paid for out of the limited funds of the hard-pressed city as a gift to the suburbs; some appropriate source must be found to share the load, and this points to an overall governmental unit of the people involved such as the county. If this line of argument is not convincing, there is no alternative for the Chicago Public Library except to reconsider the present liberal policy for out-of-city use. It is not easy to explain or excuse an ineffective library program in Chicago's ghetto at the same time that the more affluent residents of Lincolnwood and Alsip and other suburban communities get a free ride. But the matter should not become an either-or proposition—better service to the city poor or continued service to the suburban resident. The issue is not whether to provide or not provide library service for those who want it; the problem is to get equitable financing for what is needed.

The state has entered metropolitan library service on a small scale. Less than $100,000 of state money is provided to the Chicago Public Library annually to carry out its functions as Research and Reference Center for northern Illinois. The rationale for the size of the grant is not clear. If this is money to meet the direct cost of handling some 15,000 inter-library loan requests per year from northern Illinois, then a minimum unit rate of $5–$6 per transaction would about equal the compen-

sation provided. But this in no way pays for the necessary build-up of the Chicago collection in subject fields necessary if this program is to achieve its purpose. It in no way finances essential additions to the "research and reference" service—the handling of difficult reference questions from suburban libraries, direct inquiries by telephone from out-of-city residents, bibliographic information, and provision of copies of the printed book catalog. If the Chicago Public Library is to develop into a metropolitan center by state mandate, it would seem inequitable as well as unsound to expect this to occur at bargain-basement rates, with the out-of-city population getting a service at a fraction of what they would have to put up themselves, and the city's sources of tax revenue somehow making up the difference.

Utilization of an existing large city library as the nucleus of a metropolitan level of service can proceed on the basis of one of two assumptions. One is that such an agency already has considerable strength and should share it with those who lack a similar facility, either by free provision or with token payments. For all its appeal to the natural instincts of librarians to open and extend service, this approach does not provide a sound, long-term basis for library development in metropolitan centers, for our cities face problems of virtual survival that are straining their financial capacity to the utmost. Another approach is to recognize that the region has an asset in the large central library that has been built up over the years, that access to this resource saves the surrounding areas substantial outlays, and an equitable distribution of costs should therefore be found—not by draining off the limited financial base of the large city library, but by contributing to and reinforcing that base in the interest of the city and suburb and metropolitan region alike.

12 Priorities for the Period Ahead

No final and completely logical sequence can or should be laid down for the development of the Chicago Public Library. Both priorities and schedules depend on several variables, from changes in the city itself to success or failure of experimental programs initiated by the Library. The essential and most urgent requirement is to get moving at whatever points are amenable to early response, and from this start enthusiasm, confidence, and momentum will grow and spread to other parts of the organization. Effecting change in a large and long-established institution is not easy, but the Chicago Public Library has shown fresh life in the past two years even with its limited resources of money and personnel and will respond even more to determined leadership in the future.

The outline and sequence presented in this chapter are therefore suggestive rather than definitive. In the face of all that should be done, a start must be made somewhere; likely initial moves are indicated for a first year of preparation and launching of a new program. Then, with resources in hand, action must be pushed not on one but on many fronts; these are suggested for the five-year period 1970–1975. Even when the enterprise is moving on many fronts, continual direction is needed, not only to maintain quality but to evaluate progress and identify false starts and dead ends. As a guide to this ongoing development, a recapitulation of the basic policies which should prevail is given for a 1975–1980 "Phase III" period.

Three ingredients are essential at the outset as well as later on—the will to change and develop, money to pay the way, and personnel to get the job done. Without these the total program developed in this report and the specific priorities suggested in this chapter will be no more than theory. Therefore the first and preliminary step proposed is involvement of Board, administration, and staff in discussion and review of the survey report itself. The object of the exercise is not to ferret out recommendations with which some individuals may disagree or proposals that must be put off for the present—of course there will be such in any broad plan projected—but rather to identify the areas of agreement and to nurture commitment to those chosen for early action.

Because money and staff are required in any case, these figure prominently in the early phases. Indeed some progress in this direction was achieved before the survey report was completed—the position of Chief Librarian has been exempted from civil service and put on a "cabinet" basis; a national search has started for the administrative director of the library in the period ahead; and the state-imposed pegged levies for both operating funds and capital improvements have been removed and the state-wide support rates for libraries applied to Chicago, thus opening the way for an increase in operating revenues by some $2 million in each of the next two years, 1970 and 1971, and by an increase in the capital commitment from $800,000 to $2,250,000 annually.

Not every recommendation detailed in this

report has been fitted into the outline of priorities. Many specifics can be acted on as the opportunity arises. And the plan as presented here is only in compressed outline form and simply gives a checklist of project items within the broad program. As each item is considered for action, reference should be made to the appropriate presentation and discussion within the body of the report.

PHASE 1. *Preparation for Action, 1969–1970*

1. As an interim measure, obtain removal of the $9 million pegged levy on operating funds and put the Chicago Public Library on the prevailing state-wide base of 1.2 mill for library support. *(Already accomplished)*

2. Similarly obtain removal of the $800,000 pegged levy on the annual capital improvement appropriation and get the library on the prevailing state-wide base of .2 mill for library improvements. *(Already accomplished)*

3. Exempt the position of Chief Librarian from civil service and handle it as a "cabinet" post for direct Board selection. *(Already accomplished)*

4. Search out on a national basis the person best qualified to serve as Chief Librarian for the period ahead.

5. Make contact with (1) community groups, (2) city-wide groups, and (3) subject groups in order to start planning library development with the people to be served.

6. Have the Board of Directors come to a decision about the alternatives for a new central building, so that financing can be explored and preliminary plans made by the end of 1970.

7. Establish a committee of historians and cultural leaders in Chicago to review the G.A.R. location in the Central Library building and explore the possibility of combining its exhibits with those of the Chicago Historical Society.

8. Fill the position of Assistant Chief Librarian for Personnel, so that the total personnel program can go forward; this should be at the Librarian VI level and open to applicants on a national basis.

9. Create two distinct senior positions (at the Librarian IV level) in the Personnel Office for (1) recruiting, and (2) in-service training as a further step in preparing for an intensified personnel program.

10. Extend the Technician position into a career sequence at three levels, with recruitment at both the junior college (Technician I) and college graduate (Technician II) levels.

11. Make an extraordinary effort to recruit librarians from the class of 1970 in graduate professional schools across the country, by attracting them with a vital overall service program, definitely competitive salaries, and challenging job assignments.

12. Search out and create where needed Librarian III *service* positions (as distinct from management jobs) and promote present Librarians I and II, thereby opening opportunities for junior professionals now with the library and establishing a more attractive career prospect for graduate librarians in the Chicago Public Library.

13. Select ten senior and principal library clerks and provide thorough supervisory training for them, to prepare them for management assignments in recordkeeping, technical, and processing operations.

14. Build closer employee-administrative relations and establish clear channels for grievance procedures.

15. Broaden the scope of and then complete

the compilation of the statement of book selection policies which is now underway, in the process reviewing and including policies not only for the present middle range of materials now held by the library but also for the acquisition of basic sources for persons of limited education and advanced sources for persons of specialized interests.

16. Create an interstaff committee to explore the diffusion of audio-visual materials throughout the library, going on in 1970 to experimental programs in at least one branch (perhaps Woodlawn) and one central department (e.g., Education).

17. Consider and adopt several educational "themes" (e.g., racial understanding, consumer information, the younger generation) and push them in appropriately different ways in different communities (avoiding a standardized centrally-structured program) throughout the library system.

18. Consolidate and streamline information service, in person on the premises and by telephone, in the Central Library, as evidence of the "new" Chicago Public Library, thus creating an Information Center to take its place in the life of Chicago.

19. "Tighten up" on attitude, courtesy, and thoroughness of any and all staff members who have direct contact with the public.

20. Create two top-level extension positions (at the level of Librarian VI)—Assistant Chief Librarian in charge of branches and Assistant Chief Librarian in charge of regional library centers—hire outstanding national leaders for the positions, and open central city-wide offices for branch and regional service throughout Chicago.

21. Shift the present Regional Librarians, as soon as the central extension offices are opened, from detailed management duties to planning and coordinating functions in the field, starting with the creation of professional task forces—those for the ghetto areas to be formed first.

22. Study the prospects and locations for small neighborhood individualized storefront units in disadvantaged areas, at least two or three to be opened by early 1970.

23. Create two system-wide coordinator positions (at the Librarian V level), one for children's service and one for young adult service and hire outstanding national leaders for these positions.

24. Initiate and carry through in 1970 a program budget for 1971 with the involvement of department heads and branch librarians, general officers, and the Board of Directors.

25. Commission a step-by-step analysis of accounting and purchasing practices and procedures, looking toward modern automated methods and more adequate internal controls.

26. Change the frequency of Library Board meetings from semimonthly to monthly, with thorough staff analysis and preparation of action proposals between meetings to be made available to Board members in advance of each meeting.

27. Create a Citizen's Committee for the Chicago Public Library, derived from the lay group that advised on the present survey.

28. As an early and ongoing project, carry out an enlarged publicity program about the library, designed not so much to create and sustain an "image" as simply to inform Chicagoans, all Chicagoans, about the resources of the agency, how the agency can serve them, and the new activities and facilities being inaugurated along the way.

PHASE 2. *The Big Push, 1970–1975*

1. Put into operation an internal system-wide ·

and continuing review of every existing service unit from the user's standpoint, to make these units inviting to the visitor and easy to use, and effective in the service delivered.

2. Stress intensified service in the ghetto, built on experimentation, accessibility, variety of program, new media, and planning with local groups; open by the end of 1970 at least ten new store-front libraries or study centers or information centers or cultural centers.

3. Build and open two regional library centers each year beginning in 1971.

4. Start and continue the endeavor to strengthen, extend, and broaden the central subject collection in conformity with the new statement of selection policies.

5. Reorganize the central subject departments into five divisions (Science and Technology, Social Sciences, History and Travel, Art and Music, and Humanities), thereby simplifying and balancing the subject service structure.

6. Add genuine "specialities" within the reorganized subject departments, in the form of subunits (both staff and collections) devoted to such fields as business, education, American literature, African history and culture, religion, steel and electrical industries, and the like.

7. Add a bibliography unit to the Information Center which is recommended for immediate development, thereby creating a strong Information-Bibliographic Center.

8. Establish the two recommended cosmopolitan media centers in the Central Library—the Contemporary Media Center based on the Popular Library and the Family Materials Center based on the Thomas Hughes Room.

9. Decide upon selected fields for research

acquisitions (e.g., urban planning and development, Negro literature, Chicago authors) in consultation with other scholarly libraries, and start building the Special Collections section of the Chicago Public Library.

10. Organize the "Business Sponsors" of the Chicago Public Library, composed of firms and industries making regular use of the library, to carry part of the cost of the service they receive.

11. Complete the staffing of four professional task force groups for the branch program, to develop fresh and creative services over the city by working through branches staffed mainly by technicians and clerks.

12. Enrich service for both children and young people, in increasingly closer coordination with the schools.

13. Draw on local, indigenous personnel—mothers, part-time college students, even high school students—as aides to the professional core in working individually with users.

14. Expand the in-service training program for staff, reaching all levels from supervisors to new high school aides.

15. Specialize staff by encouraging selected members to go on to graduate subject study and by bringing in workers from such related fields as adult education, visual media, and community relations.

16. Improve service to the blind and the physically handicapped by means of reference and advisory as well as the present supply functions, and by provision of a central facility to which some of the handicapped could go directly for materials and service.

17. Revitalize the deposits program, bringing to groups of people where they assemble selected and varied collections.

18. Proceed with recruiting of staff on all

fronts during this period—professionals over the country, technicians in the Midwest, clerks in the Chicago area.

19. Establish the Computer-Communications Center, with responsibility for applications of new technology to the library.

20. Proceed with automation of computerization of acquisitions, cataloging, and physical preparation of books.

21. Build a communications network, with branches, libraries in the Chicago area, and out to centers beyond the metropolitan region.

22. Relocate the technical service divisions outside the central building, in an industrial-type building with provision for assembly-line processing and direct one-level delivery.

23. Produce a printed book catalog by computer as an alternative to the card catalog.

24. Shift to the Library of Congress classification for current acquisitions and selected older titles in the interest of long-term economy and efficiency.

25. Open formal contact with the school systems, research libraries, and suburban library systems and establish the Office of Metropolitan Library Relations for this purpose.

26. Commission a review and clarification of legal relations between the Chicago Public Library and the city government.

27. Promote revision of state-wide legislation affecting libraries, in the direction of the state maintaining a minimum but not imposing a maximum on library support.

28. Review the state designation as Research and Reference Center for northern Illinois, to clarify scope and level of responsibility and to establish an equitable basis for financing.

29. Establish the position of Deputy Chief Librarian, with broad responsibility under the Chief Librarian for advancing and implementing the new library program in the 1970s.

30. Establish the position of Assistant Chief Librarian for Program Planning and Evaluation, to serve as staff officer to the Chief Librarian in designing and redesigning service activities and in conducting research and evaluation to determine what has been accomplished.

PHASE 3. *Holding to Course, 1975–1980*

By 1975 the Chicago Public Library, under the program outlined in this study, should exhibit focus and quality in its program—that is, clarity as to what it is seeking to accomplish and at least a degree of effectiveness in carrying out its functions. At that point two underlying principles should guide its planning, administration, and operation: (1) whatever is done should be maintained at a high level and with impact and not be just another likely service provided to a limited extent for a fraction of the people who seek it, and (2) whatever is done must be subject to review and change as the character and problems of American life change. These broad principles alone may be enough to hold the ship to course, but their applications as developed in this report may be worth recapitulating here as markers, in the channel, which may continue to apply five and ten years hence.

1. The library within four walls will have given way to the concept of the library as an immediate and integral part of the lives of people—on the block where they live, in the groups with which they associate, in the jobs they hold, in the cultural and recreational activities which give lift and color to their existence.

2. Central library resources in Chicago will

have been built up to and be maintained at an advanced and specialized level between the working collections in schools and colleges and the research collections in a few universities and scholarly libraries.

3. Intermediate subject and media resources will be available to students and adults conveniently within the section of the city in which they live.

4. Highly diversified library programs responding to local neighborhoods will exist in 100 or more locations throughout Chicago and change as neighborhoods change.

5. At whatever level, library resources will be as much film as print, as much sound as words, as much leaflet as book.

6. The Chicago Public Library will be the nerve center in the Chicago area for contemporary information, in substance functioning as the fact bank, information switchboard, and special library for the general populace.

7. Service to distinct groups will be intensified (that is, mobilized, aimed, and delivered), whether to preschoolers or senior citizens, businessmen or parents, college students or community leaders, skilled workers or professionals.

8. In the world of creative cultural expression, in art and music and literature and theater and dance and handicrafts, the Library will be the recognized source of the record and of reproductions of the new as well as the old.

9. The Library will have a place in the (hopefully disappearing) ghetto as well as in near-suburban areas, and particularly in the many workingmen's communities.

10. The Library will be a resource for the sophisticated cosmopolitan as well as the cultural initiate.

11. The librarian will be "specialist," whether in the industries of Chicago or the literature and culture of Africa, contemporary poetry or foreign travel, American history or home maintenance, avant-garde literature or the sports world.

12. The librarian will also be "advocate," promoting and guiding the use of resources on selected social concerns—racial understanding, urban renewal, consumer buying, crime and drugs, pollution of the environment, the search for values—or whatever issues mark a given time.

13. The Library will be staffed by a diversity of personnel matching the diversity of its programs: specialized librarians, nonlibrary professionals devoting their skills to library service, technicians recruited at the college level, clerks in a satisfying career sequence, local residents attracted to the cause.

14. A service program planned jointly with the schools will meet the instructional and the noninstructional needs of children and young people, with a review scheduled as to future balance of school library and public library provisions for younger readers and students.

15. The various outlets and units of the Chicago Public Library will be linked by communications connections for sight and sound which will make resources available rapidly at any point in the system.

16. The Chicago Public Library will function within a metropolitan network, performing its role as a large library with advanced resources, and in turn connecting the metropolitan complex with materials across the country.

If many or most of these qualities are achieved by mid-decade, the Chicago Public Library will be a considerable influence in the life of its city and region, and will at the same time be in a good position to change course as conditions change.

Appendix

Methods

A survey of a large multipurpose agency such as the Chicago Public Library naturally moves through several stages. Clarification of scope and purpose of the project comes first; a key group participating in this initial definition was a committee composed of the President and three members of the Board of Directors of the Library. A period of sensitizing follows, when the surveyors seek to absorb the nature and temper and individuality of the institution and its social environment—perhaps the little-used term "ethos" best describes what is sought at the outset. In the process issues and limitations and potentialities are identified; these serve as a guide to the next step of developing a research design.

Systematic gathering of data—to describe conditions, analyze processes, probe for weaknesses, and verify or modify impressions—constitutes the bulk of the work and provides a solid base on which conclusions can stand. Sometimes hard facts lead directly to recommendations. More often they do no more than describe the present situation objectively, at which point there is no alternative except to call on the judgment and imagination of the surveyors to suggest what should be. An essential source at this point in studying a service agency should be the people served, the present and the potential users of the library. And the surveyors would do well to try out their conclusions on policy makers and operating staff and clientele before freezing them into a final report.

These various steps and stages were applied in the study of the Chicago Public Library. A roomful of data was acquired. Yet in the end it is not the specific and fragmentary and static facts, but understanding of a functioning institution and empathy with the people served that count most. The director of the survey was born and grew up in Chicago, and worked for nine years in the Chicago Public Library; during the study itself he lived for four months in Chicago. The two research directors each lived in the city for almost a year. The senior consultant had recently been head of the Department of Development and Planning of Chicago for five years.

This appendix briefly summarizes the various methods used for gathering data. No account can readily be given of the continuing and subjective effort to comprehend the Chicago Public Library and the city it serves.

No one source or fact-finding instrument will record the whole story of a complex service agency with a user clientele now approaching a million people and the potential of twice that number. The widest possible range of approaches was used in studying the Chicago Public Library, from the more formal and obtrusive to the more functional and unobtrusive.[1] Thus there were detailed interviews with staff members on the one hand and informal discussions at coffee breaks on the other. Part of collection evaluation rested upon objective checking of standard lists, but part upon the subjective judgment of subject bibliographers. The formal personnel program set forth in an official Staff Manual was analyzed, and this theoretical statement was offset with the comments of staff members on the job and in exit interviews. When the essential matter of actual service rendered was considered, there was

[1] Eugene J. Webb. *Unobtrusive Measures; Nonreactive Research in the Social Sciences* (Chicago: Rand McNally, 1966).

what the librarian said and also what the user found. All sources add to the search for strength and weakness.

Several guiding principles were adopted at the outset. Every effort was made to avoid premature conclusions and to let the evidence accumulate before making any evaluations. Not one person's judgment but the combined view of survey staff and consultants prevailed. Internal checks on reliability were built into question forms, and information obtained from one source was cross-checked against that from other sources on the same topics. Wherever possible the Chicago Public Library was studied in action—at the point of service performance, in regular staff and board meetings, and actual community contacts. And all resources and services were examined not only from the standpoint of approved library practice but also of user response. The impressions of surveyors about limitations in service performance were not solely relied upon, but these observations were verified by sending anonymous "shoppers" into the Library.

The field work, spread over a ten-month period from June 1968 through March 1969, moved generally through a definable sequence. An initial period was spent in preliminary visits to departments and branches, casual observation of service, and informal talks with staff members— a sensitizing period, to perceive the measure of the project and the character of the institution. The first concentrated work was on population and community life and trends, partly from cold figures and partly from visits and discussions in the fascinating neighborhoods of a metropolis in transition. Then staff members of the Library were consulted systematically and in detail, to capitalize upon their knowledge of the institution and to obtain a sense of their attitudes and values. At about the same time records of board meetings, personnel, circulation, and acquisitions were assembled and analyzed. Buildings were studied for size, spacing, design, and usability. The survey staff was then ready for systematic observation of the Library in action—setting policies, selecting and cataloging books, planning operations,

providing service—and ready also to move into collection evaluation. Relatively late in the process the emphasis shifted more to use and users, to determine response to collections and staff and services and buildings. The sequence was not as orderly as this account implies, and certain basic considerations—of social purpose and impact of the Library, of staff morale, of public image of the institution, of the decision-making processes —necessarily ran throughout the project and were not scheduled as such for study within a limited period.

Some methods used were quite standard and orthodox, and others somewhat innovative. Field visits followed the usual pattern of discussion with department heads and branch librarians (and with junior staff as well), sampling of materials on the shelves (in selected topics germane to the individual community or subject group), examination of circulation and reservation files, sitting for a period at the reference desk, and observation of users. Visits out in the city were aided by extensive community studies prepared by the University of Chicago and area redevelopment plans issued by the city's Department of Development and Planning. All visits were recorded on standard forms; for example, item 1 on the following pages shows the form used in branch visits. Where it was possible to have several survey staff members visit certain units of the Library at different times, each getting an impression of the unit visited, the observation sheet was refined into an evaluation form, as shown in item 2.

Contact with staff members took place through various channels. An effort was made to keep all staff members informed about the progress of the survey by means of brief monthly bulletins; items 3 and 4 are examples of these communications. Staff members filled out question forms, one version (item 5) for those in public service positions and another (item 6) for those in technical services. Completed questionnaires were returned by 92 percent of the staff. Then during a six-month period just under 300 staff members were interviewed; these included senior administrators, middle managers, younger people with special responsibilities, individuals who responded to an invitation to arrange an interview, and all newly appointed and all resigning or retiring staff members. Some structure was given to the interviews, while still leaving freedom for individual expression, by means of prepared questions; items 7, 8 and 9 show the points of inquiry in formal interviews with the Acting Librarian, department heads, and regional librarians, while items 10 and 11 were used for entrance and exit interviews with regular staff members.

To see the Library in operation, survey members attended staff meetings and board meetings, not just once but throughout the duration of the study. The activities of working committees were followed, such as the staff group compiling selection policies within the Chicago Public Library and the informal organization of suburban library system directors out in the metropolitan region. Where the Library was in contact with community groups, survey staff members attended sessions, and in addition contacted community groups on their own. Narrative summaries were prepared for all such staff and community meetings. As another look at the organization in operation, all staff bulletins, directives, memos, and the like were systematically read, so as to participate in the on-going communication process.

Evaluation of library collections proved particularly difficult. The difficulty derived in part from wide variation as to what materials are right or best for different reading publics; there is no one collection suitable for the many different groups and communities of a diversified city such as Chicago. Even when the appropriate type of resources for one or another reader group or local neighborhood became clear, there were no validated instruments available for measuring what was provided. As a result the approach to collections was both objective and subjective. Standard lists were checked (for example, the Queens Borough Public Library *Reference Book List for Branch Libraries,* the American Library Association *Books for College Libraries,* the Eakin *Good Books for Children* compilations,

the New York Public Library list on *The Negro in the United States*, and lists in specific fields such as education, music, art, science, religion, and other subjects referred to in chapter 4, pages 53–55). Compilations of recent publications were used, such as the "Outstanding Books" from *Choice*, and the American Library Association annual selections of notable books, business books, and science-technical books.

Such lists by and large represent the combined and, in some cases, traditional consensus of librarians as to proper library resources. Further, any list lacks other and equivalent titles which a library may possess, and treats all titles included as though they had equal value. Thus the results from checking were indicative but static. To get an appraisal of holdings in subject fields, bibliographers were used, individuals who have devoted their lives to fields of literature. The seven subject bibliographers brought in did not cover all parts of the collection but they did probe into aspects of the several broad fields of knowledge. The orientation statement given these subject bibliographers is shown as item 12. Each of these specialists then prepared an analytical and evaluative report within the range of his competence. Seeking further appraisal of collections, users were questioned; potentially this provides a revealing approach to collection evaluation, but it is clear that many readers cannot readily explain just where the available resources did or did not serve them.

What users can state is their own background, what they sought, how they used the Library, and whether they were satisfied. The patrons of the Central Library and a sample of ten branches were studied by means of the question form shown as item 13. The test period was one week in November, and within the week a selection of morning, afternoon, evening and Saturday hours. By passing out the forms as users entered and then asking individually at the exits for the return of completed forms, data were obtained from just under 90 percent of users in the test periods. The total amounted to 9,500 returns. A supplementary group of user responses was obtained from 36 special libraries in the Chicago area, as a sample of this more specialized clientele; the form for this purpose is shown as item 14.

For a closer approach to the actual contact point between library and reader (in current jargon, the institution-patron interface), a panel of representative users (and previous nonusers) was hired and sent into various agencies of the Chicago Public Library on designated quests. Some of these were simple inquiries for books by title, some original applications for library cards, while others became more complex in the form of reference questions and requests for reading guidance. Some inquiries were also made by telephone. The anonymous "shoppers" reported their experience and the service provided, on item 15 for specific questions and item 16 for advisory inquiries. As anticipated, it proved easier to get students and housewives to serve on the user panel, but more difficult to get representatives of minority and specialized groups. This technique needs refinement as a means of library evaluation, to realize fully its promise for getting at real performance with actual library patrons; work has been and is proceeding along this line at the Graduate School of Library Service of Rutgers University.

It was necessary along the way to watch for unanticipated issues and unanswered questions and then to devise means to get relevant data, thus supplementing the original research design. For example, when some branch librarians commented on delays in getting catalog cards from the central processing divisions, the question form shown as item 17 was distributed. As another example, when indications came in that children might not travel as far as adults to get to branches, a separate check was made of the home addresses of juvenile users in a sample group of agencies.

The Chicago Public Library in the past had a Friends group, but the organization had been inactive for several years prior to the survey. A Citizen's Committee was therefore organized explicitly for this study. It was composed of 140 individuals, some city-wide cultural and civic and educational leaders and others more active within local communities, including ghetto areas. The group met three times during the course of the survey. The first session was devoted to orientation and suggestions for design of the project, and led as a follow-up to the policy-question form shown as item 18. The second meeting was a working session, called when considerable data had been assembled; discussion groups considered the implications of the information. The third session was devoted to a summary of major findings and recommendations, before the final report was written. Members of the Citizen's Committee took steps to have this survey advisory group reorganized into a continuing lay commission for the development of the Chicago Public Library. Thus the ranks composed of trustees and staff are reinforced by a public group committed to the goals and general program presented in this report.

BRANCH VISITS

Form to be filled out for <u>every</u> branch visit, even if some items not observed.
Supplement on separate copy of form if second visit made. To be deposited with
Miss Strohm.

*****

Branch _____   Visitor _____   Date _____

General impression of community:

_____

_____

_____

_____

_____

Building or other branch quarters--size, arrangement, visual impact inside and
    out, state of repair:

_____

_____

_____

_____

_____

Location--in relation to traffic, shopping, other branches:

_____

_____

_____

_____

_____

Future plans for building, expansion, re-location:

_____

_____

_____

_____

_____

Service program--reference, reading guidance, children's, community relations:

_____

_____

_____

_____

_____

Collection--visual impression, non-book materials, etc.:

_____

_____

_____

_____

_____

How collection, program, staff adapted to particular community:

_____

_____

_____

_____

_____

Impressions of branch librarian and staff:

_____

_____

_____

_____

_____

Most serious problems:

_____

_____

_____

_____

_____

What potential?

_____

_____

_____

_____

Chicago Public Library Survey

DEPARTMENTAL OBSERVATION RECORD

Date _____

Dept. _____

Observer _____

Very Good	Good	Fair	Poor	
				GENERAL IMPRESSION Comments:
				TRAFFIC FLOW, FURNITURE Is information desk appropriately located? Can room be supervised from desk? Other comments:
				SIGNS (Including kinds of material and services)
				Directional
				Shelf identification (Dewey no's. – Subjects) Desk identification
				HOUSEKEEPING
				Windows clean? Books dusty? Floors Paint
				LIGHTING
				Seating-No. of seats ____ Occupied ____ Quality
				DISPLAY
				Periodicals Books
				SHELVES
				Overflowing ___ Full ___ Some space ___ Much space ___ Books in order?
				STAFF
				Appearance
				WORK SPACE

THE CHICAGO PUBLIC LIBRARY SURVEY

78 East Washington Street
Chicago, Illinois 60602

Telephone:
312-CE 6-8922 — Ext. 46

SURVEY BULLETIN NO. 7 FOR CPL STAFF

Personnel in CPL

A large part of our study of personnel has now been completed. Thus far, we have analyzed records in the Personnel Office, distributed question-naires to <u>all</u> of the technical services staff, and recently also question-naires to all librarians, trainees and technicians in both the Main Library and the branches. One-third in the last group have not returned question-naires as yet. SO WILL ALL THOSE STAFF MEMBERS WHO HAVE RECEIVED QUESTION-NAIRES AND HAVE NOT YET RETURNED THEM, PLEASE DO SO AS SOON AS POSSIBLE.

Several clerical employees have expressed concern that the Survey is for-getting them. This is not true. All clerks in the technical service de-partments were asked to complete questionnaires. For others, we have gone to records in the Personnel Office for information. We know that clerical staff members have constructive ideas about the Library, and we will be planning an open meeting with the clerical group within the next few weeks.

Among the many revealing facts about personnel are a few about <u>careers</u> in CPL in which you may be interested. In the past a staff member has moved from Junior Library Clerk on the average in $3\frac{1}{2}$ years, and then to Principal Library Clerk in $6\frac{1}{2}$ years more. This means that a person entering CPL as a beginning clerk at the present salary of $4,092 could reasonably expect ten years later to be a Principal Library Clerk making $5,472-$8,472. For professional librarians it has taken 7 years on the average to move from LI to LII, and 8 years more to go to LIII. At present salary levels, a professional starting at $7,320 could expect 15 years later to be some-where in the LIII range of $8,064-$12,528 (present scales).

That is the past record. Now the job of the Survey is to decide whether this constitutes a suitable career, or whether adjustments in salaries and in promotion opportunities must be made.

One related circumstance bearing on careers in CPL is the present age distri-bution of staff. Including all librarians (LI and above), over half are 50 years of age or older, while less than one in five is under 30.

The Survey will seek to define both a <u>service program</u> and a <u>career structure</u> that will make employment in CPL both personally stimulating and financially rewarding.

Thomas Shaughnessy
November 22, 1968

THE CHICAGO PUBLIC LIBRARY SURVEY

78 East Washington Street
Chicago, Illinois 60602

Telephone:
312-CE6-8922 — Ext. 46

SURVEY BULLETIN NO. 8

Information Service

The CPL reports having answered nearly four million "Reference and General Information Questions" in 1967, almost one question for every two books circulated. Over fifty percent of these questions were asked at the Main Library, where an increasing share of the total effort is produced. The size of this activity indicates a substantial commitment on the part of the staff at dozens of reference and information desks all over Chicago. Thus the Library responds to the need for information on the part of many Chicagoans.

The evaluation of that response is complicated, and should test collection depth, staff qualification, and actual service. Collection strength has been diminished by a long period of inadequate book money, some flaws in the selection procedures and sources, and serious loss by theft and delinquency. The lack of qualified staff in sufficient numbers is especially critical in Branch reference service, with only an average of three librarians per branch and high turnover throughout the system. The service climate varies, of course, but there is a widespread reluctance to go beyond the first step in reference work. Referral to another agency or department, or to the Tribune Public Service Office, becomes a passing of the buck.

Actual service has been evaluated by test questions, and by asking patrons their opinion. Many questions have been answered quickly and correctly, a few with imagination, but too often the service is perfunctory, and unnecessarily limited to answers found in published reference books. Thus on questions which require some "current awareness" on the part of the staff member, the responses suggest that this awareness is lacking. To a question requiring current knowledge about the U.N. members, ten agencies gave a total of five different answers, none correct. Another question went unanswered by nine agencies before a sub-branch provided the correct answer. One question asked on successive days in a Main Library Subject Department drew two different answers, one correct and one incorrect. The level of some service at the Main Library is not noticeably higher than at some branch libraries, despite the greater collections and staff qualifications.

Evidently more and better training is needed in modern reference techniques and attitudes; trained personnel must be recruited to allow flexibility in staff assignments, time for training, and completion of other duties. Perhaps most important is the principle of periodic or continuous evaluation with corrective feedback to the appropriate supervisors. Personal service can make or break the library over a period of time; there must be a mechanism for judging the quality of that service, at least for such factors as courtesy, self-confidence, and basic reference knowledge.

Terence Crowley
December 30, 1968

Chicago Public Library Survey

CONFIDENTIAL

Civil Service   Department or
Grade (LI, LII, etc.)_____   Agency_____

QUESTIONNAIRE FOR CPL
LIBRARIANS, TRAINEES, TECHNICIANS

Because of the key roles which librarians, trainees and technicians play in the operations and service programs of CPL, we are asking your cooperation in completing and
returning this questionnaire as soon as possible. We cannot overemphasize the importance of your help, for the information you supply will enable us to form a more complete profile of your backgrounds, experience and qualifications. At the same time,
the questionnaire offers you the opportunity to express your opinions and judgments
about your work and related matters. If, in addition, you would like to be interviewed by the Survey staff, please check here_____. All information will be held
in strictest confidence.

1. Name:_____ 2. Age:_____

3. Number of hours per week scheduled_____

4. Type of Service (adult, branch, children's, technical processing, etc.)_____

5. Position (Head Assistant, etc.)_____

6. Date of appointment to present position_____

7. Higher Education:

Name of school or training class	Years attended	Total Credits	Major	Degree or certif- icate received and date*
_____	_____	_____	_____	_____
_____	_____	_____	_____	_____
_____	_____	_____	_____	_____
_____	_____	_____	_____	_____

*Note: Please do not indicate degree as received if any requirements (e.g., thesis)
        are not yet completed.

8. Foreign languages read with a dictionary or better:_____

9. Current membership in professional library organizations:

____Chicago Library Club   ____Chicago Regional Gr. Tech. Proc. Librarians
____Illinois Library Assn.   ____Catholic Library Assn.
____American Library Assn.   ____Other (specify)
____Special Library Assn.   _____

10. Current membership in other professional organizations (e.g., A.A.U.W., L.W.V., N.E.A.)

    _____

11. Library experience other than CPL:

    Library   Location   Dates   Position
    _____   _____   _____   _____
    _____   _____   _____   _____
    _____   _____   _____   _____

12. Articles published (give full citations):

    _____

13. Book reviews published (give citations):

    _____
    _____

14. Current member of the Staff Association?   _____Yes   _____No

15. Current member of the union (AFSCME Local 1215)?   _____Yes   _____No

16. If you have <u>less</u> than five years experience with CPL, describe how you found out
    about positions here_____
    _____

17. What Civil Service examinations have you taken in the last 10 years:

    Examination   Year   Pass - Fail

    _____   _____   _____
    _____   _____   _____
    _____   _____   _____
    _____   _____   _____
    _____   _____   _____

18. Professional conferences or conventions attended in the last 24 months:

    Name   Date   Place

    _____   _____   _____
    _____   _____   _____
    _____   _____   _____
    _____   _____   _____

    If CPL paid <u>all</u> expenses, indicate with an (A). If CPL paid <u>part</u> expenses, indi-
    cate with a (P). If you received <u>leave</u> <u>with</u> <u>pay</u>, indicate with an (L).

19. Please list the professional journals that you read regularly:_____
    _____
    _____

20. List other periodicals and newspapers read regularly:_____
_____
_____

21. In the space below, please list and briefly describe your <u>main</u> duties, and in the column to the left, indicate the percentage of your time spent weekly at each task. (For example, 35% - Reference desk, 20% - Reading shelves, 33% - Handling reserves, 12% - Other miscellaneous work, = 100%.)

    Percent of time   Main duties
    spent weekly

    _____   _____
    _____   _____
    _____   _____
    _____   _____
    _____   _____

22. Generally speaking: a. what percentage of your work is professional?_____%
                           b. what percentage requires a college education, but not
                              a graduate degree?_____%
                           c. what percentage could be accomplished with a high school
                              education, and without much experience?_____%

23. How would you describe the staff spirit or morale in your department or agency?

High	Above average	Average	Below average	Low

    Give reasons for your answer, if possible:_____
    _____
    _____
    _____

24. Please describe any work you are not assigned, but feel you could do:_____
    _____

25. Describe any work you are doing and feel you should not do:_____
    _____

26. Are the physical conditions of your work (ventilation, lighting, equipment, work space, etc.) satisfactory or unsatisfactory? Please explain your answers.

    _____
    _____
    _____

27. Do you have enough responsibility to make your position attractive to you?_____
    _____

28. How frequently do you receive assignments and instructions from your supervisor?
_____

29. Do you receive too much supervision?   _____ Yes _____ No
    sufficient supervision?   _____ Yes _____ No
    not enough supervision?   _____ Yes _____ No

30. How many staff members do you supervise? _____professionals, _____sub-professionals, _____clerks?

31. How often does your supervisor discuss your service rating with you?_____

32. Please describe any in-service, or on-the-job training, or orientation sessions you've had in the last 5 years, giving dates, purpose, and names of persons conducting the training. _____
_____
_____
_____

33. Was such training useful or valuable? _____Yes _____No. In what respects?
_____

34. Do you feel a need for additional in-service training? _____Yes _____No. If yes, in what areas?_____

35. Do you ever make any suggestions for improving services or routines? _____Yes _____No. If yes, what has been reaction to these suggestions?_____
_____
_____

36. Do you usually receive recognition for your ideas, for a job well done, etc.? _____Yes _____No.

37. How often are staff meetings held in your department or agency?_____

38. What's your opinion of your present salary? ____High; ____Adequate; ____Low.

39. In your opinion, what are the major problems now facing the Chicago Public Library:
_____
_____
_____

40. Please comment on any matters not covered in the above questions.
_____
_____
_____
_____

Chicago Public Library Survey

QUESTIONNAIRE FOR CPL
TECHNICAL SERVICES STAFF

DIRECTIONS

1. Please read over the entire questionnaire to get an idea of the
    kinds of information we need.

2. For the next two or three days, as you do your work, think about
    how you are going to answer the questions, especially the last
    question. You might want to keep a "score card" yourself for a
    few days to get an idea of what percentage of your time you spend
    doing various tasks.

3. Please try to answer the questions as completely and as thought-
    fully as you can.

4. Do not ask your supervisors or the department head for help in
    answering the questions. Please refer your questions to Mr. Shaugh-
    nessy in the Survey Office, or when he visits your department.

5. When you have completed the questionnaire, please return it in the
    sealed brown envelope to the Survey Office--either personally or
    through the house mail. All questionnaires should be completed and
    returned NO LATER THAN SEPTEMBER 6th.

6. IMPORTANT. This information will be used by the Survey Team <u>in
    strictest confidence</u>. No one except Survey analysts will have access
    either during or after the survey is completed.

THE CHICAGO PUBLIC LIBRARY SURVEY

(Technical Services)

A. Personal Data

   1. Name _____

   2. Department _____

   3. Position or Title _____ 3a. Rank _____

   4. Daily Schedule (Hours) _____

   5. Annual Salary _____

   6. Length of time in present position _____

   7. Length of time with The Chicago Public Library _____

8. Education	Name of School	Years Attended	Subject Major	Degree
a. High School	_____	_____	_____	_____
b. College	_____	_____	_____	_____
c. Graduate School	_____	_____	_____	_____
d. Library School	_____	_____	_____	_____

   9. Foreign Language Specialties _____

  10. List memberships in national, regional, state, local library
      organization, or other relevant societies _____

      _____

      _____

  11. Do you belong to the staff association? Yes _____ No _____
                        The union? Yes _____ No _____

B. Supervision

  12. Name of immediate supervisor _____
      (person who assigns work, gives instructions)

  13. How frequently do you receive assignments and instructions from
      your supervisor? _____

      _____

CONFIDENTIAL

14. In what ways are you allowed initiative on your job? _____

    _____

    _____

15. Is your work revised?   (Check items that apply)

    While in progress _____   Upon completion _____

    By your supervisor _____   By other depart- _____
                                  ment members

    Is not revised _____

    Name of supervisor or revisor _____

16. Do you supervise other members in department?

    Yes _____   No _____   How many _____

    If yes, indicate the nature of the supervision (e.g., revising,
    giving assignments, time scheduling) _____

    _____

    _____

17. What comments would you make about the following items? Please be
    specific, and again, if you need an extra sheet, please do not
    forget to place your name on it. Mark the number of the question
    beside each answer if a second sheet is used.

    a. Nature of your work (simple, routine, difficult, done under
        pressure, etc.)

        _____

        _____

        _____

    b. Physical conditions of work (ventilation, lighting, equipment).
        Note if any aspect is satisfactory, unsatisfactory, etc.

        _____

        _____

        _____

CONFIDENTIAL

2

c. Responsibility of position (do you have enough responsibility
    to make the position attractive to you, etc.?)

    _____

    _____

    _____

    _____

d. List specifically any work that you are doing that you feel
    you should <u>not do</u>:

    _____

    _____

    _____

e. Work that you feel that you <u>could do</u>:

    _____

    _____

    _____

f. How would you describe the staff spirit or morale in your
    department?

    High, good spirit _____
    Above average   _____
    Average   _____
    Below average   _____
    Low, very poor   _____

    Give reasons for your answer, if possible _____

    _____

    _____

    _____

g. Please comment on any matters not covered in the above
    questions. _____

    _____

    _____

<u>CONFIDENTIAL</u>

3

Name _____

DETAILED STATEMENT OF DUTIES

Prepare a statement of duties and estimate the percentage of time spent on each. Follow the form below. Please be specific, and make a special effort to assign percentages to the amount of time spent weekly. This part of the questionnaire is MOST important: If some of your duties are infrequent or occasional, show this with an X.

Percent of
time spent
  weekly   LIST AND DESCRIBE TASKS PERFORMED
_____

_____

_____

_____

_____

_____

_____

_____

_____

_____

_____

_____

_____

_____

_____

_____

_____

_____

Name _____

DETAILED STATEMENT OF DUTIES - cont'd.

Percent of
time spent
weekly   LIST AND DESCRIBE TASKS PERFORMED

_____

_____

_____

_____

_____

_____

_____

_____

_____

_____

_____

_____

_____

_____

_____

_____

_____

_____

_____

CONFIDENTIAL

QUESTIONS FOR ACTING LIBRARIAN

Thinking of the next 2-3 years, what do you see as the major priority problems confronting the Library?

Are there additional different long-range (5-10 year) problems?

What are the major alternatives in policy before the Library--what services should be stressed--which played down or dropped?

Going back to immediate problems, what progress on each in the last ten years--which being solved, which marking time, which worsening?

Any difference in progress on each--more, less--in last 18 months?

What are the most important changes occurring in Chicago--in population composition, educational programs, economic life, physical rehabilitation-- and how does each affect the Library?

How do developments in school libraries relate to public library--discernible effect yet--what anticipated?

Of the following, which are now receiving most attention and greatest effort to improve--collection, reference service, adult education activities, children's service, branch buildings?

What were the basic causes of breakdown in public confidence in the Library 2-3 years ago--what back of campaign against the Library?

What is the public "image" of Library today--how changed?

What should be done next--first--to continue rebuilding image of the Library?

With what civic, educational, governmental, cultural groups and organizations is the Library working actively at present--how--with what results?

Where is the personnel strength of the Library, and where are the weaknesses?

1. coordinating officers above department heads and branch librarians

2. main library department heads

3. regional librarians

4. branch librarians

5. "older" professionals-- with Library 10 years or more

6. young professionals--recruited last three years

7. seasoned clericals

8. new clericals

How successful is Library in recruiting young professionals--how many
vacancies--what turnover--how many Negroes?

What are the realistic prospects for needed money in the future--from
what sources, for what programs, based upon what kinds of appeal?

What is the morale of staff now--what degree of enthusiasm--what chief
grievances--what done to improve morale?

What formal policy statements does the Library have on book selection,
censorship, personnel programs, metropolitan area role?

Chicago Public Library Survey

QUESTIONS FOR ASSISTANT LIBRARIAN AND CENTRAL DEPARTMENT HEADS

For whom, for what categories of readers, are the subject departments designed--whom are they not designed to serve?

What level and depth of materials and service are aimed at--what resources provided and not provided?

Are the departments planned to serve students--which students--in what way-- how are student needs determined--what adequacy of resources and services for this group?

Which are the departments that come closest to achieving their objectives-- which furthest from their goals--and in each case why?

What kind and scope of collection on open shelves--what there, what in stacks? Are open subject shelves weeded?

What of total central collection--where is it heading, how large should it become in next 20 years--in what form?

How is professional staff selected for subject departments--what level in experience--what subject background?

What check or control is exercised as to quality of service given by staff-- accuracy of reference information, thoroughness of guidance to readers, help when patrons have difficulties?

Where does the general reference department fit in--what is its function, limits, relation to subject departments?

How are relations maintained between departments--as to allocation of border- line topics, reference materials held, referral of readers, contact with special interest groups?

How do the subject departments relate to specialized collections in and near Chicago--what contacts, agreements, referrals, interlibrary use?

What is the connection between central subject departments and branches--as to policy, materials acquired, interunit services given, information about resources provided?

How well do readers find their way among the various service units of the main building--what recurring problems--new users in particular?

What does the general reader seeking "good reading" do in Central--both persons seeking current popular literature and those seeking cultural material and intellectual publications?

What is the aim of the Young Adult section on the first floor--who uses-- what problems?

To what extent do subject departments' staffs work in and with subject in- terest groups in their respective fields--is this encouraged--with what re- sults? Similarly, work with institutions, museums, etc.? What lists pre- pared for specific groups?

How are incoming telephone calls for information handled--general, specific, subject, etc.? Telephone calls encouraged or discouraged?

Where would one find material on Negro history and culture in the main library--how strong are holdings--how made available?

What resources and services do Central Library departments provide in Chicago's fight against poverty and inner city problems--what resources, used by whom, how called to attention of potential users?

What is policy and practice in acquiring nonbook materials in subject departments--serial publications, documents, reports, etc.--what depth of nonbook holdings--how handled?

What about service to business--what is aim--to what extent achieved-- which groups reached and not reached--how could service be improved?

What particularly do central departments do for civic and cultural leaders in Chicago--in government, education, health and welfare, the arts, religion?

Other than space, what is the most urgent and immediate problem confronting the main library service departments--what should be done first?

Chicago Public Library Survey   <u>ITEM 9</u>

<u>QUESTIONS FOR REGIONAL LIBRARIANS</u>

Given present trends and plans, what will the Chicago branch program be in 1980--assuming present and contemplated programs are carried out, how many units by then, where located, of what size?

What are the three or four most effective, most distinctive branches--why--how did they get that way? Which are the least effective?

How exactly do branches differ in low-income ghetto areas and in middle-class neighborhoods further out in the city?

What is the standard or goal for size of branches--what minimum collection and staff, what maximum collection and staff?

How large are collections in regionals--how large should they be?

Three regionals the right number--why?

How far apart does Library aim to place branches--on what evidence--same in all parts of city--same for adults and children?

In branches, what provision of paperback books, magazines, government publications, recordings, art works, films?

Any use of programmed and other self-instruction materials--if not, why not?

How strong are the branches in the following categories of personnel--branch librarians, experienced professionals, children's librarians, young professionals, clerical staff?

How closely do branch staffs work with community groups--how do local people share in branch policies, book selection, etc.?

What is the conception of information and reference service in the branches--do all have reference desks--who staffs them?

How much interunit service--interbranch loans, interbranch reference, co-ordinated acquisition--from branches to regionals to central library?

How does the average person learn about the existence and service of his local library--what publicity, contact with agencies, with schools?

How has library reached out to low-education neighborhoods--what priority put on this--who does the work--what results to date?

What is the single most promising development in the branches today--what the most serious problem, and what is being done about it?

Date _____   Grade _____

                                                 Agency _____

Chicago Public Library Survey

ENTRANCE INTERVIEW

                                                 Expected
Name _____ Began _____ Duration _____

College _____ Major _____

Work experience

Library experience

Why CPL?

Entrance information?

Job expectations

LS interest?

    None

    Some

    Strong

Date _____   Grade _____

Chicago Public Library Survey

EXIT INTERVIEW

                                                    Length of
Name _____ Termination _____ Service _____

Agency _____ College _____

Experience in CPL: Main ____ Regional ____ Branch ____ Subbranch _____

Reason for leaving

Entrance

Preview

Duties   % Clerical

                                                    % Subprofessional

                                                    % Professional

Responsibility

Supervision

    Recognition

    Suggestions

Advancement

Recent developments

Leadership

Best part of job

Worst part of job

CHICAGO PUBLIC LIBRARY SURVEY

BACKGROUND AND GUIDELINES FOR COLLECTION CONSULTANTS

I.   Background - The following summary is made to familiarize the
     consultants with some of the historical events and current
     practices which have influenced CPL collection development.

     A.   A cooperative agreement for a "division of fields" among
          the John Crerar Library, the Newberry, and the Chicago
          Public Library was approved in 1896. It is difficult to
          gauge the total effect this agreement had on the
          collecting policies of the Chicago Public Library,
          particularly in those areas for which Newberry and Crerar
          were given responsibility. The report stated: "The
          limitation proposed for the purchases of the Public
          Library is not of subjects but of character of books."
          Presumably, the agreement offered CPL a good reason for
          excluding specialized research type material, especially
          during the time when book budgets were severely limited.
          Recently, the agreement has been further modified in
          practice, if not in theory, by the increasing restrictions
          imposed by Newberry, and by the movement of the Crerar
          Library to the IIT campus some distance from downtown.
          Below the doctoral level, Newberry specifically excludes
          students except in special cases where they must obtain
          a letter from the librarian of their institution.
          Crerar continues to offer its services freely to the
          public, but its position in an academic milieu is bound
          to affect future development. In any event, the succession
          of CPL department heads since 1896 have subjected the
          agreement to a variety of interpretations; hence
          generalizations are hazardous.

     B.   In 1963 CPL was designated as one of four "Reference &
          Resource Centers" in Illinois. By 1965, nearly $60,000
          had been received to augment the library's holdings as
          a reference center. This money was originally used to
          increase the number of copies of selected titles rather
          than to increase the number of titles acquired, but
          during the last year an increasing share of the money
          - now $125,000 per year - has gone to "fill in gaps"
          as well as add expensive items not heretofore purchased.
          The departments probably vary widely in their use of
          this money.

     C.   The overlap characterizing all subject departmentalized
          libraries is a matter of special concern. Duplication
          is inevitable, but more importantly we should watch for
          areas which are neglected because of the division of
          responsibility. A breakdown of subject department
          responsibilities is enclosed.

D. Comments culled from interviews and from observation of
the selection procedures:

1. Single copies of titles are purchased only in the case
of reference books and in special subject fields such
as Art; the normal minimum order is 3 copies for Main.

2. Selection sources most frequently mentioned were
Publishers Weekly, Library Journal, a few standard
general periodicals and local newspapers, and the
approval books, as supplied by McClurg's (the book
jobber).

II. General Guidelines and Assumptions

A. As a Public Library CPL has a wider scope than an academic
library in form and content. The importance of the nonacademic areas will vary from subject to subject, but we
must underscore the unique responsibility for collecting
in these areas. The consultants should keep this in mind
as they study the comprehensiveness and scope of the
collections. For the student, there is nearly always
recourse to an academic library; for the non-student,
CPL often has the sole responsibility.

B. A second aspect of the many responsibilities of CPL
is the difference between extension - the promotion
of good reading through the branches - and research
- the search for and discovery of new knowledge in the
Main Library. These two functions are largely separate
and, in book selection, they polarize along the lines
of "many copies" vs. "many titles". Because of the
pressure generated by circulation statistics, Public
Librarians by nature are more conscious of the former
than the latter, and hence the research function runs
the risk of being submerged by the extension work.

C. It may be useful to outline three levels for research
library collections. These levels correspond to or are
based on various degrees of coverage of the literature
in a field.

The first level consists of a collection adequate for
the needs of the casual reader as well as the person
wishing to pursue a subject interest to some depth,
or for the needs of those interested in somewhat specialized subject areas. At this level would be many adults
interested in informally continuing their education, in
developing or cultivating subject interests. Also included are high school students and college students. At
this level would be the popular treatments of more specialized subjects and somewhat specialized treatment of less

arcane subjects. Bibliographies and guides to the
literature at the first level would include <u>Books for
College Libraries</u>, <u>the Julian Street Catalog</u>, <u>the Catalogue</u>
of the Lamont Library, <u>Guide to the Literature of the
Social Sciences</u>, American Universities Field Service
<u>Select Bibliographies</u> on Asia, Africa, Eastern Europe,
Latin America.

The second level is characterized by comprehensiveness -
a collection which includes all the materials in the
previous category, plus a wider selection of books,
periodicals, and other resources having value to the
graduate student in a subject field. This collection
would support current as well as retrospective research,
including materials in all languages. The emphasis here
is on both range and depth, greater specificity in subject areas, and inclusive background materials. Second
level bibliographies would include the <u>Harvard Guide to
American History</u>, the <u>London Bibliography of the Social
Sciences</u>, the annual bibliographies in PMLA & similar
scholarly journals, the A H A <u>Guide to Historical
Literature</u>, and Chamberlin's <u>Guide to Art Reference Books</u>.

The third level is characterized by exhaustivity - a
collection which attempts to include everything written
on a subject, regardless of quality. It includes all
editions, all translations and all languages. Perhaps
there are a few areas where The Chicago Public Library
might assume responsibility for acquiring everything
written in a specific subject, but thus far it has not
attempted to do so. Consequently, CPL should not be
evaluated against the ideal of absolute completeness.
Third level bibliographies might be Bosterman's
World Bibliography of Bibliographies, the reprint catalogs
of various research libraries published by G. K. Hall,
and the National Union Catalog.

Admittedly these levels are only constructs, and cannot
be rigidly applied. Neither can corresponding "levels
of need" be isolated or precisely defined. These levels
of coverage are obviously interrelated and do not have
sharply focused beginnings or ends. Moreover, there
is a whole range of material which is not covered by
these levels, for example, CPL's extensive holdings in
fiction, in popular reading material; collections of
"how-to-do-it" books, sports and recreational material,
and inspirational books. While these are not research
collections, they do constitute an important part of
the library's service program. Popular bibliographies
in this range include the <u>Standard Catalog for Public
Libraries</u>, the <u>Fiction Catalog</u>, <u>How-to-do-it; a selected
guide</u>, and many metropolitan Public Library lists .

The purpose in delineating these levels of coverage is to provide a framework to guide your evaluation. There are three parts to your assignment:

1. Description of that part of the collection for which you have contracted, reflecting strengths as well as weaknesses.

2. Evaluation of the collection based on your professional judgment and the use of authoritative bibliographies, if appropriate.

3. Recommendation of alternative means of reaching necessary levels of resource strength in view of CPL's state-wide research library responsibilities.

Your report should emphasize the research adequacy of the collection in your area. In other words, levels one and two: basic subject materials of range and some depth, and comprehensiveness in both the primary sources of research, and bibliographic tools to locate additional material. CPL is not expected to be exhaustive, or virtually complete in any area. Please mention special collections, if any, including pamphlet and document files, but do not spend too much time on these.

The report should be a fairly detailed comment on the adequacy of the collections to sustain research, running perhaps six to eight pages. We are less interested in assigning blame than in pointing out specifically where and how CPL can function as a research resource.

On the other hand, you do not need to make specific recommendations on branch library collections, or about the administration and staffing of the departments, except as it may affect the collection. Since we want the report to be useful to the library you might also wish to include any significant gaps in the sources which they use for selection, and offer comments on such topics as the advantage of using specialized jobbers for special materials, the use of paperback books, and similar aspects which affect the collection.

If there is any checking of bibliographies you wish done in advance, please let us know as soon as possible.

We estimate that a visit of three days should be sufficient, including two to three hours interviewing the department head. These three days may be broken up and would normally not include time required to write your report. The report would hopefully be in hand within two weeks of your library visits.

If you wish us to obtain any bibliographies for your use,
please contact Miss Marion Strohm, our executive secretary,
at the Survey Office. Other questions should be referred
to Mr. Crowley.

In addition to your per diem retainer, we will reimburse
you for any normal expenses incurred. Unfortunately,
there is a four-to-six week delay in paying consultants,
since the check must be processed through city offices.

We look forward to a productive relationship.

TC:gw
8/29/68

BRANCH QUESTIONNAIRE

To improve the services of The Chicago Public Library, we need your cooperation in filling out <u>both</u> <u>sides</u> of this questionnaire. It is very important that we receive a completed questionnaire from <u>everyone</u>. Do not sign your name.

1. Have you come to the library today to:

    _____ check out books, records or pamphlets
    _____ use reference books, such as encyclopedias, almanacs,
          dictionaries or other materials which cannot be taken
          from the library
    _____ read magazines or newspapers
    _____ bring and read your own books or materials
    _____ return books only
    _____ other use:_____

    _____

2. For what kind of reading material or information did you come to the library today? Check only the <u>one</u> category which best describes your main interest <u>today</u>:

    _____ books or information on a specific subject. (What subject:_____
          _____)
    _____ current fiction
    _____ current non-fiction (biographies, current events, etc.)
    _____ older standard works (classics, histories, biographies, etc.)
    _____ others (please describe: _____

    _____

3. Do you have an unexpired Chicago Public Library borrowers' card? ___yes ___no

4. Do you regularly use any other branch libraries or suburban libraries?
    ____ yes ____ no Which:_____

    Any school, college or business libraries? ____ yes ____ no
    Which:_____

5. Do you live in Chicago? ____ yes ____ no If no, where:_____

6. Do you work or attend school in Chicago? ____ yes ____ no

7. How far away do you live from this library?

    _____ 0-½ mile (4 <u>long</u> blocks)   _____ 1½-2 miles
    _____ ½-1 mile   _____ 2-3 miles
    _____ 1-1½ miles   _____ 3-5 miles
                                            _____ over 5 miles

8. How old are you?

    _____ 0-14 years   _____ 25-39 years
    _____ 15-19 years   _____ 40-59 years
    _____ 20-24 years   _____ 60 years or older

9. Education: If you have finished school, circle the highest grade you've completed. If you are still in school, circle the grade you're now in.

Grade school	0 1 2 3 4 5 6 7 8
High school	1 2 3 4
Business school	1 2 3 4
College	1 2 3 4
Graduate school	1 2 3 4 5 6
Other school	1 2 3 4

    (What kind?_____)

10. Occupation: Check only the <u>one</u> position showing where you spend most of your time.

    _____ student
    _____ housewife
    _____ unemployed
    _____ retired
    _____ professional, manager, proprietor, official
    _____ sales or clerical
    _____ craftsman, foreman, driver, operator, repair, maintenance, laborer, or similar work
    _____ other; please give: _____

PLEASE DO NOT ANSWER THE FOLLOWING QUESTIONS UNTIL YOU ARE READY TO LEAVE THE LIBRARY

---

11. Did you check for books or other material in the card catalog? ____yes ___no

12. Did you ask anyone on the library staff to help you? ____ yes ____ no
    If yes, were they helpful and courteous? ____ yes ____ somewhat ____ no

13. Did you find what you were looking for? ____ yes ____ partially ____ no

14. If dissatisfied, what caused your dissatisfaction?
    _____
    _____

15. Please make any other suggestions you may have for the library below.

THANK YOU VERY MUCH. PLEASE RETURN THIS QUESTIONNAIRE TO THE STAFF MEMBER WHEN YOU LEAVE.

Chicago Public Library Survey

QUESTIONNAIRE FOR SPECIAL LIBRARIES
Name of Library_____

1. Have you contacted the main Chicago Public Library for any information or materials
    in the past year? No____ Yes____. If yes, by telephone?____, in person?____
    If in person, have you used the following?

	weekly	monthly	a few times
books			
periodicals			
newspapers			
films			
pamphlets			
maps			
government documents			
other_____			
_____			

    If you have not used C.P.L., skip to question 11.

2. Has your use generally been weekly____, monthly____, once every several months____,
    rarely____?

3. During the past 5-10 years, has your use increased____, decreased____, remained
    the same____?

4. Do you usually ask questions____ or try to locate materials____?

5. Does Chicago Public Library usually answer your questions? Yes____ No____.
    Supply the material? Yes____ No____

6. Which department(s) do you use most often?

7. Has the service been satisfactory? Yes____ No____. If no, in what way was
    it unsatisfactory?

8. In which subject area(s) has C.P.L. been most successful in answering your
    requests?

9. What types of materials have you been most successful in getting?

10. Have you requested any materials from C.P.L. through Interlibrary Loan in
    the past year? Yes____ No____. If yes, were your requests usually filled?
    Yes____ No____.

11. Does the C.P.L. collection influence your decisions to include or exclude
    materials in your collection? Yes____ No____. If yes, in what way?

12. What other libraries or sources of information have you found most able to
    supply your requests for information or materials?

13. During the period in which you have been associated with your special library, has there been any improvement or deterioration in the collection or services of C.P.L.? Please comment.

14. Are there any aspects of the collection or service which you find particularly useful?

15. Do you have any suggestions for improving the service in your subject area?

16. Would a book catalog of the C.P.L. collection be useful to you? Yes____No____

17. Any additional comments?

Chicago Public Library Survey

REACTOR PANEL FORM

Branch: Date: Approximate
                                                              Time:

Question:

Background:

Was the branch _____ attractive and inviting? _____ neutral?
                _____ cold and unappealling?   _____

Was the branch clearly identified from the outside? _____

Had you been inside this building before? _____

Did you have to wait long before finding someone who would help you? _____

Was the staff member confident _____ yes _____ somewhat _____ no
                      courteous _____ yes _____ somewhat _____ no
                      friendly _____ yes _____ somewhat _____ no

Other comments:

What questions did she ask?

What answer was given to your basic question?

Did she suggest another library as a possible source?

If this had been your own question, would you have been satisfied? _____

Do you have an overall impression of this branch?

                                    Signed_____

PLEASE RETURN ONE OF THESE SHEETS FOR EACH BRANCH VISIT.

READERS' ADVISORY SERVICE
EVALUATION FORM

Library _____ Subbranch _____
                                                  Branch   _____
                                                  Regional _____

Investigator _____

Date _____ Day of week _____ Time _____

Librarian's name or position (if offered) _____ _____

Questions posed were numbers: _____

ACCESS

   Approach used (describe): _____

   First confrontation was: _____

   Location of librarian in charge of R.A. function: _____

   _____.

Describe sequence to librarian in charge of R.A.: _____

   _____

   _____.

SERVICE ATTITUDE

   Working atmosphere:

               Very busy _____ Slack

    Personal manner of librarian:

     Very pleasant, warm _____ Very unpleasant, cold

   Handling of query was:

               Confident _____ Lacking in confidence

   Did librarian probe:

      _____ personal interests?

      _____ educational background?

      _____ reading ability?

   Was users' name of library card number requested? _____

HANDLING OF QUERY

"Filter" questions to clarify or narrow scope of query were:

_____ used very efficiently.

_____ asked but not purposeful; lacking in direction.

_____ not asked at all.

Comment: _____

_____.

Material/information offered was (enumerate):

_____   _____

_____   _____

_____   _____

Material offered was:

Very relevant _____ Totally irrelevant

Very useful _____ Not at all useful

At disposal _____ Not available

Well interpreted _____ Not interpreted

Comment: _____

_____.

Did librarian inquire into the usefulness of material/advice:

_____ At time material/advice was offered?

_____ After user had opportunity to examine material?

Was persistence required on the part of the user to obtain the desired information or reading material? _____

SUMMARY, EVALUATION, ADDITIONAL COMMENTS:

_____

_____

_____

HANDLING OF QUERY: DIAGRAMMATIC REPRESENTATION

Information
and/or Material

Filter   Interpretation
Queries

USER

Bibliographic   Instruction-in-
Tools   use

CHICAGO PUBLIC LIBRARY SURVEY

QUESTIONNAIRE ON TECHNICAL SERVICES FOR BRANCH LIBRARIES

To improve technical services to branch libraries, we need your co-operation in completing this question form. It is very important that we receive this information as soon as possible, so please try to return the questionnaire to the Survey office by January 8th. If you have any questions, please call Mrs. Leonard or Mr. Shaughnessy at CE6-8922, extensions 46 or 76.

1. Name of branch _____

2. In your order file, please count:

    a. total number of book titles on order but not received _____
    b. number of book titles not yet received which have been on order over two months but under six months _____
    c. number of book titles not yet received which have been on order six months or longer _____

3. During the past year, has the service of the Accessions, Bindery, or Catalog Departments speeded up, slowed down, remained the same, or changed in any way? _____

    _____
    _____

4. Please describe the general physical condition (e.g., cards soiled, torn, etc.) of your adult card catalog _____

    _____

    juvenile card catalog _____

    _____

5. Are you up-to-date in filing catalog cards? ____ yes ____ no
   If no, approximately how many sets of cards are waiting to be filed___?
   Are you up-to-date in withdrawal of cards? ____ yes ____ no

6. Do catalog cards usually arrive within a few (2-3) days of the arrival of the book? ____ yes ____ no

7. If the books arrive first, do you make temporary catalog cards and/or shelf list cards to use until the permanent cards arrive? ____ yes ____ no

8. If you do not make temporary cards, how many titles are you holding pending the arrival of catalog cards? _____

9. How many sets of catalog cards do you now have which you received in advance of the book? _____

10. Is there any difference in the time lapse between receipt of catalog cards and receipt of fiction, non-fiction, or juvenile books?

   _____
   _____
   _____

11. Do you have any suggestions for improving technical services to your branch by the:

   Accessions Department _____

   Catalog Department _____

   Bindery Department _____

12. Any other comments you wish to make regarding technical services.

Citizens' Committee
Survey of The Chicago Public Library
October 11, 1968

QUESTION FORM ON BASIC PUBLIC LIBRARY POLICY

The public library today serves primarily two groups in the population, in addition to the large number of children who respond naturally. The two adult groups are students in high school and college, and the relatively small proportion of adults who are regular book readers. Together these groups make up less than 25 percent of the population over 12 or 13 years of age.

This is the proportion that usually prevails in larger cities. We are still in process of getting exact use figures for Chicago, but present data indicate a similar percentage of adult library use here.

A basic policy question for a public library is whether to concentrate on improving conventional services to existing users, or to reach out with fresh forms of service to additional groups, or to try to do better on both fronts. In addition to students and regular book readers, one can think of various other groups which might be served by an expanded and less traditional library program:

> Persons of limited educational background who do not turn readily to books.

> Persons of whatever educational background who seek factual information rather than reading as such.

> Specialists who need unique and research-type materials.

> Persons of varying background who have an interest in personal or civic or cultural or leisure-time matters, but who do not find the usual library program suited to their needs.

Another way to put this is to say that the public library typically reaches a middle range or band. Individuals who do not turn to the usual book sources do not find the library of much value to them, and on the other side, persons who need advanced and specialized materials do not find the public agency equal to their needs.

Thus basic policy questions arise. Should The Chicago Public Library "stick to its last" and concentrate on improving traditional service? Should it devise fresh programs in order to serve more of the people? If it should reach out, can money be found to do an effective and continuing job, as against occasional and short-term projects financed from a little leftover money? And in answering these questions, we should bear in mind that some existing services are deficient.

The survey team needs your views on these fairly basic considerations. We have set down several open-ended questions on the attached sheets. Please give us your opinion, straight out and at whatever length you believe necessary. We will be going over each response carefully and with an open mind.

Please mail your responses to: Library Survey Office The Chicago Public Library,
78 East Washington Street, Chicago, Illinois 60602

1. In your judgment, should The Chicago Public Library concentrate on <u>improving</u> conventional services to existing and potential users, or should it consciously and intensively <u>reach</u> <u>out</u> to additional groups and segments of the population-- or must it do <u>both</u>?

2. If in your view the Library should reach out and develop beyond its present program, which groups or types of potential users should receive priority?

3. If it were to cost quite substantial sums to reach each of these groups with any real effectiveness (for example, a million dollars a year or more to serve the ghettos with fresh patterns of service), would you still recommend that The Chicago Public Library launch the necessary programs (the Library currently spends approximately $9,000,000 per year on operations)?

4. What basic policies or methods strike you as most promising for improving library service to the groups you have indicated--in fact, what direction of development do you consider most important for the Library for any part of its program?

Name_____

Index

DESIGNED BY
VLADIMIR REICHL

PAPER IS A SPECIAL PERMANENT DURABLE STOCK
DEVELOPED FOR ALA